ANTEBELLUM AT SEA

Antebellum at Sea

· · · ·

Maritime Fantasies in
Nineteenth-Century America

Jason Berger

University of Minnesota Press
Minneapolis
London

Portions of chapter 1 and the Introduction were previously published as "Antebellum Fantasies of the Common Sailor; or, Enjoying the Knowing Jack Tar," *Criticism: A Quarterly for Literature and the Arts* 51, no. 1 (Winter 2009): 29–61. Copyright 2009 Wayne State University Press; published with the permission of Wayne State University Press.

Portions of chapter 2 were previously published as "Killing Tom Coffin: Rethinking the Nationalist Narrative in James Fenimore Cooper's *The Pilot*," *Early American Literature* 43, no. 3 (November 2008): 643–70.

An earlier version of chapter 5 was previously published as "*The Crater* and the Master's Reign: Cooper's 'Floating *Imperium*,'" *The James Fenimore Cooper Society Miscellaneous Papers* 27 (2010): 7–10.

Frontispiece: W. D. Hammond, *Sea chest*, 1996. Oil on wood. Auckland Art Gallery Toi o Tāmaki, gift of the Friends of the Auckland Art Gallery Acquisitions Trust, 1998.

Copyright 2012 by the Regents of the University of Minnesota

All rights reserved. No part of this publication may be reproduced, stored in a retrieval system, or transmitted, in any form or by any means, electronic, mechanical, photocopying, recording, or otherwise, without the prior written permission of the publisher.

Published by the University of Minnesota Press
111 Third Avenue South, Suite 290
Minneapolis, MN 55401-2520
http://www.upress.umn.edu

Library of Congress Cataloging-in-Publication Data

Berger, Jason.
Antebellum at sea : maritime fantasies in nineteenth-century America / Jason Berger.
Includes bibliographical references and index.
ISBN 978-0-8166-7706-1 (hc : acid-free paper)
ISBN 978-0-8166-7707-8 (pb : acid-free paper)
1. Sea stories, American—History and criticism.   2. American literature—
19th century—History and criticism.   3. Seafaring life in literature.
4. National characteristics, American, in literature.   I. Title.
PS217.S4B54   2012
810.9'32—dc23   2012027703

Printed in the United States of America on acid-free paper

The University of Minnesota is an equal-opportunity educator and employer.

20 19 18 17 16 15 14 13 12   10 9 8 7 6 5 4 3 2 1

For Sarah and Jonah

Contents

Acknowledgments — ix

Introduction: Bewitching Sea — 1

I. Fantasy and the Common Sailor

1. Fantasies of the Common Sailor; or, Enjoying the Knowing Jack Tar — 25
2. Tarrying with the National: Fantasizing the Subject of State — 57

II. Polynesian Encounters Redux

3. Tattoos in *Typee*: Rethinking Melville's "Cultural Grotesque" — 97
4. Melville's "Porno-Tropics": Re-Sexuating Pacific Encounters — 123

III. Ocean-States of Exception

5. *The Crater* and the Master's Reign: Cooper's "Floating *Imperium*" — 175
6. The Sublime Abject of Democracy: Melville's "Floating *Imperium*" — 197

Epilogue: Incomplete Sea — 239

Notes — 247

Index — 305

Acknowledgments

THERE ARE MANY PEOPLE who have made this book possible. If not debts, I have indeed accrued benefits from interactions at various stages of composition. My earliest conceptions of the project were formed while I was a graduate student at the University of Vermont, and I am, on many levels, grateful to the English Department faculty there. At the University of Connecticut, Jerry Phillips and Wayne Franklin were instrumental in every phase of the book's development. I want to thank them here for their critical insight and professional guidance as well as for giving me the latitude to pursue a vision that entailed pushing, however slightly, certain methodological conventions. Robert Tilton provided valuable commentary and support throughout. In addition, Sharon Harris and Mary K. Bercaw Edwards offered thoughtful suggestions that undoubtedly improved the book. I would also like to thank my current colleagues at the University of South Dakota. In particular, Emily Haddad, John Dudley, Skip Willman, Ron Ganze, and Darlene Farabee volunteered to read portions of the manuscript and helped move the final revisions toward completion. Commentary from anonymous readers for the University of Minnesota Press was invaluable in helping to shape the finished project. And I am grateful to Richard Morrison for his early interest in and consistent support for the book.

This would have been a very different book had it not been for the camaraderie of D. Michael Jones and Stephen Lucasi, two fellow Bostonian travelers. If Emerson's rather pragmatic notion of friendship is correct, that a friend's "office is closing" when he or she has fully "become an object of thought," then I am sorry to say that I shall be seeking your company and conversation for some time to come. Well before I pursued an academic path, my parents provided me with an incredibly loving and supportive home. To them, and to my brother and sister, I am forever grateful. And if there is a center to the person I have become, it is continually forged through the space and time I am lucky enough to share with Sarah Ehlers. She is the catalyst and not-so-silent partner in so much of this.

· INTRODUCTION ·

Bewitching Sea

There is a witchery in the sea, its songs and stories, and in the mere sight of a ship, and the sailor's dress, especially to a young mind, which has done more to man navies, and fill merchantmen, than all the pressgangs of Europe.

—Richard Henry Dana Jr., *Two Years before the Mast*

ON NOVEMBER 25, 1842, an eighteen-year-old midshipman named Philip Spencer approached another crew member on board the USS *Somers*. Taking the sailor, Mr. Wales, aside, Spencer quietly bound him to secrecy and then pulled a piece of paper covered in Greek writing from his razor box. Explaining that he was "leagued with about twenty of the crew to get possession of the brig, murder the commander and officers, and commence piracy," Spencer offered as proof the paper, which recorded the crew members who had assented to mutiny and detailed how the plan would be carried out.[1] This clandestine meeting occurred on the *Somers*'s return voyage to New York from the coast of Africa, during which Captain Alexander Slidell Mackenzie saw his crew's behavior progressively worsen. After Spencer left him, Mr. Wales quickly made his way to ranking officers and informed them of the mutiny plot. By November 26, Spencer was in irons, and the next day two of his main conspirators, boatswain's mate Samuel Cromwell and seaman Elisha Small, were also being held. After an impromptu court-martial, the officers found the three men guilty and hanged them from the yardarm.

When the *Somers* docked in New York shortly after, word of the executions spread quickly. Soon the event, which was picked up by a myriad of newspapers, developed into a national sensation. The story interested readers both because the potentially precipitous use of martial force was carried out just two weeks' sail from the New York Naval Shipyard and because the ringleader of the event, Philip Spencer, was the son of John Canfield

Spencer, then secretary of war under President John Tyler. Captain Mackenzie was soon exonerated in a naval court, and many in the press defended his actions, condemning both the rebellious young Spencer and, interestingly, the sea narratives by James Fenimore Cooper that had presumably inspired the mutiny attempt. The *New York Herald* asserted: "Spencer reads the pirate works, has his imagination fired, and wants to sail a Red Rover." The *New York Courier* similarly condemned the desires spawned by Cooper's pirate romances, claiming: "Could young Spencer now be heard from, we doubt not but he would point to Mr. Cooper's *Red Rover* as one of the most prominent causes for his determination to war against civilized society."[2]

This famous affair links two of the main writers this book will explore: James Fenimore Cooper, who never directly responded to the accusations against his pirate novels but did side with Spencer in his 1844 review of Mackenzie's court-martial, and Herman Melville, who read of the *Somers* incident during his adventures in the Pacific and sympathized with the executed seamen in his novel *White-Jacket* (1850), a telling position for Melville, considering that his cousin, Guert Gansevoort, had been a lieutenant on the *Somers* and an active agent in the hangings. More broadly, the incident and the media's response reveal a significant political relationship among fantasy, desire, and maritime experience in antebellum America. The connections among these concepts, however, are not as clear-cut as the *New York Herald* would have us believe. In this dynamic era of rapid economic maritime expansion, sea narratives did indeed engender desire for fantastic and unruly experiences on the high seas, but they also evinced a complex array of much more formative sociopolitical valences.

The economic landscape of this age took shape when the large-scale development of commercial cities and maritime industries began flourishing in the 1740s. By this time, for example, New Englanders owned roughly 1,500 vessels, and their neighbors to the south in New York and Philadelphia were also quickly expanding their merchant-maritime infrastructure.[3] Such trends continued as oceanic routes stabilized and colonial projects in the Americas and the Caribbean developed, forming, by the onset of the nineteenth century, a veritable Atlantic-maritime empire of trade. The antebellum era, especially after the naval victories of the War of 1812, saw unprecedented proliferation of commercial, naval, and scientific maritime activity and a correlative growth in the production of sea-based narratives.

To the *New York Herald* and *Courier,* some of these narratives, even a national romance such as *The Red Rover,* were vehicles for subversive imaginary ideas. These claims convey lingering eighteenth-century conservative skepticism about the mysterious and utopic functions of the imagination, but they also respond to the growing number of early American texts that vividly depicted foreign places and adventures. In fact, it was common for authors of such narratives, or their characters, to portray how reading sea tales had prompted their desire to go to sea in the first place. An apt example can be found in Captain Benjamin Morrell's *A Narrative of Four Voyages to the South Seas* (1832). After explaining that hearing and reading maritime narratives "excited" his initial "desire" to run away to the sea, Morrell recounts how watching the French bombardment of Cadiz years later he realized "what [he] had so often heard and read and dreamed of."[4] Yet, importantly, Richard Henry Dana Jr.'s words in the above epigraph make it clear that not everyone viewed the "witchery" of the sea as yielding either exhilarating adventure or dissent from the status quo. In *Two Years before the Mast* (1840), Dana portrays the crew on board the merchant ship *Pilgrim* being forced to chant the decidedly unromantic "Philadelphia Catechism," "Six days shalt thou labor and do all thou art able, And on the seventh—holystone the decks and scrape the cable," as they pound the anchors.[5] Melville also challenges romantic conceptions of sea experience in *White-Jacket* when his narrator, after exclaiming, "Oh, give me the rover's life—the joy, the thrill, the whirl," includes the qualifying aside: "But when White-Jacket speaks of the rover's life, he means not life in a man-of-war, which, with its martial formalities[,] . . . stabs to the heart the soul of all free-and-easy honorable rovers."[6] The enigmatic lure of the sea, so often dramatized and commented upon in the antebellum era, is here joined by the markedly darker underside of regimented merchant-maritime labor and martial duties. This simple disjuncture thus casts the maritime world as not only a field of new economic and cultural experiences but also a differentiated scene of desire.[7]

This book examines how antebellum maritime narratives structure such desire, but in a way that shifts the grid, so to speak, of the above dichotomy. From a Lacanian psychoanalytic perspective, "Desire is not something given in advance, but something that has to be constructed—and it is precisely the role of fantasy to give the coordinates of the subject's desire, to specify its object, to locate the position the subject assumes in it."[8] It is my wager that considering the social function of fantasy will provide a nuanced means to examine how maritime narratives operated in the political landscape of nineteenth-century America. Throughout these years, a developing maritime economy interfaced with and produced ideological fantasies about sea space, including the long-standing notion that experiences "beyond the line," a term first coined in the Elizabethan era to denote the outer reaches of the maritime world, were exotically dangerous and chaotic.[9]

Consequently, maritime fantasies have significant political import in this era, for they emerge (or reemerge) to organize, condition, and respond to experiences in which social, political, and economic antagonisms often occurred or came to a head—many of which opened up irreconcilable fissures in existing symbolic coordinates. Cesare Casarino poignantly notes how the nineteenth-century sea narrative often responded to and participated in such antagonisms and, in turn, "constituted a crucial laboratory for that crisis that goes by the name of modernity."[10] Figuring the genre as a "laboratory" for responses to crises within the early development of global capitalism might yield a metaphor for the act of producing or complicating fantasies—with "crisis" representing a conceptual or affective response to breakdowns within dominant ideological narratives. In this sense, the problem of the sea, if we can call it that, stems in part from limitations writers face when attempting to represent it as a coherent cultural and imaginative space.[11] Such a notion is articulated in the journal entries Ralph Waldo Emerson penned while crossing the Atlantic in 1833, where he reflects: "No wor[d] suits the sea but I hope. Every sign fails."[12] But this scenario is compounded, as I will show, when one considers the specific ways that fantasy operates. In this regard, antebellum writers not only struggled to maintain and produce fantasies in the face of new and sometimes troubling sociopolitical arrangements, but in the process they also often glimpsed the tenuousness of antebellum sociality, and, by implication, of material reality itself. When considering maritime fantasies, to paraphrase Adrian Johnston paraphrasing Jacques Lacan, one quickly sees how abstractions have sea legs.[13]

From Witchery to Fantasy

If we are to take Richard Henry Dana Jr.'s claim seriously, we might refocus it a bit and ask more generally how such bewitching maritime stories participate in the nineteenth century's conception and construction of a world in flux. In discussing how a modern critic might approach the nineteenth century, a century characterized as a *"Zeit-traum,"* or "dreamtime," Walter Benjamin suggests that the dialectical method mediates between the historical situation of the past and the present, whereby the "object" of the past is "concretized in itself and upraised from its former being into the higher concretion of now-being."[14] In a similar fashion, I view the theoretical development of the conception of fantasy in our own age as a means to take up and illuminate aspects of the nineteenth-century world. Although a Lacanian view of fantasy departs in important ways from nineteenth-century notions of the imagination, using it to read these earlier texts affords the opportunity to subsume the antebellum content and conceive of it in new ways. In other words, because of the very fact that a modern critical perspective radically breaks from previous contexts, using it to read antebellum texts creates a historical short circuit that may allow us to reconceive the structures of meaning inherent in nineteenth-century narratives.

In this section, I provide an overview of the Lacanian notion of fantasy, including Slavoj Žižek's more contemporary modifications and inflections. While such a summary briefly takes us away from the sea, as it were, it is indispensible for the way the following chapters will analyze maritime narratives. Readers familiar with Lacan's and Žižek's work may wish to skip ahead to the last section of the Introduction, "Fantasy and Antebellum Maritime Narratives," where these theoretical topics are linked to antebellum maritime concerns.

The term "fantasy," or "phantasy" in the European version, has been traditionally defined within the discipline of psychoanalysis as an "imaginary scene in which the subject is a protagonist, representing the fulfillment of a wish (in the last analysis, an unconscious wish) in a manner that is distorted ... by defensive processes."[15] Adhering closely to Sigmund Freud's work, such a conception of the term couples the German *Phantasie*, meaning imagination or the "world of the imagination," and the French *fantasme*, which refers more specifically to "imaginary production."[16] Freud no doubt built upon both the ancient concept of phantasia and the romantic notion of the imagination when developing the psychoanalytic view of fantasy in the late nineteenth and early twentieth centuries.[17] His discussion of these concepts begins in his first seminal work, *The Interpretation of Dreams* (1899). In addition to portraying dreams as a "symptom" and "the (disguised) fulfillment of a (suppressed, repressed) wish," he also correlates them with the notion of fantasy, especially in his explication of daydreams.[18]

Freud defines the daydream as "the dream's equivalent in waking life"—constituted as a wish fulfillment, based largely on infantile experiences, and "[enjoying] a certain relaxation of . . . censorship."[19] These concepts are developed in subsequent essays, such as "The Relation of the Poet to Day-Dreaming" (1908). In this well-known piece, Freud correlates fantasy, daydreaming, and poetry. According to Freud, "Unsatisfied wishes are the driving power behind phantasies."[20] A poet "disguises" his own desires and fantasies in a composition, thereby offering the reading public pleasure through the "release of tension in [their] minds."[21] These points are picked up again in "Formulations Regarding the Two Principles in Mental Functioning" (1911). Moving toward definitions he will develop later in his career, Freud locates the "act of phantasy-making" in the context of the reality and pleasure principles—where fantasies can be seen as a site split off from reality and "subordinated to the pleasure-principle alone."[22] It is in the subsequent *Civilization and Its Discontents* (1929) that Freud more fully realizes this theory, viewing fantasy as a "palliative measure" or "substitute satisfaction" within a society that is plagued by a delimiting reality principle.[23] In such a society, "satisfaction is obtained from illusions," and "at the head of these satisfactions through phantasy stands the enjoyment of works of art."[24]

Jacques Lacan's notion of fantasy incorporates many of these elements, but they are developed in new ways as he progressively reconceives of and fills important lacunae in Freud's work.[25] Despite Lacan's original goal to "return to Freud," therefore, his project pioneers radically new approaches to psychoanalytic concepts and interpretation.[26]

On the most basic level, Lacan's conception of fantasy is based on the interplay of three registers: the Imaginary, the Symbolic, and the Real. The three functions can be conceived separately, but should be seen to function together, forming what Lacan refers to in his later work as a knot. The Imaginary relates to the visual dimension. As Lacan makes clear using the now ubiquitous example of an infant's experiences before a mirror, the Imaginary provides a means to fill the gap between a "virtual complex [a child's image in the mirror] and the reality it duplicates—namely, the child's own body and the persons and even things around him."[27] In other words, the Imaginary acts at the foundational site of ego constitution to provide an illusory sense of wholeness; in so doing, it covers over essential "discordance with [one's] . . . own reality" and thereby prevents us from seeing essential gaps and absences in these constructions.[28]

This idea is developed in Lacan's *Seminar XI*. Here he gives an account of being disturbed while on board a fishing boat when a fisherman, pointing out a floating sardine can, jokingly says: "You see that can? Do you see it? Well, it doesn't see you!" Pondering this, Lacan is led to the conclusion: "The picture, certainly, is in my eye. But I am not in the picture."[29] By this, Lacan gestures toward the way that the domain of vision commonly prevents us from seeing the central gap in reality that is constituted by the viewing subject himself or herself.[30] Consequently, when we view the world, we often miss the "stain" or "spot," to employ Lacan's terms, that designates our own presence within the scene.

The subject is a gap or void—one, again, that is in part occluded by the Imaginary—due to the function of the symbolic order. This order can be conceived as a structure that sustains and regulates society. Drawing on Saussure's structural linguistics and Lévi-Strauss's cultural anthropology, Lacan presents this system as a linguistic field that undergirds what we commonly view as reality. In discussing the formative role of signifiers, Lacan reveals language's function in shaping how we think about and view ourselves, but also the attendant conceptual structures, such as the law, that directly shape identity. One's identity, therefore, is always shaped primarily by one's "symbolic identity," or position in the symbolic register. According to Lacan, this is because "socially we define ourselves with the law as a go-between. It is through the exchange of symbols that we locate our different selves [*mois*] in relation to one another."[31] This, then, is the foundation for the Lacanian notion of symbolic castration and the view that the subject is a barred, divided subject. In Lacan's terms: "Because it is in so far as the symbol allows this inversion, that is to say cancels the existing thing, that it opens up the world of negativity, which constitutes both the discourse of the human subject and the reality of his world."[32]

Such openings in the symbolic order evidence the fact that this system is itself incomplete. As Yannis Stavrakakis points out, "Lacanian theory is indispensable in showing that understanding social reality is not equivalent to understanding what society is, but what prevents it from being."[33] What this means is that a Lacanian view of social reality starts with the premise that such reality is predicated upon impossibility. Lacan conceives of the Real as manifesting at these places where linguistic and social systems fail. In his early teachings, he claims that the Real is that which "resists symbolization absolutely."[34] But he later seems to distance the concept from run-of-the-mill Kantian noumena, arguing that it "can only be inscribed on the basis of an impasse of formalization."[35]

Slavoj Žižek's contemporary work productively builds on this latter formulation. Using the notion of the parallax view, or the "constantly shifting perspective between two points between which no synthesis ... is possible," to reconceive of the Real, Žižek effectively relegates this register to a placeholder marking the incommensurability of symbolic perspectives on reality.[36] In Žižek's words:

> The parallax Real is thus opposed to the standard (Lacanian) notion of the Real as that which "always returns to its place"—as that which remains the same in all possible (symbolic) universes: the parallax Real is, rather, that which accounts for the very *multiplicity* of appearances of the same underlying Real—it is not the hard core which persists as the Same, but the hard bone of contention which pulverizes the sameness into the multitude of appearances. In a first move, the Real is the impossible hard core which we cannot confront directly, but only through the lenses of a multitude of symbolic fictions, virtual formations. In a second move, this very hard core is purely virtual, actually non-existent, an X which can be reconstructed only retroactively, from the multitude of symbolic formations which are "all that there actually is."[37]

As such, the Real "is just a gap between two points of perspective, perceptible only in the shift from one to the other."[38] Žižek argues that this is in keeping with Lacan's own developing formula, where he moves from the "Real *qua* Thing to the Symbolic (the Real as the inaccessible traumatic core around which symbolic formulations circulate ...) to the absolute inherence of Real to Symbolic (The Real has no substance, ... it is *nothing but* the inherent inconsistency, gap, of the Symbolic)."[39] What remains to be seen, however, is the way that this Real operates in society, or, in slightly different terms, the way society structures itself in relation to its own parallactic failures.

Žižek's conception of the parallax Real is precipitated by his development of a new (or at least reinvigorated) form of "dialectical materialism," a type of materialism, as Adrian Johnston explains, based on a reinterpretation of Hegel as a "thinker of material inconsistency."[40] Using this perspective, Žižek conceives of "the Real of being *an sich* as internally self-splitting, ... auto-dividing. Hence, the very gap between noumena and phenomena is immanent to being itself."[41] This theoretical position, one that asserts "an ontological gap" in the "very heart" of material reality,[42] adds an important level of nuance to Žižek's earlier modification of Marx's famous definition of ideology as false consciousness: *"They do not know it, but they are doing it."* Emphasizing the second aspect of the equation, Žižek previously argued that the primary modality of ideology is the "doing" and not the "knowing."[43] Accordingly, "ideology is not simply a 'false consciousness,' an illusory representation of reality, it is rather this reality itself."[44] Žižek's brand of dialectical materialism thus provides a conceptual model for how this ideological reality is structured: with a dialectical relation connecting an incomplete ontic plane, symbolic functions, and manifestations of the Real.[45]

And this is precisely where fantasy comes into play. Like the traditional Freudian conception of the term, fantasy in a Lacanian sense is a narrative form of wish fulfillment that both structures desire and, ultimately, remains unconscious.[46] Lacan, however, translates these elements into his own system, which allows him to more specifically trace both the ideological and the potentially disruptive elements of its functions. Since the symbolic order and, thus, all ideological systems are structured around inevitable limits and breakdowns, the basic role of fantasy is to make people misrecognize these potential failures. As Lacan makes clear, "It is in relation to the real that the level of phantasy functions. The real supports the phantasy, the phantasy protects the real."[47] Fantasy acts to protect the Real by functioning, in Lacan's terms, as "the screen that conceals."[48] In this important sense, fantasy and ideology dovetail. According to Žižek, ideology is, itself, "a fantasy-construction which serves as a support for our 'reality' ... : an illusion which structures our effective, real social relations."[49] On the most basic level, therefore, ideology is our social reality supported by fantasy. Unlike the traditional view that fantasy is merely a means for the pleasure principle to escape the confines of reality, in Žižek's formulation, "the phantasmatic narrative does not stage the suspension-transgression of the Law, *but the very act of its installation,* of the intervention of the cut of symbolic castration."[50]

As the following chapters will explore antebellum maritime narratives using various aspects of a Lacanian notion of fantasy, it is here important to specify two foundational characteristics of the concept: its relation to desire and, even more important, its relation to the Real. For Lacan, desire is associated with the space opened up by the lack in the symbolic order. In this sense, desire—the state of wanting something—is ultimately impossible to satiate. This is because no object, experience, or concept can effectively stand in for the lack or split in the subject that gives rise to desire in the first place.[51] Lacan refers to the objects with which we attempt to fill the symbolic fissure as, conceptually, object *a* (throughout Lacan's work this concept is referred to as *objet petit a*, but is often translated as object *a*, object (a), or simply *a*). It is in this context that the title of Žižek's first major book, *The Sublime Object of Ideology*, refers to the role of object *a*: an object-cause of desire that sustains the subject and ideology by structuring their inconsistencies.[52]

In this schema, fantasy has the central role of allowing objects to occupy temporarily the impasse where the (parallax) Real manifests. In a simple sense, therefore, an object of desire is merely a variable shaped by fantasy to fill a structural symbolic gap. This is the context for Žižek's point that "fantasy mediates between the formal symbolic structure and the positivity of the objects we encounter in reality: it provides a 'scheme' according to which certain positive objects in reality can function as objects of desire."[53]

But the stakes are higher when this scenario is contextualized in its social ideological setting. Žižek's conception of the relationship between fantasy and the Real should here be emphasized: "The psychoanalytic notion of fantasy cannot be reduced to that of a fantasy-scenario which obfuscates the true horror of a situation; the ... relationship between fantasy and the horror of the Real it conceals is much more ambiguous than it may seem: fantasy conceals this horror, yet at the same time it creates what it purports to conceal."[54] In an appended footnote, Žižek expounds on this point, arguing that ideas of horrors, as such, can act as a "phantasmatic screen enabling us to avoid confrontation with the [true] social antagonism."[55] This view aligns with Fredric Jameson's well-known formulation in *The Political Unconscious* that a text or artwork is a "formal resolution in the aesthetic realm" of "real social contradictions."[56] Since Jameson's Marxist view of history is informed by a notion of the Lacanian Real, such "resolutions" can be viewed as fantasies, or at least as manifestation thereof.[57] Jameson gestures toward this when he claims: "The social contradiction addressed and 'resolved' by the formal prestidigitation of narrative must, however reconstructed, remain an absent cause, which cannot be directly or immediately conceptualized by the text."[58] In both scenarios, fantasy acts to occlude a Real that is linked to an "absent cause" and, at the same time, shadows forth its presence.

In his more recent work, Žižek links this foundational social antagonism qua absent cause to the concept of "economy." Following the parallax logic of dialectical materialism introduced above, economy is portrayed as "non-all," a site of contradiction that acts as the "cause of the mutual contamination-expression of [political] struggles."[59] Thus, "politics is . . . a name for the distance of the 'economy' from itself. Its space is opened up by the gap that separates the economic as the absent Cause from the economy in its 'oppositional determination,' as one of the elements of social totality."[60] We might, in this way, locate ideological fantasies in this space of politics—as a means to structure and (falsely) define the contradictions of the non-all of economy proper. In using this context, one can begin to see the way fantasy's relation to desire and the Real might function ideologically in a given historical reality, especially in terms of antebellum maritime fantasies. Reminiscent of Dana's reference to sea stories' conservative "witchery," maritime fantasies often occlude foundational antagonisms and redirect potentially revolutionary desires; however, as is clear in the media's portrayal of *Red Rover*'s role in the USS *Somers* mutiny, such texts can also be seen to possess radical imaginary potential.[61] According to Žižek, fantasy is typified by such a dual nature, being "simultaneously pacifying, disarming (providing an imaginary scenario which enables us to endure the abyss of the Other's desire) *and* shattering, disturbing, inassimilable to our reality."[62] Put differently, fantasy screens the Real by providing a schema for desire, and yet, in so doing, potentially engenders various complications. Such complications include: promoting a desire to transgress the law (at the same time that fantasy instantiates and supports the law), producing forms of enjoyment that threaten to overwhelm a fantasy schema's confines, and, perhaps more significant, revealing the falsity or failure of ideological fantasies themselves—which illuminates both the function of fantasy and (parallactically) the unsteady ground of a reality predicated on foreclosed antagonisms.

Stepping back, I would like to close this section with a comment on the link between this theoretical model and the historical–theoretical methodology I employ in this book. To consider historical narratives in terms of fantasy is perhaps most basically to view literature as a means to reveal social and ideological *work*, as opposed to social and ideological content. This is why, rhetorically speaking, a Žižekian brand of anecdotal discussion will not necessarily serve the type of historical analysis I propose. Anyone familiar with Žižek's corpus undoubtedly comes to expect a rapid-fire style of reference, where complex theoretical concepts are artfully and usefully translated into pithy examples culled from the realms of popular culture. As Žižek himself explains, this approach allows him to "achieve the greatest possible clarity" and, at the same time, to gauge whether or not he has fully achieved a "proper grasp" of the "Lacanian concept" at hand.[63] Although I at times follow suit, I am working primarily in the opposite direction, using Lacanian and, indeed, Žižekian concepts to clarify and illuminate specific historical ideological fantasies. But just as Žižek's work should not be misread as constituting simply a series of exempla for abstract concepts, theoretical analysis of historical fantasies should be seen as more than an exercise in teasing out the complications in an era's ideological narratives.[64]

To bring Jameson back into the fold, this difference might be clarified by taking into account the distinction between deconstruction and what Jameson calls the dialectic. According to Jameson, the "dialectic proceeds by standing outside a specific thought—that is to say a conceptual conclusion about a problem . . . —in order to show that the alleged conclusions in fact harbor the workings of unstable categorical oppositions." Next, the "antimonies . . . and ultimately contradictions then historicize the previous moment of 'conclusion' and enable a new dialectical 'solution'" to form.[65] Jameson suggests that this dialectical process, moving "jerkily from moment to moment," is in some ways consonant with deconstruction and its tendency to "dizzily fast-forward."[66] But he notes a crucial divergence:

> Where the dialectic pauses, waiting for the new "dialectical" solution to freeze over in its turn and become an idea or an ideology to which the dialectic can again be "applied" (as it were from the outside of the newly reformed system), deconstruction races forward, undoing the very incoherence it has just been denouncing and showing that seemingly analytic result to be itself a new incoherence and a new "contradiction" to be unraveled in its turn.[67]

The significance of waiting or pausing to let the dialectic operate resonates on interconnecting political and methodological levels: in terms of the former, in a desire or willingness to construct a reality in light of incompleteness (something approaching praxis), and regarding the latter, in a perspective adept enough to follow the conceptual, temporal, and spatial "zigzag" logic of historical becoming.[68]

In this light, examining nineteenth-century maritime literature's function in terms of fantasy entails more than reading it as a symptom, where one might, presumably, follow the path of positivistic historicism and move seamlessly from text to historical context, or the path of deconstruction and jump from a given narrative toward either a negative space of play or, for some, the Holy Grail of the Real.[69] Employing a dialectical approach, and better yet, a dialectical materialist approach, means one has a different analytic horizon. One is concerned not only with unraveling the disguised contradictions of given historical narratives, but also with the way these narratives function within their own impossible moment's construction.[70] As we will see, such analysis negotiates traditional historical and literary content, but it is able to reconceive of this material by foregrounding the very real but ephemeral concepts of desire and enjoyment.

Fantasy and Antebellum Maritime Narratives

To assert that early nineteenth-century maritime narratives played a crucial role in conceptualizing economic and social transitions in the developing global market system perhaps belabors the obvious.[71] And yet, just what roles these narratives played and, moreover, what they may reveal about an era marked by immense change has yet to be fully considered. In the antebellum years, the Western world's symbolic realm was expanding—or, more accurately, being resituated—with each exploratory expedition and as commercial crafts ventured further and further into Pacific, Asian, and Arctic waters. Although John L. O'Sullivan's now ubiquitous term "manifest destiny" first appeared in the *United States Magazine and Democratic Review* in 1845, the spirit of a similar form of expansion had infused the economic maritime development of the United States since its inception. After naval victories during the Revolutionary War, skirmishes with France, conflicts with the Barbary States, and triumphs in the War of 1812, a nationalist fervor fused with ongoing and burgeoning maritime commercial interests. According to Thomas Philbrick, the cessation of hostilities with England in 1815 commenced "the golden age of American shipping, a period of thirty-five years during which American seamen came to challenge and even to displace the British hegemony of many of the most important areas of maritime activity."[72] This maritime ascension is evidenced in the first volume of Alexis de Tocqueville's *Democracy in America* (1835), where he notes that, since the American Revolution, "the number of Union vessels has increased almost as rapidly as the population."[73] But his account of U.S. maritime development goes further than mere statistical references. In surmising potential causes of this growth, Tocqueville provides a narrative sketch of the "heroic" aspects of the American mariner: "He sets sail while the storm still rages; by night as well as day he spreads his full canvas to the wind; he repairs his storm-damaged ship while still under way; and when at last he comes to the end of his voyage, he continues to make for the coast at full speed."[74]

Such narrative accompaniments to maritime expansion can be seen throughout the era's numerous travel and geographic texts.[75] Their popularity was, in part, facilitated by the incredible growth of magazines, which often encouraged submissions of sea narratives of various kinds. By way of a canonical case in point, Henry David Thoreau, who in *Walden* famously calls for inward travel as opposed to foreign exploration, had, according to his journals, read and enjoyed Melville's *Typee* (1846) during his stay on Emerson's land at Walden in the fall of 1846.[76] Sea narratives were thus a popular and commercially viable means of reporting on encounters with new places, peoples, and social arrangements in the developing maritime economy.

In a broader context, this time of rushing to outer borders and of increased commercial, military, and tourist maritime activity began shifting the Eurocentric geopolitical alignments established between the fourteenth and eighteenth centuries. According to Carl Schmitt, U.S. political and economic development in the nineteenth century—development linked to the broader coalescence of modern capitalist relations—ushered in the end of what he calls the *nomos,* or conceptual and judicial order, established by European spatial coordinates linking state terrestrial territories and the vast "free" sea space.[77] We might reconceive of this nineteenth-century historical transition and its modification of spatial and political structures by locating it at the end of a shift between what Fredric Jameson terms the first phase of capital, classical or market capital, and the second phase, monopoly or imperial capital. In the first phase, the world undergoes a shift from use value to exchange value and a concomitant "desacralization of the world." In the second phase, capital begins to move into a global market. According to Jameson, this new global network creates a gap or contradiction between "lived experience and structure." Using the example of London, he describes how life in the city becomes reliant on economic realities in places such as India or Hong Kong; as a result, "structural coordinates" for social and economic reality "are no longer accessible to immediate lived experience and are not often even conceptualizable for most people." Importantly, this new modern era's art includes "forms that inscribe a new sense of the absent global colonial system."[78]

Jameson's historical schematic provides a basic way to illuminate how antebellum maritime narratives may operate within a broader process of "cognitive mapping," or symbolically locating and conceiving of new global economic and social experiences.[79] As Gunnar Olsson makes clear, "Just as the map . . . is our privileged means for finding the way, so the travel story is the most effective device for transporting our imaginations from the utopian No-where to the actual Now-here."[80] Such functions pertain to a Lacanian notion of fantasy in their role of providing narratives that fill gaps in the symbolic order, narratives that help structure responses to various experiences within the development of capital and its attendant expansion of Western domains. From the perspective of what we might call a parallax reading, maritime narratives relate to this process of cognitive mapping in a twofold manner: performing the operation of cognitive mapping *stricto sensu* by recording or narrating experiences in global settings and, at the same time, supporting and/or complicating cognitive mapping by mobilizing or forming underlying ideological fantasies.

In contextualizing antebellum maritime activity within the volatile transition to the second phase of capital, it is important to remember Edward Said's point that "imperialism and the novel fortified each other."[81] Although Said does not discuss U.S. maritime narratives, his study of how nineteenth- and twentieth-century Oriental travel texts became a central means to "bring the Orient closer to Europe, thereafter to absorb it entirely and—centrally important—to cancel, or at least subdue and reduce, its strangeness and . . . hostility" is quite relevant to the way maritime texts aid the conceptual mapping of foreign spaces and experiences.[82] In these terms, and in keeping with the aforementioned ideological nature of fantasy, the various forms of sea narratives that proliferated in the antebellum period are directly political in effect, if not intention. But this intention does at times become apparent. For example, when Charles Wilkes was about to set off in command of the hugely publicized United States Exploring Expedition in 1838, he received a letter from the secretary of the navy explaining that the military viewed the expedition as a mission "to extend the empire of commerce."[83] The letter also included the telling instructions that Wilkes should not allow any of the sailors' journals to be published without the "authority" and "supervision" of the U.S. government. To ensure this, the letter directed Wilkes to collect all such journals, writings, and drawings before the ships reached home at the close of the expedition.[84]

As should be clear by now, not all intentionally political maritime texts are conservative. An interesting example of this can be found in the fourth sketch, "A Pisgah View from the Rock," of Melville's *The Encantadas, or Enchanted Isles* (1856). Melville opens by describing what you should do "if you seek to ascend Rock Rodondo" in the Galapagos Islands:

> Take the following prescription. Go three voyages round the world as a main-royal-man of the tallest frigate that floats; then serve a year or two apprenticeship to the guides who conduct strangers up the Peak of Teneriffe; and as many more, respectively, to a rope-dancer, an Indian Juggler, and a chamois. This done, come and be rewarded by the view from our tower. How we get there, we alone know. If we sought to tell others, what the wiser were they? Suffice it, that here at the summit you and I stand.[85]

Although this passage puts forth a correlation among working-class forms of labor, experience, and knowledge—a topic I will explore more fully in chapter 1—it also reveals an important gap between the experience of space and its geographic or symbolic translation. Melville gestures mockingly toward the notion of place-as-experience—a notion inherently yoked to concepts of class and labor. Furthermore, he casts knowledge of this "other" space as being directly untranslatable, even if in terms of a refusal to tell ("we alone know"). The narrator's leap to the phrase "suffice it, that here at the summit you and I stand" reveals a veritable schism between the impossible or withheld knowledge of how to get to the rock via experience in the world and the hypothetical premise that the audience is now there. This gap is further widened in the next paragraph, when Melville shifts to the role of tour guide, pointing out sites using geographic coordinates. Thus, one can see the process through which geographic forms of discourse retroactively fill the gap between experience, on the one hand, and knowledge in the symbolic order, on the other.[86]

Melville's passage clearly relates to the developing gap between lived experience and society's newly globalizing social structure. Whereas, in the case of Wilkes's directives, the navy attempts to fill this gap with sanctioned narratives, Melville's piece conversely brings this very tension into the foreground. We might, in this way, read Melville's tale as exemplifying Žižek's rather romantic assertion that "the artifice of 'true art' is . . . to manipulate the censorship of the underlying fantasy in such a way as to reveal the radical falsity of this fantasy."[87] Edgar Allan Poe's "A Tale of the Ragged Mountains" (1843) may provide a helpful correlative. Stumbling upon a fantastic Eastern city à la the *Arabian Nights* in the midst of the Virginia mountains in 1827, the morphine-addicted narrator suspects that he is dreaming and reflects that "Novalis errs not in saying that 'we are near to waking when we dream that we dream.'"[88] Although the Novalis reference takes up the simple dichotomy of dreaming and waking, a dichotomy I will later discuss in terms of Walter Benjamin's thought, it nonetheless aligns with Žižek's logic—where a dream or fantasy moves toward an outside or new perspective when it begins to become conscious of its own functions. In a similar fashion to Melville's narrative, the Poe tale is more complex than first meets the eye, with the narrator's experience of the city ultimately resulting from a time schism that connects his current life with a previous-life role in a colonial insurrection in the Indian city of Benares in 1780.

The two tales thus share a chiasmic relation—with Melville's distant maritime scene being interrupted conspicuously by domestic mainland concerns (in the form of the audience) and with Poe's domestic mainland scene being disrupted by the improbable appearance of a foreign colonial conflict. The relation between such schisms and surrounding fantasy structures typifies the conflicts and complications that are seen in the antebellum United States' transition into the modern world, conflicts and complications that often directly involve maritime settings and scenes. Across the following six chapters, which consider various sites of such conflict, *Antebellum at Sea* examines how maritime narratives reveal and negotiate disturbing experiences of the new. These sites include: the plane of knowledge and the role of sailors' know-how within an era undergoing a transition into codified scientific knowledge; the plane of cultural and national identity and the anxiety produced by conflict between gender- and culture-specific forms of enjoyment; and the plane of law, and how maritime space and legal practices illuminate devastating juridical paradoxes at the heart of Jacksonian and Polk-era political life.

Such a project contributes to a variety of contemporary areas of scholarship within the fields of American Studies and American literary studies. Broadly speaking, it builds out of postnational and transnational paradigms of analysis.[89] Addressing antebellum literature and culture, it operates in the spirit of historical-theoretical studies of the era by scholars such as Russ Castronovo, David Kazanjian, and Christopher Castiglia.[90] In considering the social landscape of the period, I implicitly and, in chapter 4 at least, explicitly take up historical analyses of ideological gender formations in relation to travel narratives. As Amy Kaplan convincingly argues, however, traditionally gendered demarcations of space are inadequate for considering the political construction of empire in the nineteenth century. Instead, as she demonstrates using the case of Maria Cummins's *The Lamplighter* (1854), male adventure narratives and issues of female domesticity are often "intertwined."[91] Thus, I am interested not only in building on productive studies of conventional concerns of gender in antebellum America, such as those articulated in Dana Nelson's conception of "national manhood," but also in theoretically shifting gears, in a way, and attending to aspects of gender associated with more elusive topics, such as enjoyment.[92]

In terms of studies of early American and nineteenth-century maritime narratives and contexts, this book closely aligns itself with theoretically informed attempts to reconceive of nineteenth-century maritime sociopolitical events, most notably Ian Baucom's *Specters of the Atlantic: Finance Capital, Slavery, and the Philosophy of History* (2005) and Cesare Casarino's *Modernity at Sea: Melville, Marx, Conrad in Crisis* (2002). Such studies stand out amid what is a burgeoning scholarly focus on sea space, themes, and experience. In fact, the development of maritime-based studies across fields now denotes what a *PMLA* theories and methodologies forum has dubbed "oceanic studies."[93] Recent monographs that can be loosely associated with this trend include Margaret Cohen's *The Novel and the Sea* (2010) and Hester Blum's *The View from the Masthead: Maritime Imagination and Antebellum American Sea Narratives* (2008). As I will discuss to some degree in chapter 1, these books typify recent historical and literary approaches to maritime themes and texts. Though there is a wealth of such historical studies, I am most indebted to the cultural and political analysis found in the work of such scholars as Samuel Otter and Wai Chee Dimock and to the class-based analysis found in Peter Linebaugh's and Marcus Rediker's works.[94] While each of the following chapters intervenes in a different locus of various above-mentioned scholarship, my general aim is to analyze selected maritime texts and contexts in a manner that shifts the conceptual and methodological terrain offered by predominant historicist approaches.

Antebellum at Sea is composed of three thematic parts, each of which includes a pair of chapters. While addressing a variety of texts, the chapters focus on at least one primary case study. Throughout, the focal texts are those of either James Fenimore Cooper or Herman Melville—whose differing but shared complex status in terms of maritime labor experience, the political landscape, and the literary marketplace makes them an apt platform from which to study the relationship between maritime narratives and the world they present. Although the chapters address the canonical works of both authors, I focus mainly on their less-studied publications as a means to open up a broader consideration of the age as well as to contribute to critical understandings of Cooper and Melville. Such books include Cooper's *Ned Myers; or a Life before the Mast* (1843) and *The Crater; or, Vulcan's Peak: A Tale of the Pacific* (1847), and Melville's *Mardi: and a Voyage Thither* (1849) and *White-Jacket; or The World in a Man-of-War* (1850).

Part I, "Fantasy and the Common Sailor," conceives the figure of the common sailor as a flash point for prevalent ideological fantasies of the age. Chapter 1, "Fantasies of the Common Sailor; or, Enjoying the Knowing Jack Tar," explores how anxiety relating to the authenticity of maritime narratives can be seen as a symptom of foundational antebellum fantasies about class and labor experience. Looking specifically at Richard Henry Dana Jr.'s *Two Years before the Mast* and James Fenimore Cooper's *Ned Myers; or, a Life before the Mast*, I examine these fantasies by rethinking the apparent impasse between antebellum maritime narratives and the experiences they seek to depict—ultimately finding that the position of the common sailor acts a fantasmatic locus of enjoyment. Chapter 2, "Tarrying with the National: Fantasizing the Subject of State," uses James Fenimore Cooper's first maritime novel, *The Pilot* (1824), as a centerpiece to explore the conflicts, contradictions, and tensions inherent in constructions of maritime national narratives. The chapter opens with an analysis of Walter Scott's maritime romance *The Pirate* (1822)—which Cooper, in his 1849 preface to *The Pilot*, sets up as the impetus for his own novel—and explores the fantasy mechanisms that carry a Waverley-esque youth into an identification with and position in the national symbolic register. I then turn to Cooper's novel, using the seemingly precipitous death of the common sailor Tom Coffin as a lens for rereading the narrative. In essence, I suggest that formative class and national mandates may contribute to the narrative excision of Coffin.

Part II, "Polynesian Encounters Redux," uses Melville's novels and a wide range of primary texts to reconsider scenes of cross-cultural encounter from a Lacanian perspective. Chapter 3, "Tattoos in *Typee*: Rethinking Melville's 'Cultural Grotesque,'" focuses primarily on Melville's *Typee* and seeks to rethink contemporary scholarly approaches to both the novel and the topic of Polynesian tattooing. The first section relocates the climactic trauma from chapter 30's scene of anxiety about facial tattoos to the novel's appendix and its account of political events in Honolulu. In so doing, I argue that while the tattoo's threat to Tommo's face is a manifest fear in the text, the appendix's account of the colonial failure to control natives' bodies and desires potentially reveals a related and more formative peril. The second section more closely examines this fantasy scenario and its implications. Chapter 4, "Melville's 'Porno-Tropics': Re-Sexuating Pacific Encounters," uses Melville's three Pacific-island novels and contemporaneous nonfictional Pacific narratives to explore the ideological elements that shape representations of Polynesian women. More specifically, it traces how figurations of native women negotiate and reveal the tenuous mechanisms and limits of fantasy. The first section rethinks gender issues surrounding antebellum maritime narratives and introduces Lacan's notion of "sexuation"; the second section provides a relative genealogy of traditional "phallic" fantasies about Pacific Island women; and the third section uses Melville's novels to reveal the occluded problematics—especially those relating to notions of female jouissance—inherent in Pacific fantasy structures.

Part III, "Ocean-States of Exception," explores how maritime narratives illuminate legal fantasies within the antebellum era's volatile political landscape. Chapter 5, "*The Crater* and the Master's Reign: Cooper's 'Floating *Imperium*,'" and chapter 6, "The Sublime Abject of Democracy: Melville's 'Floating *Imperium*,'" place Cooper and Melville even closer on the same stage. These chapters present how both authors' dystopian novels from the late 1840s and early 1850s—*The Crater* and *White-Jacket*, respectively—reveal shared but divergent attempts to negotiate an early transition into contemporary political formations that include an apparent loss of law within democratic structures. Chapter 5 situates Cooper's novel amid a Polk era that sees Cooper's thought progressively taking an antagonistic and admonitory tenor in regard to domestic politics. Here, I argue that Cooper's novel not only manifestly favors vesting power in constitutional law over Whig-backed congressional agency, but also, in so doing, fantasmatically defends the broader master signifier of the law and its political valences. Chapter 6 examines how Melville's martial man-of-war world reveals bizarre and repugnant excesses that sustain a new manifestation of normative law. In this vein, I demonstrate how White-Jacket's experiences expose a traumatic ontological shift into what can be seen as a nineteenth-century naval totalitarian realm. Reading central events in the novel, especially those pertaining to labor and flogging, in light of a Lacanian conception of perversion, I argue that it is not only democratic law or fantasies of such law that are threatened aboard the *Neversink*, but also the foundational locus of the fantasizing subject as such.

In discussing the dream interpretation model Walter Benjamin used to shape his methodology in *The Arcades Project*, Howard Eiland and Kevin McLaughlin explain that "the nineteenth century was the collective dream which we, its heirs, were obliged to reenter, as patiently and minutely as possible, in order to follow out its ramifications and, finally, awaken from it."[95] Benjamin describes this process by writing: "The realization of dream elements, in the course of waking up, is the paradigm of dialectical thinking."[96] Quite humbly, I enter this dream world with fantasies of my own. I propose that we try to follow out the ramifications of the collective dream that is the nineteenth century, but also, perhaps, disturb this slumbering state a bit. As Melville makes clear in his *Moby-Dick* chapter "The Mast-Head," the site of sleeping and waking has consequence. There is danger in sleeping above the ocean, he suggests, for while "this dream is on ye, move your foot or hand an inch, slip your hold at all; and your identity comes back in horror."[97] In my own reverie, it is possible to not only awaken from the maritime dreams of this fascinating age (as Benjamin writes, "Remembering and awakening are most intimately related"), but also to awaken in them, in a sense, even if to horror.[98]

I

Fantasy and the Common Sailor

· CHAPTER 1 ·

Fantasies of the Common Sailor; or, Enjoying the Knowing Jack Tar

> *He holds him with his glittering eye—*
> *The wedding-guest stood still,*
> *And listens like a three years' child:*
> *The Mariner hath his will.*
>
> —Samuel Taylor Coleridge, *The Rime of the Ancient Mariner*

> *The renewed emphasis on the knowledge of the exploited seems to me to be very profoundly motivated structurally. The question is knowing whether this is not something that is entirely dreamed up.*
>
> —Jacques Lacan, *Seminar XVII*

COLERIDGE'S WELL-KNOWN SCENE in which a hoary mariner's enchanting presence arrests the attention of a young wedding guest unintentionally pinpoints a salient aspect of the future American antebellum literary marketplace: the developing role of the author in catching and holding the attention of a growing market of consumers. Though here the old mariner is a fictional storyteller, as genres of maritime narratives develop and proliferate in the years after the War of 1812, the interface, or to use Deleuze and Guattari's term, interference, between the roles of author and sailor becomes a central issue.[1]

Framing the positions of author and sailor in such a way suggests an element of ambiguity within the dynamics of their relationship. Indeed, antebellum maritime narratives include an array of possible structural relations between the two, with lifelong sailors writing of their adventures and plights; relative middle-class and upper-class writers portraying their own experiences at sea; authors transcribing or translating common sailors' stories; and other writers, in the tradition of the romance, penning fully fictional and semifictional maritime accounts.

Reading such narratives through a Lacanian notion of fantasy, I explore in this chapter the links between antebellum maritime narratives and maritime labor, and argue that the literary marketplace's anxiety about the issue of authenticity is, in part, a symptom of foundational fantasies about class and labor experience. Focusing on such texts as Richard Henry Dana Jr.'s *Two Years before the Mast* (1840) and James Fenimore Cooper's *Ned Myers; or, a Life before the Mast* (1843), I examine these fantasies by rethinking the apparent anxiety-ridden impasse between maritime narratives and the experiences of common sailors they seek to depict. Ultimately, my line of argument shifts away from the popular theoretical perspective that views this gap as the result of a symbolic failure to represent a heterogeneous or liminal "other." Instead, I explore how, paradoxically, such failures may be a necessary prerequisite for the fantasies that undergird and constitute these very narratives. In this vein, I argue that, within these maritime narratives, the position of the common sailor becomes a fantasmatic locus of enjoyment. Grounding this position in a historical transition that sees the domain of knowledge shifting from what Lacan describes as the "master's discourse" (a social link where the slave is the source of knowledge) to the "university discourse" (a modern arrangement in which institutions condition knowledge), I explore the tenuous dynamics of how these narratives may attempt to garner jouissance (surplus enjoyment) from the sailor's supposed experiences. Such an approach reframes standard considerations of the antebellum literary marketplace by examining more closely how maritime texts may have operated in the era's symbolic economy of knowledge and desire.

The early nineteenth century marks a new horizon in the way common sailors were popularly figured, as well as the way their tales functioned in society. Departing from Francis Bacon's seventeenth-century presentation of sailors as a threatening horde and a monstrosity, and Tobias Smollett's eighteenth-century comical dupe, this era often found the sailor in the role of both romantic hero and purveyor of knowledge.[2] Whereas the sailors' tales circulated among port cities were a source of information about foreign peoples and experiences throughout the seventeenth and eighteenth centuries, such knowledge took a different form and played a different function in an antebellum era marked by the proliferation of published maritime narratives. That is to say, while sailors' knowledge most assuredly included information about alternative experiences—of cultural others, of geographic spaces, of laboring experiences, and of social formations—it is also important to consider how this knowledge operated in popular maritime narratives produced in the early nineteenth century.

As noted, from the early-modern period through the nineteenth century, the common sailor's experience and knowledge played a salient role within symbolic processes. The broad contours of an apparent shift in the form of this knowledge, as well as the roles it assumed, can be discerned, however, in the difference between late eighteenth- and early nineteenth-century Barbary piracy narratives and sea narratives published after the War of 1812. As scholars have convincingly portrayed, these earlier narratives by sailors held captive by Barbary States such as Algiers and Tripoli were often written to provide specialized and serviceable information for other seamen.[3] Sea narratives produced in the antebellum era, however, not only circulated within a maritime laboring and reading community, but also were progressively addressed to a larger domestic readership.

This transition is apparent in the way texts such as *The Mariner's Library or Voyager's Companion* (1833) existed in an ambiguous realm between intended audiences. In the preface to this compendium of sea narratives "from Columbus to the present day," for example, the publisher suggests: "To transient passengers across the deep, it is hoped, that the volume will not be an uninteresting and unsought-for companion; while to that very respectable class of persons who live on shore, it will be found to present an ample and genuine representation of the habits and excitements, the pleasures and perils of a mariner's life."[4] While referring to common sailors as passengers might inadvertently bespeak the text's shift toward casting readers as literal and metaphoric tourists, it is the passage's latter series of concerns that most inform questions addressed in this chapter. In an age that viewed the sailor, in Ralph Waldo Emerson's terms, as "the man of his hands, ... all eye, all finger, muscle, skill and endurance," what is the value of such a laborer's knowledge?[5] That is, how do notions about a common sailor's excitements, pleasures, and perils shape the way these laborers' experiences and knowledge operate in maritime narratives of the age?

These questions have ramifications for a contemporary scholarly interest in maritime knowledge or, as Margaret Cohen puts it, sailors' "know-how."[6] For example, Hester Blum's *The View from the Masthead: Maritime Imagination and Antebellum American Sea Narratives* (2008) provides an invaluable focus on the writing and reading practices of common sailors, but her analysis is perhaps limited by her conceptual frame of "maritime epistemology." Blum predicates the direction of her nuanced historical discussion on a romantic conception of the "sea eye," or the "experiential view" offered by laboring at sea. According to Blum, this view creates a "knowledge system" in which "the material practices of nautical labor serve as the experiential and rhetorical foundation for imaginative speculation."[7] Such a straightforward and conclusive association of labor experience, imagination, and literary production is antithetical to a reading informed by a Lacanian notion of fantasy. The potential implications of Blum's construction can be gleaned when she discusses Cooper's and Melville's claims about the relation between their literary works and their experiences laboring at sea, bluntly stating that she takes them "at their word."[8] As we will see, much is at stake in such trust.

Margaret Cohen's more recent *The Novel and the Sea* (2010) takes up notions of maritime labor in a similar fashion, setting up a generic comparativist examination of sea novels based on the desire to revise critical assumptions about, in her terms, the novel's "lack of interest in work" as well as its biased focus on land-based events.[9] Focusing her wide-ranging analysis on the notion of a sailor's "craft," what she describes as the "skills and demeanors [that] comprise the mariner's excellence in action," Cohen presents manifold ways that the genre of sea fiction presents elements of "practical reason."[10] From my perspective in this chapter, such a focus on labor is incredibly welcome and productive. Cohen's conceptual frame for this study, however, relies on a methodological approach that is manifestly critical of and defensive toward "Marxist thinkers" and perspectives. When critiquing Adorno and Horkheimer's reading of Odysseus, for instance, she develops the claim made in her introduction that political and cultural critics in the twentieth century evince a "hydrophasia," or a tendency to reduce sea experience to "allegories of processes back on land."[11] Lumping Adorno and Horkheimer with said "Marxist thinkers," Cohen argues that they "perpetuate a key feature of Cartesian models of knowledge: the privilege accorded the mind over the body, attended by the denigration of embodiment, applied knowledge, and practical reason."[12] Though I do not intend to wade into a point-by-point dialogue with Cohen's rich work, I would like to draw attention to potential problems with her critical perspective, which seeks to carve out a positive categorization of maritime labor, across great spans of time, that is marked by a rather basic partition between land and sea as well as between varying forms of skillful embodiment and conceptual "abstraction."[13] As I will show, in the early to midnineteenth century, this experiential knowledge included not only a new and potentially radical focus on nautical labor but also acted as an enigmatic lure within foundational ideological fantasies of the age.

In returning to antebellum contexts, it is important to situate the positions of author and sailor more specifically within a marketplace that saw a burgeoning middle class of white-collar workers. By midcentury, for example, roughly fourteen thousand young men clerked in various Manhattan offices alone.[14] With a steady and growing market developing for American writers, authorship formed as one of these tenuous new professional callings. As scholars have often explored in recent years, the notion of antebellum authorship is a study in vocational, cultural, and political anxiety. Michael Newbury explains, for instance, how in order to distinguish themselves various antebellum authors and authorial affiliations employed competing rhetorical paradigms of labor—with literary middle-class and upper-class writers seeking to differentiate themselves from popular writers of dime novels, magazine pulp, and domestic fiction by associating the latter such authorial activity with industrial or slave labor.[15] While a general overview of the complex political and social landscape of the antebellum literary scene need not be redrawn here, as we will see, many of its tensions are illuminated by how it negotiates maritime concerns.[16]

The role of the common sailor was far more static, at least in terms of its symbolic parameters. As Peter Linebaugh and Marcus Rediker argue, the birth of the modern world in the early seventeenth century in many ways begins with the production of capital via enclosing public lands to expropriate labor power and push the masses into new maritime and colonial projects.[17] As the Atlantic maritime world of the seventeenth and eighteenth centuries developed, it was fueled by the energies of laborers from all nations and races. With the growing domains of colonization sweeping the globe, and slavery and impressment to fall back on, national powers and capitalists alike created, in Rediker's terms, an ongoing "process of proletarianization," whereby, in essence, an international working class was forcibly assembled to fulfill maritime-related labor needs.[18]

Although the vast majority of these sailors remained nameless and faceless Jack Tars, as they were popularly called, some attempted to peddle narratives of their experiences. Going further than those sailors who could be found selling peeks at their "skin art" on piers and in taverns, these mariners catered to the era's taste for adventure tales set at sea or amid exotic isles. Inspired by the maritime nationalism spawned by the War of 1812, newly formed publications such as *American Monthly Magazine* and *New-England Magazine* often dedicated pages to sea stories—from simple nationalist naval tales such as William Leggett's "A Burial at Sea" (1829) to sentimental pieces such as Catharine Sedgwick's "Modern Chivalry" (1827). Other periodicals, such as *Niles' Weekly Register*, were almost exclusively devoted to factual accounts of maritime piracy, especially events relating to American vessels.[19] Many of these tales and longer manuscripts were wholly fictional or ghostwritten, but quite a number were the legitimate work of various sailors and ex-sailors. In fact, in addition to popular books by ex-sailors like Cooper, Dana Jr., and Melville, there are at least sixty antebellum autobiographies by sailors on record.[20]

An interesting schism can be seen, however, between the autobiographical work of former working-class sailors, such as Horace Lane or John Nicol, and the maritime narratives by ex-sailors such as Cooper, Dana, and Melville, who possessed a higher social and class status, had relatively limited maritime experience, and often moved into the realm of literary genres such as romance.[21] While the autobiographies and exposés of lifelong sailors reveal much about antebellum and maritime social conditions, the work of popular writers who identify as both professional authors and ex-sailors (to differing degrees) may best reveal complex issues relating to the symbolic construction of the antebellum maritime world, authorship, and class experience. That is to say, though a broader study of the narrative and historical components of sailors' autobiographies would undoubtedly reveal elements about antebellum maritime labor, the structural relations between the positions of author and sailor within maritime narratives by writers with limited or no shipboard experience call attention to and generate anxiety about the issue of experiential authenticity. As we shall see, taking this anxiety as a starting point for analysis may lead to important reassessments of how these narratives harness desire.

The Author as Authentic Sailor?

At the same time that antebellum middle-class authors tended to strive for genteel or professional status, writers of maritime narratives often were forced to cut back toward the domain of manual labor. An example of this can be seen with Evert Duyckinck's Young Americans' association: just as this influential group sought to lift and professionalize authorship, Melville—a member of Duyckinck's cohort in the late 1840s—found himself having to legitimize his working-class maritime experiences to a skeptical public.

Authenticity was a central issue for the genre because—like slave narratives—maritime texts were often constructed within the paradigm of autobiography. The writer is presumably one who has experienced events and places that are foreign or extraordinary to the mainstream reading public.[22] This salient role of reporting on new places and experiences may account for part of the anxiety antebellum audiences evince when the authenticity of one of these narratives is called into question. In other words, while maritime romances obviously offered imaginary travel into fantastic and exotic realms, such fictional tales existed within a broader field of narratives that provided one of the only means to learn about and process a physical and symbolic world that was rapidly expanding.[23]

James Fenimore Cooper's first maritime novel, *The Pilot* (1824), is an early and popular example. In the 1849 preface to a new edition of the novel, Cooper shifts from his original assertion that the aim of the novel is primarily nationalistic to focusing on its efforts at maritime realism. While Cooper doesn't mention Richard Henry Dana Jr.'s *Two Years before the Mast*, which positioned itself as the first realist sea narrative and was popularly received in 1840, it is clear that maritime fiction's move toward verisimilitude influenced his approach. His new preface sets up *The Pilot* as a corrective to Walter Scott's *The Pirate* (1822). In what appears to be both a claim for paternity of the burgeoning genre and an attempt to distance himself from Scott's passé romantic project, Cooper argues that Scott doesn't go far enough to depict actual sea experience and that one of *The Pilot*'s merits is its ability "to present truer pictures of the ocean and ships."[24] Comparing Scott's employment of illusion-producing "vraisemblance" with his own use of legitimate details culled from personal experience in both the merchant and naval service, Cooper claims that he even "selected" a "seaman" for a critic and that this "old messmate" gave him the "gratifying assurance that the work would be more likely to find favor with nautical men, than with any other class of readers."[25] This concern can be seen even earlier in an 1834 preface to his pirate romance, *The Red Rover*. Here, Cooper focuses not on the veracity of events in the plot but on the accuracy of his depiction of maritime labor: "The object of the book is to paint sea scenes and to describe nautical usages and nautical character, and not at all to embody any real events."[26] As the antebellum years progressed, then, Cooper made an effort to resituate his romantic fictional narratives in response to a market that desired realism. Even more pertinent for my interests, however, is the way this move toward legitimacy focused on the knowledge and sanction of the common sailor—seen here in Cooper's own maritime past and in his prefatory use of other sailors to bolster and supplement his text's content.

Such concerns are at the heart of Herman Melville's public relations difficulties surrounding the reception of his first book, *Typee*. Melville composed the narrative after having returned in 1844 from a now well-known adventure in the South Seas, and sought to sell his manuscript when the New York publishing industry was still wary of public frustration over the "hoax" Edgar Allan Poe purportedly pulled with the extravagant adventure tale *Narrative of Arthur Gordon Pym of Nantucket* (1838). As Hershel Parker writes, Melville first approached the Harper brothers, who rejected his manuscript "on the ground that 'it was impossible that it could be true and therefore was without real value.'"[27] Though such pointed rejection obviously stung Melville, his brother, having accepted a diplomatic post in England, took the manuscript to London, where he was able to sell it to the publisher John Murray after assuring him that the tale was legitimate. But upon publication in Murray's Home and Colonial Library series, the book came under siege by English reviews that raised questions about its authenticity. These challenges to the veracity of the narrative focused not, as with the Harpers' criticism, on the events themselves, but on the apparent gap between the quality of the writing and the advertised fact of the author's identity as a sailor. In the prominent *London Times*, for example, a critic viewed *Typee* as a ruse, referring to it as a "very clever production . . . introduced to the English public as authentic, which we by no means think it to be." After citing the book's erudite references and moments of "masterly" prose, this critic argues that it is preposterous to think of the author as "a poor outcaste working seaman" and posits: "We have called Mr. Melville a common sailor; but he is a very uncommon sailor."[28] This sentiment was shared by others. One London reviewer, for instance, asserts: "We have not met with so bewitching a work as this narrative of Herman Melville's. . . . Like Robinson Crusoe, however, we cannot help suspecting that if there be really such a person as Herman Melville, he has either employed Daniel Defoe to describe his adventures, or is himself both a Defoe and an Alexander Selkirk."[29] While the first reviewer uses "uncommon" to distance the author of *Typee* from such a laboring position (he is an uncommon sailor tout court), the second views this amalgamation of author and sailor (Defoe and Selkirk, respectively) as an impossibility.

In his "Herman Melville: Uncommon Common Sailor," Walter Bezanson explores this dichotomy between positions of author and sailor, ultimately framing Melville's experiences as legitimate (though much exaggerated) "adventures" that he intentionally sought out as fodder for his writing.[30] In Bezanson's words, "Even a quick summary of the Pacific years ... reminds us of the layers of action and excitement Melville compounded for future exploitation."[31] Might this figuration, however, act to conveniently close the troublesome gap between the positions of author and sailor? That is to say, instead of illuminating this symbolic flash point as a structural-social problem, doesn't Bezanson's logic essentially explain how the latter reviewer's closing proposition was actually correct? By shifting the reviewer's term of "uncommon sailor" to "uncommon common sailor" doesn't he put forward that Melville *is* both Defoe and Selkirk?

Although Bezanson's claims are accurate in terms of historical context, I'm interested in how his apparently innocuous thesis acts to occlude the anxiety-ridden relationship between working-class maritime labor experience and authorship. As Melville's biography makes clear, his mix of patrician heritage and family maritime experience (such as his father's extensive business travels, his uncle Captain John D'Wolf's famous excursions into Siberia, and his cousin Thomas's trip into, ironically, the Taipi Valley) supports such a hybrid constitution. Yet, Melville's correspondence from the time complicates this premise on a more foundational level, as can be seen in a telling and comical letter Melville writes to his brother Allan (whom he mockingly refers to as "Sergeant") after returning from his first maritime experience on the merchant ship *St. Lawrence*:

> My Dear Sergeant,
> How is you? Am you very well? How has you been?—As to myself I haint been as well as husual. I has had a very cruel cold for this darnation long time, & I has had and does now have a werry bad want of appetisement.—I seed Mrs Peebles tother day and she did say to me not to fail to tell you that she am well
>
> No more at present
> from you friend
> Tawney[32]

Quite clearly, Melville's mocking corruption of language seeks to parody the station from which he had just returned, foregrounding a foundational difference between himself and his laboring maritime companions.[33] While I will discuss the topic of maritime narrative form and style later in this chapter, it is important here to note the way Melville's parody draws attention to not only the gap between class identities (a gap officers often sought to close in their writing by employing various forms of such "plain style" language) but also the slippage effected between the positions of sailor and common laborer (with all its symbolic import). His signing off as "Tawney" furthers the class divide with racial implications.[34] Might this letter, then, act in part as a "return of the repressed," where Melville's initial symbolic return to his mainland life establishes, on the surface, his new identity as a sailor, yet at the same time (re)inscribes the original impossibility of this class transfer within the same formal enunciation? If so, we might call Bezanson's schematic into question in terms of its ideological implications. For here a class divide is evidenced that cannot be completely bridged, even if the experience of labor in the Pacific or elsewhere was legitimate. In other words, we might ask whether Melville ever really fully experienced the position of common sailor.

To be clear, Melville did obviously labor for a time in the role of a so-called common sailor. Nonetheless, the public anxiety surrounding Melville's authenticity reveals that there are deeper issues at play. Since this tension seems to arise as critics place Melville's work within an ambiguous realm between fiction and nonfiction, we might question more directly the threat such (potential) fiction poses to the ideological function of maritime narratives. What if, paradoxically, it reveals the spuriousness of authentic accounts themselves? Ultimately, might the public's angst in responding to Melville's *Typee* gesture toward the possibility that notions of authenticity in relation to authorial working-class maritime experience are, themselves, ideological fantasies?

Asking this question in the context of the apparent gap between class experiences of the antebellum world might be seen to recapitulate aspects of Gayatri Chakravorty Spivak's seminal postcolonial inquiry, "Can the subaltern speak?" Spivak reveals a gap between subaltern subjectivities and the discourses used to represent them, and in a similar way I am asking whether the antebellum anxiety related to authenticity signifies that something is repressed in its maritime narratives: namely, again, that a genuinely authentic representation of the common sailor's experience may be impossible.[35] Though a very different political project than Spivak's, Cesare Casarino's *Modernity at Sea* analyzes notions of class and representation in *Moby-Dick* (1851) along similar lines. Whereas Spivak claims that traditional class formations are inadequate because they are conceived via male and racial domination, and thus occlude the heterogeneous identities of their members, Casarino argues that the whaling crew aboard the *Pequod* is, itself, too heterogeneous to be articulated by traditional notions of class. In this case, Casarino views the diverse living body of the crew as the "other limit" of capital, in that it is not a single "shared class" but a "shared potential for the overcoming of capital."[36] This collective body, according to Casarino, forms modes of existence that are not recognized by traditional categories of hermeneutics and language. As Casarino observes, "The fact that Ishmael can ultimately understand Ahab far better than he can understand either the crew or himself qua member of that crew should give one pause."[37] Melville, via Ishmael, cannot fully or accurately represent the crew because they, themselves, resist traditional notions of bourgeois subjectivity.

Although I am not following Casarino's lead in theoretically tracing the outlines of this potentially revolutionary class's (and I use the term loosely here) identity, his analysis clearly supports my claim that an unresolved tension exists between working-class maritime experience and literary maritime narratives. For Casarino, this tension appears to be caused by the material and social formation of the heterogeneous crew itself.[38] Scholarship on the nineteenth-century sailor tends to support this view, though in a less theoretical context. For example, after claiming that "the eighteenth-century deep-sea sailor is still by and large an unknown man," Marcus Rediker cites Gary Nash's point that early American seamen "are perhaps the most elusive social group in early American history because they moved from port to port . . . , shifted occupations, died young, and, as the poorest members of the free white community, least often left behind traces of their lives."[39] Yet, one must also contextualize the formation of this group within the symbolic matrix and structure of capital and the fact that it is capital's systems that simultaneously produce and fail to conceptualize these laborers.

By figuring this narrative deadlock in terms of a rather elementary symbolic class divide, I do not intend to reduce the heterogeneous complexity of subject formation or negate the ontic or ontological identity of one of these groups (most centrally, the working class). Instead, I am interested in revealing how such narratives may function within a literary market and a broader symbolic order that seek both to conceal and maintain class antagonisms *and* to feed off of the workers' experiences and desires, along with their laboring bodies. By viewing notions of authenticity as an antebellum fantasy, one can begin to see how maritime narratives, wittingly and unwittingly, use the very gap between class and experiential positions to structure a desire for knowledge about the common sailor's labor and experience.

Richard Henry Dana Jr.'s *Two Years before the Mast* is remarkably telling in this regard, as well as influential in how subsequent authors negotiate issues of authenticity. Dana's hugely popular "accurate and authentic" narrative of his two years as a merchant sailor on the *Pilgrim* is one of the first antebellum sea narratives to foreground the issue of class, with Dana positing in the preface that most maritime narratives are written by "naval officers . . . or passengers" and that these perspectives "take a very different view of the whole matter from that which would be taken by a common sailor."[40] The conditional tense "would" here relates to Dana's subsequent claim that though much attention has been focused on the common sailor (presumably in terms of temperance) "with the single exception [of *Mariner Sketches* (1830)] . . . there has yet to be a book written, professing to give their life and experiences, by one who has been of them, and can know what their life really is. *A voice from the forecastle* has hardly yet been heard" (3). This passage highlights the text's—and, one can argue, the antebellum world's—foundational premise that the common sailor is largely unknown. On the most basic level, *Two Years before the Mast* enacts the fantasy that this can be changed—that a nonsailor can be "of them" and "know what their life really is."

At first glance, the book is manifestly successful in accurately depicting shipboard labor; yet, we might explore to what degree Dana actually succeeds in "knowing" the experiences of a common sailor. Framing the text as a fantasy in the context of Jacques Lacan's conception of the term, however, allows such potential inconsistencies to coexist: where knowing and reporting some elements of a sailor's life masks the structural impossibility of completely achieving this very task. As discussed in the Introduction, according to Lacan, fantasy is a narrative that acts to "screen" the failure (designated by the notion of the Real) of linguistic and social systems. In this view, such a process structures reality by providing coordinates whereby a subject desires something (object a).[41]

In the case of *Two Years*, the common sailor, a figure Dana goes out of his way to portray as largely unknown, is clearly invested with a type of object *a*—an undefined aspect that arouses Dana's desire. In Lacan's well-known schematic, because desire is based on a certain misrecognition (a nonknowledge of the function of object *a*), a central paradox of fantasy is that an element of distance is required between the subject and his or her object of desire. Although I will explore the dynamics of this relationship in more detail later, here it is important to observe more generally the way Dana navigates the distance between himself and the liminal figure of the sailor.

We might, therefore, safely take this text at its word and say that its primary desire is to know the common sailor. This manifests throughout the narrative, most notably in chapter 28's aside to the reader: "We must come down from our heights, and leave our straight paths, for the byways and low places of life, if we would learn truths by strong contrasts; and in hovels, in forecastles, and among our own outcasts in foreign lands, see what has been wrought upon our fellow-creatures by accident, hardship, or vice" (244). Central to this call is the assumption that one can "learn" of those living in "low places" by merely "seeing" their conditions. This foundational assumption alone might be seen to undergird a wide variety of both nineteenth- and twentieth-century down-classing projects.[42] Yet the passage also blatantly includes an obfuscation of class conflict: identifying the cause of such low stations as a result of "accident, hardship, or vice." Of course, "hardship" might be correlated with broader economic systems, but couching it between abstract and fatalistic "accident" and self-imposed "vice" tends to diminish this association.

Though Dana's book does not readily or intentionally present the potential untruth of its fantasies, there are moments when they are complicated in important ways. These complications often derive from scenes in which Dana's symbolic identity and class position are shown to be incommensurate with that of the crew. The book opens and closes with such divides: in chapter 1, even when Dana claims that with his new sailor dress he can "pass very well for a jack tar," he notes that the crew could easily see the difference (5); and, in chapter 29, any temporary closure of the gap between positions is formally breached when Dana uses money to procure a transfer onto a homeward-bound vessel and, in turn, the crew scornfully views him as a "gentleman's son" and as assuredly not "one of them" (256–57). Besides these emphatic ruptures, other events relate to a more subtle difference in regard to class associations of learning and social etiquette. This can be seen, for instance, when the cook is upset at Dana's skepticism about his supernatural tales and says: "You think, 'cause you been to college, you know better than anybody" (39), or when Dana feels a strong connection to George Marsh, another "well born," "gentleman" sailor (243).

But even more salient are the times when Dana figures his own position within the crew in qualified forms of difference. This commonly occurs when he presents his current immersion in the crew in terms of past or future separation or restored divergence. In this sense, his belonging acts as a precarious (and, I argue, fantasmatic) moment that bridges symbolic and chronological divides. In chapter 14, for example, when the ship's return to Boston is delayed, he laments with the crew the prospect of remaining in California for three years, thinking that such a lengthened stay would be even worse for him, one "who did not mean to be a sailor for life; having intended only to be gone eighteen months or two years. Three or four years would make [him] a sailor in every respect, mind and habits, as well as body—nolens volens; and would put all [his] companions so far ahead of [him] that college and a profession would be in vain to think of" (88). His fear of not only losing ground within mainland professional society but also of fully and permanently becoming a sailor testifies to his not already inhabiting such a position. This schematic resurfaces when, sitting alone on the rocks by the shore, he rejoices when his "better nature returned strong upon [him] . . . and [he] experienced a glow of pleasure at finding that what of poetry and romance [he] ever had in [him], had not been entirely deadened" (133).

In her analysis of *Two Years,* Hester Blum uses an 1841 *North American Review* passage in which the author praises the "truth" of Dana's narrative to set up her argument that "the achievement of antebellum sea writing lies in its author's ability to make the 'truth' of sea labor a productive compensation for any loss of the reader's romantic notions of sea life."[43] On closer examination, however, truth's "compensation" for fancy is less a simple exchange as much as a relative isomorphic shift. That is, Blum's historically sound observation misses the fact that this "truth" is itself structured by fantasy and thus denotes merely a qualitative shift in the ground of a reader's "romantic notions of sea life." Ultimately, therefore, Dana's fantasy casts the sailor as a type of object of desire that provides a means to bridge the divide between symbolic class positions—an enigmatic other who is yet to be completely known and, as such, maintains a position of surplus, of being more than he appears. Yet it remains unclear how, exactly, the sailor's experience operates in this equation. Such fantasies, in fact, may desire not just knowledge about the lives of common sailors but access to something else that resides within that supposed knowledge.

The Sailor Knows . . .

Long-standing European and American tropes figure the sea as a threshold between the known and the unknown. As mentioned in the Introduction, since at least the early sixteenth century, experiences "beyond the line" were popularly viewed as exotically mysterious and dangerous.[44] According to Greg Dening, "The most important knowledge . . . was that of a seaman who had gone where others had not been, beyond that point, beyond that cape, beyond that sea."[45] A late eighteenth- and early nineteenth-century sailor's experience of such spaces was, of course, marked and mediated by a variety of shipboard rituals. But how was this "knowledge" defined, mediated, and articulated outside such practices?

Here, we return to the conceptual rub I presented in terms of a basic symbolic class divide: can the sailor speak of what he has experienced? Since the problem of representing experiential knowledge is as much a social one as it is a conceptual one, it might be better illuminated via the four discourses, or social arrangements, that Jacques Lacan establishes to explain different types of human relations: the master's discourse, the hysteric's discourse, the analyst's discourse, and the university discourse. Each of these discourses is structured by the links between four functional positions: agent, other, truth, and product.[46] Depending on the arrangement, these positions are occupied by four different concepts: the master signifier (represented as S_1 and connoting both the traditional master and the ideological quilting point), knowledge (represented as S_2), the divided subject (represented as S and connoting the human subject after symbolic castration), and surplus enjoyment (represented as a and connoting both jouissance and the object-cause of desire). Each of the discourses, therefore, denotes a different social alignment based on issues of agency, knowledge, subjectivity, and enjoyment.

The master's discourse is the most relevant for initially considering the position of the common sailor. In addition to the fact that Lacan locates this schematic within the historical development of modernity, the configuration of its constitutive elements correlates loosely with the antebellum literary market's relation to sailors.⁴⁷ This social arrangement is shaped by a master (again, doubling as an ideological quilting point) who addresses an other/slave who is in the position of knowledge.⁴⁸ In part following Hegel's master–slave dialectic, Lacan claims that the slave is traditionally "characterized as the one who is the support of knowledge" as he is the one with "the know-how [savoir faire]." Consequently, when considering modern social formations of knowledge, philosophy is placed in the role of master and, according to Lacan, its history is shaped and supported by "stealing slavery of its knowledge."⁴⁹

Using this context to view antebellum maritime concerns, we might say that sea narratives attempt to conceive of and represent (via a form of translation or "transmutation") the new and expanding world, in part through the knowledge and experiences of maritime laborers. In placing this dialectic within the modern era, Lacan reads the master as a capitalist and observes a veritable "modification of the place of knowledge" whereby the slave (as the "proletariat") is "dispossessed" at a new level—for now "capitalist exploitation effectively frustrates him of his knowledge by rendering it useless."⁵⁰ Consequently, a paradigm shift establishes a "new tyranny of knowledge" based on the master's knowledge. But this shift is not a simple reversal. According to Lacan, although knowledge is now vested in the position of the master, the master "does not know what he wants" and, paradoxically, must rely on the slave for this direction. In Lacan's words, "The slave knows many things, but what he knows even better still is what the master wants, even if the master does not know it."⁵¹

This modern paradigm shift in the location of knowledge gives birth to what Lacan refers to as the university discourse. Although I will discuss this discourse and its relation to the master's discourse in the final section of this chapter, suffice it to say here that the antebellum era might be seen as completing a transition into this latter structure, where the position of agency is occupied by knowledge (for in the university discourse, institutional knowledge reigns). As this process is still incomplete during the early nineteenth century, the figure of the sailor within the more traditional master's discourse might be seen to fantasmatically supplement such "university" knowledge (as we'll see, veiling its shortcomings as well as giving form to excesses that resist it). On a basic level, Lacan's schematic might account for why the antebellum market desires the sailor in the first place. For just as the master needs the slave to, in a sense, close the circle of knowledge, antebellum society as it plays out in the literary market seems to need the sailor to maintain its fantasies about itself and the expanding maritime world.

This also provides a possible reason why the antebellum era's symbolic order fails to fully know sailors and their experiences. Complications arise not only because of properties of this other, per se, but also because the symbolic is conditioned by the developing aegis of what can be seen as a contemporary master's discourse. As mentioned, in Lacan's discussion of the master–slave dialectic, it is the master's position that conditions the knowledge that the slave provides him or her with. As such, the structural gap between the two positions might be seen as tantamount to a gap within the master himself.[52] This is not to suggest that the sailor-as-slave does not possess his or her own knowledge—knowledge that is often intricately linked to specific and vital nautical skill sets as well as to various maritime social encounters. Rather, the point is that the master's discourse addresses and views this other subject and its knowledge from the position of agency; thus, the master can never fully conceive of the other's knowledge because it is, in a way, trapped by its own gaze. The previous question of whether the sailor can speak of his experiences, therefore, might be reconceived as "Can the sailor speak of his experiences in a way that the master desires?"[53]

By placing Dana Jr. and other authors of this age who sought authentic representations of a sailor's experiences in the position of a relative master, the underlying structure of their fantasies may be better illuminated. According to Lacan, the master's discourse is structured by an object a that "is precisely identifiable with what the thought of the worker, Marx's, produced, namely what was, symbolically and really, the function of surplus value."[54] In this way, Lacan directly connects Marx's notion of surplus value with the concept of surplus enjoyment, or jouissance.[55] A crucial aspect, therefore, is that the master seeks not merely the surplus value or knowhow produced by the worker's activity, but also the thing (a) generated as a by-product of this activity: surplus enjoyment.

As mentioned, this entire process is predicated upon impossibility. Structured by fantasy, such a relation is sustained by a desire for surplus enjoyment that is associated with a worker's experiential knowledge, and access to such supposed knowledge is clearly not feasible within the fantasy's own terms. For, according to the Lacanian truism, access to knowledge precipitates a correlative loss of jouissance.[56] Yet, just because such full surplus enjoyment is only "perceived in the dimension of loss" does not mean such fantasmatic searches for it do not elicit forms enjoyment per se.[57] The impossible task of procuring jouissance qua the sailor's knowledge engenders a lower-level type of enjoyment that Lacan terms "phallic enjoyment," a form of blind enjoyment produced by and associated with language and fantasy.[58]

Ultimately, then, the gap between full knowledge and its object, the frustration of knowledge, if you will, is both the origin and necessary structural prerequisite for desire and fantasy. In terms of the common sailor, maritime narratives can be seen to create fantastical searches for an enigmatic other whose very distance (from knowledge) enables such narratives to approach a second-level goal: enjoyment. Yet, as we see within the antebellum literary marketplace, this enjoyment and its manifestation within a negative condition of knowledge generate anxiety that is often articulated in terms of authenticity; thus, maritime narratives of this era evince a shifting paranoid attempt to address these inner complications: manifestly seeking to close the gap of (authentic) knowledge, and, at least structurally, to maintain it so that the constituting fantasies may continue.

Such fantasies manifest in maritime narratives of the age in various ways and degrees. For example, in Poe's short story "MS. Found in a Bottle" (1833), the protagonist is a maritime passenger who is one of only two survivors of a mysterious storm. Even though the fact that the foreign crew ("consisting principally of Malays") was swept away clearly presents an antebellum racial fantasy scenario, what happens next in the tale is more relevant.[59] Floating into uncharted southern waters, they slip aboard a massive ship of antiquated form. The narrator's uncanny experiences on the old vessel culminate when he learns that the oddly dressed crew with the strange language cannot see him. As the narrator explains, "I made bold to trust myself among a group of the crew. They paid me no manner of attention, and, although I stood in the very midst of them all, seemed utterly unconscious of my presence."[60] On the surface, Poe's experience of these "incomprehensible men" appears to complicate Dana's project—dramatizing a passenger's complete inability to know or even communicate with the laboring crew.[61] Yet, this very scene might also be viewed via Lacan's schematic as a supplement to the foundational fantasy found in Dana's work. For the ambiguity surrounding who is haunting whom, in a sense, potentially casts the strange sailors in a position of power—a position of being able to refuse to acknowledge the narrator. This figuration places the sailors outside the narrator's, and therefore the symbolic order's, domain of control. In this context, the sailor is still embodied with an enigmatic object *a*, as in Dana, but here the distance between symbolic positions is acknowledged. It is as though Poe's narrative constructs a fantasy of the sailor that can operate without the concomitant fantasy of authenticity that conditions so many antebellum narratives. In terms of Lacan's discussion of the master's discourse, does not Poe's narrative erect a fantasy whereby the sailor (or slave) retains his classic position and role as source of knowledge? By placing the sailors beyond the range of the narrator's symbolic reach, these men—literally from an earlier age—become the potential bearers of both knowledge and enjoyment that are impossible if this gap is closed. This distance, then, might be seen to fortify the foundational fantasy expressed by Dana. One must ask, however, whether Poe's fantasy is sustainable in a narrative bound by verisimilitude. Although he is able to slip the constraints of authenticity, this is achieved by displacing the potentially irreducible gap between sociosymbolic positions via an imaginary time gap.

In this light, Poe's narrative gestures toward a consciousness of the desires surrounding narrative authenticity. While the story might be read as an attempt to quell the demand to bridge the gap between author and sailor, it nonetheless brings this very divide into the foreground. Other maritime narratives of the era also depict a relative cognizance of this tension. In Joseph C. Hart's historical novel *Miriam Coffin; or, The Whale-Fishermen* (1834), the Nantucket whale ship the *Grampus* finds itself "the rage" of London after ramming a French naval schooner in self-defense and then making it to England.[62] In a comical spirit, Hart presents how the two chief London playhouses, with their numbers dwindling, sought to capitalize on public interest by staging dramatizations of the Nantucket crew's exploits. Most revealing in this scenario, however, is how the manager of the playhouse intentionally seats the members of the *Grampus*'s crew directly below the stage in order to "[enable] the audience to get a full and better view of the Jonathan-looking boys, who had performed the bold action which was about being commemorated in mimic display."[63] This effort to authenticate the dramatic narrative by having the real-world referent, of sorts, directly on hand pays off, as "cheer followed cheer in quick succession."[64] The ironic scene's apparent critique of the maritime market's need for authenticity is furthered when a playful dispute erupts between the American sailors—especially the ship's vocal proprietor Jethro Coffin—and the star of the theatrical event itself.

Telling Yarns; or, Ned Myers Does Not Exist

The awareness of the role of authorial experience can be correlated with the developing notion of celebrity in the antebellum world. As Newbury makes clear, by midcentury a "new kind of conspicuously public space for the celebrity" had developed that included pushing authors into a "field of the publicized personality."[65] In terms of maritime literature, this may have exacerbated the anxiety surrounding authenticity by making the author's experiences (or lack thereof) a relevant topic of public discourse. Moreover, it might account for the prevalence of forms of translation during this era.

On a basic level, narratives involving translation and transcription might be seen as a last resort to sustain fantasies that bridge the symbolic gap between class and experiential positions. Transcribing or editing a sailor's story offers a unique way for an author to traverse the space between positions merely on the plane of knowledge. All previously mentioned fantasies are, therefore, upheld—most important, that of the sailor as a distant and enigmatic bearer of knowledge. At the same time, the gap between positions is acknowledged. Ultimately, the notion of translation in terms of maritime experience can be seen as a last line of fantasy over the Real, where out of necessity the symbolic rupture is, itself, forced into the fantasmatic narrative fabric. In terms of the master's discourse, the position of sailor (slave) keeps a safe distance from the position of author/editor (master) and maintains the appearance of agency (in his possession of experiential knowledge).

Fantasies of translation, however, also include notions about the rhetorical form this knowledge assumes. As Casarino claims in terms of Melville's *White-Jacket*, there is a tendency in this era to figure sailors as "the last tribe of storytellers."[66] Though he may come close to romanticizing the communal nature of shipboard life, Casarino aptly contextualizes the antebellum maritime labor market as an outlet for artisans who were forced from mainland jobs with the acceleration of industrialization in the 1830s and 1840s. With its heterogeneous mix of laborers from various cultures and traditions, including traditional storytellers from the mainland United States, "the ship becomes ... one of the last sedimentary spaces for the residues of oral narrative traditions."[67] In an age dominated by the proliferation of print culture, the yarn becomes a romantic vestige of traditional means of communication and social networks. As Mark Simpson elucidates in terms of Poe's *Narrative of Arthur Gordon Pym*, "Pym's account makes the creation and reception of travelers' tales individual, intimate, knowledgeable, desiring, face-to-face—an immediate exchange of mediated experience." Although such sailors' yarns undoubtedly existed, their function within the maritime literary genre can be seen, in Simpson's terms, as "a pointed fantasy *about* narrative."[68] Not only is the sailor's knowledge via experience viewed as valuable and rare, its very method of communication also constitutes an enigmatic lure.

An example of such a yarn/fantasy can be found in chapter 54 of *Moby-Dick*, "The Town-Ho's Story." This chapter, first published in 1851 in *Harper's New Monthly Magazine,* includes a playful presentation of a yarn's successful translation and dissemination. Ishmael tells the reader about a time in Lima at the "Golden Inn" when he presented a group of Spanish friends with a tale he heard on the *Pequod* from the crew of the whaling ship the *Goney.* Thus, the chapter frames itself as a series of retellings of the yarn. Interestingly, Melville's schematic negotiates fantasy elements on multiple levels, furthering the premise that the translation of such a story is possible and, at the same time, emphasizing the mysterious nature of such storytelling events. In fact, his emphasis of the yarn's inscrutable source might be seen as an attempt to call such fantasies into question.

While the content of the yarn (the sailor Steelkilt's escape from and ascendancy over the captain's power) is relevant here, the way Melville invests the tale itself with enigmatic value is even more significant. According to Ishmael, "secret" information in the form of a tale was imparted to Tashtego by "three confederate white men" of the *Goney* during a "gam" between the two whale ships. Melville foregrounds the fact that this tale "never reached the ears of Captain Ahab or his mates" or, for that matter, the captain of the *Goney.* The class divide is again underscored when Melville describes the tale as the "private property" of the three white sailors.[69] Such constructs clearly place sailors' tales and their messages in a zone beyond the bounds of authority, which is subsequently emphasized when the crew, after hearing the tale, agrees to keep it from the officers.[70] Yet, Melville furthers this divide on a conceptual level by casting the source of the tale's transmission to Ishmael and the rest of the crew as Tashtego's "rambl[ing] in his sleep."[71] Although the tale is known to the crew alone, they originally have access to it only through the muddled and displaced echoes of another sailor's unconscious thoughts.

In these terms, one should not separate fantasies about the content of a sailor's story from fantasies about the form of his story. Instead, the tale should be viewed as a dialectical whole—portraying, in Fredric Jameson's terms, how "form is itself but the working out of the content."[72] Like the "plain style" of many maritime narratives, where sailors' technical nautical jargon and concise syntax links them to their position as laborers, here such narrative form portrays how, in Blum's terms, "sailor narratives foreground their own materiality."[73] That is to say, maritime plain style was popularly associated with the sailor's specific technical knowledge (both at the level of officer and of Jack Tar), and also with the notion that this language somehow represented an organic development, directly spawned from sea-based experience. This link between plain style and something approaching the romantic conception of the poetic "organic principle" can be seen, for example, in a dialogue Margaret Fuller includes in *Summer on the Lakes, in 1843* (1844) between "S" and "J," presumably herself and James Freeman Clarke, one of the friends with whom she was traveling. In a discussion of the topic of lakes, Fuller has "J" comment: "That is why sea-slang is so poetical; there is a word for everything and every act, and a thing and an act for every word. Seamen must speak quick and bold, but also with the utmost precision. They cannot reef and brace other than in a Homeric dialect."[74]

In the anonymously published (and most likely ghostwritten) trilogy titled *The Female Marine,* distributed first in pamphlet form between 1815 and 1818, this relation between laboring station and language is dramatized in an interesting manner. The tale is presented as a personal narrative by a woman named Lucy Brewer, who, at one point, moves quickly from being a land-locked prostitute living in Boston's "Negro Hill," to a cross-dressing marine aboard the USS *Constitution* during the War of 1812. Thus, the narrative depicts implicitly fantasies of experiential transformation that Dana later takes up—here adding gender to the mix (a topic I will discuss in chapter 4). While this transition itself is plausible, the narrative's shift in rhetoric—in the space of a single page—draws attention to surrounding fantasy structures. The narrative is written in the form of a standard first-person autobiography while set on land but moves abruptly into the mode of plain-style writing when Lucy depicts events at sea. Just paragraphs after recounting how, in joining the crew, "new scenes now opened to [her] view," Lucy includes passages such as: "On the 19th, at 2 P.M. a vessel was discovered at the southward; our ship instantly gave chase, and soon gained on her. At 3 P.M. it could plainly be perceived that she was a ship, under easy sail, close hauled to the wind."[75] Since the action leaps forward a vague number of months once Lucy joins the *Constitution,* the chronotopic logic of the narrative allows for the acquisition of the technical knowledge required to "plainly" discern the foreign vessel's nautical maneuvers. Yet, in the feverish speed with which the narrative switches rhetorical codes and in the apparent ease with which Lucy picks up and employs plain style, the story may complicate the broader fantasies of experience that undergird this very rhetoric. Thus, on one level, plain or technical style directly links linguistics to class station and nautical know-how, and on another, it is charged with fantasies about both these forms of labor and the language form itself. In the case of translation, therefore, especially as it relates to the sailor's yarn, one should attend to the way form relates to narrative plot elements as well as to the qualitative aspects of the sailor's supposed experiences.

This can be seen in Dana's *Two Years* when whaling ship captain Job Terry comes on board the *Pilgrim* and begins a "'yarn' ... which lasted, with but little intermission, for four hours" (34). In fact, Dana goes so far as to claim that the tale "probably never would have come to an end, had not a good breeze sprung up, which sent him off to his own vessel" (34). Here, the yarn might be figured as a story that can temporarily break from the surrounding confines of the symbolic world, including its elements of time and space. As a potentially perpetual tale, this yarn also acts as a relative schizophrenic break from the broader context. Unlike a traditional Lacanian schizophrenia, however, where there is a breakdown in the signifying chain itself, here there appears to be a fantasy in which the yarn offers a veritable leap into a synchronically alternate or parallel signifying system. A central aspect of this construction is that the formal difference is based on the content of the tale. This is apparent when Dana explains that Terry's tale was "all about himself, and the Peruvian government, and the Dublin frigate, and Lord James Townshend, and President Jackson, and the ship Ann M'Kim of Baltimore" (34). The apparent randomness of topics should be viewed as symptomatic of this sailor's real-world material life—which includes schizophrenic-like movement across international waters. Thus, a longtime sailor's experience is a Job Terry–like life of circulation, a life one cannot know or represent based on the events of a single journey or even a series of journeys. This is why elements of the translation of common sailors' autobiographical tales may offer an important structural supplement to antebellum fantasies.

Indeed, antebellum narratives that employ legitimate and performed translations abound. These include self-proclaimed joint efforts between authors and sailors, as with Cooper's *Ned Myers; or, a Life before the Mast*, as well as adaptations of previous sailors' tales, such as Melville's *Israel Potter: His Fifty Years of Exile* (1854). Although Cooper and Melville both explicitly refer to themselves as editors in relation to these texts, such projects had a tenuous status in the antebellum literary market. In terms of Cooper's book, which was popular in 1843 but quickly faded from sight, scholars such as Hugh Egan see its ambiguous genre status, "which hovers between straight autobiography and first-person fiction," as the reason for its ultimate lack of success.[76] One should go beyond Egan's astute observation, however, and ask why exactly such narrative ambiguity poses a problem. Of course, issues of basic authenticity are relevant here. Yet, the text's blurring of the positions of author and sailor might be read more in terms of the fantasies that structure these relations. If one looks at Cooper's work in this context, it is apparent that *Ned Myers* paradoxically complicates the very fantasies with which it seeks to operate.

As mentioned, Cooper's maritime romances during this era are set up and repackaged to emphasize their authentic representation of maritime experience. *Ned Myers* is no exception, published in 1843 after Cooper collaborated and composed it with his eponymous former shipmate earlier that year. The two first met in 1806 when both signed on for a voyage bound from New York City to London aboard the merchant ship *Stirling*. While Myers's purportedly autobiographical account includes many interesting events—from his youth in Nova Scotia and ties to Prince Edward to his merchant and naval adventures during the War of 1812—it is the book's textual relationship between Cooper and Myers that best illuminates issues pertaining to fantasies of class experience.

By the time of the book's publication, Cooper had solidified his career as a prolific and influential American author. Even though *Ned Myers* is about Myers's life, Cooper's thoughts and experiences figure prominently throughout—especially in the editorial preface. Besides setting up the moral purpose of the tale, Cooper tellingly uses his own maritime experience as a means to authenticate his old shipmate's—a pronounced and paradoxical shift in light of previous discussions of the position of knowledge. He explains that he first met Myers "in the year 1806, [when] the editor, then a lad, fresh from Yale, and destined for the navy, made his first voyage in a merchantman."[77] As Wayne Franklin makes clear, such a summary is in many ways an idealistic revision of the past; Franklin elucidates: "'Fresh from Yale' was certainly an evasion, and only in retrospect could the expelled ex-student claim that in 1806 he already was 'destined for the navy' or had anything like a 'profession'—which the navy never became for him in any case."[78] Though Cooper did serve in both merchant and naval maritime posts, he had technically seen the end of his firsthand maritime activity in 1810, subsequently acting only as a recruiting agent and later as a New York militia leader. While his innocuous romanticizing of the past is of little consequence in itself, its relation to a broader process of historical and narrative character construction is.

This can be seen in the opening paragraph of the preface. After recounting an aphorism about how any "faithfully told" account of "the life of any man" holds didactic import, Cooper suggests that such a belief "has induced the writer to commit to paper, the vicissitudes, escapes, and opinions of one of his old shipmates, as a sure means of giving the public some just notions of the career of a common sailor" (1). Just as Dana's immensely popular *Two Years* should be viewed as the paradigmatic context that Cooper is working in and responding to—seeing Dana's two years of experiences and raising him a sailor's lifetime—so, too, should the role of Job Terry's yarn in Dana's tale. Using Myers's lifelong experience as a common sailor enables Cooper to "commit to paper" a Terry-like yarn that his own maritime experiences could never produce, replete with its perpetual and complex "vicissitudes."[79] That Cooper may be intentionally negotiating such fantasies of the yarn can be seen early in the book in the way he rhetorically figures the audience. Interestingly, both Cooper's preface and the first chapter of *Ned Myers* argue that the moral lessons of the narrative might benefit readers who are also common sailors (1, 5). Although sailors undoubtedly read such narratives, the book is obviously also intended for a mainland market of readers.[80] This stated philanthropic aim can be seen, therefore, as a fantasy structure for a broader audience, with the reading public rhetorically placed in the position of the common sailor. Such a setup enables Cooper/Myers to mimic the structure of a yarn: establishing a veritable fantasmatic voyeur's scene where a narrative purportedly for an inside crowd is opened up for an outside one.

The most revealing aspect of the narrative, however, is the symbolic relation between the self-proscribed roles of Cooper-as-editor and Myers-as-narrator. While the simple premise that Cooper may be more than just an editor in this project is interesting, merely questioning whether Cooper is using Myers as a legitimating working-class prop fails to attend to underlying fantasies related to translation and class experience. This is because such a question operates within the logic of translation itself. Instead, the very ambiguity of their relation should be centered. And such ambiguity is apparent in the opening of the first chapter. Myers's narrative persona is complicated in the very first line, when he opens by referring to his identity in the third person and recounts how he wants to "lay before the world the experience of a common sailor" (5). Taken on its own, this rhetorical distancing is inconsequential; yet when considered in the light of Cooper's preface and Myers's own subsequent comments, it might be seen, ironically, as the truth of the narrative at large: that Ned Myers's narrative subjectivity does not coincide with itself. The rhetorical gap in the first sentence between Myers's narrating first-person subjective "I" and his figuration of his experiences in the same narrative as relating to a third-person "common sailor" might be seen to reveal the very split that constitutes his broader identity in the book.

In one sense, this scenario can be viewed in relation to a general Lacanian conception of subject formation, where the subject is divided due to the function of the symbolic order.[81] The playful claim in my subtitle for this section, that Ned Myers does not exist, refers to the common Lacanian notion that the subject does not exist but "ex-sists"—that is, existence as such is distorted or split by the function of the symbolic order. This more general and formal schematic, however, is here carried out within a historical and material social reality: Cooper's renarration of Myers's story. It may be more accurate, therefore, to view Myers as a subject who functions in a role approximating the slave in Lacan's master's discourse: as a locus of knowledge and enjoyment that is foundational to the narrative's broader fantasy constructions.

Yet even this traditional schematic is called into question by the way the preface establishes the relation between Cooper's and Myers's positions. While in the second paragraph Cooper sets himself up as a strict amanuensis in his role as editor, he later complicates this scenario, writing, "In a few instances he has interposed his own greater knowledge of the world, between Ned's more limited experience and the narrative" (2). This line is significant in its reversal of the qualitative aspects of the traditional translation scenario. Since the narrative is of Ned's vast experience as a common sailor, Cooper clearly can't be referring to worldly maritime experience—for although he, too, was a sailor for a time with Myers, he hasn't nearly the "life before the mast" that his friend does. Therefore, Cooper must be invoking his symbolic position as author. In fact, his language at the end of the passage, perhaps unintentionally, directly contests his earlier claims of functioning as an editorial translator. As Cooper clearly says, it is not that he as editor has "interposed" his knowledge between Myers's comments in the narrative—as in, say, editorial asides—but "between" Myers's "experience and the narrative." In other words, such an editorial role would presumably act not only as an intermediary source of supplemental information, but also as a screen of interpretation between Myers's life and the very language of the narrative. If translation can be seen as a fantasmatic means to account for symbolic and experiential impasses by moving the divide into the formal structure of narrative, Cooper goes one step further, also moving to the fore of the narrative the reality that it is the author (or editor) who structures the knowledge of the laborer.

It is in this precise sense that we might more fully recontextualize the social link of the master's discourse with Lacan's notion of the university discourse. As noted, Lacan and, to an even greater degree, Žižek cast the four discourses as developing within a historical progression. The university discourse is the structure that follows directly after the master's discourse, with its formula constituting a counterclockwise rotation of the mathemes.[82] As a result, this discourse finds knowledge (S_2) in the position of agency addressing the other of object a. Here we see a formal account of the oft-discussed transition in the master's knowledge during the modern era. In fact, Lacan goes so far as to refer to the university discourse as the "modernized master's discourse," where knowledge is "put in the master's place" as opposed to the slave's.[83]

Thus, the "transmutation" of knowledge in the modern world caused by philosophy and science's usurpation of the slave's place of knowledge leads to an ambiguous "opposition between know-how and what is *episteme* in the strict sense."[84] To put it another way, there is a tension between the experiential knowledge of the laborer and the now dominant "purified" knowledge of the scientist or scholar. Such a shift in the domain of knowledge can be accounted for in part by the development of scientific discourse during the early nineteenth century. In terms of maritime knowledge, by the 1840s, when Cooper was working on *Ned Myers*, many eighteenth-century and contemporary "discovery" voyages were available to the public, and Charles Wilkes's much-publicized national exploratory expedition was completed in 1842. With national and economic interests pushing the terrain of science to map the globe, it is easy to see the antebellum era as existing in a tenuous realm at the latter end of a shift toward codified and bureaucratically dominated systems of knowledge. But such systems are, of course, incomplete (both quantitatively, in terms of hard knowledge, and qualitatively, in terms of symbolic constraints). And, as noted, it is here that the common sailor might be seen to function as a fantasmatic means to both address and control that which exceeds this new field of knowledge.[85] Cooper's narrative provides an interesting case that, more than the other previously mentioned maritime texts, foregrounds a transitional play between symbolic positions and domains of knowledge.

Quite clearly, then, the tension between Cooper's and Myers's positions stems in part from the way Cooper presents Myers as a narrating source of experiential knowledge that is ambiguously under the aegis of Cooper's own editorial knowledge and control. This indeterminate play between positions is also seen on the first page of the narrative, where Myers describes the role Cooper, his "old shipmate," plays in being "disposed to put into the proper form the facts which ... [Myers] can give him" (5). Here, we have the mise-en-scène of ostensible translation. Yet, what a cursory reading misses is that this very narrative voice that is addressing us is, in fact, formally mediated by Cooper—and not Cooper as merely an amanuensis but an empowered authorial screen.

In this context, Cooper's editorial footnotes become interestingly charged, for they appear not only to provide basic supplemental information but also to create a fantasy of separation between the positions of editor and narrator. That is to say, if Cooper's editorial role at times includes the reconstruction of Myers's narrative voice and persona, doesn't inserting editorial asides help displace this synthesis by creating an overt formal break between narrative subject positions? Such explicit divisions might be seen as supplements to in-text rhetorical divisions between the two—such as in chapter 1 when Myers, surmising about the place of his father's death, states, "My old shipmate, the editor, however, thinks it must have been in Canada" (7). Compositional ambiguity prevents us from knowing definitively who crafted what lines, so presumably Myers could have uttered or written this aside. Yet reducing the problem of ambiguity to the literal terms of *whodunit* avoids the symbolic reality of the text and its fantasmatic functions.[86]

By exploring these ambiguities in the narrative, I do not intend to reduce this rich text to such constructs. There is much of value in the book—especially for the political and historical concerns of a study like my own. Instead, I want to foreground the elements of fantasy that both structure the way the narrative's content is presented and, to go even further, shape the conditions of the text's very creation. In his preface, Cooper makes it clear that Myers has the relative cultural capital to "speak for himself"—pointing out he had "held intercourse with persons of a condition of life" "not much below" "the rank of gentleman" (2). Given this, one can ask whether Cooper is really needed for the project. In short, why doesn't Myers follow the example of other ex–common sailors before him, push beyond the impediment of a "want of habit" (2), as he puts it, and pen his own tale?

Two basic explanations seem appropriate. The first is that Myers doesn't have the learning requisite to write a coherent narrative for the market—essentially Cooper is right to say that he has greater knowledge of this than Myers. Strictly speaking, this may be the case, for, as Egan suggests, while Myers could read, it is possible that he was not proficient in writing, as evidenced by the fact that one of his pension files includes an "X" for his signature.[87] For the second explanation, one might more radically ask whether Myers can be, structurally, both the author of and the common sailor in the narrative. For if Myers were to be sole author, his *subject* would change on two levels relating to the function of fantasy: he would no longer completely inhabit the position of common sailor, and, as a result, the necessary distance between the narrative and the desired object would close.

In these terms, though it is, of course, possible for common sailors to write their own tales, perhaps Cooper's *Ned Myers* reveals that these narratives' formal qualities prevent them from effectively structuring the underlying fantasies and desires that give rise to the texts in the first place. This is in part evidenced by *The Athenaeum*'s 1843 review of *Ned Myers,* in which the reviewer opines, "Together with the charm, we find in it some of the tediousness of a true tale; and, compared with young Dana's book, this can rank but as second in the marine library."[88] Scholars who blame the book's authorial ambiguity for its poor market showing might, therefore, be correct, but for different reasons than they realize. Paradoxically, although *Ned Myers* may optimize its own fantasmatic effect, it may just do this too forthrightly and transparently. The construction of Myers's narrative persona may be an effective means to approach and harness enjoyment, but the explicit rhetorical foregrounding of this construction in the ambiguous relation between Cooper and Myers might threaten the process by revealing the fantasy's logic. In short, the problem stems from the fact that their relationship blatantly vacillates between structural links that resemble Lacan's master's and university discourses.

On one level, the fantasy operates in a mode similar to that of the master's discourse, with Myers and his experiential knowledge constituting a means for appropriating an end—ultimately an instrument for Cooper and the narrative to approach *a*. On another level, Cooper's manifold presentations of his authorial activity paradoxically complicate the narrative's construction by realigning the positions of knowledge into a relation closer to that of the university discourse. Accenting the agency of his own knowledge, Cooper essentially reveals the notion of translation as such to be a fantasy. That is, by divesting Myers of the position of knowledge, Cooper radically alters the structure of the fantasy that seeks access Myers's experiences.[89] Thus, *Ned Myers* may unintentionally traverse the fantasy that translation is a means to capture true knowledge of sailors' experiences, laying bare such narratives' approach to jouissance and radically complicating the entire process.

Ultimately, the common sailor plays a central role in antebellum fantasies of the maritime world. As we've seen, however, this figure is more than merely a screen onto which America projects its desires about experience in a developing global age. Instead, it constitutes a valuable locus through which these desires are harnessed and mediated. Pointing out how certain conspicuous failures and ruptures within such fantasies retroactively reveal the imaginary construction of the sailor should not be seen as a cynical condemnation of either antebellum or subsequent historical attempts to understand the experiences of these laborers. Rather, if we loosely view the representation of the common sailor's subject position as a concept, then my attempt to focus on its symbolic seams might be read in the spirit of Adorno's negative dialectics, where the initial theoretical gesture is to "change ... [the] direction of conceptuality, to give it a turn toward nonidentity."[90] In my view, this negative move has distinctly positive aims and effects. In the spirit of Jean-Luc Nancy's claim that "compassion is not altruism, nor is it identification; it is the disturbance of violent relations," I see my work as a provisional attempt to reveal the "systemic violence" that conditions both the lives of and our critical approaches to nineteenth-century common sailors.[91]

Consequently, I hope that my arguments here will not be seen as a simple extension of Spivak's embattled thesis. As scholars have rightfully suggested, the liminal voices and experiences of the oppressed—both present and past—can and should begin to be accessed through various forms, including translation and mediation.[92] What my analysis adds is the central caveat that such processes must be rigorously (and, hence, theoretically) self-reflexive, commencing from a position that considers its own fantasmatic coordinates: those that undergird it and those it propagates. In this sense, as Lacan begins to ask in the second epigraph to this chapter, the question remains open whether "know-how at the level of manual labor [can] carry enough weight to be a subversive factor."[93]

When exploring antebellum notions of the common sailor, then, we might underscore the questions Melville's conspicuous old prophet Elijah asks Ishmael and Queequeg as they follow a troop of shadowy sailor specters toward the Pequod early one morning in *Moby-Dick*. Stealing up to the anxious pair, Elijah asks, "Did ye see anything looking like men going towards that ship a while ago?" And then, "See if you can find 'em now, will ye?"[94] Like men, indeed.

· CHAPTER 2 ·

Tarrying with the National: Fantasizing the Subject of State

Fantasy has been where statehood takes hold and binds its subjects, and then, unequal to its own injunctions, lets slip just a little.

—Jacqueline Rose, *States of Fantasy*

These waves, to me, are what the land is to you; I was born on them, and I have always meant that they should be my grave.

—James Fenimore Cooper, *The Pilot*

IF THE SAILOR IS A SPECTER-LIKE CATALYST for antebellum maritime fantasies, then for many of this era's related narratives, the nation might be viewed as a common symbolic denouement. Indeed, maritime endeavors were paramount to the young country's economic, military, and spatial development, playing a salient role in both how and why its mainland domains rapidly expanded via the Louisiana Purchase and the subsequent appropriation of Mexican territories. This process of expansion included, by the time of the Civil War, the construction of a navy that could have menaced the dominating fleets possessed by England and France during the Napoleonic era. Though North American merchants had created piecemeal a veritable flotilla of private men-of-war as early as the 1740s, the rapid creation of an official naval force was quite a feat if one considers that it did not begin until 1794 and then only with the construction of a meager six frigates.[1]

Economic and scientific expansion into Pacific, Asian, and Arctic maritime regions during the early nineteenth century, therefore, was directly tied to state military power. In fact, American merchants' initial push into the Pacific during the late eighteenth century stemmed from a dire need for open markets when the British banned American ships from its colonial ports after the close of the Revolutionary War. In the antebellum era, such direct connections between merchant and national maritime registers are apparent in the military instructions to Charles Wilkes's 1838 United States Exploring Expedition, as mentioned in the Introduction, where the secretary of the navy writes that Congress had voted to finance the mission in order "to extend the empire of commerce."[2] Antebellum-era citizens eagerly read of Wilkes's experiences and were also familiar with Benjamin Morrell's account of South Pacific and Arctic exploits (1822–31) as well as Captain David Porter's narrative of Pacific activity (1812–14). The mainland public, in other words, was quite conscious of the concerted and ongoing national effort to both physically and empirically extend the nation's command over foreign and largely unknown maritime regions.

It is thus easy to see why many antebellum maritime narratives take up the subject of the nation—especially in the years following the politically divisive War of 1812, when surprising naval victories offered fodder for nationalistic fantasies. Even maritime texts that do not ostensibly treat national or naval issues negotiate such topics through their contexts' broader implications. Examples of this abound in early-American maritime texts. Royall Tyler's *The Algerine Captive, or, The Life and Adventures of Doctor Updike Underhill* (1797), for instance, ends a rather stock captivity narrative of abduction, internment, and escape from a Barbary "pirate" state with a charged call for military and naval power, asserting that the events in the tale evince the "necessity of uniting our federal strength to enforce a due respect among other nations."[3] Such sentiment is also voiced in Owen Chase's *Narrative of the Most Extraordinary and Distressing Shipwreck of the Whale-ship Essex* (1821). Chase opens the harrowing tale of a sperm-whale attack by discussing British competition in the developing Pacific whale fishery, and explicitly states that "recent events have shown that we require a competent naval force in the Pacific, for the protection of this important and lucrative . . . commerce."[4] These repeated calls for the use of concerted national force—obviously heeded by the time of Wilkes's expedition—depart distinctly from political views dominant during the Federalist era, which, though favoring the construction of a navy, opted for political neutrality within international and foreign waters so as to allow American merchant shipping to profit from Europe's splintered allegiances.[5]

Timely national issues within antebellum maritime narratives, however, extend far beyond concerns of military naval power proper. In Melville's early adventure narratives *Typee* and *Omoo*, for example, he repeatedly delves into the nuances and complexities of national colonial projects and missionary endeavors in Polynesia. As Bruce Harvey elucidates, such concerns do much more than merely color these tales with political verisimilitude. Depicting the fraught but successful inroads of Western codified law and missionary projects in places like Hawaii and Tahiti during an age in which domestic slavery cleaved the coupling of morality and jurisprudence, these tales reassured Americans that such foundational crises could and might ultimately work out.[6]

In terms of fantasy, the age's maritime historical romances offer a particularly rich presentation of national themes. Just as Georg Lukács aptly observes that the characters and struggles within the nineteenth-century genre of historical romance—particularly those found in the work of Walter Scott—exemplify "historical social types" as well as "social trends and historical forces," the fantasies in and of these texts might be seen to reveal issues paramount to the age's conceptual construction of the nation.[7] More broadly, if the rise of the novel in the eighteenth century coincides with the rise of the modern bourgeois *homo economicus,* then the development of the historical romance in the nineteenth century undoubtedly accompanies the development of the modern bourgeois nation-state.[8] Indeed, scholarship has examined, prodded, and deconstructed the concept of the nation to such a degree in the past twenty-five years that there appears to be little theoretical work to be done in this vein. Such work—from Benedict Anderson's *Imagined Communities* (1983) through Homi Bhabha's *Nation and Narration* (1990) and David Noble's *Death of a Nation: American Culture and the End of Exceptionalism* (2002)—productively traces and challenges the various ways that the modern nation-state and its subjects are constructed. Yet, in our own historical moment, as J. Gerald Kennedy so aptly puts it in terms of the United States, "The resurgence of jingoism thus compels renewed attention to the phantasm of American exceptionalism that still haunts us like an ominous bird of yore."[9] Despite the fact that theoretical projects have conquered the ideological edifices of the nation and its past, the nation heedlessly pushes on. Such laudable theoretical projects thus appear to function like an unwitting Benjaminian *Angelus Novus,* looking back at the fantastical and violent construction of nation-states and national identities while being carried along in the wake of such structures' stubborn march forward.[10]

The nation, therefore, remains a timely theme. And timely in more senses than one.[11] In terms of the field of American Studies, even if we've now answered Janice Radway's question, "What's in a Name?," we still quite obviously need to revisit both how this name—this national construction of subjectivities and communities—continues to operate and develop.[12] Central to this project is an ongoing exploration of how the nation perpetuates itself, a topic Donald Pease has productively taken up in terms of the contemporary U.S. political landscape in *The New American Exceptionalism* (2009). As Homi Bhabha makes clear, the notion of time is foundational for all national identities: "The passage of time is always marked in the *prefix*, as an anteriority, something that is placed behind the sign of the nation's contemporaneity to signal its precarious progress. This moment of the turn of the nation's subjects to a past then re-turns, rushes past— indeed, projects *the past*—into a paradoxical position of futurity."[13] The symbolic location of the nation in the present is, in this way, irrevocably linked to the renarration of its past. In Bhabha's terms, the perpetuation of a nation is thus achieved in part via an "invention of . . . [a] national past," which acts as an "interregnum, a place-holding position constructed as the passageway to modernity."[14]

This process is carried out through official histories and various forms of print culture, including novels and newspapers. According to Benedict Anderson, these narratives occlude "inequality and exploitation" by concomitantly conceiving of community as a "deep, horizontal comradeship" and renarrating the abstract and multifarious present as "steady, anonymous, simultaneous activity."[15] Quite clearly, such operations involve more than positivistic constructions of citizenship and community. As Žižek notes, "National identification is by definition sustained by a relationship toward the Nation qua Thing."[16] Since here "Thing" denotes "enjoyment incarnated," or object *a*, we might rearticulate Bhabha's reference to the "placeholding" role of the national past in terms of the function of fantasy. In other words, national identities and communities are ineluctably predicated on the function of fantasy, whereby national narratives of various forms (quilting pasts, presents, and futures) provide coordinates for identifications and exclusions. It is in this context that we might read Žižek's point that "[a] nation exists only as long as its specific enjoyment continues to be materialized in certain social practices."[17]

In addition to Pease's *The New American Exceptionalism*, which directly employs a Žižek-inflected notion of national fantasy, Bhabha's persistent focus on the topic of racial and cultural foreclosures within the production of national subjectivity often aligns with a Lacanian perspective.[18] His discussion of the "moments of disavowal, displacement, exclusion, and cultural contestation" inherent in any national fiction is subsequently developed when he examines the "splitting" of the national subject within narrative construction.[19] After setting up the role of the nation's past as "the passageway to constituting, and confronting, the problem of its modernity," he uses a Lacanian notion of anxiety as a twisted border to discuss the "temporal disjunction" between a nation's past and the way it is taken up and used by the present.[20] In a passage ripe with significance for my project, Bhabha writes:

> If one can say that nation*ness* is the Janus-faced strait gate of modernity, and all who enter shall look backwards—in what we may now call an *anxiety of the antecedent*—then one must also point out, following Weber, that that experience "is to be caught in the space between two frames: a double frame, or one that is split . . ." (p. 167). What enters this double frame of the nation's anxiety is not the naturalized, harmonized unchosen of the *amor patriae*—which is also the love of the nation-people—but its double: those who are the "unchosen," the marginalized or peripheralized non-people of the nation's democracy.[21]

Such a reading of the anxiety affixed to national identity clearly aligns with my discussion of angst and authenticity in chapter 1. More important, Bhabha delineates the political tensions inherent in all national fantasies of the past, tensions that spring from a residual uneasiness about that which is obliterated in the process of constructing modern identity. Bhabha subsequently gestures toward the potential utopic twists in the "future's fold" of this anxious border, where because the past and future are retroactively constituted by the present, there is always the possibility for an opening of new experiences and identifications. But it is the originative, negative foreclosure at the root of national fantasies that most interests me in relation to antebellum maritime historical romance. Twisting Bhabha's terms just bit, instead of solely looking to the future for "reparation of the present and the revision of the past," we might initiate such a process by using the vantage of our own moment to explore how the nineteenth century negotiates its acts of peripheralization.[22]

In what follows, I will explore two influential nineteenth-century maritime historical romances that emphasize the concept of national identification: Walter Scott's *The Pirate* (1822) and James Fenimore Cooper's *The Pilot: A Tale of the Sea* (1824). As mentioned in chapter 1, although Scott's text is not an American work per se, it was well read throughout the Atlantic world and directly inspired Cooper's novel. More pointedly, however, in different ways and to different effects, both romances dramatize scenes of national identification and exclusion in historical settings contiguous to the creation of their respective contemporary moments. As such, these narratives present interesting and formative fantasies about the construction of national fantasy itself.

The Pirate, Symbolic Capital, and Entrance into the Political Realm

Since Georg Lukács's *The Historical Novel* (1937), twentieth-century scholarship has explored Scott's political positioning as well as his novels' depictions of history. Building on Lukács's view that Scott promoted a conservative "middle way" "between the wavering extremes" of bourgeois modernism and an aristocratic past, Avrom Fleishman cites Scott's "ambivalence toward the values of Scotland's past and those of its present."[23] According to Fleishman, this ambiguity creates "dramatic tension" in Scott's novels; in this context, he writes: "However much they are brought to happy endings by melodramatic plot involutions, Scott's novels are set in motion by conflicts that are universal and real, polarities not only of the time but of all periods of transition."[24]

In the case of *The Pirate,* this transition is seen on multiple levels as the traditionally insular Zetland Island community's ongoing interface with the broader global political sphere accelerates as the plot progresses. The novel purportedly sprang from a voyage Scott took in 1814 on an "armed yacht," on which he "join[ed] a party of Commissioners for the Northern Lighthouse Service" as they toured Scotland's islands.[25] Citing Scott's diary from this voyage and his experiences on Fair Isle and the Orkneys, George Dekker reveals Scott's uneasiness about the conflict he saw between the inhabitants' feudal economy and the various inroads of modernization. After initially feeling optimistic about modern "improvements," Scott becomes skeptical when he sees the extent of overpopulation and poverty.[26] Though Scott's corpus might be read as reflecting a similar angst about civilization's ongoing transition into the nineteenth-century world, scholars have noted how these narratives often work toward resolving such historical tension.

In this vein, Nicola Watson suggests that Scott's novels "[carry] out an essentially counter-revolutionary remaking of the national past."[27] Although Watson does not directly address *The Pirate,* through analysis of *Waverley* and *Redgauntlet,* she argues that Scott "rehistoricizes" the past "within a socially sanctioned version of the real"; moreover, she suggests that he "[dramatizes] the failure of individual reading in the face of an 'official' quasi-historical rereading of past events."[28] Although critiques of the conservative elements in Scott's novels are clearly warranted, might their inherent insistence on these plots' closures obscure consideration of the strained nature of such denouements? Even more important for my purposes, might this focus on conclusions in general—conclusions that often take the form of characters' interpellation into dominant national identities—ignore the import of beginnings and the mechanisms that initiate and condition these conservative transitions? In other words, does fetishizing endings and closures per se come at the expense of considering how these novels are set in motion through characters' various entrances into different sociosymbolic fields?

In this section, I will explore how the pirate Cleveland's interactions with Mordaunt Mertoun and Jack Bunce engender fantasies about movement into and between social and political identities. In so doing, I argue that these characters' foundational fantasies about entering the broader economic and political realm are motivated by a desire for "symbolic capital," a term Pierre Bourdieu uses to describe "economic or political capital that is disavowed, misrecognized and thereby recognized, hence legitimate, a 'credit' which, under certain conditions, and always in the long run, guarantees 'economic' profits."[29] The drive for such capital is predicated on the idea, in the case of Mordaunt, that maritime military experience can be valuable in its conversion into narrative, and achieved, in terms of Bunce's plight, through a tenuous and potentially dangerous public performance. Though *The Pirate* ultimately represents a typical nineteenth-century historical romance, moving toward squaring an aristocratic and artisan past with the economic and social imperatives of the modern nation-state, its dramatization of the process might be seen to complicate this aim. Similar to Cooper's approach to underlying fantasies about the knowledge of the common sailor in *Ned Myers,* we might read Scott's novel as bringing to the foreground the fantasmatic elements that push individuals toward becoming national subjects. Further, if, in Bhabha's terms, the nation's anxious imagination of the past is carried out in order to erect a clear antecedent to justify its present-future, what might we make of the way *The Pirate* seems to leave the door ajar between such epochs?

The plot of Scott's novel begins to take form in chapter 7, when Mordaunt and his father, while overlooking the sea from atop a stretch of cliffs on one of the Zetland islands, spy a ship foundering in the surf. Soon after, the vessel is wrecked against the rocky coast and a single man is seen floating toward shore. The survivor is Clement Cleveland, the pirate commander of the *Revenge* and, as we learn late in the tale, the lost son of Basil Mertoun and Norna (a.k.a. Ulla Troil). From the moment Cleveland arrives, he is shown to be a disrupting force in the relatively closed society of Zetland. The scene of Cleveland's rescue is particularly telling in this regard, for the very act of saving him goes against the belief structures of the island. Scott earlier refers to how the island "was as yet a little world by itself" where "ancient northern superstition remained."[30] One of these superstitions is a long-standing dictum not to save a drowning man. This is seen when Bryce, a local merchant, chides Mordaunt for saving Cleveland, explaining: "If you bring him to life again, he will be sure to do you some capital injury" (98). Scott's depiction of the island's economic dependence on the "wrecking system" (107), claiming goods washed ashore from wrecked vessels, grounds this superstition in material concerns. Consequently, Bryce's warning that saving sailors will engender "some capital injury" might more aptly be read as an injury *to* capital.[31] In this light, Cleveland's arrival becomes the deus ex machina of the island's formal immersion in and acceptance of the broader political order.

This movement first manifests in the relationship between the typical *Waverley* figure of Mordaunt Mertoun, a romantic youth who has come of age on the island, and the pirate Cleveland. After saving Cleveland, Mordaunt is impressed by the sailor's gentlemanly demeanor and his "bold, sunburnt, handsome countenance, which seemed to have faced various climates" (110). The last aspect of this description is germane to the events that follow. Though only incipiently, Mordaunt's correlation of world travel and the appealing physical signifiers of masculinity qua experience gestures toward the schematic of social and economic identity with which he begins to redefine himself.[32] Cleveland's presence can thus be seen as a catalyst for Mordaunt's redefinition—ushering him into the political realm that structures movement toward and experiences in the "various climates" that Mordaunt reads in Cleveland's face. This is apparent when Cleveland gives Mordaunt his "beautiful Spanish-barrelled gun" as a gesture of payment for saving his life (113). This gun, with its exotic Spanish origin and "unusual length," acts as a flash point for Mordaunt's entrance into Cleveland's world. After feeling anxious about accepting the gift, a "successful day's shooting reconciled him" to it (117). In fact, after using the gun, "all other pieces" seemed "but pop-guns in comparison" (118). This dialectical shift is drawn out in a pivotal passage in which Mordaunt laments:

> But then, to be doomed to shoot gulls and seals when there were Frenchmen and Spaniards to be come at—when there were ships to be boarded, and steersmen to be marked off—seemed but a dull and contemptible destiny. . . . His ambition had formerly aimed no higher than at sharing the fatigues and dangers of a Greenland fishing expedition; for it was in that scene that Zetlanders laid most of their perilous adventures. But war was again raging. The history of Sir Francis Drake, Captain Morgan, and other bold adventurers . . . had made much impression on his mind; and the offer of Captain Cleveland to take him to sea frequently recurred to him. (118)

This reasoning highlights an obvious divergence between activities and social positions available in Zetland society and those afforded by warring on the high seas. Life in Zetland is split between earning income from the occasionally hazardous labor of fishing and eliciting excitement from, ostensibly, recreational hunting, while naval warfare is able to unite both qualities on a single, romantically heightened plane. Moreover, this comparison highlights the mechanisms at play in the way Mordaunt reconsiders his identity.

Reading this scenario in the context of a Lacanian notion of identity formation illuminates issues relating to both Mordaunt's and the greater Zetland Islands' transition into the modern national register. As discussed earlier in different terms, fantasy functions to assist the subject's entrance into a symbolic order by working to temporarily shield gaps inherent in the system. Without unnecessarily rehashing technicalities of this theory here, in Lacan's later work, the void in the symbolic order (which we should read in terms of a plural, or parallax, Real) takes on the guise of a "big Other." In a metaphorical sense, this big Other is itself a fantasy structure that stands in for the Real and confronts each individual with the question

"Che vuoi?" or "What do you really want?" Fantasy acts to answer this unbearable question and thereby structures the subject's desire. In so doing, it acts as a screen that conceals the ultimate lack of the symbolic order's big Other, or what Žižek refers to as the "abyss of the desire of the Other."[33] Fantasy is about the other's desire—with objects and people filling the empty space that constitutes the big Other's desire. It is, therefore, an intersubjective figuring of oneself based on one's perceptions of what others want.

Yet, how does one—such as Mordaunt—enter a sociosymbolic order via fantasy? According to Žižek, it is through the "interplay of imaginary and symbolic identification under the domination of symbolic identification."[34] Concomitant with the process of fantasy construction, a subject—on the "level of meaning"—must identify with an imaginary other. By "imaginary identification" Žižek means "identification with the image in which we appear likeable to ourselves," whereas the more important and determining "symbolic identification" is "identification with the very place *from where* we are being observed, *from where* we look at ourselves."[35]

Using this schematic to view Mordaunt's experiences, it is possible to see Cleveland and his gun as providing a sociosymbolic field shift—one that places Mordaunt in an anxiety-ridden and liminal space between realms. That is to say, with Cleveland's arrival, Mordaunt's conception of himself changes, and this change clearly operates on both levels of identity formation. First, the locus of Mordaunt's symbolic identification shifts, as seen in way he recontextualizes his local society (fishing and hunting) via the focalization of a national and political one. This move toward a broader geopolitical perspective corresponds to an attendant shift in his imaginary identification. Here, Mordaunt abandons the "dull and contemptible" image of himself as a Zetland fisherman for the romantically charged notion of becoming a maritime adventurer in "raging" wars. Such latter images, Scott makes clear, were first forged through stories Mordaunt had previously read of adventures—so, arguably, this broader identification had already been tenuously established; yet, importantly, it is Cleveland's body, gun, and existence in the reality of Mordaunt's world that establishes them as legitimate options.

As mentioned, this theory of identity formation is structured around an intersubjective concept of desire, in which both forms of identification are based on one's view of what others want. This becomes relevant when, later in the same passage, Mordaunt links his desire for the exploits of war with the cultural cachet such experiences might yield. Mordaunt ruminates: "With what pleasure . . . would he embark in quest of new scenes and strange adventures, in which he proposed to himself to achieve such deeds as should be the theme of many a tale to the lovely sisters of Bugh-Westra—tales at which Minna should weep, and Brenda should smile, and both should marvel!" (118). It thus becomes clear that the primary reason he longs for international maritime experience is the potential value it holds once transferred into "tales" to be used in Zetland's marriage market.

This aspect is reinforced when Cleveland subsequently becomes a rival for the sentiment of the Troil daughters. In a conversation with Norna, Mordaunt laments that Cleveland "can tell them of battles, when [he] can only speak of birds' nests—can speak of shooting Frenchmen, when [he] can only tell of shooting seals. . . . Such gay gallants as [Cleveland] can noose the hearts of those he lives with" (137). The Troil girls, themselves, later comment on the influence of such tales when Minna defends Cleveland to her sister, arguing: "He really has been in many distant countries, and in many gallant actions; and he can tell them with as much spirit as modesty" (213). In this context, Mordaunt does not merely want to enjoy adventures on the high seas; he desires, in a sense, to become a narrative—to be translated into the future past of his new imaginary identification. Thus mobility and war experience can be seen as a Bourdieuian form of "symbolic capital." While there is no direct evidence that Mordaunt desires to exchange, or later recognize, this symbolic capital as social hegemony, it is not at all improbable. Considering especially Magnus Troil's bloodline and feudal reign over the inhabitants of the island, being associated with him, as well as potentially one day replacing him, would most definitely proffer such social power. There is, as well, the more obvious material capital that marrying into the Troil family would yield in the form of an ample dowry. Although Mordaunt's intentions are consistently portrayed as being motivated solely by romantic interest, such sentiment exists in a marriage market that is clearly mediated by concerns of capital and proprietorship.

Mordaunt's initial foray into the political realm, however, is shown to be replete with danger. In the symbolically loaded scene when he fires the Spanish rifle across a Zetland lake—causing animals to flee—he reflects: "Wheel, dive, scream, and clamour as you will, all because you have seen a strange sight and heard an unusual sound. There is many a one like you in this round world. But you, at least, shall learn . . . that strange sights and sounds, ay strange acquaintances to boot, have sometimes a little shade of danger" (129). This danger, of course, becomes real for him when he is later near-fatally wounded by Cleveland. Paradoxically, this injury effectively excises him from the plot just as the arrival of the British man-of-war *Halcyon* brings the very scenes of battle he had longed for to the shores of Zetland.

The movement toward the political realm is echoed in the experiences of another character in the novel, Jack Bunce. Bunce is a secondary character who enters the narrative in chapter 31, when Cleveland is reunited with his pirate crew. While it becomes clear that Bunce's fantastical adoption of a rover's life shares many qualities with Mordaunt's desire for maritime war, there are distinct differences that reveal salient aspects about Scott's presentation of political identity.

Like Mordaunt, Bunce appears to have desired to go to sea and enter the global fray in order to garner symbolic capital. This is seen in his constant reference to class (with his view that rovers—especially Cleveland—are "gentlemanly") and in his glorification of combat and death (seen, for example, when he reflects that there "was some credit in being hanged" [416]). Also like Mordaunt, Bunce's admission into the pirate world was spurred by Cleveland (Bunce reverentially tells his captain: "It was you who first . . . turned me from a stroller by land to a rover by sea" [414]) and achieved through a shift in imaginary identification. As mentioned, however, it is the differences between Bunce and Mordaunt that may be the most revealing. These include the qualitative aspects of his desire for a maritime life, the form of his imaginary identification as a rover, and the function of performance in his assumption of identity.

Jack Bunce enters the narrative already assuming the identity of a pirate. In the passage just cited, he gestures toward his previous life as a "stroller by land," and we soon learn that in this life he had been employed as an actor (416). That profession comes up again when Bunce watches over the captives Claud Halcro, Magnus Troil, and the Troil sisters. On learning that one of his charges was Claud Halcro, a former professional musician and actor, Bunce—having imbibed some alcoholic "punch"—fondly exclaims, "Why, you are the . . . fellow that played the fiddle to old Manager Gadabout's company!" (489). After a moment, Halcro recognizes the spirited pirate as "the very hopeful young performer who came out in Don Sebastian" and compliments Bunce on his performance (489). Tellingly, Bunce responds with the quip that as good as he was, he "was destined to figure on other boards" (489). After Halcro's continued approbations, Bunce laments: "Ah, you flatter me, my dear friend . . . ; yet why had not the public some of your judgment! I should not then have been at this pass" (490). This response, of course, reveals that Bunce's shift to a "rover by sea" comes only after his failure to succeed as an actor. Donning the identity of a rover, therefore, provides a secondary outlet for his acting ability (where he can "figure" on the "boards" of ship)—one replete with the opportunity to receive the material spoils of privateering and, as previously mentioned, the social esteem from assuming what he views as a powerful, gallant figure. Unlike Mordaunt, then, Bunce appears to be quite conscious of the performative elements of experience and identity.

This awareness of his own process of identity construction is seen in his initial appearance in the novel, when he reminds Cleveland: "I wish you would forget that name of Bunce and call me Altamont, as I have often desired you to do. I hope a gentleman of the roving trade has a good a right to have an alias as a stroller, and I never stepped on boards but what I was Altamont" (414). He goes on to fuss over the new first name as well, saying "Jack Altamont . . . 'tis a velvet coat with paper lace. Let it be Frederick . . . ; Frederick Altamont is all of a piece" (415). Clearly, Bunce chooses a name that embodies his imaginary identification with a gentlemanly rover. Yet, unlike Mordaunt in his desire for authentic war experience, Bunce reveals that he views such an identity as being completely assumed.

Such a self-conceptualization also suggests that although Bunce has generated a new imaginary identification, his symbolic perspective remains the same. That is, Altamont is always already Bunce *as* Altamont— the position of focalization he uses to view himself remains constant throughout both of his careers. This is apparent in his ability to slip between roles and allegiances (such as when he befriends Halcro and aids the Troils) as well as when Scott blatantly unmasks him in the end. After being captured, tried, and pardoned, Captain Weatherport of the Royal Navy asks: "You call yourself Frederick Altamont? . . . I can see no such name here; one John Bounce, or Bunce, the lady put on her tablets" (557). Bunce responds: "Why, that is me—that is I myself, captain—I can prove it; and I am determined, though the sound be something plebian, rather to live Jack Bunce, than to hang as Frederick Altamont" (557). Bunce thus chooses against the romantic "credit" he once saw in such a heroic death, effortlessly leaving the role of Altamont for his original place in society.

Taken together, Mordaunt's and Bunce's interactions with Cleveland and their subsequent movement into the political realm can be seen both to reveal the type of conservative narrative closure that critics have often explored and to complicate it. The end of *The Pirate* does seek a tidy denouement, where the wayward parts are relegated to their proper places and the modern world moves forward after absorbing the aristocratic values of the past. Yet the monumental strain of achieving this remains in the foreground of the narrative, creating an ambiguity that is hard to ignore. A major aspect of this ambiguity arises in the interstice, or one might say inconsistency, between the qualitative aspects of the characters' entrances into the political sphere and the dominant national narrative that attempts to close the novel. Unlike the national sentiments that conclude the narrative, Mordaunt's and Bunce's entrances into the political world are motivated by notions of symbolic capital that are not mediated through clear national markers—capital in the form of international (explicitly with Bunce and implicitly with Mordaunt) worldly experience. In addition, this ambiguity can be seen in the divergent, chiastic-like trajectories of these characters' relations to the dominant national narrative that closes the novel.

Although Bunce's experiences may appear potentially radical—with the explicit performative nature of his own political and national identities complicating such identities in toto—the way his play, in both senses of the word, between social positions is delimited by imperial rule at the novel's close calls any semblance of subversion into question. Quite clearly, the state's physical power to enforce and enact its symbolic mandates is shown to close the liminal space where unsanctioned alternative social positions are possible.

Alternately, Mordaunt's entrance into the political realm can be seen as potentially conservative. Any subversive aspects related to the fact that Cleveland is a pirate—existing outside national identity—are tempered by the fact that Mordaunt does not initially know that Cleveland is a rover and later negated when Cleveland, himself, formally accepts a traditional position within the national symbolic order by joining the British navy. Nonetheless, Mordaunt's movement toward the political is mitigated by the action of the novel. After being removed from the climactic events in the narrative when recovering from his wounds, Mordaunt, in the end, returns to his original place as a pseudo-aristocratic figure on the isolated island. While Cleveland is subsumed within a national power system that is rapidly tightening its hold on the modern world, Mordaunt, the Waverley-esque character, slips out of the political signifying chain, spending the rest of his days in Zetland with Brenda where he "laughed, sung, danced, daffed the world aside" (563).

We find, then, a strained bifurcation: where on the one hand, modern national empires progress with Cleveland and, on the other, the aristocratic order lives on, somehow, on the western islands of Scotland with Mordaunt and Brenda. This figuration of a rustic pastoral ideal is, of course, a long way from the "poor creatures" Scott sees on the Scottish isles in 1814 as well as from Zetland's obvious move toward modernization in the novel itself. More important, this closing chronotopic divide is yet another example of the ambiguities that lace the novel as a whole. In this light, is it appropriate to read Scott's novel as merely portraying another simple conservative denouement? Or might this vexed narrative closure more aptly reveal Bhabha's notion of "the construction of the Janus-faced discourse of the nation?"[36]

In the end, *The Pirate* functions as a fantasy of modern national interpellation of the past—where the temporarily liminal position of heroic rover is recast by being linked concomitantly to ancient Norse warriors and to the modern Royal Navy. Yet, the way Scott foregrounds the process of such narrative construction—the way he shows renarrations of identities and histories—might signal the purely provisional nature of these moves.[37] The hard-handed and, arguably, forced national denouement of the novel, coupled with the fantasmatic placement of Mordaunt in a protected bubble of antiquity within the rising tide of modernization, seem to emphasize the mechanisms of narrative peripheralization that Bhabha describes. Moreover, Scott's opening "Advertisement" to the narrative throws such movements into even bolder relief. There, Scott claims that the "purpose" of the narrative is to give an "accurate account of certain remarkable incidents which took place in the Orkney Islands, concerning which the more imperfect traditions and mutilated records of the country only tell us ... erroneous particulars" (xi). Scott then proceeds to review the government's "erroneous" historical account of the experiences of the pirate John Gow on the Orkney Islands in the years 1724 and 1725. The events, of course, are described as being almost antithetical in nature to those in the subsequent narrative: with Gow remaining stubbornly antigovernment to the end, submitting to hanging only after the court ruthlessly tortures him, and the civilian hero James Flea, who was responsible for Gow's capture, being abandoned by the government after Gow's execution, leaving him open to litigation by those acting on behalf of Gow's imprisoned crew. Highlighting the disparity between this record and the tale he is about to tell, Scott writes: "It is supposed, for the honour of George the First's Government, that the ... commonly received story ... [is] inaccurate, since [it] will be found totally irreconcilable with the following veracious narrative" (xiii).

Before the narrative even begins, therefore, Scott, signing the advertisement "the Author of Waverley," casts the project into a tenuous historical and symbolic predicament, for audiences were quite familiar with *Waverley*'s genre of historical fiction. Thus, not only does the plot itself reveal tension in characters' relations to national identities, but the advertisement rather comically illuminates the historical novel's own task as a fantasy-revision of national history—in essence, potentially parodying the real desire for and approach of national narratives themselves. Surely, from the political position of a Bhabha-like perspective, one cannot laud Scott's novel as being above the fray of national ideological work. Yet at least we might see it as dramatizing the way this work is carried out within various anxiety-ridden symbolic fronts.

Turning to Cooper's zeal to improve Scott's approach to romantic maritime narratives by presenting more realistic action, we might initially ask if such a desire is spawned by discomfort with the politically charged symbolic seams that Scott leaves open (or portrays as being tenuously closed). In addition to a new and improved version of nautical fiction, Cooper's novel may also present an attempt to clear the many desires and bodies left afloat on *The Pirate*'s stage.

Killing Tom Coffin: Rethinking the Nationalist Narrative in *The Pilot*

Set during the Revolutionary War, James Fenimore Cooper's first maritime novel, *The Pilot,* is a historical romance that follows a nascent American navy's fictitious attempt to bring the battle to England. "Long" Tom Coffin, whose words appear in the second epigraph to this chapter, is Cooper's romantically imagined natural sailor—a sea-born Nantucket whaler who stands over six feet tall and totes his harpoon into battle. The lines quoted, spoken aboard the sinking *Ariel* along the rock-strewn coast of England, are soon borne out with Coffin's self-imposed death—a death, I argue, that Cooper's nationalist intent makes necessary.

Tom Coffin's death can be viewed as intricately bound to the vexed relationship among labor, class, and national identity in the nineteenth century of Cooper's historical moment as well as the eighteenth century of which he writes. Indeed, Cooper obliquely raises this issue at the opening of the novel, when a troupe of English peasants on a field above the coast avoids contact with what turn out to be two mysterious American vessels because "the intelligence of the hot press was among the rumours of the times."[38] Opening the book with peasants' vivid fear of impressment, which entails the forceful transference from private activity to military service, often irrespective of national identity, is an apt exergue, in a sense, for themes that permeate the rest of the novel.[39]

Both traditional and recent scholarship on *The Pilot* has addressed some of these topics. For example, H. Daniel Peck's "A Repossession of America: The Revolution in Cooper's Trilogy of Nautical Romances" (1976) productively explores Cooper's political ambivalence about the American Revolution and how his early sea narratives attempt to "solve the problems that the Revolution posed for him."[40] Yet, his analysis is limited by use of reductive binaries such as sea/land and modern present/traditional past. More recently, Margaret Cohen's work—both her original "Traveling Genres" (2003) and its development in *The Novel and the Sea* (2010)—include cogent analyses of maritime fiction and its depiction of labor as "know-how."[41] Yet, her discussion of labor in *The Pilot* includes the problematic assertion that "what sets *The Pilot* apart . . . is the way it connects know-how to skilled work that is a common denominator across class."[42]

In this section, I build on the topics that Peck and Cohen raise by combining their themes of nationalism and labor and by centering the presentation of Tom Coffin in the narrative. Thus, I explore *The Pilot* in terms of how Cooper's anxiety about the American Revolution and nationalism influences his figuration of labor and the depiction of maritime heroism. Why would Cooper, as Wayne Franklin aptly puts it, make the "hasty decision" to kill off the most colorful character in the novel so soon in the action?[43] While Susan Fenimore Cooper explains that toward the end of his life her father regretted precipitously killing off Coffin and reducing him to a "sketch," I argue that, in the context of Cooper's other maritime fiction as well as his political and historical writings, this sailor's death may be more of a prerequisite for the national narrative Cooper envisions than an unfortunate oversight of character development.[44] By reading this decision loosely in the context of fantasy, an apparent literary dilemma might be shown to house deeper political and social desires.

The complex and competing social elements in *The Pilot* are a direct result of both Cooper's complicated political identity in the 1820s and the constant din of magazines such as the *Port-Folio* calling for material that promoted maritime nationalism.[45] As Peck makes clear, Cooper was uneasy about the American Revolution, viewing it as an example of "the way in which noble motive and high purpose can be distorted by the violence and chaos that inevitably accompany social rebellion."[46] According to Wayne Franklin, Cooper always viewed the war "as a civil war more than a revolution," where the colonial act of resistance "also had its own tyrannical surfaces."[47] As Franklin intimates, however, this anxiety about the Revolution is not merely about tyranny per se, but is based on deep-seated class angst. The bifurcation in Cooper's political and social thought is well documented: where a break, in many ways mirroring the structural divisions in Burke's and Scott's thought, is seen between social aristocratic values and disdain for popular revolution, on the one hand, and political support for a Jacksonian ethos, on the other.[48] Cooper's political division stems, in part, from the inheritance of Federalism from his father—a powerful member of the nouveau landed gentry of post-Revolution New York State—and his own experience of the rise of democratic republicanism in the nineteenth century.[49]

These competing sentiments, which play out across Cooper's long literary career, manifest in this early maritime romance. While the period of *The Pilot*'s composition, roughly 1822 through 1823, finds Cooper in his Republican phase of political identification, his social and economic views at this time are anything but one-dimensional. The years leading up to *The Pilot*'s publication are quite tumultuous for the Cooper family. Facing economic hardship as he dealt with various lawsuits against his father's estate; grieving for his young son, who died in 1823; and fending off his own mysterious fevers and bodily ailments, Cooper was more than once forced to delay the composition of the novel. Politically speaking, in 1823 Cooper helped found New York's Bread and Cheese Club. This expansive association gathered many of the city's most erudite and elite professionals and, as Franklin explains, acted as a "Clintonian adjunct."[50] DeWitt Clinton had served as both mayor of New York City and governor of the state during different stints early in the century. As a Jeffersonian Republican, whom Cooper's father had opposed, Clinton was formative in reworking the political landscape of New York. Welcoming former members of the dissipated Federalist Party, Clinton was able to create what Franklin terms a "hybrid movement" that synthesized aspects of both traditional Federalist and Jeffersonian sentiments.[51] Although it is imperative to locate *The Pilot* in its historical moment, the context of Cooper's affiliation with Clinton's hybrid politics does anything but pin Cooper down socially or economically.[52]

In terms of *The Pilot*'s historical material, despite a general ambivalence about the American Revolution's class and social ramifications, Cooper consistently evinces an avid patriotism. This can be seen clearly in the novel's 1823 preface, where Cooper laments that "the daring and useful services of a great portion of our marine in the old war should be suffered to remain in . . . obscurity" and asserts that, now that such bygone heroes are dying of old age, "we should be more tenacious of their glory."[53] This sentiment, as well as the romantic patriotism voiced by Katherine Plowden later in the novel, is consistent with Cooper's feverish effort to promote maritime nationalism in the early 1820s. In magazines such as *The Literary and Scientific Repository, and Critical Review*, Cooper published essays that called for the development of both a distinctly American national literature and a strong naval power.[54] His early nautical fiction evinces, in Philbrick's terms, "the meeting of maritime nationalism and romanticism."[55] As mentioned, the notion of historical romance has been explored on many fronts in past decades and is often cast as having a rich and ambivalent legacy relating to sociopolitical issues. More broadly, Edward Said goes as far as claiming that the "obsessive concern in Cooper, Twain, Melville, and others with United States expansion" represents "an imperial motif . . . to rival the European one."[56]

With Cooper, however, this "unsavory patriotism" was not some clandestine political machination, but, as noted, a concerted project.[57] According to James Wallace, from early in his career Cooper was "anxious to develop techniques for instructing [his] audience in his vision of an American culture."[58] In what follows, I seek to explore this project more closely—analyzing how the interface between Cooper's social angst, class views, and nascent patriotism manifest in his first maritime novel. More specifically, I consider *The Pilot* and its treatment of Tom Coffin in three thematic sections relating to labor, class, and nationalism—collectively constituting a shared inquiry into the multifarious social implications of the fantasy of Coffin's death. In a starkly different manner than Scott's *The Pirate*, where a constitutive process of peripheralization is explicit, here such processes of national interpellation and exclusion operate much more subtly. In *The Pilot*, therefore, we might ask if and how Long Tom Coffin haunts Cooper's narrative—marking a potentially vexed site where Cooper's social and political vision is caught writing over—or, more accurately, writing out—a romantic lower-class constituent who had risen up too far for comfort.

The Pilot and Maritime Labor: The Ideal Coffin

Because of the way that labor, class, and nationalism intersect to form the circumstances of Tom Coffin's death, it is important to contextualize Cooper's presentation of maritime labor more generally in *The Pilot*. As mentioned in chapter 1, Cooper, in his revised preface to a new 1849 edition of the novel, shifts from concerns of nationalism to concerns of nautical realism—explicitly setting up the task of the novel as a corrective to Scott's approach to maritime themes in *The Pirate*. If one uses the notion of nautical realism as a criterion of assessment, Cooper's novel does indeed seem to improve on Scott's romantic caricature of nautical scenes, which comes replete with singing Zetland *haaf* fishermen and gentlemanly rovers. Yet a close look at Cooper's depiction of sailors reveals that Scott's reductive portrayal of feudal labor has merely been replaced with a reductive portrayal of a more modern form of alienation. This is not to say that Cooper either maliciously disparages the lower-class workers on these ships or intends to reveal their plight. But the notion that the common sailor is less worthy than his romantically figured fellow laborers John Paul Jones (the pilot) and Tom Coffin (coxswain), or the gentlemanly officers, arises repeatedly in the narrative. Although many of the novel's scenes include vivid and realistic nautical experiences—such as chapter 5's meticulous account of how the pilot ushers the vessels through coastal shoals—they rely on elevating only one or two representative laboring figures.

This can be seen early in the novel, when Cooper takes care to acknowledge the vast crew that works on the frigate, referring to their curious "countenances" as the whaleboat returns with the pilot, as well as how there were "large groups of men" whose "faces were distinctly visible" (32); this gathering of subjectivities, however, soon dissipates into a mechanized mass when the ship gets under way. Here, Captain Munson's order to "Heave round!" is shown to echo down the chain of command as men repeat the directive—thus, syntactically reducing sailors to metonymic "voices" (38). Such a subtle linguistic figuration of common sailors as unified and abstract labor power continues as Cooper describes how a fife "struck up" "to enliven the labour" (38). Besides referring to men as labor as opposed to laborers, which he does again later when rowing sailors are said to resemble a "nice machine" (183), Cooper also acts to sublimate the masses into virtual nonexistence by constantly describing the ships, themselves, as having subjectivity and agency.[59] Such effacement of the common sailor, however, gives way in brief and telling moments when Cooper hints at divisions both within the labor of the lower ranks (such as the marines' "ignorance of seamanship" [36]) and between the agency of the crew and the authority of the officers (such as when Barnstable takes out his pistols to uphold the "arm of authority" over his men [276]).

It is this context from which the common sailor Tom Coffin rises to fill, for a time, the elevated space of hero in Cooper's narrative. As Philbrick makes clear, Coffin represents an "ideal" and "democratic" sailor; like Tom Tiller in Cooper's subsequent novel *The Water-Witch; or, The Skimmer of the Seas* (1831), Coffin is tall, moral, and "the epitome of seamanship."[60] This is apparent when Cooper first introduces Coffin at the opening of the second chapter. In a pseudo-dramatic dialogue, Captain Barnstable, upon exiting the whaleboat on a mission to find the pilot, introduces Coffin by pronouncing: "I would sooner trust Tom Coffin and his harpoon to back me, than the best broadside." Thus establishing the central theme of Coffin's role in bridging merchant and naval labor as well as his heroic aptitude, Barnstable then appends the romantic notion that Coffin is, quite literally, a creature of the sea: "Come, gather your limbs together, and try if you can walk on terra firma, Master Coffin" (17). Besides the initial blazon of Coffin's "elevated" frame, "well-formed body," "gigantic strength," and instinctual manner of grasping his "bright harpoon" (17–18), Cooper later furthers this seemingly overwrought notion of Tom as natural sailor by having Coffin discuss his ability to read "God's language in the clouds" and forecast an impending gale (23).

His sundry nautical abilities culminate in chapter 18's battle scene, where Coffin is portrayed as the sole reason why the small American schooner the *Ariel* defeats the English cutter the *Alacrity*. In preparing for engagement, Coffin sheds his jacket and shirt, standing by his "long gun" with his "brawny arms folded on a breast that had been turned to the colour of blood by long exposure" (194). Cooper then recounts how Tom was a "privileged individual in the *Ariel*" and that his opinions "were relegated as oracles by the crew, and were listened to by his commander" (194). In addition to his knowledge, Tom's skill is shown as a primary asset of the vessel, as his ability to aim the powerful cannon makes him the only sailor to fire at the *Alacrity* until they are within close range and vital damage has already been inflicted. The battle, however, is not only framed by Tom's ability—with his "shot" splaying out "like a shoal of porpoises" (196)—but also literally becomes his private affair when he sees the English sailors brandishing his beloved harpoon, which he had lost in a botched attempt on a whale. Appropriately, the battle terminates when Coffin recaptures his harpoon and, "looking like Neptune with his trident," launches the weapon through the English captain's chest, pinning him to the mast (200–201).

Coffin's physical abilities and nautical knowledge are subsequently coveted and respected by the English captain, Borroughcliffe, who, incidentally, also acts as a recruiting agent for the Royal Navy. When Coffin enters Colonel Howard's mansion in chapter 22, seeking surreptitiously to rescue Griffith, Borroughcliffe, in awe of Coffin's stature, exclaims: "A clear six-footer in nature's stockings! and the arms as unique as the armed!" (244). While Borroughcliffe finishes dining, he surveys "with unrepressed admiration" the "inches of the cockswain," taking stock of the potential value Coffin's labor might afford a ship's crew (244). Of course, Borroughcliffe had previously been informed of Coffin's covert intent; yet, his admiration of Coffin's body inspires him to have the American sent to his own quarters instead of to the guardroom.

In the repartee between the two men that follows, Borroughcliffe reveals that Coffin is a prisoner and informs him that the only way to avoid the prison ship or death is to enlist in the service of the king. Coffin rejects Borroughcliffe's offer and tosses him to the ground, and in describing the brief battle that ensues, Cooper juxtaposes the genteel captain and his sword and the laborer Tom Coffin and his harpoon. Not only does Coffin and his weapon win out but, having pinned Borroughcliffe with the harpoon, he grabs the other's sword, breaks the blade at the handle, and gags his victim with the silver hilt (251). Here, Cooper depicts an American sailor defeating a British soldier, and also, more important, an indecorous whaleman–coxswain defeating a refined captain in a duel-like struggle. In this pivotal sense, the harpoon trumps the sword. However, in keeping with Cooper's escalating romantic figuration of Coffin, this scene is also—

given Cooper's social and political views—inherently problematic. Coffin as romantic laborer–hero functions well in the narrative up to this point, but the harpoon's complete ascendancy engenders complications that Cooper must address. He answers, of course, by excising Coffin from the narrative one chapter later with the romantic, stormy wreck of the *Ariel*.

In chapter 24, Coffin returns to Barnstable and the *Ariel* after escaping from Borroughcliffe, and the Americans quickly make for the sea. However, as they head for the passage through the shoals a gale moves in toward the coast. Building on Coffin's previous role of leadership, Cooper presents him as feeling that "he had some right to advise, if not to command" and, fittingly, Captain Barnstable defers to his opinion on strategy (271). At this same time, soldiers manning a battery of artillery along the coast spy them and open fire. When the ship's mainmast is toppled, Cooper ushers in a pivotal turn in the narrative: with the metaphoric castration of the *Ariel*—to which, throughout, Coffin has shown excessive romantic attachment—comes the fall of Long Tom Coffin.

With its mainmast disabled, the *Ariel* is pushed by the storm back toward the rocky coast and the English artillery. Then, for the first time in the narrative, Cooper depicts Coffin and Barnstable at odds. When Barnstable asks Coffin for advice, Coffin despairingly responds: "I would have nothing, nothing" (273). After Coffin begins to speak of his prophetic vision of the wreck of the *Ariel,* Barnstable silences him, yelling: "Away with ye, ye old sea-croaker!" and tells him that if he has "sights of wrecks" to "keep them stowed in [his] own silly brain" (274). With this exchange of words, Cooper effectively exchanges heroes in the novel. Instead of the romantic, indomitable Long Tom Coffin, we get an "old sea-croaker" filled with "silly" superstitions. And as Coffin slinks away to do as he is bidden, Barnstable can be seen belting out orders to the crew. This dialectical shift, in a sense, is carried further when the gale mounts and the ship drifts closer to the coast. While Tom exhibits "the calmest resignation" to "fate," Barnstable rallies to fill the space of the hero (275–76). Breaking out his pistols and forcefully putting the men to work in order to keep them from taking control of the vessel and drowning their "apprehensions of death in ebriety," Barnstable refuses to follow Coffin's model of "cool resignation" (276). Cooper thus creates an interesting reversal, where Coffin's knowledge of the sea and association with action, elements that previously elevated him, now function, ironically, to cripple him. For Coffin is correct that there is nothing that can be done to save the vessel, and while his confidence in this assessment explains his defeatist attitude, it also pointedly reveals that his conception of the world is limited to the given reality—to ships, the sea, and the parameters of experience. Unlike Barnstable—the narrative's newly minted hero—Coffin cannot conceive of the situation, in Fredric Jameson's terms, as "anything other than what is."[61]

Responding to Coffin's complacence, Barnstable exclaims: "We must do our duty to ourselves and the country" (277). Despite the fact that resistance may be futile, such resistance *must* be offered. If Coffin's harpoon had earlier defeated the sword, here, his experience and pragmatism are surpassed by the romantic notion of unyielding national "duty." Indeed, the crew reacts with "desperate submission to the will of their commander," dropping the anchors and cutting down what remained of the masts in a futile attempt to counter the gales (277). It is clear, therefore, that a new criterion for heroism is being established, or, at least, reestablished: one that is conditioned by national sentiment and that is performed via a position of consolidated and traditional leadership. The *Ariel* soon goes down, and after tossing Barnstable into a whaleboat and refusing to depart from the ship, Coffin dies. Quite literally, the natural hero has given birth to a national one.

After Coffin's death, Barnstable and the crew scour the beach for the remains of their ship and shipmate. In dialogue replete with romantic tropes, these characters nostalgically reflect on Coffin, moving through a brief and rather formulaic process of mourning. The form of this remembering, however, has an essential and political function in the narrative. Even before the scene begins, the narrator closes the previous chapter by saying that the tide bore away "the body of the simple-hearted cockswain among the ruins" (284). Thus Cooper prefigures the qualitative aspects of how Barnstable will remember Coffin by metaphorically re-membering him. Coffin's previous identity and its association with his powerfully built body and propensity for aggressive action is replaced by correlating him with, literally, the organ of the heart and, abstractly, sentimental simplicity.

Soon after, Barnstable adds an important qualification to his sentimental ruminations about Coffin. After lamenting the loss of his "loved" ship, Barnstable tells Merry, a young midshipman: "And yet boy, a human being cannot love the creature of his own formation as he does the works of God. A man can never regard his ship as he does his shipmates" (288). Such a position pejoratively recasts Coffin's ostensibly heroic refusal to abandon the *Ariel*—figuring the maelstrom of Coffin's death as a lesson about facile and misplaced affection. In much the same way that Barnstable uses what he thought was Coffin's death to rally the crew in chapter 18's battle (crying, "Revenge Long Tom!" as his men board the *Alacrity* [199]), Coffin's actual death allows Cooper to sublimate his ideal sailor's disruptive elements back into the national tale that he set out to write.

In Coffin's death, therefore, we have a murderous (in a figurative sense) narrative coup de théâtre. Coffin's existence in the narrative undoubtedly reveals Cooper's creation—whether intentional or not—of a potentially radical literary and social common hero. Yet, looking again at the narrative as well as at Cooper's political writings, it becomes evident that Coffin's death may be an attempt to contain this fantasmatic energy: to relocate the focus from the heroic but impolite sailor to the American naval officers and the mysterious genteel pilot whom Cooper clearly wishes to play the lead role, as well as to sublimate Coffin's merchant-based roots and extranational motivations into a broader nationalist cause.

The Class Mandate

If *The Pilot* functions as a romantic narrative of the nation, one aspect of Cooper's vision that necessitates the declension of Tom Coffin is class. Philbrick pinpoints this issue in his brief analysis of the novel, suggesting that one reason *The Red Rover* is a more effective narrative is because its genteel hero "receives little competition from the lower ranks." Indeed, Philbrick goes so far as to assert that "the gentlemen sailors of *The Pilot* . . . must contend with" Coffin and his role as "the ideal seaman" and that the narrative structure of the novel "collapses" with Coffin's death.[62] While Philbrick does not assert that Coffin's death is in any way related to an element of class conflict, his reading quite clearly gestures in this direction. In this scenario, however, the genteel officers in the novel do not compete with the lower ranks on an even playing field. As we have seen, besides Coffin, who dies, and the pilot, who exists in an ambiguous space between classes, Cooper consistently effaces the common sailor. While the lower-rank laborers do surface now and again, in these spare moments, Cooper figures them as a lowly herd: evoking more of a Smollett-like caricature sans the satire or Coleridge's vision of how "slimy things did crawl with legs / Upon the slimy sea," as opposed to offering any romantic or realistic portrayal.[63]

For example, in the 1849 preface to the novel, Cooper refers to sailors as "rude beings" "of the lowest habits" and sarcastically defends the navy's use of flogging as a means of control.[64] This sentiment manifests in the aforementioned *Ariel* scene when Barnstable uses force to prevent the crew from taking over the ship, as well as more directly in chapter 30, when the American forces are marching their captives from Colonel Howard's St. Ruth house to the sea. In a passage that discloses many aspects of this issue, Cooper writes how the marines "were followed ... by a large and confused body of seamen, heavily armed, whose disposition to disorder and rude merriment, which became more violent from their treading on solid ground, was with difficulty restrained by the presence and severe rebukes of their own officers" (345). Here, Cooper keeps with his earlier mode of casting common sailors as a faceless "body" and develops both the theme of the potential danger in their predilection for "disorder" and the necessity of having "gentleman" officers actively quell their tendency toward chaos. Such competing propensities clearly relate to the mythic Hercules–Hydra dialectic, which, as Peter Linebaugh and Marcus Rediker portray, was a popular literary trope in the eighteenth and nineteenth centuries—with the Hydra, like the lowly sailors, a "symbol of disorder" and Hercules, like the officers, a "symbol of power and order."[65] In more theoretical terms, such antithetical forces depict what Deleuze and Guattari view as two poles of libidinal energy, where "flows of desire" gravitate toward either the "paranoiac," the pole of order and "central sovereignty," or the "schizophrenic," the pole of chaotic multiples where desire seeks to "escape" delimiting barriers.[66]

Cooper furthers the apparent implication that the common sailors' Hydra tendencies are linked to their class status in the following scene. Focusing on two sailors within the crowd—the only time he does so in the entire novel—he portrays how they cruelly taunt Howard's black slaves. As the midshipman Merry attempts to silence their attack, Cooper describes a "low laugh" that "passed through the confused crowd" and then, in an aside, comments on how "that abject race" of African Americans are still "the butts of the unthinking and licentious among our low countrymen" (348). The two uses of the adjective "low" here clearly conjoin the concepts of class and social behavior. In this context, Cooper's phrase "lowest habits" in the preface, which is used to describe sailors' poor etiquette, can also double for their economic origins.

Cooper's disdain for the lower class is not, however, simply one-dimensional. In his analysis of *The Water-Witch*, Dekker explores Cooper's anxiety about the rise of the commercial class in Europe and America—

where Cooper juxtaposes this group, represented in a Jewish, Merchant of Venice–like Van Beverout, and the traditional "Northern European bourgeois" Protestants.[67] The ostensible threat from the nouveau riche of the merchant class is linked to a more general notion of the lower class in Cooper's early political writings. The 1828 fictional account of a visiting European's observations of the United States, *Notions of the Americans,* has been correctly viewed as "Cooper's most explicit declaration of American Independence from English influence."[68] If, as Peck points out, *The Pilot* seeks to "solve the problems that the American Revolution posed," then *Notions of the Americans,* written four years later, vividly portrays the qualitative aspects of those very problems.[69] Framed as a correction to European distortions of America, this two-volume work portrays Americans as having a natural "tendency to the sea."[70] In terms of the Revolutionary War, however, Cooper makes important distinctions about American maritime activity. After describing the incipient U.S. marine forces as having an "extraordinary aptitude" for such service, he qualifies such accolades by citing how they were "imperfectly organized." Cooper sees this lack of order stemming from the use of merchant-class officers, saying: "Their discipline was not, nor could not well be, better than that ordinarily observed on board private vessels of war since the ships were of necessity officered by men taken from the trading vessels of the country."[71] He goes on to say that in this "mixed marine" service, where the officer ranks were supplied by men who were "masters and mates of the merchantmen," "there must have existed the utmost inequality of merit and of fitness for . . . duty."[72] The class component of this view becomes even more apparent when Cooper describes how, after 1801, the marine department had the opportunity of "making a selection among the officers."[73] This selection led to the establishment of the navy's "discipline" and "high reputation of spirit" because of the "ambitious natural character" of its men—young men "chiefly of the best families of the country." As opposed to during the American Revolution, by the time of the war with Tripoli, "officers were now first seen in the command of vessels, who had regularly risen from the lowest ranks of the service."[74]

Clearly, Cooper conceives of a need for institutionalized officers and leadership, but also for such men to derive from the traditional "best families" of the nation. Such sentiment is later echoed in Cooper's 1839 *History of the Navy of the United States of America,* in which he writes that during the Revolutionary War "there was no lack of competent navigators, or of brave seamen, but the high moral qualities which are indispensable to the accomplished officer, were hardly to be expected among those who had received their training in the rude and imperfect schools of the merchant service."[75] A distinct mandate that officers demonstrate "high" qualities, which are impossible to accrue in the "rude" merchant service, corresponds to Cooper's broader political views about governance. John C. McCloskey asserts that while Cooper did not long for a feudal society, he imagined "a constitutional republic in which men were free and equal in the law but in which the representatives were chosen on the bases of wealth and social position."[76] According to John P. McWilliams, this sentiment is more directly developed in Cooper's *The American Democrat* (1838). After seeing the dangerous rise of the masses within the Jacksonian democracy that he had earlier championed, Cooper began to fear that the "public would override the law."[77] In a revealing passage that portrays his Federalist roots, Cooper argues: "There can be no question that the educated and affluent classes of a country, are more capable of coming to wise and intelligent decisions in affairs of state."[78] This is quite bluntly prefigured in the book's introduction, where Cooper says that he "is not a believer in the scheme of raising men very far above their natural propensities."[79]

In this context, the American Revolution was a noble cause fought and won by brave seamen *despite* the fact that "mixed" officers led them. Juxtaposing this schematic with the events of *The Pilot*, we see an interesting amendment, where the class problematic is displaced onto tension between the "low" merchant-based and common sailor Tom Coffin and the relatively "high" officers. With Coffin's fall from prominence, might we see Cooper transferring the postwar move toward stable upper-class naval leadership seen in *Notions of the Americans* onto the Revolutionary War's historical moment?

Much in the spirit of Walter Scott's depiction in *The Pirate* of Minna's determination that "no whale-striking, bird-nesting" sailor could be her "lover," but only "a Sea-King, or what else modern times may give that draws near that lofty character," Cooper's eradication of Coffin appears to be highly motivated by conservative and romantic class notions.[80]

The National Mandate

Coffin's disruption, however, goes deeper than general notions of class. For in addition to his placement within the lower status of common sailors, he is portrayed as a Nantucket whaleman who romantically identifies with the space of the sea. In chapter 2, Coffin tells Barnstable:

> Give me a plenty of sea-room, and good canvas, where there is no 'casion for pilots at all, sir. For my part, I was born on board a chebacco-man, and never could see the use of more land than now and then a small island, to raise a few vegetables, and to dry your fish—I'm sure the sight of it always makes me uncomfortable, unless we have the wind dead off shore. (19)

Quite literally born on the sea and raised on an island, Coffin evinces a longing for a landless sea-space that is clearly extranational. Although Barnstable is shown somewhat to echo Coffin's sentiment, saying, "Damme, long Tom, but I am more than half of your mind," unlike Coffin, an essential other "half" of Barnstable considers the mainland United States to be home (27). Although scholars, such as Wai Chee Dimock, have cogently argued that the romantic eighteenth- and nineteenth-century American desire for "sea room" correlates to the spatial requirements for constructing an economic and cultural empire, here Coffin's totalizing longing for such space can be seen to complicate Cooper's own notions of national allegiance.[81] For example, in *Notions of the Americans,* Cooper asserts that the "lower orders" of sailors in America are able to invest in national causes because: "They are not accidents of the surface of society that are willing to float, like most other mariners, whither the current shall carry them, but they are men who can find opinions which lie at the root of all their habits, in their native land."[82] It is possible, of course, to argue that Coffin's cavalier attitude and desire for unbounded space is very much anchored, if you will, to the American ideology of individualism. Nonetheless, juxtaposing Coffin's statement from chapter 2 and this passage from *Notions* reveals an obvious tension between conceptions of what an ideal sailor may be. While Coffin portrays a dis-ease with land, itself, preferring constant oceanic movement, Cooper describes the ideal nationalistic common sailor as being inherently bound to the "native land" for the very "root" of his opinions and habits.

In this context, Coffin can be seen to fill the mode of national sailor described in *Notions*; yet, while he may be in the service of the American Navy, important tensions complicate his ability fully to embody this position. Though the pilot's (or John Paul Jones's) desire for fame and Barnstable and Griffith's pursuit of the women in Colonel Howard's charge are clearly examples of personal motivations, they all, ultimately, act on these causes within the bounds of national interests.[83] John Paul Jones's character, specifically, is an interesting example of this dynamic. Under the guise of Mr. Gray, the taciturn pilot evinces a complex array of motivations: he is essentially a Scottish-born naval commander (or "pirate," depending on one's perspective) with close ties to the court of France and fierce nationalist animosity toward George III. Although his drive for personal fame may account for why Cooper sends him off at the close of the novel in a solitary boat on the North Sea, the pilot's skill and motivations—unlike Coffin's whaling and merchant associations—clearly exist on the symbolic plane of national naval activity and are paramount to the United States' revolutionary cause. In addition to his nationalist concerns, Jones can also be seen as distinct from Coffin in terms of class position. For while Gray does literally function as a common maritime pilot in the novel's action, his subsequent identification as Captain John Paul Jones clearly invests him with a status above that of the Nantucket coxswain. Interestingly, Cooper's decision to align Jones with American revolutionary nationalism can be seen as a clear act of historical revision. As Franklin makes clear, in the early nineteenth century "British propaganda portraying Jones as a traitor and a pirate still dominated even the common American view."[84] Furthermore, considering the United States' close political and military ties to France in the 1820s, Cooper's presentation of Jones's alignment with the French may be seen to place the Scottish captain even further in the American camp.[85]

Such distinctions between Coffin and other Cooper characters that share his qualities as a common-laborer hero are important to note. This line of discussion, of course, is bound to generate comparisons with Cooper's most famous character, Natty Bumppo. On the surface, Coffin does indeed resemble Cooper's mainland hero, from their physical attributes and class status to their penchant for using "long" guns in battle. Another character to consider in this context is Harvey Birch in Cooper's *The Spy* (1821). In his introduction to this novel, Franklin notes Cooper's ability, in *The Spy* and the subsequent Leatherstocking series, to replicate "the vertical class structure of the day," and views Harvey Birch as a heroic lower-class predecessor to Bumppo, "the first great common man."[86] Though a lengthy contextualization of *The Pilot* with these novels falls outside the scope of this chapter, it is important to note that, like Jones, both Birch and Bumppo act out their respective parts firmly within the requisite political bounds of the national narrative—though, as Franklin points out, Bumppo's loyalist actions during the Revolution may have prevented Cooper from writing a sixth Leatherstocking tale set during that war.[87]

Unlike these various characters, Coffin's motivations are consistently and narrowly personal. In chapter 18 of *The Pilot*, when Barnstable spies the *Alacrity*, he says that "there is a sort of national obligation on [them] to whip that fellow" (192). While Coffin is the key component of the subsequent American victory, not once in the narrative does he voice any such nationalistic sentiment. Accordingly, Coffin's bravery and skill can be used in the nationalist cause, but his identity and motivations are never limited to it. Tension arising from this surplus initially manifests in Coffin's position of transference between an extranational preoccupation with whaling and the national duties at hand. As mentioned, Cooper repeatedly figures Coffin's harpooning and nautical skills as being a dominating force in the military arena. At the same time, however, there are moments in the text when the qualitative aspect of this very strength acts as a potential disruption to military affairs. In chapter 2, after Coffin brashly says that he could "drive" his harpoon through any prospective enemy since he has "sent it to the seizing in many a whale," Barnstable chides him, saying: "Pshaw! You are not on a whaling voyage, where everything that offers is game" (20). Barnstable's point clearly denotes the way Coffin's interests and skills are not contained by the crew's military task. Just as Coffin's desire for abstract, open space at sea exceeds the traditional geographic constructs of national identity, his merchant-based activity of hunting whales exceeds, or is out of joint with, the parameters of combat within national warfare.

Cooper stresses this point by subsequently dramatizing the dangers inherent in competing merchant/private and naval/national motivations. In chapter 17, while Barnstable and his crew row their whaleboat back to the *Ariel* after picking up Coffin, they spot what Coffin identifies as a wright whale. Coffin's description of how "he's a raal oil-butt, that fellow" (184) prompts Barnstable, whose own "youth had been chiefly passed in such pursuits" (186), to reflect on the "temptation for sport" (184). After discovering that Coffin had brought whale-line on board, Barnstable orders the men to pursue the whale—which they herald with a "spontaneous" shout. This romantic and comical adventure soon finds the whale secured and dying. Cooper quickly complicates the scene when Coffin urges Barnstable to allow the whale to perish on its own because "there's no occasion for disgracing [themselves] by using a soldier's weapon in taking a whale" (187). Despite the line's obvious syntactic ambiguity, the context of Coffin's character suggests that he is referring to the fact that the disgrace would stem from the use of base military weapons on the vaunted whale. While this depicts how Coffin's esteem for whaling surpasses that of his notions of soldiering, the events that follow evince Cooper's displeasure with such a schematic. In fact, Cooper quickly reveals that this transference between whaling and naval activity is not only incongruous but, in fact, dangerous. First, when the whale finally dies, Barnstable is shown to stand over his "victim" with "diminished excitement" and ask: "What's to be done now?" (187). Cooper thus depicts how the terminus of this "sport" reveals the utter anachronistic nature of the crew's desire—for in their current role there is no way for them to process this whale into what Melville terms a "bank."[88] Yet, while Barnstable is shown to lament his error in judgment, Coffin fantasizes about how having such a catch back in Boston "would prove the making of [him]" (188).

There is, then, an apparent divergence between Barnstable's and Coffin's sentiments at the close of the hunt: where Barnstable realizes the impossibility of combining whaling and his duties in the navy, Coffin continues to think in terms of profit. Such motivation is clearly condemned in *Notions of the Americans,* where Cooper criticizes "an object so little justifiable, and perhaps so ignoble, as gain."[89] In his later maritime novel *The Crater,* Cooper expounds upon this topic, making clear that such pursuit of profit is not necessarily bound either by or to the moral parameters of a "Christian nation." Citing the example of the sandalwood trade, he argues that "no higher offence can be committed" than by those, including American merchants and vessels, who sell such a product to China for use in pagan rituals.[90]

The global aspect of profit that, in Cooper's view, can exceed the moral and social boundaries of the nation also appears in the composite of American vessels' crews. Although in *The Pilot* Cooper only briefly mentions how many of the "rude beings" who are common sailors are, in fact, "men of all nations," this foreign aspect of the lower class of maritime laborers was on Cooper's mind (7). In a long footnote in *Notions,* Cooper addresses the fact that "possibly one-third of the common seamen employed in the foreign trade of America are foreigners" by arguing that this is not due to America's lack of propensity for nautical activity, but to "the superabundance" of outside labor.[91] Many other Americans shared Cooper's apparent anxiety about the potential physical and symbolic threats posed by having foreign sailors in the American merchant service. At the close of *Two Years before the Mast,* for example, Richard Henry Dana Jr. defends the use of corporal punishment at sea primarily because "three-fourths of the seamen in our merchant vessels are foreigners" and, therefore, "masters are obliged to sail without knowing anything of their crews," which many include "pirates or mutineers among them" (353–54). This general distrust of the common sailor's foreigner status, according to David Kazanjian, included a concerted movement at the end of the eighteenth century to cut back on the number of black and foreign mariners in both the merchant and the naval services. These efforts included "requiring that mariners carry Seaman's Protection Certificates attesting to their national identity" as well as passage of the Negro Seaman Acts beginning in 1822, which called for placing black sailors in prison while their ships were in Southern ports.[92]

In looking further at this scene in *The Pilot,* however, it is apparent that Coffin's and Barnstable's actions in whaling are not only incongruent with but antithetical to naval warfare. This becomes clear when Cooper has the English vessel *Alacrity* move in on them while they are engaged with the whale. While the Americans desperately try make it back to the *Ariel,* Cooper continues to rescue Barnstable's "honor" by having him order Coffin to throw his whale-line overboard; as Coffin casts the tub into the sea, Barnstable exclaims, "Ah! there is much of your philosophy in that stroke" and then laments: "Damn the whale! but for the tow ..., we should have been out of sight of this rover!" (189). At the close of the whaling scene, then, Barnstable—though a "mixed" officer, unlike the more genteel Griffith—can be seen to prefigure his subsequent ascendancy over Coffin by moving from his lowly merchant roots into the role of heroic naval officer. Coffin, on the other hand, remains clearly and firmly defined by his old ways.

In addition to being linked to the activity of whaling and its profits, Coffin's motivations are also shaped by his personal attachment to the *Ariel.* Even before the ultimate example in the wreck of the *Ariel,* Cooper portrays aspects of Coffin's allegiance in the scuffle between him and Captain Borroughcliffe. When Borroughcliffe asks Coffin to enlist with the English, Coffin answers: "A messmate, before a shipmate; a shipmate, before a stranger; a stranger, before a dog; but a dog before a soldier!" (250). While the context correlates the term "soldier" with "English soldier," the language indicates that Coffin views the personal bonds between messmates as the most important relationship and soldiering—commitment to a broader national cause—as the lowest. Cooper provides little information about Coffin's past, but he does reveal that he had acted as Barnstable's "father and mother on the deep" and had taught the captain "the art of [their] profession" (288). In this context, we might speculate that Coffin's impetus for engaging in this military enterprise is the fact that his closest messmate, Barnstable, has chosen to serve in the nascent navy.[93]

As noted, the personal motivations that condition Coffin's behavior culminate in the wreck of the *Ariel*. Initially, Coffin's determination to go down with his ship might be seen as adherence to the romantic correlation between ship and state. Paul David Nelson points out how, in one of Cooper's early nationalist articles, he pleaded with sailors not to forget the words of an American naval officer who died in an 1813 battle: "Don't give up the ship."[94] In addition, the name "Ariel" refers to Jerusalem ("Woe to Ariel, to Ariel, the city where David dwelt" [Isaiah 29:1]) and can, therefore, be seen to invest the ship and Coffin's actions with grand allegorical significance.[95] The text, however, does not bear out these readings. While Coffin does voice Christian sentiment for the first time in the novel during the shipwreck scene, his motivation for going down with the ship remains sentimentally personal. After throwing Barnstable into the whaleboat to save him, Coffin says: "I saw the first timber of the Ariel laid, and shall live just long enough to see it torn out of her bottom; after which I wish to live no longer" (281). As Coffin's economic activity and interests are too broad (conditioned by global capitalism and the space of the sea) to be completely contained by the idea of the national, here his affection for the ship is too narrow, for although it might have been built in the United States, his attachment to it occludes or eclipses attachment to an abstract national cause.

The scene that corresponds to this chapter's second epigraph exemplifies this notion: here Coffin answers Dillon's question of why he wishes to remain on the ship by saying: "To die in my coffin, if it should be the will of God, . . . ; these waves, to me, are what the land is to you; I was born on them, and I have always meant that they should be my grave" (282). The reference to God's will aside—which is effectively negated by Coffin's claim to have personally "meant" the sea to be his grave—this passage includes an interesting linguistic and conceptual conflation of Coffin and the ship. By having Tom Coffin view the *Ariel* as his own coffin, Cooper syntactically enacts the coxswain's desire to join the ship.

Ultimately, just as Coffin's heroism is curtailed by being transferred to Barnstable, Coffin's Nantucket surname and its association with whaling families is closed down, in a sense, by being transferred to the image of a sinking casket.

Coffin and the "Other Limit" of the National Narrative

Cooper scholarship traditionally views *The Red Rover* as his maritime masterpiece. Both H. Daniel Peck and Thomas Philbrick aptly portray how the novel's pre–American Revolution pirate, Captain Heidegger, represents a "threatening Byronic . . . hero."[96] The threat, which takes the form of raids on European and colonial vessels, is shown, however, to embody the Red Rover's prescient conception of "the drift of history," whereby his violent actions prefigure the subsequent war of independence.[97] I mention this novel because juxtaposing the disparate "threats" that the Red Rover and Tom Coffin pose to national and imperial systems provides a useful lens through which to conceptualize the nature of Coffin's role in *The Pilot*.

Cesare Casarino's *Modernity at Sea* provides a theoretical schematic that may be useful for analyzing Cooper's characters and their relation to national constructs. As noted earlier, Casarino conceives the antebellum era as a dynamic period of economic and social transition within early modern capitalism, viewing the development of modernity in this period as "the modernity of capital."[98] As discussed in chapter 1, in his analysis of *Moby-Dick* Casarino introduces the Deleuze-informed concepts of the "outer limit" and "other limit" of capital. While the outer limit is a false final terminus that "already points to yet another last limit" and, hence, defers internal contradiction by pushing outward toward an ever-expanding boundary, the other limit is "in" a concept's "own nature."[99] It is the site of immanent and internal crisis that constantly requires deferral.

In the context of Cooper's fiction, we might use Casarino's model to view the concept of the national narrative. Captain Heidegger's private war against the nations of the early eighteenth century can be viewed as a push against the "outer limit" of national constructs. Not only is his battle against nations quite literally waged in the ambiguous oceanic space between them, but the narrative presupposes that this crisis represents the birth pangs of a new national power. The Red Rover makes this clear at the end of the novel by claiming that his actions had been driven by a vision of a new state beyond the condition of the "dependant Colonists"; consequently, had its "flag been abroad . . . no man would have ever heard of the name of the Red Rover."[100]

Alternately, Tom Coffin can be viewed as a possible "other limit" of the national narrative and project. As I have shown, not only does he embody the extranational concepts of identification with the sea and motivation based on economic profit and personal allegiance, but also his class and occupational status link him to the intrinsic dangers, in Cooper's view, in American's democratic and economic systems. In Cooper's forceful containment of his natural sailor, then, we see how national disavowals and displacements can erupt in the very narratives that seek romantically to efface them. Tom Coffin begins as a working-class caricature that adds color to the naval adventure, yet he emerges as the site where the internal contradictions of the nation converge. Yes, Coffin ultimately dies for the nation, but not for the reasons that Cooper's tale would have us believe.

In these varied contexts, both Scott's and Cooper's narratives portray a historical transition into their nineteenth-century present. In both, a foundational element of the transition's drama is the creation of national subjects and heroes (Mordaunt, Cleveland, and Minna/Norna for Scott, and primarily Barnstable for Cooper). Within this process, the plots' tensions and emotional energies stem from a struggle to hone and redistribute characters' desires, or, more specifically, to interpellate characters into national fantasies. In this context, we might use Catherine Rottenberg's distinction between identification and "desire-to-be" to view the competing elements of desire seen in these texts. In her analysis of racial subjectivity, Rottenberg asserts that the traditional notion of identification—one that would presumably include the Lacanian version used in my earlier discussion of *The Pirate*—conceives of desire reductively. Referring specifically to the experiences of African Americans, she reveals how the unconditional coupling of these concepts fails to account for racial "subjects [who] are encouraged to privilege and thus desire attributes associated with whiteness, but concurrently . . . *forced* to identify as black."[101] Though the predominantly white characters in Scott and Cooper's two novels do not experience a racially informed bifurcation between desire-to-be and identification, distinguishing between these constituent elements within subject formation may illuminate issues relevant to nationalism. For, as discussed, both plots hinge primarily on characters' eventual conformity to national constructions. Consequently, these historical characters' acquisition of the *desire to be* national subjects can be seen as a formative element in the movement toward a national present. It is in this sense that Pease, citing Žižek, suggests that "national subjects can only come into existence by desiring this fantasized relation to the national Thing."[102] These historical narratives effectively align this amorphous Thing with national identity itself, thereby reifying a desire-to-be a national subject into a transhistorical constitutive element of national subjectivity.

Paradoxically, we might amend our previous comparison of the political import of Scott's and Cooper's narratives. Even though Scott portrays the transition into national identification as a tenuous and questionable process, it is Cooper's narrative that unqualitatively illuminates—even if unintentionally—one of the most dangerous obstacles facing the perpetuation of the nation: the desire of its citizens. Scott's characters may reveal that curbing or transferring desire by adopting national fantasies occurs, at times, under duress (as seen with Cleveland and Bunce) and has apparent enigmatic remainders, yet the point is that the blood of such metaphoric and fantasmatic revolutions gets quickly—all too quickly, perhaps, in Scott's case—absorbed into the national fray. Coffin, on the other hand, may exist in the national fray by laboring for the nascent American navy, yet he refuses on the level of fantasy to respond to the hail of the nation. Although he may identify as an American sailor, he never evinces a desire-to-be a national subject and, hence, must become a relic—a romantic antecedent to the present-future of the State.

· II ·

Polynesian Encounters Redux

· CHAPTER 3 ·

Tattoos in *Typee*: Rethinking Melville's "Cultural Grotesque"

THE CONSTRUCTION OF ANTEBELLUM NATIONAL subjectivity that the previous chapter begins to explore emerges in part through experiences within the era's expanding geopolitical landscape. In terms of the frequent encounters across and around the Pacific, the native tattoo constitutes a central exotic artifact and trope. Indeed, native peoples' systems of "tattowing" have fired the imaginations of readers since the earliest published account of Cook's first Pacific voyage, and descriptions of tattoos can be found throughout subsequent maritime narratives of various kinds.

In the late eighteenth century, these accounts begin to shift from simple anthropological observations by naturalists such as Joseph Banks, who compiled a graphic account of Tahitian tattoos during Cook's 1769 stay on the island, to more dramatic narratives of Westerners' encounters with the practice. By the early nineteenth century, for example, naval registers of seamen reveal that tattooing (or "pricking," as it was more commonly called) had begun to be absorbed into the rituals of Western sailors.[1] At the same time, white sailors who had been extensively tattooed by natives, such as Joseph Kabris and John Rutherford, became sensations when they appeared before European and American audiences.[2] The Western fascination with the tattoo, in fact, spawned a veritable "heads-for-weapons" trade in the late eighteenth and early nineteenth centuries: until the practice was banned in 1831, Europeans aggressively procured the tattooed skulls of New Zealand Maori natives in order to peddle them to mainland "curiosity" enthusiasts and collectors (à la Queequeg's skull trade in *Moby-Dick*).

These scenes play out in an antebellum literary market saturated with texts portraying various ramblings across remote areas of the maritime world, and they negotiate a myriad of Enlightenment and Romantic-era conceptions of noble and ignoble Pacific savages.[3] As colonial and commercial agents from Europe and, later, America arrive in the Pacific region, their notions of social and political identity are tried and tested. In this regard, J. G. A. Pocock claims:

> There is a real sense in which the most important encounter made by Europeans in the Age of Enlightenment was the encounter with themselves, with their pasts and with their own historicity, so that it was into these highly sophisticated and even self-critical schemes of historiography that they sought to integrate, or gave up trying to integrate, the cultures with which they came in contact. The Others found all the problems of European history dumped upon them.[4]

Such an assertion might reductively cast this "Other" as a mere phantom of the Western mind. Yet it reveals the extent to which Western cross-cultural maritime encounters are mediated by their own symbolic systems and narratives.

In this context, the tattoo stands out as a particularly nuanced focal point through which to interrogate how an ethnocentric and logocentric West negotiates Pacific others as well as the liminal spaces in which they experience them.[5] Using Melville's adventure narrative *Typee* as a centerpiece, in this chapter I employ a Lacanian perspective to build on and rethink contemporary approaches to both Melville's text and antebellum notions of Polynesian tattooing. To this end, the first section relocates the climactic trauma from chapter 30's scene of anxiety about facial tattoos to the novel's appendix and its account of political events in Honolulu. While the threat that the tattoo poses to Tommo's face is the manifest fear in the text, the appendix's account of the colonial failure to control natives' bodies and desires reveals a related and potentially more formative peril. Using *Typee*'s appendix as a lens through which to reread events in the novel, I explore how the West's anxiety about being disfigured and racially marked by natives' ink may act as a fantasy that displaces gaps in its own symbolic mechanisms. In the second part of the chapter I more closely examine this fantasy scenario, suggesting that the symbolic threat of the tattoo might paradoxically facilitate Tommo's desire for his own face.

Tattoo Transference and Refracted Freaks: Reframing the Aggressive-Grotesque in *Typee*

Scholars have often discussed the scene in Herman Melville's *Typee* where Tommo's fear of being inscribed by a Marquesan tattoo artist catalyzes the young sailor's desire to escape the valley of the Typees. After Karky brandishes his tattooing implements "in fearful vicinity" of Tommo's face, Tommo famously reflects: "I now felt convinced that in some luckless hour I should be disfigured in such a manner as never more to have the *face* to return to my countrymen."[6]

Melville composed this narrative after having returned in 1844 from an adventure in the South Seas that purportedly included jumping ship from the whaler the *Acushnet* in Taio'hae Bay in the Marquesas, dwelling in the Taipi Valley, joining up with the Australian whaler *Lucy Ann* (whereupon the action of *Typee* ends), staying in Tahiti until signing with the Nantucket whaling vessel *Charles and Henry*, and, finally, sailing as an ordinary seaman aboard the U.S. frigate *United States* after living for a time in Hawaii.[7] Thus, *Typee* should be set against the biographical issues of authenticity highlighted in chapter 1 of this volume. When focusing on scenes of tattooing, however, the novel should also be placed in the context of accounts of the Marquesas Islands and various antebellum experiences of Polynesian tattooing.

The Marquesas, a group of ten easternmost islands in the Polynesian archipelagoes, have been the object of European fascination since early accounts, such as Fernández de Quirós's 1595 depiction of Fatu Hiva.[8] Although France was making colonial inroads into the islands during the 1840s of Melville's *Typee,* the United States had made its own imperial foray into the island chain when Captain David Porter temporarily took possession of the region in 1813. In fact, in his own narrative, Porter acknowledges Spain's early contact with the area but argues that it was the American captain Roberts who first "discovered" many of the islands— using Roberts's patriotic appellations Adams, Jefferson, and Hamilton when referring to islands.[9] Porter arrived in Taio'hae Bay with his frigate *Essex* and a band of captured British whaling vessels that he had amassed during his War of 1812 mission to disrupt British shipping, and promptly engaged in battles with both the obstinate "Happahs" and the fierce "Typees." His difficulty with the Marquesan natives colored subsequent antebellum conceptions of the islands. In 1828, for instance, the Sandwich Island missionaries refused the instructions of the American Board of Commissioners for Foreign Missions to expand into the Marquesas (a hesitancy shared by English missionaries on Tahiti). It was not until after Charles Stewart, a chaplain on board the *Vincennes,* published a more optimistic account of the Marquesas in 1831 that the board fitted out a separate Marquesas missionary team; those missionaries, however, abandoned their efforts within two years.[10]

In addition to such grand political and ideological interactions, European and American commercial ships frequently landed on Marquesan islands and in other Pacific regions, especially in the later antebellum years. Eager mainland Americans, therefore, learned about Pacific encounters from narratives by explorers such as Cook and Langsdorff as well as from tales and artifacts provided by common sailors. The tattoo was a frequent centerpiece of these accounts. But it was much more than a simple narrative trope. In fact, tattooed seamen and natives became popular spectacles in the late eighteenth and the early nineteenth century. For example, though Cook's exploits encompassed a wide scope of exotic places and topics, when he returned to England in 1774, it was a Tahitian named Omai whom he had in tow that most fueled public curiosity. And Omai's body—especially his elaborate buttock tattoos—became the rage of London high society and scientific communities alike.[11]

Contemporary studies, such as Leonard Cassuto's *The Inhuman Race: The Racial Grotesque in American Literature and Culture* (1997) and Samuel Otter's *Melville's Anatomies* (1999), cogently take up such spectacles in terms of antebellum ethnography and racial politics, interpreting Tommo's fear of facial disfigurement as a product of racial anxiety. Melville's portrayal of the tattooed native as "a hideous object to look upon" (83) and the apprehension of being disfigured are contextualized within an age of colonial exploration and the development of the domestic freak show. Robert Bogdan explains that "as explorers and natural scientists traversed the world, they brought back not only tales of unfamiliar cultures but also specimens of the distant wonders."[12] And Rosemarie Garland Thomson notes that by the nineteenth century such "specimens" of non-Western "natives" were a staple of the rising freak-show spectacle.[13]

The tattoo was a popular subset of this type of "freak." Besides surveying tattoos on natives' bodies, beginning early in the nineteenth century, pier-goers could commonly find willing sailors displaying their "skin art" for a nominal fee.[14] And by the 1840s, tattooed white men such as James

O'Connell and the Albanian–Greek captain Costentenus became sensations in traveling freak shows, which commonly renarrated the tattoos with hyperbolic and graphic stories of abduction and tattoo-torture by natives.[15]

Melville was well aware of the phenomenon of the freak show when writing *Typee*.[16] As Leonard Cassuto points out, he was also aware of the domestic racial politics that shaped the growing spectacle market, manipulating these associations by using "facial tattooing to link the black with the freak."[17] In Cassuto's terms, Melville's presentation of tattooing is in this way an encounter with racial difference, resulting in the affective portrayal of a "cultural grotesque," or a "liminal state between human and thing, becoming variables of both."[18] In a similar line of analysis, Samuel Otter locates this discourse of racial encounter within the matrix of nineteenth-century ethnological practices. Like Cassuto, Otter proposes that, ultimately, Tommo's fear of Karky's tattoo attack relates to his fear of losing his Caucasian identity.[19]

While considering Tommo's experiences in the context of antebellum racial discourse has yielded important insight into constructs and crises that shape Melville's world, reading such discourse as the definitive source of Tommo's anxiety may in fact limit our historical perspective. The threat of being inscribed with natives' "grotesque" tattoos is undoubtedly tied to specific issues of race, but by focusing on the novel's appendix, one can see that such constructs are also shaped by a more diffuse anxiety about the ability to label and control bodies.

For example, in discussing the association of tattooing and blackness Otter cites a passage in G. H. von Langsdorff's *Voyages and Travels* (1813–14) describing how "one figure is made over another, till the whole becomes confused, and the body assumes a Negro-like appearance."[20] Although Otter's subsequent analysis of how Europeans used a racial schematic for interpreting new cultural events is quite relevant, his precipitous focus on the latter part of Langsdorff's passage—the labeling of tattoos as "Negro-like"—may occlude some of the broader sociostructural issues at play: namely, a potentially more foundational source of "confusion" engendered by the tattoo. In fact, can we not view race as a stabilizing "reterritorialization" that palliates symbolic confusion or tension engendered by the tattoo?[21]

On a basic level, the notion that tattoo anxiety may embody broader social apprehensions can be seen in the way Polynesian tattoos' qualitative aspects often trouble Western conventions of aesthetics. From the beginning of the novel, Melville uses general Western fantasies about the Marquesas as an a priori schematic for viewing the region and its people. For example, as his whaling ship nears the islands, Tommo exclaims: "The Marquesas! What strange visions of outlandish things does the very name spirit up! Naked houris—cannibal banquets—groves of cocoa-nut—coral reefs—tatooed [sic] chiefs" (5). Here, imaginary narratives of this region, which tellingly include "tatooed chiefs," inform the fantasy structure that shapes how Tommo will perceive events. As the narrative continues, Tommo consistently describes the Typees' tattoos as being "grotesque" (78, 134), "hideous" (83, 86), "blemishes" (7–8).

The underlying sentiments that shape this perspective are revealed in chapter 11 when Tommo gives a relative blazon of a Typee warrior. In Tommo's terms, "the most remarkable" aspect of the warrior "was the elaborate tattooing displayed on every noble limb. All imaginable lines and curves and figures were delineated over his whole body, and in their *grotesque variety* and infinite protrusion I could only compare them to the crowded groupings of quaint patterns we sometimes see in costly pieces of lacework" (78, emphasis added). The nature of Tommo's aversion is seen in the way he links "grotesque" with "variety," a variety that takes on a dimension of density with its "infinite protrusion." Juxtaposing this pejorative figuration of variety with Tommo's subsequent laudatory description of Marnoo's tattoos in chapter 18 emphasizes the aesthetic paradigm that Tommo is employing. In this scene, Marnoo, who has no tattoos on his face, is described as being covered in "fanciful figures, which ... appeared to have been executed in conformity with some general design" (136). Marnoo thus joins Tommo's beloved "nymph" Fayaway, a character I will discuss at length in chapter 4, in being tattooed in a manner that is far less troubling. According to Melville, Fayaway was "little embellished" (86), tattooed only on the upper lip and shoulders—a claim that Jennifer Putzi and other scholars have called into question in terms of cultural accuracy.[22] We clearly see, then, that Tommo uses a relatively neoclassical notion of form to evaluate the natives' tattoos.[23] Samuel Otter points out that with Marnoo's tattoos, the "mimesis, hierarchy, and proportion ... [are] an anomaly among the Typees" and that Marnoo's earlier contact with white men—working with Europeans as a child—has "marked" him in this metaphorical way.[24]

Yet, in comparing these portrayals, it is not merely an Enlightenment aesthetic concern with order that makes the first warrior's tattoos seem unpleasant, but also something approaching an epistemological notion of their "infinite" "variety." That is to say, the tattoo is troubling because its form seems to exceed or resist Tommo's perceptive categories.[25] Cassuto's notion of the grotesque, therefore, still applies to the effect of the tattoo on the West, in that such a concept "is born of the violation of basic categories" and "emerges from this conflict on the edges of the category system."[26] By reading the novel's appendix in conjunction with this view of Tommo's anxiety, however, it becomes clear that the "freak" nature of the Typees' tattooing may be merely one manifestation of the West's distress when its political and symbolic powers are complicated by the Marquesans.

In the appendix to *Typee*, Melville attempts to gain political capital with his British publisher and audience (as mentioned, the book was first published in England's Home and Colonial Library) by defending Lord George Paulet's actions in the Sandwich Islands. After citing French iniquities and aggression in Tahiti, Melville laments that the public—presumably an American public—has fixated on the "grossly misrepresented" deeds of Britain's Lord Paulet while he was stationed in Oahu in 1844. This setting has manifold consequences for how one should reconsider the novel. As Bruce Harvey explains, in 1840, missionaries who had been working with the natives for more than twenty years succeeded in getting the Sandwich Islands to pass a written constitution. According to antebellum periodicals such as the *American Jurist* and *Law Magazine*, such an extension of codified law into the Pacific was a cause for celebration not only among Christian supporters but among all who valued democracy. Harvey notes, however, that this constitution was far from an organic product, as it was written under the careful tutelage of the islanders' "friends in the United States."[27]

In Melville's rendition of the controversy, Paulet is sent to Hawaii after the native king presumably begins to infringe on the British subjects in the region. After Paulet arrives with the Royal Navy and threatens hostilities if the king does not comply with his demands, the Hawaiian king attempts to "entrap the sympathies and rouse the indignation of Christendom" by coyly turning over the islands to Paulet in a "provisional cession" (255). While in control, Paulet learns of the native authorities' "lamentable misrule," which includes laws that are "subject to most capricious alterations" (256). The greatest detriment to maintaining order is shown to be the "continually shifting regulations concerning licentiousness" (256). Like the tattoo's effect on Tommo, then, the natives' "variety" of shifting legal signifiers (here, after the passage of a written constitution) trouble Paulet, who views the symbolic mandates of common law as static and given.

After five months Paulet relinquishes power, and in the events that ensue, Melville reveals what should seen as the crux of Western anxiety in the novel as a whole. Having established the "law" and "brought the [native] authorities to terms," Paulet transfers power back to the local king (257). According to Melville, upon being reinvested with power, the king attempts to "secure a display of enthusiasm from the lower orders by remitting for a time the accustomed severity of the laws" (257). In this commemoration, the king calls for the masses "to celebrate ... by breaking through all the moral, legal, and religious restraint for ten consecutive days" (257). Melville describes the "Polynesian saturnalia" that ensues as including "deeds too atrocious to be mentioned," and when Europeans attempt to prosecute natives for such deviant acts, they are told that "the laws [are] 'hannapa' (tied up)" (258). In concluding this section, Melville writes: "Freed from the restraints of severe penal laws, the natives almost to a man had plunged voluntarily into every species of wickedness and excess, ... [A]lthough they had been schooled into a seeming submission to the new order of things, they were in reality as depraved and vicious as ever" (258).

The West's "new order of things" has here clearly failed to subject the natives. Unlike the missionaries and the European soldiers, the natives can quickly shed the mandates of the laws since they are not inscribed on or in them. In a dramatization of the inveterate notion of natives as Janus-faced tricksters, they are able to break "voluntarily" from their "seeming submission" into their "depraved" "reality." Suspicions concerning a resistant core within native subjectivity are seen across antebellum maritime narratives. In *Omoo* (1847), for instance, Melville portrays three young Tahitian girls playfully revealing the fact that they view themselves as "'A sad good Christian at the heart—/ A Very heathen in the carnal part.'"[28] Though this sentiment smacks of racial fantasies, it might be seen to play out within broader symbolic tensions between and within social systems.

Using this context to revisit the scene in chapter 30 where Karky threatens Tommo's "face divine," it becomes evident that although antebellum anxiety about race informs the qualitative aspects of Tommo's fear, the scene is primarily a dramatization of a symbolic anxiety similar to that found in the appendix. Consequently, we might shift our analysis from Imaginary (in a Lacanian sense) concerns about racial markings to the symbolic coordinates that shape such constructions.[29] This becomes clear when Tommo reflects: "A fact which I soon afterwards learned augmented my apprehension. The whole system of tattooing was, I found, connected with their religion; and it was evident, therefore, that they were resolved to make a convert of me" (220). Here, we see a reversal of the appendix's schematic of anxiety: the West's symbolic system does not fail to incorporate the other, but it fails to prevent the Western subject from being incorporated by the other. In both scenes, it is the West's system of logos and identity that is shown to be lacking. Yet this scene is revealing not only in its demonstration of the way the West's symbolic system fails to resist incorporation, but also in its portrayal of how this failure relates to its inability to know the cultural logic of the Typees. After expressing a fear of being converted through tattooing, Melville explains: "The nature of the connection between [tattooing] and the superstitious idolatry of the [Typee] was a point upon which I could never obtain any information" (220–21). That is, the tattoo's function as a signifier within the Typee's religious system "always appeared incomprehensible" to him (221).

Such antagonism between symbolic systems is common in narratives of Pacific interactions from this era, seen in accounts of Western institutions' struggles to translate Pacific languages and, metaphorically in *Omoo*, when Melville is "shocked" by a white man who was mysteriously infected with the "native disease" of "Fa-Fa," or elephantiasis (127–28).[30] More directly, Western attempts to override hermetic foreign systems especially play out in various missionaries' encounters with Pacific islanders, and there, too, the tattoo is a formative concern.

Tahiti provides an apt example, considering it was the first island where Christian missionaries gained a permanent foothold. In *Omoo*, Melville describes how missionaries banished traditional religious and social practices, establishing severe laws against tattooing "of any kind" (183). According to Anne D'Alleva, evangelical missionaries in Tahiti sought to curb tattooing because of the prohibition in Leviticus against marking the skin and also because it was associated with specific native religious practices and a "tacit preference for heathenism."[31] D'Alleva goes on to show how such missionaries pressured natives to enact a series of laws against the tattoo and instituted harsh punitive measures to bolster them. These punishments included blotching and disfiguring violators' tattoos. Paradoxically, the tattoo also was used as a means of corporal punishment, marking the faces of women convicted of adultery or prostitution.[32]

The reconsideration of tattoo anxiety I am forwarding can also be articulated by looking at the Polynesian myth about the origin of tattoos. In *Polynesian Researches,* William Ellis recounts the tale of Hinaereeremonoi, a daughter of the gods, who is seduced by her brothers' use of tattooing. Ellis writes: "In an effort to preserve her chastity, she was kept in an enclosure and constantly attended. . . . Her brothers, intent on seducing her, invented tattooing and punctured their flesh. . . . Attracted by the marks and wishing herself ornamented, Hinaereeremonoi left her refuge, was tattooed, 'and became also the victim of the designs of her brothers.' "[33] Otter notes how the term "design" acts as an obvious pun in Ellis's account, where the "the literal tattoo designs are contrived as part of a plot to seduce and ensnare the viewer."[34] Tommo's fear of losing his identity by being "ensnared" and inscribed by the Typees clearly parallels Hinaereeremonoi's loss of chastity owing to the role of the tattoo. Importantly, both in the myth and in the novel the loss of identity precipitated by the tattoo necessitates an a priori failure of the home. In the myth, home is figured literally in Hinaereeremonoi's protective enclosure, while in *Typee,* home might more aptly be correlated to the West's symbolic system (interestingly, "home" and "mother" are the only English words Tommo teaches Marheyo [248]). Thus, the focus might be moved away from the positive agency of the tattoo and onto the negative condition of the home itself.

By situating Tommo's fear of tattooing in the context of the appendix's issues, we might begin to conceptualize the broader mechanisms that make the tattooed person a "freak" in antebellum America. In addition to exhibiting racial anxiety, Tommo's fear should be seen as a structural symptom: a positive manifestation of a broader negative condition. On the most basic level, the negative condition is the fact that—as seen in the appendix—the West's own system of knowledge and power is not only *not* universal but also vulnerable. The Polynesians' bodies and social structures, including tattooing, are associated with the notion of the freak because they exist at the limits—in fact, they push the limits—of the West's categories. As Elizabeth Grosz makes clear, "The freak is an *ambiguous* being whose existence imperils categories and oppositions dominant in social life."[35] Similar to Leslie Fielder's notion that the disturbance engendered by freaks is "a kind of vertigo like that experienced by Narcissus," Westerners often confront themselves in the act of looking at Polynesian others.[36] Unlike the safety of the domestic freak show, where aberrant bodies are incorporated into the norm while being displayed, in Melville's text, at least, native freaks and their grotesque bodies are potentially dangerous to travelers when they are in the geopolitical space of Polynesia. We might thus reframe T. Walter Herbert Jr.'s otherwise accurate claim that Tommo "has to contend with efforts to draw him into an alien and confining social structure."[37] This drawing in should be read as a literal and aggressive act of outward inscription that evokes fear about the other social structure and also catalyzes a retroactive anxiety about one's own.[38]

Such anxiety was not, of course, uniform across mariners' experiences of Polynesian cultures. As noted, in addition to white sailors who fully "went native"—such as the tattooed beachcomber figure in the Pacific or the Christian-turned-Muslim renegade in the Barbary region—a multitude of antebellum sailors were voluntarily tattooed by both native practitioners and fellow sailors who picked up the trade. For the majority of these sailors, however, the material conditions of their encounter with the practice were quite different from the ones presented in *Typee*. As Nicholas Thomas explains, Cook's 1769 visit to Tahiti was primarily peaceful. Unlike Tommo's persistent fear of the Typees' motivations and capabilities, Cook's sailors thought of the Tahitians as benevolent friends and, thus, "had no particular qualms about placing themselves in a situation in which they might have otherwise have been considered foolishly vulnerable"— including "subject[ing] themselves to the controlled violence of the tattoo."[39] In fact, according to John Ledyard, corporal of marines on Cook's ship *Resolution*, seamen willingly received tattoos when in New Zealand, solely to make themselves more attractive to native women.[40] In both cases, the sailors remain within the bastion of their own military and symbolic positions of power and, as Thomas notes, view the tattoo as a valuable material object to be collected, owned, and used.[41] It is in this sense, William Cummings argues, European sailors with Polynesian tattoos "literally incorporated something of the otherness of Polynesians into their bodies, thereby interjecting this otherness into European society."[42]

Juxtaposing the broader symbolic anxiety addressed in the appendix and Tommo's tattoo anxiety reveals an even more complex relation than merely the latter's symptomatic relation to the former. As mentioned, the apprehension that Melville voices in the appendix relates, in part, to the inability of the West's social structures to control and contain the Polynesians—insofar as natives seem to have the ability to exist simultaneously both in and out of the West's symbolic order. More than merely denying colonial control, such resistance exposes a traumatic gap between the body and Western structures of subject formation. The Polynesians' ability to resist this inscription may, therefore, haunt the modern world, parading before it bodies that complicate its universal claims.

In turning back to the tattoo, we can see how, paradoxically, Tommo's fear of being "cut into" by Karky's "designs" mirrors the broader trauma that the colonial power experiences when natives resist being "cut into" by its social systems. And the two parallel anxieties are even more congruous than this: both ultimately relate to the West's apprehension about the failure of its symbolic systems. This is apparent when Karky's tattoo aggression is further contextualized with the role of tattoos in antebellum freak shows. According to Cassuto, the tattoo served "as the basis for a wild story," in which tattooed people or a moderator "told fantastic tales of kidnap and captivity in which the tattoos where typically forced upon them."[43] In this schematic, the tattoo clearly functions as a signified, as an object/concept that is conceived of via an outside narrative. Through such narratives, the symbolic order is able to locate—or annihilate—the tattoo by viewing it as a marker of past violence, turning a foreign signifier into merely a trace of a traumatic experience. In *Typee*, however, this routine is complicated. By portraying the tattooist in the context of Typee culture—however limited in detail—Melville acts to defetishize the tattoo, revealing aspects of the human agents and cultural implications behind it. As a result, the tattoo may begin to function as a potential signifier (as a mechanism of writing, in a Derridean sense), to have agency (mirrored by Karky's agency) to speak for itself—even if it remains "incomprehensible" to Melville.

Productive readings of Tommo's tattoo anxiety that ascribe such apprehension to race may, therefore, inadvertently transfer foundational angst, stemming from the way Polynesian encounters force Westerners to confront the outer and "other" limits of their own cultural logic, onto secondary or even tertiary notions of antebellum racial discourse. In this light, I might even suggest that a historically sound claim such as Otter's contention that Karky's tattoo aggression represents "ethnology as revenge," where the "ethnologist's dream of definitive facial geometry decomposes into an illegible nightmare," may unwittingly remain on the near side of the antebellum screen of racial fantasy.[44] For as I have suggested, if racial discourse structures the form that anxiety takes—palliating trauma by renarrating it into terms that function within the social economy of antebellum America—how are we to approach the full implications of this angst if we remain ensconced within the fantasies' original coordinates?

An important coda and caveat to my argument is its specificity to the historical and political conditions of the early nineteenth century. The antebellum ethnographic work Otter so aptly explores, along with expanding trade and colonial–capitalist development in the Pacific, gradually allows the West's symbolic system to incorporate Polynesians. In relation to tattoos, this can be seen in publications such as Willowdean Chatterson Handy's *Tattooing in the Marquesas* (1922). While living in the Marquesas, Handy meticulously studies and documents the tattooing patterns of the Polynesians, providing, in typical anthropological form, charts that "translate" tattoo systems into Western discourse. Interestingly, Handy's brief book includes many references to nineteenth-century travelers' and explorers' observations of such tattoos (including Melville's), thus setting up her analysis as an answer, in effect, to the tenuous and anxious hypotheses of previous sojourners. Similarly, Claude Lévi-Strauss's *Tristes Tropiques* (1955), although focusing on the Caduveo Indians of Brazil, demonstrates the violence such studies enact on the native body. In his own anthropologic documentation of natives' facial tattoos, he goes one step further than Handy, having women tattoo artists sketch their "face-paintings" in flat two-dimensional drawings. Lévi-Strauss thus not only symbolically transfers the natives' markings into the West's record but also, in so doing, literally excises the native face that once acted as the original canvas. Such scientific inroads into native cultures undoubtedly contribute to what Bogdan describes as the tattooed freak's fall from prominence in the early to mid-twentieth century.

Tommo's "Face Divine"; or, Narcissus Lost and Found

Shifting the focus from race to broader sociosymbolic concerns opens up the discussion of tattoo anxiety to other cultural issues that may be in play. This is not to downplay the important issue of race (neither its theoretical relevance nor the reality of racial oppression and violence in this era). Viewing the anxiety in terms of fantasy provides more than a new optic for considering the issue: it allows one to approach these concerns from a structural position that dialectically alters the scenario, where the ostensible problem of race might be seen—from a different perspective—as part of a fantasmatic solution to Tommo's symbolic quandaries.[45]

Such an approach has implications for various historical analyses of Melville's narrative. Many of the studies have examined how Tommo's conception of the "savage" relates to and complicates his Western understanding of history. For instance, building on formative readings such as Milton Stern's thesis that Tommo grows discontented in Typee because of the gap between his complex modern psyche and the static native society, John Samson, in "The Dynamics of History and Fiction in Melville's Typee" (1984), explores the way Tommo's experience of the Typees' own apparent historicity complicates Western versions of historical progress: most notably the Rousseau-influenced paradigm of a noble savage living in a worldly Edenic state, and the Calvinistic paradigm of sinful heathens that must be converted to reach an otherworldly second Eden.[46] More recently, Bruce Harvey uses a similar formula to argue that Tommo desires *not* to know about the Typees' social structure so as not to complicate his own fantasies about natural law. Harvey contextualizes Tommo's experiences within eighteenth- and nineteenth-century nature-versus-culture debates that often find the conception of historically codified law pitted against notions of transhistorical natural law. Against this backdrop, he argues that Tommo "desire[s] not to comprehend" Typee cultural practices because he "prefers his insecurity about the Typees' being cannibals to the more dreadful recognition that, if they are cannibals, their cannibalistic practice is in their terms legally and systematically regulated."[47]

Such complications to preconceived notions about primitive peoples and natural law, therefore, center on the "aggressive" cultural practices of cannibalism and tattooing. Harvey intimates how Tommo's primary concern may be that natural law, "rather than being a bulwark against transgression and a protector of individual sovereignty or the right of an intimate selfhood, can also be fundamentally invasive."[48] Reading Tommo's fear of facial tattoos in the context of the Typees' mysterious Taboo system, he suggests that Tommo believes that if he were tattooed in such a way, "his identity would be inseparable from the ritualistic marks of a foreign culture." In addition to the simple fear of "mutilation," therefore, Tommo's objection to being tattooed is linked, in Harvey's view, to the way the practice evinces an invasive law that "skirts being either consensual or nonconsensual."[49]

Although such a schematic loosely reads Melville's narrative in terms of fantasy and presents how Tommo's interactions with the Typees are attempts to "work out ... discomfort with his own culture," I would like to build on the preceding section and push Harvey's line of analysis a bit.[50] To begin with, I agree with aspects of the general movement of Harvey's reading—in which Tommo's anxious flight from modern codified law to an ideal natural law ultimately leads to an ambiguous acceptance of the former. Yet, as we see with the topic of race, methodologically grounding this anxiety in a single historical concept (here, the law) may act, paradoxically, to occlude some of the complex elements of fantasy that play out in the narrative. Harvey thus adds another specific historical fold to the way Western thought stumbles on its own inconsistencies when faced with a Polynesian other; however, his thesis may also unintentionally play down the agency of this other. That is, although Harvey figures the potentially invasive nature of Typee culture as a catalyst for Tommo's discontent, this invasiveness is contained—threatening only in the secondary sense of complicating Western fantasies about natural law. The symbolic threat of the tattoo may cut deeper, complicating not just the qualitative aspects of Western civilization's complex and competing notions about history but history in toto. In short, the threat of losing one's face might reveal the threat of losing history altogether.

By threatening Tommo's subjectivity qua face and his possible "return to ... [his] countrymen," the tattoo, in addition to complicating narratives of natural law and evincing a possible racial transformation, might go so far as to induce the possibility of a relative "historical break." Žižek uses this concept to explain how the historical process does not always adhere to simple diachronic logic. Instead, Žižek posits that, much like Althusser's notion of an "epistemological break," historical change is experienced in part via symbolic breaks that "[do] not simply designate the 'regressive' loss (or 'progressive' gain) of something, but *the shift in the very grid which enables us to measure losses and gains.*"[51] Thus Žižek conceives of such breaks in terms of fantasy, denoting shifts in the symbolic coordinates that shape perceptions of reality. The relevance of this concept for Melville's narrative becomes quite clear in Žižek's description of how this operates in relation to history itself:

> The supreme example of this paradoxical coincidence of emergence and loss is provided by the notion of *history* itself—where, exactly, is its place; that is, which societies can be characterized as properly *historical*? On the one hand, pre-capitalist societies allegedly do not yet know history proper; they are "circular," "closed," caught in a repetitive movement predetermined by tradition—so history must emerge *afterwards*, with the decay of "closed" organic

societies. On the other hand, the opposite cliché tells us that capitalism itself is no longer historical; it is rootless, with no tradition of its own, and therefore parasitical upon previous traditions, a universal order which . . . can thrive anywhere . . . uprooting and slowly corroding all particular life-worlds based on specific traditions. So history is that which gets *lost* with the growth of capitalism. . . . The solution, again, is that *emergence and loss coincide*: the properly "historical" is only a moment, even if this moment is properly unending and goes on for centuries—the moment of *passage* from pre-capitalist societies to a capitalist universal order."[52]

Without pushing this schematic too far, one can see how a formidable aspect of Karky's tattoo threat may relate to its effect of inducing (or at least projecting) not only a historical break proper, but also a break that may reconstitute Tommo's notion of history itself. It has been well noted that the antebellum era falls within the latter part of a long and tenuous transition into the modern reality of capitalism. In Žižek's postulation, this passage into the totalizing capitalist order engenders the modern notion of history—where the concept of history as such emerges concomitantly with its loss. Such sentiment can be seen, arguably, across the late eighteenth and early nineteenth centuries in their furious and anxious historicizing efforts and, specifically, in the development of competing notions of "progress" and "civilization."[53] In this context, the invasive agency of the tattoo is much more extensive than previous studies allow. Tommo's crisis is more substantial than merely an experience of, in Calder and colleagues' terms, the way "history unsettles itself" by "detect[ing] the principles of change in the stages of savage culture," or, in Harvey's, the stress accompanying a realization that the West's imaginary constructs are out of joint with the reality of a native culture.[54]

Acting as a potential "historical break," the threat of Karky's tattoo forces Tommo to, in a way, take stock of the gap between his ontic and social–ontological existence. Even further, Tommo's admission that the tattoo can in effect cause him to *lose* his face (his subjectivity/identity) and, hence, his ability to return to modern society, is tantamount to the traumatic idea that a supposedly pre- or nonhistorical moment can erase his status in (or perhaps after) history as such. In these terms, Tommo's anxiety stems partly from the fact that the Typees' system of facial tattooing reveals that history, in the teleological schema Tommo employs, is an object/concept that potentially can be lost. Consequently, Tommo's desire for history, home, and mother at the close of the narrative (the violent break achieved when Tommo dashes a boat hook into Mow-Mow's throat) derives in part from his frantic attempt *not* to traverse the fantasy of history itself—not just to avoid losing his face, but to avoid losing the foundational fantasy of his face.[55]

Within this broad parameter of concerns, Tommo's character negotiates the fantasy of his face in complex and interesting ways. Most generally, his turn toward outright and uncompromised desire for home can be seen in a Lacanian sense as a refusal to relinquish his master signifier, or, in other terms, his honor. In "On Shame," Jacques-Alain Miller discusses Lacan's observations about honor and the apparent loss of shame in the modern world. Miller explains that shame is different from guilt in that it is related to a relatively transcendent Other, one "prior to the Other that judges [one's guilt], . . . a primordial Other, not one that judges but instead one that only sees or lets be seen."[56] Using the example of Vatel's shame-induced death, Miller juxtaposes the view of *primum vivere* (a hedonistic call to "live first, we will see why later") with that of honor. By being shamed to death, Vatel portrays how, in Miller's terms, "when honor retains its value, life does not prevail over honor."[57] Honor's formidable power is thus located in an Other that is instantiated retroactively when one takes on the perspective of this Other to view oneself. Miller shows how this scenario is presented in the context of Lacan's master's discourse.[58] The master signifier designates a locus through which one becomes a subject— where one is "marked" and located in the world through a position designated by this signifier.[59] Citing the common examples of Antigone and Oedipus, Miller explains how these characters' traumatic experiences reveal a relationship to a "second death," one that is not a simple corporeal death but a possible termination of one's symbolic identity as it is constituted through a relation to a master signifier. In this sense, both Antigone and Oedipus sacrifice their lives for and before relinquishing the "dignity of the signifier that represents [them]."[60]

Like these classic figures, we can see Tommo's horrific fear of losing his "face divine" as a desire to hold onto his symbolic identity within Western society. For while the topic of cannibalism undoubtedly engenders anxiety, his flirtations with (and courting of) this danger—and corporeal death itself—never triggers sufficient fear to push him into a legitimate crisis.

The "attack on [his] face," however, obviously sends him reeling. During chapter 30's trauma, therefore, Tommo might be seen to exist in a relative "zone between-two-deaths." Miller uses this phrase to describe Oedipus's limbo-esque state between renouncing his worldly life and putting out his eyes, and experiencing a second death, or, again, a strictly symbolic one.[61] Although Tommo's corporeal life is not forsaken as Oedipus's and Antigone's were, it is clearly in jeopardy. Yet his situation might be seen as potentially homologous to the other two in an inverse way: instead of deriving from the sacrifice of worldly life for the maintenance of a symbolic one, Tommo's anxiety may relate to the fact that—with the entrance of the tattoo threat—he is nearing a second death without a first one. Tommo, therefore, feels the full force of shame.

Tommo's anxiety nonetheless seems to exceed such a register. This may be because the attack not only manifestly threatens his symbolic identity per se (the self that is constituted by being viewed in relation to an Other), but also the very agency of his Other (or master signifier) itself. Tommo's description of the consequences of being "disfigured" operates within the first level of this relationship, with the "ruin" of his "figure-head" corresponding to the judgment of his "countrymen" (219) and Western "poets" (220). Nevertheless, behind these specific publics seems to lurk a concern for the perspective of a more powerful Other. As discussed, in being symbolically attacked in a way that annihilates elements of one's identity, not only is one's identity damaged but, retroactively, so too is the "dignity" or agency of one's original symbolic coordinates. In other words, Tommo may be ashamed of the possibility of losing his face while keeping his head—but also, even more radically, ashamed *for* the potential lack of his own symbolic Other.

It is important to reiterate the Typees' influence in this scenario. At issue is both the possible wound in the West's symbolic schemas and also how this wound is precipitated by the agency of a cultural other and, in turn, dressed by Tommo. A brief scene in Melville's third novel, *Mardi and a Voyage Thither* (1849), may aptly present the dynamics at play here. In chapter 68, Melville's sailor-narrator includes a eulogy-like aside about the late king of the Sandwich Islands:

Terrific shade of tattooed Tammahammaha! if, from a vile dragon's molars, rose mailed men, what heroes shall spring from the cannibal canines once pertaining to warriors themselves!—Am I the witch of Endor, that I conjure up this ghost? Or, King Saul, that

I quake at the sight? For, lo! roundabout me Tammahammaha's tattooing expands, till all the sky seems a tiger's skin. But now, the spotted phantom sweeps by; as a man-of-war's main-sail, cloud-like, blown far to leeward in a gale. Banquo down, we return.⁶²

There is much of interest in this aside, but most relevant is the relation between the sailor-narrator, here in the guise of the Polynesian god "white Taji," and the phantom king Tammahammaha. Though Tammahammaha's majesty is apparent, the question remains as to whether the narrator is in fact acting in the position of agency, "conjuring" the Polynesian king in a role tantamount to *Macbeth*'s witch of Endor. Such a possibility is suggested in the way the Western narrator had previously appropriated the role of Taji—entering and manipulating the Polynesian symbolic structure in a ploy to win Yillah. This explains the association the narrator establishes between King Tammahammaha and Banquo. In Shakespeare's tragedy, Banquo is a Scottish thane and friend of Macbeth who becomes a threat to Macbeth's schemes when the witches inform the two men that that not Banquo but his descendants will be king. Macbeth, of course, has Banquo killed (and attempts as much with Banquo's progeny), only to be subsequently haunted by his friend's ghost. If we read Taji as playing the part of conjurer, then this aside clearly speaks to his guilt over corrupting and dominating the islanders—as seen in his remorse for slaying the priest Aleema to procure Yillah. But the ambiguity surrounding this account is paramount. Indeed, Taji—like Tommo—seems cast in a precarious position between two symbolic systems. Although both men ultimately remain ensconced in the Western camp, their anxious perceptions of and relations to the respective foreign societies and their enigmatic cultural systems is deeply unsettling. As in *Typee*, in *Mardi* we see the potential for the loss of more than just physical life in the way Tammahammaha is associated with Banquo, who begets James I's ascendancy despite Macbeth's machinations, and in the imagery of Tammahammaha's "tiger's skin" tattoos blotting out the sky, evincing an immersion into a foreign body or symbolic order.⁶³

Anxiety in both situations, therefore, is centered on a potential second death, or the loss of symbolic coordinates. Such a scenario might be further considered in the context of Derrida's notion of the "visor effect."⁶⁴ In drawing on Shakespeare in his own way, Derrida uses the example of King Hamlet's ghost to discuss how a "specter" uncannily "de-synchronizes" its audience. Focusing on King Hamlet's phantom armor, Derrida relates this effect to the way "we do not see who looks at us. Even though in his ghost the King looks like himself... that does not prevent him from looking without being seen: his apparition makes him appear still invisible beneath his armor."[65] Although such a schematic does relate in some ways to Derrida's problematic conception of "Messianic Otherness," it also correlates to the symbolic concerns outlined above—especially in the way we, in Derrida's terms, "feel ourselves being looked at by it, outside of any synchrony, even before and beyond any look on our part."[66]

The visor effect provides an apt metaphor for the emotive reality of being subject to an enigmatic Other. In these terms, we can perhaps better discern the qualitative composition of Tommo's and Taji's form of anxiety. What I am suggesting is that the ambiguous scene in which Taji imagines the foreign power of Tammahammaha presents a condensed and displaced version of Tommo's shared concerns, for what is at stake is both the potential reign of a different symbolic alignment (a different master [signifier]) and, by default, the failure of one's own. Consequently, Taji and Tommo have cause to be more unsettled by the appearance of an Other than Horatio and Hamlet do, because in their cases this Other is a foreign, supplemental one. In *Mardi*, the contours of the Other do not take the form of the familiar yet hermetic armor of one's dead king; instead, an opaque screen is amalgamated into an entire "sky" of enigmatic tattoos. And then into a cloudlike movement of a "man-of-war's main-sail." Hence, this foreign master is beyond Taji's imaginary coordinates, ultimately presenting itself as pure surface—but a mobile surface that threatens to overwhelm him. Taji's foundational anxiety, like Tommo's, may stem from the potential ability of this new foreign Other to recast his own symbolic king's reign into the defeated position of a Saul.[67]

Thus far, we've seen how Melville's narrative stages how the Typees complicate Tommo's notions of self and other. However, we have yet to fully explore this scenario in terms of fantasy. As I suggested at the outset, more than merely portraying a defensive clinging to Western fantasies, Melville's narrative may map a process whereby a rebellious, wayward Western subject learns to—or, more accurately, puts himself in the position to—desire his original identity.

Throughout *Typee*, Melville portrays how Tommo's experiences in the Marquesan valley are in part motivated and sustained by his fantasies of the natives. From the first chapter's emphatic litany of "strange visions of outlandish things" firing "an irresistible curiosity" (5) through Tommo's subsequent experiences of native women, cannibalism, and other social practices, Melville consistently emphasizes the way Tommo invests the Typees with, in a Lacanian sense, an enigmatic object *a*. In keeping with this logic, many of the minor conflicts in the narrative relate to times when his desire for these objects or experiences lead him too close to them—throwing his fantasy coordinates into jeopardy. This can be seen in Tommo's comical lamentation that stories about the Typees' violence are mere "fables"—going so far as to admit "something like a sense of regret at having ... [his] hideous anticipations thus disappointed" (128).

The symbolic trauma triggered by the threat of facial tattooing, however, goes much further than this—further even than the aforementioned way it pushes Tommo back toward his Western geographic and symbolic "home." What is missed in this reading is the way his experience of the relative void between sociosymbolic systems allows him to reconstitute his fantasy structure itself. As opposed to Herbert's description of how the dangers that Western travelers experience in the Marquesas push them back toward a familiar "supreme ordering principle" and allow them to "[emerge] from the experience reinvigorated, having vindicated civilization," Tommo's experiences suggest a more complex symbolic negotiation and realignment.[68] That is to say, while Tommo does indeed return (in all relative ways) to civilization at the narrative's close, this tidy *reverto* is anything but a simple restoration.

We might return to Miller's notion of the harrowing "zone between-two-deaths" in considering Tommo's desperate desire for escape. While his anxiety may, as mentioned, relate to the ambiguous twofold shame of the potential loss of his face and the loss of his own symbolic home, it occurs within an imaginary zone of fantasmatic projection. It is in this enigmatic and anxiety-stricken space of danger that Tommo's formative notions of self and other may be reestablished. Thus, the specific coordinates of such positions are paramount to exploring the nuances of Tommo's closing fantasies.

The notion of other (both *autre* and *Autre*) is obviously a core aspect of the Lacanian conception of fantasy and subject constitution. Like almost all Lacanian concepts, it holds multifarious meanings and functions depending on the context (including the context of Lancan's developing oeuvre). Slavoj Žižek provides a helpful overview of the concept that might assist in illuminating Tommo's experiences:

> The topic of the "other" must be submitted to a kind of spectral analysis that renders visible its imaginary, symbolic, and real aspects. It perhaps provides the ultimate case of the Lacanian

notion of the "Borromean knot" that unties the three dimensions. First there is the imaginary other—other people "like me," my fellow human beings with whom I am engaged in the mirrorlike relationships of competition, mutual recognition, and so on. Then there is the symbolic "big Other"—the "substance" of our social existence, the impersonal set of rules that coordinate our existence. Finally there is the Other qua Real, the impossible Thing, the "inhuman partner," the Other with whom no symmetrical dialogue, mediated by the symbolic Order, is possible. It is crucial to perceive how these three dimensions are linked. The neighbor . . . as the Thing means that, beneath the neighbor as my semblance, my mirror image, there always lurks the unfathomable abyss of radical Otherness, a monstrous Thing that cannot be "gentrified."[69]

Using this diagrammatic overview, we might view the Typees' tattooing system as an aspect of a symbolic Other associated with the imaginary/cultural other of the Typee.[70] This simple scenario is complicated, however, when the threat from the Typees' symbolic Other affects, on the plane of Tommo's imagination, an encounter with something closer to the Other qua Real. In these terms, when Tommo's symbolic identity is jeopardized by the tattoo, he inhabits an imaginary position tantamount to an incommensurate space between himself and himself as imaginary other. Here, on the level of the Imaginary, Tommo's anxiety stems from the fact that his subjectivity is hypothetically split. On the level of symbolic functions, Tommo's relation to himself-as-other via the partial and terrifying aegis of a supplemental big Other may thus open the space for an experience of, in Žižek's terms, "the Other with whom no symmetrical dialogue, mediated by the symbolic Order, is possible." And it is precisely in this sense that Tommo's imaginary experience approaches the Real, especially the notion of the aforementioned parallax Real, for Tommo's conception of the renarration of his identity (even if abstractly) illuminates the tenuous ground of nonbeing that subjectivity is built upon—dramatizing that the zero level of human experience is a void, or, in Žižek's terms, that "subjects are literally holes, gaps, in the positive order of being."[71] In this line of thought, consciously inhabiting this void need not be some cynical experience of nihilism. Rather, in negotiating the negative ground of existence, one might garner a modicum of freedom to produce positive effects. In this relative short circuit, therefore, Melville may dramatize how Tommo is paradoxically forced into the position of imaginatively traversing his fundamental fantasies of the Typee.

The notion of "traversing the fantasy" develops in Lacan's later thought and becomes a formative goal of clinical analytical discourse. Most generally, this process relates to the radical possibility lodged in the fact that the subject is a split (and therefore incomplete) being. In this important and romantic sense, Lacan shifts Freud's well-known dictum, "Wo es war, soll Ich werden" (Where the id was, there the ego shall be) into a rather ethical call for the subject to take responsibility for the cause of his or her desire: to, in essence, occupy or take back this position (and hence one's relation to jouissance) from the foreign sociosymbolic elements that originally shape it. Bruce Fink cogently summarizes this general process in terms of clinical experience, writing:

> The Lacanian analyst aims, not at modeling the analysand's desire on his or her own, but rather at shaking up the configuration of the analysand's fantasy, changing the subject's relation to the cause of desire: object *a*.
> This reconfiguration of fantasy implies a number of different things: the construction in the course of analysis of a new "fundamental fantasy" (the latter being that which underlies an analysand's various individual fantasies and constitutes the subject's most profound relation to the Other's desire); . . . and a "crossing over" of positions within the fundamental fantasy whereby the divided subject assumes the place of the cause, in other words, subjectifies the traumatic cause of his or her own advent as subject, coming to be in that place where the Other's desire—a foreign, alien desire—had been.[72]

Though Tommo's adventures obviously exist in a nonclinical nineteenth-century context, his experiences at the close of Melville's narrative move in a trajectory similar to the process Fink outlines—where Tommo both imaginatively moves toward "crossing over" to the place of the cause of desire or object *a* (here, the Typee) and, in the process, begins to shape a new fundamental fantasy. In simple terms, by imaginatively inhabiting the potential gap between symbolic constructions, Tommo moves closer to the enigmatic object of desire. More important, the effect of this imaginary movement is clear: by approaching the possibility of being symbolically absorbed into the object of his fantasies, his hypothetical position in relation to his former identity shifts. This is because the process of reconfiguration yielded through traversing the fantasy involves not just a simple liberation from original desires but, in Žižek's terms, "fully identifying ... with the fantasy which structures the excess resisting immersion into daily reality."[73] In other words, this process involves coming to terms with the true way fantasy functions, including the aspects of excess and symbolic lack that resist "reality." By imaginatively inhabiting the symbolic space of the Typee (the initial *a*), Tommo's old self, now at a potential distance, becomes a new locus for desire (a new position for desiring and, in this imaginative scenario, a new *a* in itself). Ultimately, therefore, Tommo not only portrays the panic-stricken longing for a return to the West that various scholars have noted, but also perhaps dramatizes how his experiences in Typee quite literally *enable* him to achieve this very desire.[74]

Is *Typee* merely another exotic travel and adventure narrative that ultimately acts to strengthen Western fantasies of itself and its others? In the context described above, it does seem to offer a veritable roadmap for desiring a Western self—a fantasmatic ride of traversing the other, in a way. But the salient role that the Typees' threatening agency plays within this process seems to raise the stakes. By pushing Tommo into the precarious zone between deaths, this threat reveals how his choice to pursue his original identity may be a forced one. And by revealing the power structures that condition Tommo's decision, the text may also illuminate the illusory aspects of any conception of pure freedom. Although Tommo evinces an ability to freely choose home and mother, the narrative also seems to foreground how such a free choice is, to employ Žižek's terms, "the choice of 'freely assuming' one's imposed destiny."[75]

It is even more significant that Tommo does not simply reestablish desire for home after being disappointed by the reality of the Typees. He achieves this desire by traversing (again, under duress) the fantasy of the other, and this process suggests an experience of the Other at the heart of identity. These encounters may function as "vanishing mediators" within Tommo's fantasmatic and literal move toward home—where Tommo's resolution for home is shaped by the process of excluding both the imaginary other of the Typees and the Other qua Real relating to his original self—but the narrative *presents* them as such.

In this light, I might risk the suggestion that the most subversive element of *Typee* may be Tommo's seemingly conservative fantasmatic return to the West, for the old Tommo that returns is constituted from a new and radically different subjective position. Acting, in a way, like a Benjaminian historian of revolution as repetition—where proper historiography realizes unactualized possibilities of the past—might Melville stage the complex subterraneous ruptures and stresses that contribute to Tommo's subsequent and ostensibly simple return?[76] As such, can we not see Tommo playing a rather clandestine Job-like role similar to that of Ishmael? Whereas Ishmael alone escapes to tell of the *Pequod*'s plight, the qualitative experience of Tommo's escape might here be telling. Indeed, the orphan that the Australian whaler *Julia* picks up at the end of *Typee* may be more of a handful than the wet and traumatized Ishmael that the *Rachel* takes aboard. Though it has been noted that the name "Tommo" is in fact a Marquesan verb signifying "to enter into, to adapt well to," one might look more closely at this beleaguered young sailor and see if, in him, Melville might not be attempting to smuggle a disruptive piece of the Real back into the antebellum world.[77]

· CHAPTER 4 ·

Melville's "Porno-Tropics": Re-Sexuating Pacific Encounters

Oh Hautia! thou knowest the mystery I die to fathom. I see it crouching in thine eye: —Reveal!

—Herman Melville, Mardi and a Voyage Thither

THIS CHAPTER OPENS WITH RAVISHMENT. And begins where it will also end: with the impassioned impasse of desire. Imploring the enigmatic native queen Hautia to reveal her connection to his lost beloved, Yillah, Melville's sailor makes a futile attempt to command an understanding of the queen's knowledge. Lured to Hautia's Polynesian isle, Flozella-a-Nina, by the memory of Yillah's beauty, Melville's heroic paramour has reached one of the last stops on his amorous quest, a quest he romantically resumes at the narrative's close. With the sailor's brash and ersatz advance standing in for anxious failure, we get a dramatization of a central aspect of Western representations of Pacific experiences in the eighteenth and nineteenth centuries: the sheer impotency of male fantasy.

Borrowing the term "porno-tropics" from the first chapter of Anne McClintock's *Imperial Leather: Race, Gender, and Sexuality in the Colonial Context* (1995), I wish to reconsider the erotically charged region of Polynesia as it plays out in antebellum maritime narratives. And what better figure in which to ground such a study than Herman Melville, the travel writer–provocateur who, in the words of a Whig reviewer in 1847, was little more than a "smart scamp" whose novels "stimulate curiosity and excite unchaste desire"?[1] Of course, Melville brazenly admits in *Moby-Dick* that he loves "to sail forbidden seas," but the public had perceived him as an experienced sexual authority since the release of *Typee* in 1846.[2] In fact, according to Hershel Parker, "*Typee* had made Melville the first American author to become a sex symbol"—as evidenced by lascivious fan mail, such as a letter penned by an Englishwoman named Ellen Astor Oxenham, who closes with the unambiguous admission: "Typee, you dear creature, I want to see you so amazingly."[3]

In this chapter I use Melville's three Pacific-island novels and other contemporaneous nonfictional Pacific narratives to explore the fantasmatic elements that shape representations of Polynesian women: more specifically, how figurations of native women negotiate and reveal fantasy structures' tenuous mechanisms and limits. While travels in the Pacific have clearly fostered romantic ideations of South Seas women since Magellan's voyage in 1521, many contemporary studies have productively moved past what they deem a reductive focus on how the colonial region was a playground for unchecked male eroticism.[4] In focusing in part on traditional phallogocentric desire, for example, Lenore Manderson and Margaret Jolly set up *Sites of Desire/Economies of Pleasure: Sexualities in Asia and the Pacific* (1997) as a collection that reframes such male fantasies by "focusing on cross-cultural *exchanges* of sexualities."[5] Centering on the contact-zone model, their collection mirrors a contemporary trend that seeks to move past both a delimiting "fatal-impact" thesis of cultural contact and a broader impasse between universalist and relativist views of sexuality. More recently, Lee Wallace's *Sexual Encounters: Pacific Texts, Modern Sexualities* (2003) moves past heterosexual economies of desire altogether, arguing that "the erotics of European interest in the Pacific have traditionally been thought of and critiqued in terms of desires adequate to hetero-sexual mapping, whereby sexual power is located without ambivalence in a masculinity to which femininity is presumed vulnerable."[6] Thus, Wallace suggests focusing on same-sex male encounters and their impact on developing Western sexual politics, conceiving of such encounters as a "hybridized structure of sexual contact" that illuminates "the disruptive force of Polynesian sexuality within European discourse."[7]

Taking Wallace's model of cross-cultural exchange as a starting point, I wish to use a Lacanian theory of "sexuation" to explore aspects of "the disruptive force of Polynesian sexuality" that Wallace's historical approach may overlook. As I will show, Lacan's conceptualization of the sexual relationship and its coordinates of phallic and feminine jouissance provides a means to drastically reconceive antebellum representations of sexual encounters—illuminating foundational disruptive elements within traditional hetero-normative fantasies. Despite the fact that the foreign trials of a colonial "polytropic man" and myths about native feminine excesses may seem like tired themes, returning to Melville's Pacific novels through a

Lacanian perspective allows us to productively reconsider these tropes by, paradoxically, taking them seriously.[8] In other words, by reading these representations in terms of fantasy and the ideological ramifications of enjoyment, the feminine figure becomes much more relevant to current scholarly interests by acting as a formative threat to Western symbolic norms.

In the first of the three following sections I examine the role of gender in antebellum maritime narratives and the contemporary scholarly approaches to them. The second section sets up a veritable genealogical survey of traditional eighteenth- and nineteenth-century "phallic" fantasies of Pacific women in nonfictional narratives. And the third section uses Melville's novels to reveal the tensions and complications implicit in such fantasies by focusing on the concept of female enjoyment.

Sex on the High Seas: The Phallus and Antebellum Narratives

Antebellum representations of Pacific women are shaped in part by the broader ways maritime genres negotiate the era's developing bourgeois gender norms. Though women were intricately involved in maritime activities throughout the eighteenth and nineteenth centuries, almost all forms of maritime narratives have defined themselves and the real-world events they represent as male-oriented affairs. As Margaret Creighton and Lisa Norling make clear in *Iron Men, Wooden Women: Gender and Seafaring in the Atlantic World, 1700–1920* (1996), this assumption of male dominance stems from the material reality of maritime economies, but also from coalescing Enlightenment notions of gender. Creighton and Norling emphasize that while women were more often passengers or human cargo than laborers at sea, the "view of the ocean as a single-sex masculine space, in contrast to a feminized and domesticated society on land, reflected the nineteenth-century projection of bourgeois social mores onto a time-honored division of seafaring labor."[9]

This can be seen in the way popular tales of the infamous female pirates Anne Bonny and Mary Read—who where captured and tried in Jamaica in 1720—dissipated as the nineteenth century and its domestic ideologies developed.[10] As Dianne Dugaw reveals, eighteenth-century popular ballads and tales of cross-dressing "transvestite heroines" who took to the seas and various battlegrounds in the guise of men shifted in the nineteenth century. Looking specifically at the cases of the eighteenth-century cross-dressing sailors Hannah Snell and Anne Talbot, Dugaw shows how Menie

Muriel Dowie, in her book *Women Adventurers* (1893), reinterpreted their bold actions through Victorian conceptions of proper domestic feminine cultivation.[11] Another example of this trend can be seen in the cross-dressing trilogy *The Female Marine,* published between 1815 and 1818. Most likely authored by a male ghostwriter, the series by Nathaniel Coverly Jr., first titled *The Adventures of Louisa Baker,* gave New England readers a first-person account of a young woman's adventures on the USS *Constitution* during its famed experiences in the War of 1812. Baker's maritime adventures, however, are couched within a *Charlotte Temple*–like plot of a young woman's youthful betrayal and pregnancy, entanglement in a Boston brothel, and eventual resurrection through marriage to a wealthy New York gentleman.[12]

We find, therefore, that antebellum maritime narratives by or about women's experiences increasingly pander to emergent gender norms that stress female domesticity. For example, Catharine Maria Sedgwick's short story "Modern Chivalry" (1827) presents an eighteenth-century cross-dressing female sailor whose captain punishes her for her deception by forcing her to work on his New Oxford plantation, until a "gallant young sailor" romantically rescues her from servitude.[13] This dynamic is reversed at the tale's end when, after years of separation, the sailor, acting as an American captain in the Revolutionary navy, is captured by the British and taken to Antigua, where the girl happens to be the distinguished wife of the governor and arranges his freedom. Thus, while Sedgwick clearly provides her heroine with multiple levels of agency, the tale definitively relocates the mode of this action to the realm of domestic authority and influence.

These two realms, of course, intersect within antebellum narratives written by captains' wives at sea. Though relatively few were published in their own time, journals and essays penned by such women as Abby Jane Morrell, Eliza Azelia Williams, Mary Brewster, and Mary Davis Wallis present, in Haskell Springer's terms, "the writers' narrowly limited, simultaneously privileged and deprived lives at sea."[14] These texts illuminate the "small places occupied by women within their husbands' definitely male world" as well as how women "found their own, ambivalently gendered ways to record that complex experience, strategically creating on paper audience-conscious lives as protagonists of their narratives."[15] I will consider Mary Davis Wallis's account in more detail later in the chapter, tracing her figurations of native bodies and sexualities in the context of male travelers' descriptions.

Even more pertinent to the figuration of Pacific sexual encounters is the way such gender positions operate within maritime romances, with women in narratives such as Cooper's pirate tales *The Red Rover* and *The Water-Witch; or, The Skimmer of the Seas* (1831) relegated either to positions of enigmatic objects of desire or stabilizing domestic entities. The romance genre's tendency to tie up all class and gender issues in a tidy and conservative denouement has been widely discussed. But the qualitative way certain types of women are both curtailed and constrained in maritime narratives is especially telling. In novels such as Walter Scott's *The Pirate* and Joseph C. Hart's *Miriam Coffin; or, The Whale-Fishermen* (1834), we see ambitious and empowered women in the line of Lady Macbeth undergo, to push the Shakespearean analogy, a *Taming of the Shrew*–like domestication. As mentioned in chapter 2, Scott's novel closes with most characters ostensibly falling in line with modern nationalist fantasies. Two of the most drastic conversions, however, relate to women: Minna, who had previously identified with feudal-era Zetland warriors, "exchang[es] the visions of wild enthusiasm" for national allegiance, and Norna, the powerful and enigmatic enchantress of the isle, dons her original name (Ulla) and trades mystic spells for a Christian Bible (564, 561).

In an even more concerted manner, Hart's novel figures the dangerous effect of female agency within the realm of the marketplace. Miriam Coffin is the ambitious wife of a Nantucket whaling ship owner who surreptitiously plots to take command of her husband's fortune while he is on an Atlantic voyage. Her machinations devolve into smuggling plots, but her aggressive tactics gain her a veritable monopoly over other Nantucket merchants. In fact, her success spawns a public revolt, which culminates in her husband's return. In the end, all of Miriam's exploits are negated by her husband's command: "Get thee gone to thy kitchen, where it is fitting thou should'st preside.... Never meddle with men's affairs more!"[16] Though Miriam's ambition takes a financial form, like Minna and Norna's "enthusiasms," we see that regardless of its particular fantasy orientation, her desiring energy, itself, is seen as posing the central danger. And Hart leaves this danger brewing even after it is formally contained, having Miriam "put on the show of content": yet, he writes, the "world never knew of the volcano fires, burning with a smoldering flame in her bosom;—nor of the yearnings for power;—nor the throbbings, struggling to be revenged upon those who had brought her house to its ruin."[17] In what follows, I will return to this notion of an excessive and smoldering feminine desire in the context of representations of Pacific women, but in a paramountly different way—looking at how male-oriented fantasies about this type of excess may paradoxically act as a defense against an even more traumatizing form of female enjoyment.

In terms of Pacific contexts, scholars have convincingly revealed the "phallic" nature (here used in the rudimentary sense) of both antebellum gender constructs and the various twentieth-century conceptions of Eros and the other used to explore them. In discussing Edward Said's formative *Orientalism* (1978), for example, Anne McClintock posits:

> For Said, Orientalism takes perverse shape as a "male power-fantasy" that sexualizes a feminized Orient for Western power and possession. But sexuality comes close, here, to being no more than a metaphor for other, more important, (that is, male) dynamics played out in what Said calls "an exclusively male providence." Sexuality as a trope for the other power relations was certainly an abiding aspect of imperial power. The feminizing of the "virgin" land, . . . operated as a metaphor for relations that were very often not about sexuality at all, or were only indirectly sexual. . . . But seeing sexuality only as a metaphor runs the risk of eliding *gender* as a constitutive dynamic of imperial and anti-imperial power.[18]

Said's analysis of the Western imperial imagination paradoxically operates within the logic of the fantasies it seeks to censure. According to McClintock, while Said may accurately reveal how such fantasies dovetail with imperial power, the strictures of this analogy may cause the category of gender to drop out of view. Lee Wallace's *Sexual Encounters* takes up this line of thought in important ways. Maligning what she views as a continued "tendency to heterosexual metaphorization," she revisits "documents of discovery" in an effort to work against assumed heterosexual constructions of experience by focusing on the male body.[19] Yet, while Wallace and others are justified in claiming that "in order for the power relations of empire to be normalized, they must first be heterosexualized," a Lacanian perspective allows us to explore the precarious manner in which such heterosexualizations are constituted and maintained.[20] Within traditional "hetero-normative" representations of native women we might find an overlooked traumatic kernel that perpetually threatens gendered imperial constructs. But first it is necessary to pause and set up Lacan's conception of sexuality and enjoyment in some detail, in order to use such elements to revisit Pacific narratives.

Many scholars have noted that Lacan's *Seminar XX* marks an important development of his earlier discussions of desire, knowledge, and jouissance. According to Suzanne Barnard, however, this popular text—with its notorious claims that "there is no sexual relationship" and "woman does not exist"—has been misread and derided by readers who for years had access only to partial English translations.[21] In looking at sexual relations, Lacan focuses on the traumatic gaps that erupt when one tries to account for sexual difference as such. As Renata Salecl explains, sexual difference is, in fact, "the name of a deadlock, of a trauma, of an open question, of something that *resists* every attempt at its symbolization."[22] This difficulty, to put it lightly, stems from the fact that, in Lacan's view, the sexual positions of male and female have less to do with biology (in fact, one might say they have little to do with it) and more to do with how each subject position exists in relation to jouissance.

As I will explore various nuances of this theory in my discussion of Melville's novels, it is appropriate here to establish two central components: sexuation and jouissance.[23] "Sexuation" is Lacan's term for the relation of what might be called a masculine structure of enjoyment and a feminine structure of enjoyment. The claim that there is no sexual relation should be read in terms of his more specific postulation that "sexual jouissance has the privilege of being specified by an impasse."[24] This impasse, the symbolic deadlock Salecl mentions, is a result of the fact that "there's no such thing as a prediscursive reality."[25] Since the symbolic order establishes "existence" as such, if—as Lacan claims—the sexual relation cannot be written, then it follows that it also cannot formally be.[26] As Bruce Fink notes, this view breaks from a deep-seated Western fantasy of a potential harmony between the two sexes that dates back as far as Plato's *Symposium*.[27]

As discussed in chapter 1, "jouissance" is Lacan's term for surplus enjoyment, an enjoyment that is directly linked to Marx's notion of surplus value.[28] Using the notion of symbolic castration, one can view jouissance as an element that is lost with the acquisition of language. As a subject, one submits to the function of the symbolic order, and a result of this "separation"—as Lacan refers to it—is that one can never directly experience or know full jouissance. In the context of antebellum narratives, Melville frequently gestures to such a full experience of enjoyment in his novels, but always in negative terms and often in reference to a cultural or social other's experience. This can be seen in *Typee*'s appendix, where he claims that the Sandwich Islanders' "deeds [were] too atrocious to be mentioned" (258), or in another scene in which he describes how the dancing bodies of the Typee women were "almost too much for a quiet, soberminded, modest young man" (152). Although, on the one hand, such sentiments can relate to a form of experience outside the bounds of Western decorum, on the other, they can also outline the contours of a fantasy about enjoyment beyond the domains of civilization's linguistic and sociopolitical structures. Bruce Fink puts this in simple terms by describing the way language and knowledge affect an unavoidable tendency to "judge our jouissance against a standard of what we think *it should be,* against an absolute standard.... In other words, language is what allows us to think that the jouissance we obtain is not what it should be."[29]

This is a helpful way of beginning to approach Lacan's conception of the relationship between language and enjoyment. Without delving too far into specifics, one can view the implementation of language as the master signifier's reign over reality, sometimes figured metaphorically as the father's *"No!"* to the child's desire. Knowledge as mediated by language, therefore, comes as a response to this injunction and the correlative loss of forbidden jouissance. Thus, the subject is cast into a futile mode of "repetition," whereby one seeks this lost enjoyment in replacement objects and experiences. This is where the function of fantasy becomes paramount. As Lacan notes, when jouissance is lost, "in the place of this loss introduced by repetition ... we see the function of the lost object emerge, of what I am calling the *a*."[30] So even if true jouissance is beyond the symbolic order proper, through the very knowledge and language that impede full enjoyment, one can still experience a diluted form of this concept. And this form of enjoyment is what Lacan refers to as "phallic jouissance."

This concept and its constituent elements of the phallus and enjoyment are, again, directly related to symbolic castration and shape the process of sexuation. In Lacan's work, he often designates the symbolic order as *le grand Autre,* or the big Other. As briefly discussed in chapter 2 in the analysis of symbolic identification, we as subjects address this big Other (or "A") in our everyday lives even if we do not consciously realize it—the A acting as ballast for the construction of written and unwritten codes and rules (or, if you will, the position from which we view ourselves). Lacan's concept of the Real, however, clearly reveals that this system is not complete. Thus, the A that stabilizes the symbolic order must be lacking. And it is in this context that Lacan refers to the A as a divided or barred Other (Ⱥ). In fact, Lacan makes clear that since there is ultimately no big Other per se, this lacking A should be viewed as a master signifier, or S(Ⱥ) in his formula: designating the signifier of the lack of the Other. This is why Lacan refers to S(Ⱥ) as "the dead Father in the Freudian Myth" and, for all intents and purposes, a signifier with no signified.[31]

One's sexuation is contingent on how one is positioned vis-à-vis this Other, and the resultant type of enjoyment afforded. The concept of phallic jouissance is the type of enjoyment related to the male structure and the now familiar function of fantasy. Here, a barred subject is completely subsumed under the master signifier. As such, he fills in his own lack in being, and that of the master signifier through which he is constituted, with an object a.[32] In Lacan's terms, what men "deal with is object a, and . . . the whole realization of the sexual relationship leads to fantasy."[33] As a result, whenever two people get together in a sexual relationship, they are never alone, for their experience and desire of each other is always mediated by a third element.

This brings us to Lacan's modification of the concept of phallus. Where Freud associates it (at least in an imaginary way) with the physical penis, Lacan instead correlates it with the subject's relation to symbolic castration. Essentially, the Lacanian phallus is a signifier for the way the male structure operates (or compensates) via fantasy. Using the Greek letter phi to denote this concept, he breaks it into two functions: the lowercase $-\varphi$ for the imaginary and the uppercase Φ for the symbolic. While a discussion of the technical operations of Lacan's graph of desire is not required here, the imaginary $-\varphi$ denotes a relation to castration—literally, an imagined loss of the penis or agency—while the symbolic Φ connotes a key transformation of this lack into positive terms.[34] Just as the object a acts as a positive stand-in for the lack of the Other, illusorily filling the gap in the male's being, the phallus signifies, in Bruce Fink's terms, "this very sublation or positivization of loss that language performs."[35] Renata Salecl's summation aptly ties these various functions together:

> The phallic signifier *is* the direct signifier or operator of the symbolic castration. That is to say, against the standard notion of phallus as the siege of "natural" male penetration–aggressive potency–power (to which one then opposes the "artificial," playful prosthetic phallus), the point of Lacan's concept of phallus as a *signifier* is that

phallus "as such" *is* a kind of "prosthetic," "artificial" supplement: it designates the point at which the big Other, a decentered agency, supplements the subject's failure.[36]

This "supplement" to "the subject's failure," again, corresponds to the male structure's indomitable reliance on fantasy to maintain its existence. With this understood, we can turn to the most important aspect of this discussion: the female structure and its relation to Other jouissance.

Unlike the rather simple male structure, which is fully subsumed by the master signifier and maintains itself via phallic enjoyment, the female structure is more complex on both accounts. In Lacan's schematic, he infamously writes "woman" struck through with a bar (W̶o̶m̶a̶n̶) to argue that the notion of "woman" per se is "not-whole." This claim has generated a wealth of valid criticism. A typical example of this can be found in McClintock's *Imperial Leather*, where she accuses Lacan of making the imperial gesture of casting women into a pre-Oedipal past and limiting them to functional objects of male fetishism.[37] While engaging the rich history of gender scholarship that critiques and extends Lacan's work is outside the scope of this chapter, I want to note it here before discussing Lacan's specific views. I believe looking at his points about sexuation remain useful, in light of scholars who have adapted them, and valid, despite those who have impugned them.[38] More specifically, Lacan's formulations may be especially useful for examining antebellum constructions of fantasy relating to imperial advances in Pacific regions.

The notion that woman does not exist and is not-whole does not mean that this position is merely some phantasmagoria of male desire, for the concepts of "existing" and "whole" need to be read in the context of symbolic functions. That which is defined and shaped by language is whole (at least in appearance) and exists; alternately, that which escapes or eludes language (the domain of the Real) ex-sists. Lacan makes it absolutely clear what he means by being not-whole when he writes, "When any speaking being whatsoever situates itself under the banner 'women,' it is on the basis of the following—that it grounds itself as being not-whole in situating itself in the phallic function."[39] But if the feminine is not wholly subsumed under the phallic function and its domain of fantasy, how is it constituted in relation to jouissance?

Lacan answers this question by insisting that a subject sexuated as a woman is "doubled," having access both to phallic jouissance and what he terms Other jouissance. This is suggested when Lacan asks: "For one pole, jouissance is marked by the hole that leaves it no other path than that of phallic jouissance. For the other pole, can something be attained that would tell us how that which up until now has only been a fault (*faille*) or gap in jouissance could be realized?"[40] Although the male pole operates by blindly and futilely filling its symbolic gaps with a fantasmatic object *a*, the other pole here seems to offer a different experience of this "fault" or gap. This is where the notion of Other jouissance should be situated: as a form of enjoyment that does not exist (in language or fantasy) but ex-sists. As Lacan makes clear, fantasy, and its phallic jouissance, "is not related to the Other as such" (9); but a woman is. And it is this ability to have a "relationship" with the Other, instead of merely maintaining a denial of its lack through fantasy, that provides access to that which is beyond the symbolic, beyond the existing (81).

This is the central paradox of the feminine structure.[41] Though Lacan clearly establishes that the male "has" the phallus while the female "is" the phallus, this *being* the phallus yields a potential surplus of enjoyment. It should be reiterated that the positions of having and being the phallus are not necessarily bound by biological gender concerns—as we will see with Mary Davis Wallis's account of Manicola men, whereby their exposed physical penises act as the feminized phallus that she, herself, fantasmatically "has." By positing that the woman is the phallus, therefore, Lacan refers to her role in embodying the object *a* that the male uses to plug the gap, if you will, of his own symbolic lack. Yet, in this function the woman is anything but a fetishized object, for two reasons: her relation to castration affords a surplus of enjoyment, and she is not reduced to a deficient reliance on phallic fantasy. In terms of the former, Lacan states over and over in various ways that women have "a supplementary jouissance compared to what the phallic function designates by way of jouissance."[42] In terms of the latter, Lacan goes so far as to claim that in the scenario of phallic fantasy it is women "who possess men" (73). As Jacques-Alain Miller argues, this is the case because being the phallus "corresponds to . . . [a] variation of being the hole in the Other by giving it a positive form. One must note that the expression 'being the phallus' implies a certain depreciation of the virile Other's having, a reduction of the Other's having to a semblance."[43] Thus, even though woman's supposed excess of jouissance is not directly discernable, her function within and relation to the phallic structure may illuminate in a negative way the incompleteness and desperation of male fantasy.[44]

By way of an example from the context of antebellum literature, E. D. E. N. Southworth's novel *The Deserted Wife* (1850), which comprises a domestic plot shaped in part by maritime themes and concerns, offers a particularly nuanced representation of phallic desire and its potential limits. A central character in the story is Agatha, who is nicknamed Hagar owing to "her wild, dark beauty."[45] Even as a child, the orphaned heiress Hagar, cared for by her aunt, is figured as desiring in an excessive and phallic manner, which is often coded in terms of her "wild eyes" (40) and "falcon glance" (60, 73). From the start, this apparent excess is directed toward Raymond Withers, the son (from a previous marriage) of her aunt's husband, Reverend Withers (who, in his own grotesque display of phallic desire, had forced Hagar's aunt away from a departing naval lieutenant and into marriage, telling her: "Your hand is the *one* thing that I wish on earth, and I *must, must* have it—*will* have it" [29]). Upon his deathbed, Reverend Withers spies the child Hagar standing with her hands clasped around Raymond's. Perhaps disturbed by the way "her crimson cheek and glittering eyes display[ed] more excitement than awe," Withers pulls her close and implores her to "love him—gently" (62).

Soon after, Southworth describes an interesting exchange between Hagar and a suitor named Gusty, a young naval officer. Fawning over Hagar, Gusty exclaims that he "like[s]" her "better than [he] like[s] [his] ship" and, in an exemplary display of phallic desire, informs her: "There is a—a—an attraction—a something in your face that fascinates—that—that *draws*, that *pulls*, that *nails*, that *rivets*" (65). Responding with laughter, Hagar retorts: "I don't know how it is that I always laugh when other people would cry. I believe I am a lineal descendent of the laughing philosopher. Now, Gusty, my childhood's friend, I am laughing at your phantasy. You do *not* love me; it is a mere illusion of the imagination. Your heart is cheating itself with the semblance of love in default of the substance" (65). As opposed to earlier in the narrative, where she is figured as a potentially dangerous phallic lover, in her role as a "laughing philosopher" Hagar operates in a mode we can at least conceptually associate with the feminine structure of sexuation—where her knowledge of the "illusion" and "semblance" that constitute Gusty's "phantasy" ironically converts his expression of love into a comic and pathetic display.

Joan Copjec's discussion of female jouissance provides a helpful framework for conceiving of this scenario. She writes: "The jouissance of the woman of which Lacan speaks has nothing to do with her capacity to transcend the symbolic or exist outside language. In fact, if woman has easier access than man to the God of jouissance, this is because she is less susceptible than he is to the lure of transcendence."[46] Copjec here suggests that the female's experience of being the phallus affords a relative liberation. Unlike male fantasy's pervasive material belief in the big Other via its use of object *a* to maintain its masquerade, females' knowledge of the lack of the Other through their function of temporarily standing in for the Other yields not (fantasy) transcendental insight, but something approaching an understanding that between the sexes lies only, to use Žižek's description of the Real, "the gap between two inconsistent phenomena."[47]

In Southworth's novel, Hagar not only avoids the lure of transcendence—a lure Gusty has certainly swallowed, evidenced by his overwrought demonstration of phallic love—but, perhaps more significantly, her potential existence outside of this structure manifests as a critical and threatening censure of what to Gusty is the zero level of affection and desire. Hagar maintains this critical distance later in the novel when she critiques her aunt's advice to submit to Raymond, chiding her: "You, Sophie, have a propensity to worship, and a very decided vocation for martyrdom, which . . . under existing circumstances, *I* have not" (98).

But Hagar's possible embodiment of female enjoyment and its attendant perspectives is seemingly negated from the start—acting as something like an accidental fold in a narrative spun from decidedly phallic material. Even in the scene with Gusty, Hagar's radical position is retroactively altered when her criticism of Gusty's love is shown to be leveled not from a qualitatively distinct or outside position, but from a distant point on the same conceptual plane. This is because, as we soon learn, Hagar is passionately and desperately in love with Raymond. Indeed, from this early point in the plot, the primary conflict in the novel concerns the struggle between what turns out to be two überphallic lovers: Raymond, on the one hand, who is attracted to Hagar's excess (at one point telling her: "Use your wildness as you do your hair" [102]), who forcefully subdues her will, and who leaves her after their marriage for a woman we later learn is his lost sister; and Hagar, on the other, who painfully submits to Raymond's will, who channels her libidinal excesses into a traditional mode of jealousy over Raymond's advances toward another woman, and who continues to pursue Raymond even after being abandoned and subsequently becoming a celebrity vocalist in Europe. The close of the novel finds Hagar in a position of agency, returning to her original domestic space in Maryland to reunite with an embarrassed and crestfallen Raymond.

The way Southworth's novel potentially reveals a form of female enjoyment, however fleeting and tempered it may be, in the guise of an implicit critique of the function of male fantasy provides a simple and useful model for how I wish to use Lacan's theory to explore maritime narratives. Instead of taking a McClintock-like view that Lacan's feminine jouissance relates to a primordial womanly excess, or affirming Butler's claim that such a theory upholds the transcendental rule of Law, we will see how the figure of the woman may exist as a troublesome bone in the throat of phallic fantasy.

In sum, antebellum maritime texts that figure Pacific encounters are not merely phallic qua masculine—in the reductive sense of being shaped by male-dominated heterosexism—but are, in a Lacanian sense, examples of phallically oriented fantasy constructions. This conceptual shift yields three significant considerations. First, it directly situates representations of seemingly private and erotic experiences within broader symbolic historical contexts. Second, it automatically complicates the simple paradigms of gender and sexual orientation that still limit some historical analysis, adjusting the way we view the positions and effects of native females within Western fantasies. And third, it views these various forms of narrative as desperate endeavors—serving a type of enjoyment that can exist only by reducing the other to a partial object in an attempt to sustain precarious symbolic coordinates.

Encounter with a Partial Native

As historians have rehearsed, European eroticization of the Pacific islands and their peoples began in the sixteenth century and bloomed with the commencement of full-scale colonial projects during the eighteenth century. While both male and female natives of various Pacific cultures have been subjected to the erotic gaze of the West, the island woman has been especially prevalent within colonial discourses. This is not to downplay the role of male bodies and sodomitical activities—which, as Wallace has shown, permeate the era's narratives in ways that had manifold effects on Western sexual discourse and practices. As I have suggested, however, in looking more closely at how Westerners closely looked at the ubiquitous figure of the desiring island "nymph," we may discern elements of anxiety and danger that have not yet been adequately addressed.

Antebellum representations of Pacific native women clearly exist within a nexus of Western sexual discourses on gender and race. In terms of gender, in addition to the topic of domestic ideology, there is a rich web of myths that shape eighteenth- and nineteenth-century views of native females. Edenic references, of course, abound. Travelers saw in these women's nudity and apparent openness to sexual activity a form of prelapsarian fullness and enjoyment.[48] Such sentiment informed secular accounts of native women in the eighteenth century as well, with writers such as Voltaire and Diderot ennobling the supposed erotic behaviors of Tahitian women by associating them with natural fecundity. These laudatory depictions also linked to American native heroines, such as Pocahontas and Sacagawea. While these *belles sauvages*, as Raymond Stedman dubbed them, were not exalted for their natural eroticism like their Pacific counterparts, their bodies and desires were still used in the West's narratives of self-evaluation and validation.[49] As Patty O'Brien argues, "These women were supreme objects of imperial desire due to their perceived willingness to facilitate and lend legitimacy to colonial activity and their safeguarding of imperial endeavors at their own people's expense."[50] As we will see in what follows, accounts that depict such a relationship with native women reveal much about underlying ideological fantasies, for in a Lacanian sense, a central aspect of object *a* (here, clearly the respective *belles sauvages*) is "the Other's desire for me" or how one imagines oneself in terms of the Other's desire.[51] Yet, such female desire also exists within a Western tradition that, since Tiresias's claims about women's superior enjoyment, is threatened by a potential excess of feminine pleasure. An ambiguous and anxious play between condoned and respectable desire can be seen in a 1773 satire of Joseph Banks describing the Tahitian sovereign Oberea as both a "queen" and "a common whore."[52]

This ubiquitous "wild woman" trope has clear racial coordinates. Although Victorian iconography is rife with general associations between women and various monsters, in the eighteenth and nineteenth centuries native and African women were avidly and consistently correlated with perverse sexual excess.[53] From common depictions of eager island women swarming visiting ships, to the caged performances in Europe of the South African "Hottentot Venus" Saartjie Baartman, the racialized female body has often been an eroticized one.[54] As David Eng has convincingly argued, such sentiments later take shape, among other places, in Freud's *Totem and Taboo*. According to Eng, Freud unintentionally sanctions "colonial exploitation through a rhetoric of modernization" with his thesis that "savage" peoples have no unconscious and, therefore, act on impulses that civilized minds censure.[55] Thus, Freud's work gives an early twentieth-century voice to Enlightenment and Romantic-era notions that ineluctably fused sexuality and race.

Although many scholars have deconstructed and dismissed most imperial representations of racial and gendered excess, I seek to take this topic up from a different perspective. In a Lacanian reading, the belief that racial and gendered others possess an excess of desire might be seen as a means to fantasmatically project the dominant (phallic) symbolic position's lack onto another. Though conceptually quite simple, the implications of this process are profound. For one, we should not conclude our analysis of nineteenth-century fantasies that link excessive desire to psychological and moral failings of "lower" orders (race, gender, class, and so on) by merely highlighting their function as an excuse for colonial projects (through their de facto appeal to teleological notions of civilization, for example). Instead, we should include a requisite critique of how these constructions operate on the level of enjoyment. As scholars of Lacanian psychoanalysis have professed for years, a key teaching of Lacan's later thought is that symptoms have a way of continuing even when knowledge is gained about their causes. This is why "traversing the fantasy" at the close of analysis does not mean simply eradicating constructions of desire through coming to some epiphany about the illusory nature of one's ideas, but, in a way, identifying with one's symptom—coming to terms with how one's relation to jouissance is structured. Consequently, we should add a crucial subsequent step to studies that unearth gender and racial constructions' ideological and political functions: a consideration of how they operate as a means for dominant modes of phallic jouissance to perpetuate themselves.

In an attempt to do just this, I use this section to present a relative tableau of various eighteenth- and nineteenth-century nonfictional Western representations of Pacific encounters with native women. Such a stage, of sorts, should give rough shape to the contours of paradigmatic fantasy elements that influenced Western perceptions of and interactions in the colonial Pacific. My contention is that these fantasies, though evincing anxiety of various kinds, represent a veritable closed symbolic network—the product of phallic schemas having worked through denying or converting aspects of feminine jouissance and other potential perils related to both others (*autre* and *Autre*). In the last section of the chapter we will use Melville's three early Pacific-island novels (*Typee, Omoo,* and *Mardi*) as a means to explore how these paradigmatic fantasies may have been constituted in the first place. Taking the well-known Lacanian notion that "truth has the structure of a fiction" at its word, I use Melville's novels to illuminate retroactively the tension-wrought way such phallic operations struggle to implement and maintain their own systems of enjoyment.[56]

We must start, however, with the base. And I use this term both as a noun, signifying in a Marxist sense the foundational role of economic and material historical realities, and as an adjective, gesturing to the repugnant sexual violence that European relations with native women often engendered. Sexual violence against Carib women was endemic during Columbus's second voyage to the Caribbean between October 1493 and June 1496. A particularly vivid account of such interactions is seen in Michele de Cuneo's narrative of raping a native woman. Evincing his age's belief that, in Patty O'Brien's terms, "rape of unguarded women was acceptable practice," Cuneo dispassionately recounts how he took the naked woman into his cabin to "execute" his "desires" and was forced to "thrash her well" with a rope to quell her resistance. After describing how he beat her into submission and had his way, Cuneo observes: "I can tell you, she seemed to have been raised in a veritable school of harlots."[57]

While the ideological landscape of male sexuality had seemingly shifted toward bourgeois standards by the imperial era of the eighteenth century, one can argue that little had changed in terms of the power dynamics between the sexes. Exemplifying Marx's point that with the advent of bourgeois society relations between humans "take on the form of a social relation between products of labour," the ethical mediation of contact with native women through mechanisms of trade and commerce might be seen to mask earlier social power dynamics.[58]

Nonetheless, this formidable shift can be seen in the behavior of Samuel Wallis's crew in their 1767 stay on Tahiti. Citing the journal of George Robertson, the second master of Wallis's *Dolphin*, O'Brien recounts how after initial hostilities the crew voiced desire to have access to the "handsome" native women who, although seemingly afraid, were viewed as willing sexual partners. Wallis, however, banned all contact until an intermediary shore station was established. According to Robertson, shortly after, "a new sort of trade" sprang up in which men exchanged goods such as nails for sex with women. Robertson notes how an Irish boy was initially punished for such trade, not because of the nature of the activity but because he and the men had not executed it more discretely or, in Robertson's words, "in a more decent manner, in some house or at the back of some bush or tree."[59]

Captain James Cook's global voyages began shortly after Robertson and Wallis's stay on Tahiti. The renown of Cook's adventures—in their various narrative accounts—is testament to how profoundly they have shaped readers' views about the Pacific from the late eighteenth century up until our own time. Surprisingly, there are few passages when Cook directly comments on the bodies of native women.[60] Two instances of this, however, reveal his clear ideological immersion in modern Western codes. In one, Cook employs a common racially structured hierarchy of beauty, offhandedly calling the natives of Malekula (New Hebrides) "the most ugly and ill-proportioned" due to their "dark Chocolate Colour," "Monkey faces," "woolly hair," and "thick lips and noses."[61] Potentially more significant, though, is an earlier passage, in which Cook has observed a naked native woman of New Holland (Australia) through his spyglass and, instead of commenting on her "natural" condition, records: "Even those parts which I allways [sic] before now thought nature would have taught a woman to conceal were unconver'd" (153). Thus, in Cook's eyes, black natives appear "monkey-like" and are quite obviously below civilized standards, owing to their supposedly archaic level of development. But here complete feminine nudity is markedly *un*natural. Besides complicating any clear notion of historical development and revealing tints of a Protestant ethos, this assumption also locates the zero level of a "natural" woman's body as already conditioned by the male gaze. It seems that for Cook nonanimalistic humans exist after a historical break, where even when one lives in the state of nature, one must negotiate the proper social and bodily behavior toward others (and, therefore, the big Other).[62] Here, women are clearly born into a world of phallic fantasy and, therefore, pose little symbolic threat— for in this schematic there is absolutely no opening for feminine jouissance whatsoever.

As with Wallis, however, it is commerce that primarily structures how Cook portrays encounters with native women. Indeed, Cook shows early in his first voyage that he takes measures to initiate contact with natives through the mediation of commodity exchange, leaving "several articles such as Cloth, Looking glasses, Combs, Beeds[,] Nails &c" on the shore in New Holland in order to entice islanders to approach his crew (125). Such seemingly innocuous behavior should ground analysis of his broader experiences with various indigenous peoples. For example, the oft-cited

Tahitian sexual encounter in 1769, when a young native girl has sex with an island man outside the walls of Cook's fort while being instructed by Queen Oberea, occurs on the heels of a similar scene that is directly tied to commodity exchange. On the day previous to this event, Cook describes how a native man and two women came to the gate of the fort and presented Cook's men with various plants. The man, who seemed, Cook wrote,

> to be only a Servant to the 2 women, . . . took several pieces of Cloth and spread them on the ground, one of the Young Women then step'd upon the Cloth and with as much Innocency as one could possibly conceve, expose'd herself intirely naked from the waist downwards, in this manner she turn'd her Self once or twice round, I am not certain which, then step'd of the Cloth and dropped down her clothes, more Cloth was then spread upon the Former and she again perform'd the same ceremony; the Cloth was then rowled up and given to Mr. Banks and the two young women went and embraced him which ended the ceremony. (52)

Quite clearly, in Cook's view this erotic "ceremony" entailed transferring something—one might safely refer to it as an object *a*—from the women's bodies to the cloth spread below them, with the two uniting at the close with the gift of both the product and physical embrace. Cook's correlation of native desire and commodities is explicitly corroborated in the next entry. Directly before the sexual encounter involving the young native girl, he states: "The Iron and Iron tools daily in use at the Armourers Forge are temptations that these people cannot possibly withstand" (52). In this light, it seems plausible to conclude that Cook does indeed view the natives as excessively amorous, but only in terms of desire for Western products. We should, therefore, pull the above-mentioned child-eroticism scene into this context, reading it, too, as—in Cook's eyes at least—a means for the islanders to incite a reciprocal desire in his crew for native products and bodies.

Yet, it is important to see how this gap between women's bodies as a source of object *a* and the commodities that natives proffer is closed in most other instances. Repeatedly, Cook describes scenes where women willingly enter into trade with his crew, offering their bodies as a commodity to exchange for various European goods.[63] In an uncharacteristically reflective aside during his stay in New Zealand on the second voyage, Cook comments on how the women of this country are "more chaste than the generality of Indian women" for "whatever favors a few of them might have granted to the crew of the Endeavor it was generally done in a private manner and without the men seeming to interest themselves in it" (276). Such thoughts are quite telling: here "chastity" and, one would presume, womanliness are linked to distinctly antimarket sexual encounters—where such acts are "privately" "granted" to some of the crew. The "men" Cook refers to at the close of the passage are, of course, the native men related to the women. And it is his subsequent judgment of them that most reveals his feelings on the matter. Here Cook writes:

> We find the [native] men are the chief promoters of this Vice, and for a spike nail or any other thing they value will oblige their Wives and Daughters to prostitute themselves whether they will or no and that not with the privacy and decency seems to require, such are the consequences of a commerce with Europeans and what is still more to our shame civilized Christians, we debauch their Morals already too prone to vice and we interduce among them wants and perhaps diseases which they never before knew and which serves only to disturb that happy tranquility they and their fore Fathers had injoy'd. (276–77)

Although European commerce is depicted as a corrupting system, exacerbating native propensities for vice, it is interesting to note how Cook views the desire of native men as the root cause for native women's licentious actions. Here the previous figuration of native women's irresistible want of Western products is reframed in terms of their male relatives' desires. In this way, Cook goes even further in subtending the potential desire of women—casting them as mere pawns acting out the wishes of native men in a marketplace controlled by Europeans. What is quite important is that Cook's perceptions of largely unknown Pacific cultures are conditioned by a fundamental fantasy in which native female behavior and desire are viewed as completely immersed in a phallic economy.

A similar schematic can be seen in the journal of Edward Robarts, an English sailor who lived in the Marquesas from December 1798 to February 1806 after fleeing his ship to avoid participating in a mutiny. Much like Cook, in his accounts Robarts effectively reduces native women to the function and position of an object *a*, but without the mediation of either commerce or native men. In this sense, Robarts makes an important move toward acknowledging the existence of the desire of the other (and Other) within the native woman. He does this, however, only in short asides at the beginning of the journal, vaguely citing how the natives "are remarkably fond of strangers" and that "a white man was a great novelty among them."[64]

If Robarts goes further than Cook in considering the desire of women within the fabric of his own fantasies, this desire ultimately manifests as an abstract and a priori assumption. That is, female desire remains at a safe distance, as an open invitation, of sorts, that allows him to freely choose and condition experiences with women. Interestingly, his interactions with such women display an implicitly defensive approach toward the central concept of object *a*. Although often detailing scenes of phallic desire, Robarts consistently manages to do so while avoiding addressing this concept, in two related ways: by shifting the focus from the explicit cause of desire to a general description of an object of desire and, in so doing, by controlling and minimizing the role of the gaze in his narrative. Although Robarts often comments on natives' bodies and behavior, when describing women he tends to itemize their attributes in a veritable chivalric blazon. This can be seen when he introduces a native woman who takes him into her home. Robarts opines:

> This lady surpassed her sister in beauty. Her hair was an Aubourn brown color and very long. When loosed, [it] would flow in ringlets below her waist. Her eyes brows finely archd, her countenance open and smileing, her manner and conversation captivating, this lady was formd to please. . . . She was extremely fair, and a fine blush on her cheeks. (86–87)

This description clearly seeks to account for the source of the woman's alluring nature with a detailed list of physical particulars. While the racial implications of auburn hair and a "fine blush" are interesting, mirroring Cook's racial hierarchy and a tendency seen in many Western travelers to praise natives that have European physical traits, it is here most important to note the structural form Robarts's description takes: a series of attributes that may relate to his fantasy's object *a*. As discussed, such an object remains at least partially unconscious in one's fantasy and need not be a singular physical trait per se. Despite the fact that Robarts, as above, often focuses on markers such as a woman's hair, it is unclear what exact attribute or quality catalyzes his desire. In some respects this point seems of little importance, for an object *a* has no substantial consistency in itself, and Robarts's amorous taxonomy of feminine traits unquestionably signals that his encounters with women are mediated through fantasy structures that locate them safely within his system of desire. Moreover, even when he surmises about women's psychological interiors, he inevitably codes them with the logic of object *a:* with the above woman's "conversation" being a "captivating" lure and elsewhere their voices taking the form of lulling and melodious songs.[65] Nonetheless, this seemingly natural act of fantasmatically particularizing native women becomes conspicuously defensive when one considers the way he presents (or, more aptly, does not present) the concept of the gaze.

The Lacanian notion of gaze differs from ubiquitous ideas about the agency of male-dominated focalization. For Lacan, the gaze corresponds to the potentially disruptive role of the object *a* in the field of the Imaginary. Todd McGowan's summary of the concept—a concept I will return to when looking at Melville's novels—is worth quoting at length:

> Lacan comes to conceive of the gaze as something that the subject (or spectator) encounters in the object . . . ; it becomes an objective, rather than a subjective, gaze. Lacan's use of the term reverses our usual way of thinking about the gaze because we typically associate it with an active process. But as an object, the gaze acts to trigger our desire visually, and as such it is what Lacan calls an *objet petit a* or object-cause of desire. As he puts it in *Seminar XI*, "The *objet a* in the field of the visible is the gaze." This special term *objet a* indicates that this object is not a positive entity but a lacuna in the visual field. It is not the look of the subject at the object, but the gap within the subject's seemingly omnipotent look. This gap within our look marks the point at which our desire manifests itself in what we see. What is irreducible to our visual field is the way that our desire distorts the field, and this distortion makes itself felt through the gaze as object.[66]

Typifying the role of object *a* within phallic enjoyment, here the object-cause of desire is linked directly to the symbolic lack that male-sexuated subjects attempt to occlude. The paradox is that at times the subject encounters this extraordinary object within the visual plain when the object, itself, seems to look back at him or her—potentially revealing how the subject's desire infiltrates and anamorphically distorts reality.

Just as Robarts foregrounds his relative phallic-structural process of reducing native women to requisite partial objects (objects of desire) but never attempts to address the more enigmatic object *a* (object–cause of the desire) in them, his descriptive accounts of scenes in which he actively appraises these women never includes anything like an encounter with the Lacanian gaze. Instead, we get something more akin to the traditional notion of an empowered surveyor.

While Robarts acknowledges native women's desire to some degree—making references such as how a woman's "fine ... black eyes ... [could] pierce thro *a*damant" (86)—this desire never goes further than being an invitation for his own advances. In the context of the Lacanian gaze, however, this may reveal an anxious caution on Robarts's part. For instance, he describes the scene when he first meets the native woman he subsequently marries by recounting: "One day I was returning from up the valley. I espyd a fine figure of a young lady [j]ust as she was comeing out of the water from bathing. She could not see me. I stood among some low trees. I viewed her with a partial eye" (122). Quite clearly, Robarts desires the young woman and her "fine figure"; yet, the scene remains self-consciously voyeuristic—with Robarts describing his own perspective as a "partial eye." Considering the function of object *a*, one cannot help but mark the irony in Robarts's phraseology here. As in other episodes, such as when he watches women gather wood in the rain to observe "their shapes and blemishes" (139), Robarts consciously removes himself (and his desire) to a position tantamount to a fortified "imperial gaze." Thus, while he playfully admits that he views women through a partial eye—hinting perhaps at potential complications to this process or, at least, to the structural contingencies that shape it—like Cook, Robarts consistently presents a male-structured phallic enjoyment that is perfectly complete.

The fantasy constructions seen in Cook and Robarts play out in various degrees across antebellum nonfictional narratives of Pacific encounters. In David Porter's discussion of the Marquesas in *Journal of a Cruise* (1815), for example, native women are concertedly propped up as a lure to propel the crew to labor toward the island chain. According to Porter, his men "could talk and think of nothing but the beauties of the islands ... ; everyone imagined them Venus's, and amply indulged themselves in fancied bliss."[67] Little changes when they make landfall. Here, women are initially figured as commodities offered by the male natives ("they assured us, by the most expressive gestures, the vahienas, or women, were entirely at our service"), and Porter treats them as such, having their "heads and privates" shaved before they are allowed to approach the crew.[68] Similar to Robarts, however, Porter does briefly acknowledge these women's potential desires, but in the frame of his crew's perspective—writing that "the girls ... showed no disinclination to grant every favour we might be disposed to ask" and commenting on their "willingness to gratify every wish."[69] In fact, one of the most revealing scenes of female desire in the entire narrative is when a native woman is shown to cry when Porter prevents her from boarding his ship.[70]

Not all narratives of similar encounters are even this gracious to native women. In *Narrative of the United States Exploring Expedition* (1850), for example, Charles Wilkes dismissively quips that the native women in Madeira are "ugly."[71] This assessment continues when the *Vincennes* reaches Tahiti. Addressing popular fantasies about the island's women, Wilkes comments: "I hesitate to speak of the females of the island, for I differ from all who have gone before me in relation to their vaunted beauty. I did not see among them a single woman whom I could call handsome." While he acknowledges their famed "soft sleepiness about the eyes," he follows with his own particularizations: "Their figures are bad, and a greater part of them are parrot-toed!"[72] In fact, one of the only native women that Wilkes admits any longing for is a fifteen-year-old daughter of Chief Malietoa on the island of Upolu. And such desire is clearly honed to address proper American domestic racial and gender norms—with the chief bearing "a striking resemblance to General Jackson" and the girl, "Emma," being "as intelligent as she was pretty."[73]

Mary Davis Wallis's *Life in Feejee* (1851) displays a markedly different tenor, yet includes similar fantasy coordinates to those found in Wilkes, Robarts, and Cook. Despite being a woman, Wallis portrays a masculine sexuation in her figuration of native women and men. There is, however, an interesting aside that gestures toward a relative notion of feminine jouissance. Evincing a romantic conception of exotically unfettered sea space, Wallis writes: "I sometimes desire to be far away on the deep blue ocean, with nothing but the heavens above, and the waters beneath, that I may give utterance to thoughts that have dwelt in the depths of my heart from childhood, and which it would be a profanation for the gross ears of mortals to hear."[74] Although such sentiment can be read as a Christian yearning for intimate discourse with God (a phallic fantasy), the ambiguity of the language also makes it lean plausibly toward notions of an "Other" enjoyment (existing in a space with no apparent big Other and consisting of words only possible there). Nonetheless, Wallis's depiction of native women shares the common structure seen thus far in other Western narratives of such encounters. Though her immersion in a missionary community precludes rude notions of trafficking women, Wallis still particularizes their bodies, such as when she describes King Thakombau's "rather good looking" wives as "quite a light color . . . ; rather fleshy, but [with] . . . a fine eye and handsome features."[75] A similar scene is described when she appraises young native men on the island of Manicola. All travelers mentioned thus far, of course, itemize and exalt certain male bodies along with female ones. Yet, Wallis's language interestingly reveals the way her fantasy structure operates both within and despite particular gender differences:

> These islanders are a very handsome race, light colored, no beards, and fine black hair, which they wore long. . . . The young men resembled, at a little distance, very pretty girls, and such we at first thought them. Several wore flowers in their ears, and all had pieces of native cloth, but were not particular in its arrangement till I appeared on deck, when all who were in the canoes proceeded to cover their persons in a proper manner.[76]

In addition to the now-familiar practice of cataloging beauty, Wallis's second sentence foregrounds two salient aspects of her phallic scene of viewing: the requisite distance between the privileged vantage of the fantasizing subject and its object of desire (apropos Robarts) and the manner in which this desired other is feminized. The latter point is ironically telling, as the passage delicately makes clear that Wallis observes, at least to some degree, the native men's penises. Thus, we clearly see how even a literal phallus can act as a feminized Lacanian phallus within a woman's masculinely structured fantasy scenario.

Although only a provisional sample, these various nonfictional narratives portray a rather uniform fantasy structure when addressing the bodies and desires of Pacific natives. As seen, however, even such relatively closed economies of desire at times betray tensions within their own underlying fantasmatic processes. By way of a transition to considering such complications via Melville's novels, a scene in William Ellis's *Polynesian*

Researches (1842) helpfully (and unintentionally) shows how these seemingly indomitable fantasy scenes are predicated on tenuous ground.

Ellis opens discussion of his missionary experiences on the Society and Sandwich Islands by recounting how Cook's journals had rendered the Pacific a "sort of elysium" for readers, "where highly favoured inhabitants, free from the toil and care, the want and disappointment, which mar the happiness of civilized communities, dwelt in what they called a state of nature, and spent their lives in unrestrained enjoyment."[77] Besides the obvious recapitulation of Rousseau-like notions of noble savagery, Ellis also touches here on the view that, free from social constraints of civilization, natives can literally enjoy more. Yet Ellis departs from this familiar premise in his effort to convert the natives. He writes that when islanders surmised about how wonderful England and America must be, he would tell them that

> the difference was not so great between the countries, as between the people—that, many ages back, the ancestors of the present inhabitants of England and America possessed fewer comforts than the Sandwich Islanders now enjoy; wore skins of beasts for clothing; painted their bodies in various colours; and worshipped with inhuman rites their cruel gods—but that since they had become enlightened and industrious, and had embraced Christianity, they had been wise and rich.... [In fact, Civilized people] owed all their present wealth and enjoyment to their intelligence and industry—and then, if the people of either country were to neglect their education and religion, and spend as much of their time in eating, sleeping, ... and jesting, they would soon become as poor and ignorant as the Sandwich Islanders. [The islanders] said perhaps it was so, perhaps instruction would make them happier and better, and, if the chiefs wished it, by and by they would attend to both.[78]

This figuration is quite distinct from the way Wilkes portrays islanders regretfully lamenting the old days of polygamy, and from the tension seen in Wallis's account of, on the one hand, island females choosing to convert to Christianity in order to avoid violent traditional customs, and on the other, native complaints about the implementation of Western social codes.[79] Unlike Ellis's passage above, their accounts allow for a modicum of *qualitative difference* in enjoyment. That is, they acknowledge, in a qualified manner, that natives' traditional customs afford them an enjoyment shaped by a foreign sociosymbolic order that remains at least partially beyond the scope of Western knowledge. Thus, we might transcribe a loose analogy between Lacan's conception of Other jouissance and native enjoyment, for Lacan's analysis privileges a monolithic symbolic order and, therefore, does not seem to address cross-cultural encounters in a colonial era that predates Western symbolic dominance of foreign languages and practices. In a similar way that "woman," in Lacan's figuring, is not wholly subsumed under the master signifier and thus has access to the "*jouissance* of the Other," here the other (imaginary realm) of the native is not wholly subsumed under the West's master signifier and hence has access to a jouissance that is possibly both other and Other (symbolic realm).

Ellis's postulation that educated and industrious citizens enjoy more than primitive peoples should be seen, therefore, as more than a simple conversion ploy. This is because Ellis's reversal subtly effaces any acknowledgment of a qualitatively different form of enjoyment, framing the cultural comparison in quantitative terms based on his own phallic realm of knowledge. Put simply, for Ellis, more knowledge and more material goods result in more enjoyment. When one considers this position from the context of the pervasive racist coupling of native/other and excessive desire, an interesting schism opens up. Instead of the notion that natives' excessive enjoyment constitutes an obstacle to civilization that can be eradicated by imparting or developing a tempering moral–psychological compass (in Freud's terms, the unconscious), Ellis's schematic advances an incommensurate notion that those with such a moral–psychological apparatus actually enjoy more. And, as we will see with Melville, it is this necessary conceptual denial of native enjoyment that might illuminate formative aspects of Western fantasies that undergird representations of Pacific natives.

Staging Phallic Desire's Stage: Melville's Excessive Women

If one takes seriously the well-known Lacanian premise that one is closer to the real world of subjectivity (the real of one's desire) in dreams than in waking life and, in turn, that reality is structured by the "fiction" of fantasy, then Melville's pseudo-fictional works *Typee* and *Omoo* and his imaginatively zany *Mardi* may provide a more nuanced portrayal of the issues at play in scenes of Pacific encounter than their earlier nonfictional counterparts. Moreover, as scholars have carefully delineated, Melville crafts these works in part by culling scenes and descriptions from many of the aforementioned nonfictional accounts. In this way, the palpable discursiveness within Melville's novels and their manifest intertexuality lend material weight to the claim that such fiction illuminates wide-ranging elements of fantasy.

My argument here is a simple one: that Melville's Pacific-island novels offer an interestingly transparent portrayal of their own fantasy structures, especially in relation to figurations of native women. Though these texts remain firmly ensconced in the phallic schematic seen across nonfictional narratives of encounter, what they add, to varying degrees and in different ways, is a subtle portrayal of a problem: the desire of the native woman. As we will see, the very fact that this desire *is* a problem makes all the difference. Furthermore, Melville's novels make a pivotal gesture toward staging this desire in terms of enjoyment.[80] In these narratives, native females are perpetually located within the bounds of phallic enjoyment in that they remain enigmatically other or inaccessible (maintaining the position of object *a*). In this process, however, where a potentially threatening feminine unknown acts to strengthen phallic desire, the qualitative way females' desires and enjoyment are experienced by male narrators or characters paradoxically threatens phallic fantasy schematics by subtly illuminating their structural coordinates—and, therefore, their tenuousness.

Corresponding to their respective narrative approaches, the more realistic *Typee* and *Omoo* (Melville claimed they were completely autobiographical) establish the ground for the more daring and fantastic presentation of feminine desire in *Mardi*. Even in the first two relatively straightforward narratives, however, Melville goes much further in depicting scenes of desire than the authors of the nonfictional accounts previously discussed.

The anxiety-ridden give-and-take between Western and native symbolic systems seen in the previous chapter's consideration of tattoos in *Typee* also exists in the presentation of Tommo's interactions with native women. After prototypically citing "Naked houris" at the novel's opening, as the first of a litany of exotic associations with the Marquesas, Melville soon presents a rather different scene involving the native female body. He recounts how French officials were mortified when the queen of Nukuheva brashly lifted her skirts to display her tattooed buttocks amid a formal ceremony intended to flaunt French colonial tutelage of the parvenu native–colonial royal couple. This brazen baring of skin, however, may not be the most troubling aspect of the scene for French colonial decorum.

Melville vividly portrays how her own exposure is predicated on her spirited and unchecked interrogation of a tattooed sailor. Upon gaining the deck, the queen:

> singled out from [the crew's] ... numbers an old *salt*, whose bare arms and feet, and exposed breast were covered with as many inscriptions of India ink as the lid of an Egyptian sarcophagus. Notwithstanding all the sly hints and remonstrances of the French officers, she immediately approached the man, and pulling further open the bosom of his duck frock, and rolling up the leg of his wide trowsers, she gazed with admiration at the bright blue and vermillion pricking.... She hung over the fellow, caressing him, and expressing her delight in a variety of wild exclamations and gestures. (8)

Although the queen's social standing clearly places her within a phallic position—providing her the fantasmatic means to "single out" a sailor's body parts with her "gaze" and the political clout to manually strip him of his clothes—her "wild exclamations and gestures" suggest that her enjoyment of this process may be somehow different from an otherwise standard male-oriented scene of desire. Put differently, while this early episode in the narrative figures the queen's excessive desire using traditional phallic signposts, it does not definitely limit it to such. This enigmatic and seemingly innocuous feminine enjoyment, however, is soon borne out in a markedly different amorous setting.

As the *Dolly* coasts into Nukuheva Bay, Melville proffers a stock erotic scene in which scores of "whihenies," or young native girls, swim toward the ship to greet the crew. Yet Melville turns this scenario on its head by focusing on his narrator's struggle to understand the behavior and experience of these girls. As the veritable tide of women moves toward the ship, the narrator "imagined" the mass to be "a shoal of fish." And as they arrive closer, he fancies them "nothing else than so many mermaids" (14). This mystical collective takes on a more pointed otherness as the ship sails "into the midst of these swimming nymphs," who "boarded ... at every quarter; many seizing hold of the chain-plates and springing into the chains; others at the bob-stays, and wreathing their slender forms about the ropes, hung suspended in the air" (14). While clearly not posing a dire threat to Melville's fantasy coordinates or schemas of knowledge, these girls are figured as lingering at the limits of such. For not only do the whihenies playfully exert a level of agency in the scene ("boarding" and "seizing"), but they also seem to exist in a different manner than the crew: their numbers combine into a strange homogeneous multitude that easily crosses the spatial borders of the ship only to disarmingly occupy it without displacement—as an otherworldly presence hanging, as it were, "suspended in the air." Such existence might be seen to short-circuit the phallic mode of desire that operates in a series, where, according to Lacan, man can only approach the other "one by one."[81]

Melville tellingly links this behavior directly to enjoyment when he recounts how the girls "hung, sparkling with savage vivacity, laughing gaily at one another, and chattering away with infinite glee" (14). It is no stretch, therefore, to read this scene in light of Lacan's point that feminine enjoyment is engendered from being not-whole. As Joan Copjec makes clear, "The woman is not-all because she lacks a limit, by which [Lacan] ... means she is not susceptible to the threat of castration." According to Copjec, the Lacanian woman marks the "failure of the limit" of the symbolic order itself.[82] Although this enigmatic gathering of girls initially only pushes the limits of Melville's notions of basic physical ontology, this shifts during the last passage into a potentially more troublesome zone of pleasure. Hanging in the air, on the ship but also not quite on the ship, the girls evince a relative hermetic bundle of enjoyment by ambiguously laughing "at each other" with "infinite glee." That is, Melville makes the cause of their merriment (and even the concept of cause itself) a mystery, and in so doing renders the qualitative nature of their "glee" a foreign and limitless "infinite" experience. This point is crucial: while the girls' enjoyment may be of the phallic variety—focused on the men and on themselves as bearers of an object a—it is not necessarily so. Thus, Melville presents these others' unfathomable foreignness as a catalyst for desire, but at the same time portrays how their strange performance of enjoyment is not necessarily bound by this same logic.

Melville immediately tempers any threat from this laughing crowd by fitting it into a phallic scenario in which the girls are a "temptation" to the "bachelor sailors," musing how the men could, if they had only wanted, "[tumble] these artless creatures overboard" (15). But he concludes the scene by returning, perhaps unintentionally, to their poignant difference in terms of the experience of bodily–sexual behavior. In describing the "wild grace" of the girls' dancing, Melville opines: "The Marquesan girls are beautiful in the extreme, but there is an abandoned voluptuousness in their character which I dare not attempt to describe" (15). The interesting break between the two clauses—with the first relating to male fantasy and the second to the potential limits of symbolic knowledge—paradoxically hinges on the meaning of "voluptuousness." Clearly, here the term refers not only to the visual register of the first clause but also to the musing in the second about the girls' own sensual gratification and delight—a form of gratification that is projected into the very "character" of the girls. In keeping with the scene's previous descriptions, Melville presents their experience of this enjoyment as being "abandoned," or beyond the pale in a rather Dionysian sense, the degree to which such elation abandons standard limits rendering it too risky for Melville to even "dare" pen it.

This form of feminine enjoyment is quickly set off against the male crew's typical phallic excess when Melville laments how "the grossest licentiousness and the most shameful inebriety prevailed" (15). In the context of symbolic concerns and the topic of enjoyment, however, such a lamentation might be seen as a palliating recourse to displacement, for the subtle discussion of how native feminine enjoyment may be different from Western symbolic social modes is immediately eclipsed by a description of male excess *within* the bounds of such modes. Here Melville describes how "not the feeblest barrier was interposed between the unholy passions of the crew and their unlimited gratification" (15). Although potentially overstepping moral bounds, these passions and gratifications are clearly grounded in traditional fantasy coordinates. Consequently, the symbolic complications that might ensue from facing the inconceivable "infinite glee" of native females is immediately and conveniently dwarfed by the "ruin" these men supposedly "inflict" upon these "unsophisticated" women in the form of "unlimited gratification" engendered by a seemingly endless variety of sexual acts (and, hence, fantasies).

Despite the narrative's vicissitudes, Tommo's interactions with the Typees tend to operate smoothly on the most foundational levels of fantasy—as seen in his painstaking, phallic itemization of and desire for "the most beauteous nymph Fayaway" (85–86) and various male natives, such as Marnoo (135–36). Yet, recalling aspects of the initial scene of contact with the ephemeral whihenies, there is a subtext of anxiety that appears especially in Tommo's early interactions with Typee women. The crisis of identity related to the tattoo (explored in the previous chapter) may be foreshadowed in Tommo's early impressions of the native feminine experience of enjoyment.

An example of this can be seen in chapter 11, when Tommo and Toby wake on their first morning in the Typee village. After recounting his apprehension about the famed "treachery" of such "savages," Tommo opens his eyes to find a number of native "eager countenances" bending over him. These countenances, of course, belong to a band of young females, "who gazed upon [him] as [he] rose with faces in which childish delight and curiosity were vividly pourtrayed" (77). Taking a more corporeal form than the nymphs on the *Dolly*, the girls are at first cast in a traditional phallic economy. This is seen when Tommo describes how they "gave full play to that prying inquisitiveness which time out of mind has been attributed to the adorable sex." But the girls' subsequent enjoyment pushes Tommo and Toby into discomfort, and then they are figured as "unsophisticated young creatures," who, according to Tommo at least, "were attended by no jealous duennas" (77). Though "duenna" refers to an adult female chaperone, one might here read it as a more general stand-in for a symbolic figure of authority. Thus, the girls' actions are not only "void of artificial restraint," as Tommo comments, but seemingly without symbolic restraint as well. And this state of being not-whole or not-all within symbolic limits is quickly shown to afford "mirth" that is "so uproarious" that Tommo feels "infinitely sheepish ... and Toby [is] immeasurably outraged at their familiarity" (77). Tommo's subsequent conclusion that his "feelings of propriety were exceedingly shocked" by the girls' "having overstepped the due limits of female decorum," should be read, therefore, primarily in the context of a breeched limit of enjoyment as such. For while the act of giving "full play to prying inquisitiveness" sits nicely with phallic notions of feminine excess, an unchecked "mirth" seems to trigger marked anxiety on the part of the men.

The potential threat posed by this type of feminine excess is depicted elsewhere in the novel in a way that might complicate the traditional phallic itemization seen across Pacific-encounter narratives. In discussing how young Typee girls commonly dance in the moonlight before their huts, Tommo highlights how their bodies and movements engender a disturbing excess. According to Tommo, the dances "all consist of active, romping, mischievous evolutions, in which every limb is brought into requisition. Indeed, the Marquesan girls dance all over, as it were; not only do their feet dance, but their arms, hands, fingers, ay, their very eyes, seem to dance in their heads" (152). Such multiple dancing parts complicate a simple fantasmatic isolation of partial objects or aspects in the other. Perhaps even more disturbing is the ambiguous agency coordinating such multiform dancing. That is, the passage suggests a scene of demonic possession, but leaves the commanding locus (the big Other) that "requisitions" the mobile anatomical parts undefined. While the possibility remains that a strange Other may catalyze such dancing—dancing that reaches into the very head and eyes, the ground of Western subjectivity—what if this Other is none other than the girls themselves? Such bizarre agency obviously disturbs Tommo: "In good sooth, they so sway their floating forms, arch their necks, toss aloft their naked arms, and glide, and swim, and whirl, that it was almost too much for a quiet, sober-minded, modest young man like myself" (152). Indeed, here the women are grammatically cast as controlling the movements, and the result is an experience that seems to overwhelm Tommo. Metaphorically tying this scene to others before it, he closes his description by saying that the women "look like a band of olive-colored Sylphides on the point of taking wing" (152). Poised on the physical limits of the world yet pushing them (the directionality of this movement itself remaining ambiguous), the women are figured as mythical Sylphides, soulless beings of the air. Despite adhering to the phallic requirement of distant inaccessibility, their indeterminate existence in relation to their own enjoyment throws off Tommo's fantasy coordinates.[83]

Like these events in *Typee*, Melville's second novel and sequel *Omoo: A Narrative of Adventures in the South Seas* (1847) presents scenes in which the narrator and his Western companions encounter troubling native feminine enjoyment. Recounting adventures on colonial Tahiti after an escape from the Typee Valley, Melville's tale acts in many ways as a standard travel narrative that fills out the adventurous journey commenced in the first book. Though structured like the first novel in terms of fantasy, *Omoo* remains even more ensconced in phallic schemas—including fewer and less-intense encounters with troubling native others. As I will discuss below, the material and political conditions of Tahiti undoubtedly shape this fact. Nonetheless, the novel includes relevant and significant scenes that should be coupled with the experiences in *Typee*.

In chapter 33 of *Omoo*, for example, local natives are shown to be greatly entertained by observing Melville and his mutinous crew members' imprisonment in the Tahitian "Calabooza Beretanee." Though identifying with the *Julia*'s crew and condemning the British consul as "Ita maitai nuee, or very bad exceedily," the natives are figured as simple onlookers who, with "the vivacity of their race," at times grow "unnecessarily excited" at the spectacle of pinioned Westerners (129). Tahitian women are described as taking special interest in the men: "gazing at [them] with eyes full of a thousand meanings, and conversing with marvelous rapidity" (129). Such mysterious qualities adhere to the depiction of women in *Typee,* allowing for troubling excess yet ultimately falling into the realm of phallic terms. But it is again their laughter that disquiets Melville.

This begins when he recounts how many of the women "laughed outright at [them], noting only what was ridiculous in [their] plight" (129). On the surface, this "ridiculous" "plight" might be relegated to racial and political irony: put simply, it is funny to see white men held in a small prison by Tahitian guards. But contextualizing the sailors' situation gives this feminine mirth a more pointed cause. Backing up a bit, the *Julia* arrives in Tahiti just as the French and their infamous Du Petit Thouars are vying to crowd out British influence. In this ambiguous space of shifting symbolic power, the local British consul, Mr. Wilson, steps in to maintain the rule of British law, which governs Melville and his crew, since they were bound to an Australian ship. This Mr. Wilson, however, is shown to be both a partial arbiter (siding with his friend Captain Guy) and a capricious ruler (in Melville's eyes, holding grudges against the men). Thus, with the lowly Wilson in charge of an island being enveloped by the French, the symbolic power of the central agents on Tahiti is extremely tenuous.

In returning to the laughing women, one might use this symbolic context to suggest that while they find pinioned whites ridiculous *stricto sensu,* these particular pinioned whites are ridiculous *for submitting* to the local authorities, representatives of a faltering or absent sociosymbolic big Other. Melville gestures to this possibility in his comical account of the prison's lack of command: it constituted "a mere shell" that was "still unfinished" and that used "clumsy" "out of date" stocks to restrain prisoners (116). In fact, Melville goes as far as to hint that the primary reason the men did not rebel and escape—especially while out bathing—was their fondness for the jovial Tahitian overseer "Capin Bob" and the potential shame they would feel in attempting such an easy feat (118). In these terms, it becomes more than plausible that the native women are laughing not at the sailors' incarceration but at their self-incarceration—at their phallic need for a relation to castration via the symbolic, as such. Even if the men know that the local authorities are lacking in both legal and physical means, unlike the women in the scene, they definitively act as if this is not the case. In short, the native women's mirth may here be an ironic comment on the men's symbolic limitations and, therefore, the limitations of their fantasies, themselves.

Melville quickly raises the stakes of this mirth, having "a wild, beautiful girl burst into the Calabooza, and, throwing herself into an arch attitude, [stand] afar off, and [gaze] at [them]" (129). Taking a clear phallic posture, this "mischievous young witch" glances "from one to another, in the most methodical and provoking manner possible" (130). With the men physically and legally restrained, the woman is able to give full vent to what appears to be phallic enjoyment. Even on this rather safe plane, the traditional gender reversal is unnerving to Melville, who anxiously plays the part of object *a*, trying to discern and embody what she might want: "Ere her glance fell upon me, I had, unconsciously, thrown myself into the most graceful attitude I could assume, leaned my head upon my hand, and summoned up as abstracted an expression as possible" (130). Though he is at first thrilled that she does not mock him as she does the others, he soon blushes (affecting a traditional maidenly response) at her reaction: "There she was; her great hazel eyes rounding and rounding in her head, like two stars, her whole frame in a merry quiver, and an expression about the mouth that was sudden and violent death to any thing like sentiment" (130). Unlike her "heartless" laugh at the other prisoners, here her hilarity morphs into a more disturbingly silent enjoyment.

This scene—similar to one in chapter 71 in which the mysterious laughter of "three mischievous, dark-eyed young witches" miffs Melville (268)— depicts an encounter with a form of feminine enjoyment that not only unsettles the narrator but retroactively illuminates the fantasy structures he employs. Nonetheless, this phallic structure remains the unscathed model of the narrative at large. From exhilarating images of frolicking mermaids (64) to the "beautiful and unsophisticated women" of the village of Tamai (234), *Omoo* resounds with phallic fantasies. The political condition of Tahiti itself, however, is shown to play a role in this, with Melville arriving at the island as French cannons herald its "forced session" (69) and stepping ashore with a trove of sensational tales in his head of earlier explorers' exotic adventures (66).

Indeed, Tahiti of the 1840s is figured as a historical quilting point for both imperial control (economic and ideological) and exotic fantasies. Whereas this "classic" isle is already shaped by Western society, the Marquesas, in contrast, are portrayed as maintaining a relative ability to fend off complete colonial influence. In *Typee,* therefore, Melville is shown to have to work a bit more to establish and live out, as it were, his fantasy structures within the social reality of native life. This can be seen in an interesting exchange in chapter 18. Having convinced some local men to carry a canoe from the sea for recreation on the inland lake, Tommo is disappointed to find that the native women are forced to stop bathing there owing to a taboo prohibiting them from the waters where canoes are in use. Missing the "mermaids" and desiring to "test" the strictures of the taboo system, he applies to Chief Mehevi for permission to take Fayaway on the canoe. The fact that Tommo is granted an abeyance of the law is less relevant than how he uses this canoe space. From the beginning, he frames the situation in terms of bringing masculine courtly decorum to the island, saying that "it was high time the islanders should be taught a little gallantry" and commenting that it was "ridiculous . . . that the lovely creatures should be obligated to paddle about in the water, like so many ducks, while a parcel of great strapping fellows skimmed over its surface in the canoes" (133).

And what does Tommo do with this gallant new opportunity? He puts Fayaway in the stern of the canoe, of course, reclining with her in this space and fawning over her "delicately formed hand" or the way she has of "placing her pipe to her lip," as his trusty "valet" Kory-Kory paddles the lovers around (133). Unlike the overwhelming experience of swimming amid a school of native girls, the canoe seems to provide Tommo with the necessary fantasy coordinates to desire Fayaway in an even more effective manner. This is underscored by the way Tommo emphasizes particularizations of Fayaway's body and behavior while in the craft. Furthermore, the scene culminates with Tommo adorning her calico dress, which makes her look "something like an opera dancer" (134). Ultimately, with the structure of the boat and the trappings of Western dress, Tommo is able to move a great distance from the disorienting scene earlier in the chapter; he ends his discussion of their escapades by fittingly noting that the dress reveals a conspicuously small portion of Fayaway's leg: "The most bewitching ankle in the universe" (135).

In moving to Melville's third Pacific novel, *Mardi* (1849), we move from bewitching to outright witching. Although the figure of Hautia reigns supreme in this shift, the change in the degree of feminine disruptive agency is also inseparably linked to the ineffectual structures of male desire itself. Similar to the way that the imaginative elements in Melville's two early novels reveal subterranean fantasy elements within previous nonfictional Pacific narratives, we might view *Mardi's* more pronounced fictional mode as allowing it to further illuminate the fantasmatic structures seen in the more realistic *Typee* and *Omoo*. Of course, *Mardi's* tenuous popular and critical status as a wacky metaphysical romance is well documented. The book's uneven and bulky nature has turned many critics away, and those who have ventured in often revert to simple readings, tracing how its components are sophomoric literary examples of how Melville is beginning to "feel his hand" en route to the mastery demonstrated in *Moby-Dick.* While such romantic historiography is inconsequential, Melville's own conception of the project as a romance is not. For example, in a letter of March 25, 1848, to John Murray, Melville states his plans for *Mardi*: "To be blunt: the work I shall next publish will in downright earnest [be] a 'Romance of Polynisian Adventure'—But why this? The truth, Sir, that the reiterated imputation of being a romancer in disguise has at last pricked me into a resolution to show ... that a *real* romance of mine is no Typee or Omoo, & is made of different stuff altogether."[84] As mentioned, this "real" romance includes more pronounced fictional components—including the presentation and negotiation of fantasy scenes surrounding Polynesian women. Melville more generally signals as much later in the same letter, writing: "I have long thought Polynesia furnished a great deal of rich poetical material that has never been employed hitherto in works of fancy."

In its day, the fanciful *Mardi* confounded readers—as seen in a London *Literary Gazette* reviewer's quip that the novel "has struck our head like one of those blows which set everything glancing and dancing before our eyes like splintered sunrays."[85] Here, I am interested in how the novel may in some ways confound its own foundational fantasies. Paradoxically, one of the main reasons it may do this is the relative simplicity of the narrative. Although the plot is a sprawling multilayered affair, it is driven by a totalizing phallic quest for the lost native woman, Yillah. And as we will see, this simple quest births a web of relations that sketch the contours of the most radical form of feminine enjoyment yet seen in antebellum Pacific narratives.

The novel's adventure is in part catalyzed by the sailor–narrator's daydreams of the distant Kingsmill Islands and the "voices of maidens" as he sails along the Pacific line aboard the monotonous, boring *Arcturion*.[86] The first native woman he meets, however, is less than idyllic. After jumping ship with his Norseman "chum" Jarl and venturing out in an open whaleboat, the narrator comes across an abandoned, drifting brigantine. Upon it they find the one-armed Samoa and his wife, Annatoo, who had managed to resist the mutinous efforts of a band of "half-breed" Cholos and to steer the vessel, the *Parki*, to sea after the captain and the whites on board were murdered. From the start, Annatoo is shown to embody traditional masculine traits—having, for example, skillfully worked the rigging aloft in order to hasten the ship to sea during the Cholos' attack (71). Soon after, the narrator describes her "costuming" herself in the captain's extensive wardrobe, "bedecking herself like a tragedy queen: one blaze of brass. Much mourned the married dame, that thus arrayed, there was none to admire but Samoa her husband; but he was all the while admiring himself, and not her" (75). Like a Lady Macbeth or Queen Gertrude, then, Annatoo wields power within a phallic economy where her symbolic position and possessions warrant (if not elicit) the desire of others.

But Annatoo is shown to be excessive within the bounds of this system. After cutting off her husband's damaged arm for him with three strokes of an axe (castration writ large), she is depicted as jealously coveting stores of beads (83), destroying nautical tools in an attempt at "scientific inspection" (93), and fancying herself the captain (110). At first, Melville's protagonist recognizes the use value of Annatoo's aggression. Nevertheless, he deems it "indispensable that she should at once be brought under prudent subjugation; and made to know, once and for all, that though conjugally a rebel, she must be nautically submissive" (90–91). This "tigress's" rebellion primarily takes the form of removing all manner of objects from the brig and collecting them in her separate private quarters—from sails and hatchets (80) to "the screw bolts that held together the planks" (92). And when the narrator confronts her with the fact that "neither the vessel nor aught therein was hers," she "went off in a fit of the sulks" sitting down "swaying from side to side" and giving "utterance to a dismal chant" that "sounded like an invocation to the Cholos to rise and dispatch [them]" (92).

Yet, Annatoo's power is shown to be curtailed from the start, with the narrator commenting that the ship's hull would hold her if need be (92) and comically contemplating with Jarl whether she should be "sacked and committed to the deep" (115). Most significant, however, is the sudden and inconsequential manner of her death—when a storm causes one of the lanyard's blocks to strike Annatoo in the forehead, knocking her into a whirlpool. Fittingly, Melville describes the men's response in three short clauses: "Samoa shrieked. But there was no time to mourn; no hand could reach to save" (117). Not a word more about the troublesome woman who, it seems, is both easily dispatched and easily forgotten.

The next two native women that emerge, however, redirect and complicate the narrative in intricately related ways: the first as an ideal lost object that highlights the narrative's fantasy structures and the second as a mocking witness to a type of enjoyment and knowledge that exceeds Melville's sailor. This begins when the three men encounter a large native double canoe with a concealed, tented area in its center. Upon talking to the natives and their priest, Aleema, they learn that the enclosed region is restricted from outsiders. Referring to how the space contained, for him, "Eleusinian mysteries," the narrator explains how this information "roused [his] curiosity to unravel and wonder" (131). Upon pressing the natives, they learn that a "beautiful maiden" is housed inside the tent and that she is being transported to be sacrificed. Such a scene needs little explication: the veiled tent creates an enticing mystery that is animated when an exotic damsel in distress rises up to fill this enigmatic space.

The mystery does not last long. Bent on rescuing and revealing the maiden, the narrator kills the priest with a cutlass. Though he gains access to the tent ("the interior was revealed to [his] gaze") and possession—albeit temporary—of the fair Yillah, he is haunted by remorse over his actions, asking himself, for reassurance: "Am I not rescuing the maiden?" (135). Though his guilt remains, the narrator soon completes his conquest, inserting himself into the priest's mythic narrative about Yillah's origins by adopting the identity of the god "white Taji." Here, Melville not only dramatizes a scene that metaphorically presents the function of fantasy but also takes it to the next level—revealing how fantasy often structures cultural encounters: with the West penetrating natives' physical and symbolic space in an attempt to control it.

But Yillah's role in the narrative goes much further than this. Even after being pulled from the interior of the tent, she maintains an enigmatic lure owing to the mystery of her European appearance: "Did I dream?—A snow-white skin: blue, firmament eyes. Golconda locks.... I could not link this mysterious creature with the tawny strangers. She seemed of another race. So powerful was this impression, that unconsciously, I addressed her in my own tongue" (136–37). In this economy of desire, her white skin seemingly functions as a second veiling, of sorts: a type of mask that props up the mystery of her origins, allowing her to function as object a.[87] This mystery remains intact even when Taji later learns from Aleema's sons that Yillah is, indeed, white—having come in "a mighty canoe, full of beings, white, like ... Taji" (307)—because the questions of where she is and what she desires remain unanswered. In short, Yillah is from the beginning an ideal feminine semblance. And because of this Taji's fascination with her white skin should not be read as merely replicating Western travelers' partiality for Caucasian-like native traits. Rather, Yillah's whiteness provides a convenient means to project a safe imaginary feminine imago onto her—where this mask at once effects a mysterious past *and* locates a controlled site of feminine otherness in a cultural other.

Yillah's position and function, however, are anything but completely safe for Taji. Though Taji attempts to break Aleema's fantasmatic hold on Yillah by inserting himself into the narrative of her so-called island home, Oroola, even (or especially) in death the priest is shown to act as a stubborn and active ego–ideal for Yillah. As briefly discussed in chapter 2, for Lacan, the process of identification is carried out in a dialectic between the functions of the ideal ego, the projected image of how one sees oneself (and others), and the ego-ideal, the introjected symbolic coordinates of language and law that reshape and reconstitute the ideal ego.[88] When Lacan writes that "it's one's own ego that one loves in love," he refers to the way that love "reopens the door" to imaginary identifications by provoking "a veritable subduction of the symbolic, a sort of annihilation, of perturbation of the function of the ego-ideal."[89] In other words, through loving another (or some thing in another) one is experiencing the alteration of both one's ego-ideal and one's ideal ego. In Lorenzo Chiesa's terms: "Every new love will correspond perfectly to the intervention—at the imaginary level—of a new ego-ideal."[90]

We see such notions at work in the interactions between Taji and Yillah. Despite his efforts to bring Yillah toward him, Taji laments that "so etherealized had she become from the wild conceits she nourished, that she verily believed herself a being of the land of dreams" (159). Aleema's role in shaping Yillah's ego-ideal is apparent in the way his figure is woven into her imaginary self-conception:

> And now, at intervals, she was sad, and often gazed long and fixedly in to the sea. Nor would she say why it was, that she did so; until at length she yielded; and replied, that whatever false things Aleema might have instilled into her mind; of this much she was certain: that the whirlpool on the coast of Tedaidee prefigured her fate; that in the waters she saw lustrous eyes, and beckoning phantoms, and strange shapes smoothing her a couch among the mosses. (159)

This mirror scene, one repeated in chapter 62 when Yillah "[gazes] intently into the lagoon" (189), clearly delineates aspects of her identity's foundational fantasy. Looking at her own image in the sea, she presumably sees the "lustrous" eyes of Aleema—and admits that his narrative of her "fate" remains the symbolic frame that conditions her views.

In failing to dislodge Yillah's ego-ideal, therefore, Taji fails to definitively harness her desire (after gazing into his eyes, for instance, Yillah signals that Taji is "dwarfing down to a mortal" [159]). Paradoxically, this distance between them, this mystery of her true desire, acts as a catalyst for Taji's own fantasy space. In spinning myths that he, too, heralds from the isle of Oroola, Taji begins to form and introject an interesting identification with Yillah. For example, Taji claims that, in his dreams, "her own lineaments had smiled upon [him]; and hence the impulse which had sent [him] roving after the substance of this spiritual image" (158). The trappings of love in a Lacanian sense clearly abound here, as well as in Taji's subsequent claim that Yillah was the "earthly substance of that sweet vision . . . that haunted [his] earliest thoughts" (158). This complex web of identifications culminates with Taji seeming to adopt Yillah's own foreboding narcissistic fantasies: "Her dreams seemed mine. Many visions I had of the green corse of the priest, outstretching its arms in the water, to receive pale Yillah, as she sunk in the sea" (159).

Prophetic visions, it turns out, for after a brief idyllic repose together on the islet of Odo, one morning Yillah mysteriously disappears. After the initial shock of her sudden absence, Taji recounts how "for a time [he] raved. Then, falling into outer repose, lived for a space in moods and reveries, with eyes that knew no closing, one glance forever fixed" (194). Taji refers to this time as "bereavement," but his actions signal otherwise. Although the fact that he is not initially "roused" by dancing girls adheres to normal bounds of mourning, this state of being "fixed" on Yillah is soon shown to be symptomatic of his general constitution. Thus, he resolves that he "must hie from Odo, and rove through-out Mardi; for Yillah might be found." The initial tension within his terminology—figuring a search for a missing person in terms of a more general "roving" or wandering—is grounded a bit with the chapter's closing line: "But hereafter, in words, little more of the maiden, till perchance her fate be learned" (195). The paradox is that this permanent loss occurs less than a third of the way through the novel—a novel whose manifest content for the next five hundred pages is this wandering and inept search.

The movement of the search, and therefore of the narrative itself, is constituted in relation to a certain notion of inevitable failure. In other words, the prominent and, one might say, obsessive focus on the earthly failure of his relation to Yillah before her disappearance should be read not as merely a love-sick paramour's renarration of the past, but rather as an essential element of the narrative's fantasy structure in toto.

As mentioned, the foreshadowing of this loss often links Yillah's gradual despondency and distance to a paradoxical augmentation of Taji's desire: "Day by day, did her spell weave round me its magic, and all the hidden things of her being grew more lovely and strange. Did I commune with a spirit?" (193). In this way, we might correlate Taji's desire for Yillah with the function of melancholia. Unlike mourning's process of "testing reality" while withdrawing libido from attachments to a lost love object, melancholy, for Freud, involves a complex response to a more mysterious loss. In fact, as Freud makes clear, in melancholy "the object has not perhaps actually died, but has become lost as an object of love."[91] Accordingly, we might read Freud's point that melancholia "is in some way related to an unconscious loss of a love-object" through Žižek's assertion that in such a condition, loss is not an actual loss of an object but the loss of our (unconscious) desire for it.[92]

This is not to suggest that Taji experiences such a melancholic loss of desire, but that the fantasy that structures his desire seems to negotiate a homologous terrain. As Giorgio Agamben explains, "Melancholia offers the paradox of an intention to mourn that precedes and anticipates the loss of the object." This is achieved via "the imaginative capacity to make an unobtainable object appear as if lost," thus allowing melancholy to "[open] a space for the existence of the unreal."[93]

Taji appears to build a fantasy of Yillah that from the beginning incorporates her bodily loss into its fabric. As a result, a form of melancholia seems to structure the mise-en-scène of his fantasy space. One can account for this in part through the way he adopts her identification with Aleema's perspective, but it might also be seen as a radically transparent rendition of the way his narrative's foundational fantasy is structured. As is quite familiar by now, the object *a* emerges as it is lost, where fantasy, in Žižek's terms, "occludes this paradox by describing the process in which the object is first given and then gets lost."[94] In crafting the narrative in this manner, therefore, Melville draws attention to the function of its primary fantasy and, more than that, puts pressure on it by making it the sole motor-force of the plot.

As if this were not enough, Melville precedes the chapter in which Yillah vanishes with a sketch of the way the island of Odo's tranquil appearance masks a corrupt underworld of slave labor. While King Media and the upper classes—including Taji and Yillah—dwell in a garden-strewn bower of a city, Melville describes how "in [Odo's] inmost haunts, dark groves were brooding" where "serfs, . . . Helots, [and] war-captives held in bondage . . . lived in secret places" (191). One need not push too hard to align this horrific underworld beneath the alluring facade of the isle's surface with Taji's anxiety about the (fantasmatically necessary) mysteries behind Yillah. In other words, like Odo, her secret world might be threatening in some qualitatively unpleasant way, or, *per negativum*, potentially threatening in its quantitative nonexistence (where perhaps there is no secret at all). This latter notion is recalled by the way Taji imagines a terrifying zone that lacks desire, where in the "inmost haunts" of the isle, "infants [turn] from breasts" (191).

What does Taji really want, then? The easy answer, it seems, is desire itself. But of more importance is the specific way this commonplace psychoanalytic truism plays out in relation to Yillah and the narrative at large. It is quite clear that with Yillah's disappearance her previous role reaches its logical end: materially enacting the very distance that has been firing Taji's desire since their first meeting. While the degree of transparency surrounding these psychological issues clearly complicates the narrative— illuminating the requisite impossibility that undergirds Taji's fantasies—an even more disruptive element is revealed in the mix: Yillah's desire. The unbearable questions surrounding this concept (Why did she leave? Where did she go?) seem to haunt Taji, driving him forward in his desperate quest. And it is at this precise impasse that Queen Hautia enters the narrative, acting as a supplemental fantasmatic screen for and obstacle to the lost Yillah. Moreover, in this process, which constitutes perhaps the most radical turn of the narrative, Hautia reveals elements of feminine desire and enjoyment that unmistakably threaten Taji's symbolic coordinates.

Exit Yillah. Enter Hautia. The two are linked on the very morning of Yillah's disappearance, when right away "there chanced to arrive" a band of messengers from abroad bearing Queen Hautia's renewed invitations to "visit various pleasant places" (194). This conspicuously timed return evokes her initial innocuous visit to Odo three chapters before Yillah's departure. In fact, the earlier chapter, titled "An Incognito," should be seen as extremely telling in light of later events in the novel. In a retroactive way, we might see this two-page entrance of Hautia as subtly establishing the contours of her subsequent role in the narrative. First, of course, is her absent presence as the mysterious incognito dressed in a dark "close-plaited robe" exposing only a "solitary eye" (186). This stranger's gaze upon Yillah and Taji unnerves Taji, who refers to the gazing "fathomless eye" as a foreign "world." Though at the time this staring incognito remains unknown, we learn much later, in chapter 192, that the figure is none other than Hautia. Thus, her entrance in the narrative is a form of interference, a symbolic wound or problem that takes the explicit form of a gaze. The yet unnamed and unknown Hautia here clearly operates in a phallic mode; besides having the agency of desiring and particularizing sight, this incognito is shown to be "sacred"—with the symbolic authority inscribed in the dark robes preventing Taji or King Media from forcing the incognito to identify him or herself (187). This has two implications we will return to in light of the end of the novel: first, Hautia operates in a position of power within a phallic economy, threatening Taji from the outside as a competing desiring subject; second, on a different plane, she acts as a bizarre and disruptive object in Taji's own experience, complicating his fantasy scenario from the inside. Although he tries, Taji is unable to fit Hautia into his fantasy space, and this scenario is prefigured here in a dramatic enactment of the Lacanian gaze. Unlike Robarts's ability to function as a distant imperial eye, smoothly surveying the bodies of native women, Melville's sailor is placed in a scene with an unknown native woman who manifests as a single surveying eye. Here, the way this enigmatic object literally looks back at Taji forces him to address how this eye/object, again borrowing McGowan's terms, "is not a positive entity but a lacuna in the visual field."[95] This experience is apparent in the way Taji anxiously depicts the eye as "incorporeal," as an object that so disturbs his conceptual apparatus that it "seemed no eye, but a spirit, forever prying into [his] soul" (186).[96]

In addition to these potential complications, this early chapter also prefigures another more ambiguous way Hautia complicates Taji's scene-of-fantasy. In accepting a series of exotic flowers from Hautia's representatives, "three black-eyed damsels" (evoking the three "dark-eyed young witches" in *Omoo*), Taji flippantly tells them: "This is too sweet; thanks to Hautia for her flowers. Pray, bring me more." The women promptly reply that he "mocks... [their] mistress" and depart by "gliding" away, leaving Taji "alone and wondering" (187). We might ask: Mocks how, exactly? Indeed, this seems to be the question Taji is left asking at the chapter's close. In a Lacanian sense, Taji's playful demand for "more" mirrors the very title of Lacan's seminar on feminine sexuality: *Encore* ("more"). Lacan uses this term to signify, in his words, "the proper name of the gap *(faille)* in the Other from which the demand for love stems."[97] In keeping with the discussion of phallic enjoyment, this call for more relates to the necessary cry, "That's not it," "by which the jouissance obtained is distinguished from the jouissance expected."[98] As one may recall, for Lacan, object *a* is a mere stand-in for the void in the Other, a stand-in that must ultimately fail to satisfy this role. In other words, "That's not it" is a frustrated call for a proper "object that could satisfy jouissance."[99] In *Mardi*, this scene may present a shadow of Hautia's enigmatic power: an ability to operate in the mode of phallic enjoyment (gazing at Taji and Yillah and beckoning to them) and, at the same time, the ability to resist the requisite economic need for "more" that sustains this very system of desire. The damsels' conviction that in requesting more flowers Taji is mocking Hautia may, in this context, have less to do with his possible insinuation that Hautia is not "it" or enough, and, as the close of the novel portrays, more to do with their own possible misreading of the supposed god Taji's abilities. They may suppose that he, too, has a qualitatively different relation to desire than that of the typical phallic orientation, which, in turn, would cast his request for "more" as an obstinate and ironic one. It is precisely the tension-wrought play between these modes—Taji's phallic enjoyment and what I'll refer to loosely as Hautia's feminine enjoyment—that structures the end of the novel.

The final movements of the novel begin in chapter 189, when Babbalanja (Melville's Mardian historian–philosopher) proclaims his journey to be over and implores Taji to likewise end his quest: "Yillah thou wilt hunt in vain; she is a phantom that but mocks thee" (637). Babbalanja goes on: "Taji! be sure thy Yillah never will be found; or found will not avail thee" (638). Astutely reading the true contours of Taji's desire, Babbalanja thus observes that Yillah functions in Taji's imagination as an ideal lost object that can never be found; for even if she is somehow located, her earthly existence would no longer fit with her figuration in Taji's fantasy. Forced to confront this, Taji clings even more fiercely to his fantasy, exclaiming: "She I seek, still flies before; and I will follow, though she lead me beyond the reef; . . . and into night and death. Her, will I seek, through all the isles and the stars; and find her, whate'er betide!" (638). Uttering such grand ambitions and acknowledging their dubious potential, however, brings Taji dangerously close to the limits of his fantasy; though holding to his designs, he closes the chapter with thoughts of blasphemy and the ominous imagery of laughing hyenas.

This potential crisis in fantasy—communicated in metaphysical terms—is immediately answered with the arrival of Hautia's "phantoms," figured first as an "Iris flag" moving in from the darkness of a starless night (640). The short scene sharply delineates two aspects of Hautia's function in these final pages: her role as a fantasy supplement relating to Yillah, and her ability to operate in a strangely different mode of enjoyment. Indeed, out of the nihilistic darkness of Taji's precarious fantasy space, where he flirts with accepting the futility of his quest, comes an iris flag that we might read as a metaphor for a fantasmatic screen with which to sustain his desire. This notion is demonstrated when Hautia's "sirens" bear her suggestion that "through [her], perhaps, [Taji's] Yillah may be found" (640). This explicit offer of fantasy—of proffering herself as object *a*, as a veritable semblance for and means to Yillah—is coupled with an element of danger for Taji. Initially answering in the negative, Taji responds: "Tempt me not by that, enchantress! Hautia! I know thee not; I fear thee not; but instinct makes me hate thee" (640). Here Hautia should be seen not merely as an unknown subject, but as an unknown system—one that "instinctually" repulses Taji. Yet when he realizes this may be his "last hope of Yillah," Taji assents to follow the sirens—even if their "lure be death" (641). This mix of themes is developed in the melodramatic finale staged on Hautia's island, Flozella.

Before the travelers land on the island, Taji's reflections work toward clarifying the complex relation between Hautia and Yillah. His musings are rich and confused:

> But how connected were Hautia and Yillah? Something I hoped; yet more I feared. Dire presentments, like poised arrows, shot through me. Had they pierced me before, straight for Flozella would I have voyaged; not waiting for Hautia to woo me by that last victorious temptation. But unchanged remained my feelings of hatred for Hautia; yet, vague those feelings, as the language of her flowers. Nevertheless, in some mysterious way seemed Hautia and Yillah connected. But Yillah was all beauty, and innocence; . . . —and Hautia, my whole heart abhorred. Yillah I sought; Hautia sought me. One, openly beckoned me here; the other dimly allured me there. Yet now was I wildly dreaming to find them together. (643)

It is apparent that Yillah remains the ultimate object *a* for Taji—continuing to "allure" him from a distant "there." At the same time, Hautia "beckons" him from the immediate "here." While Hautia is thus in possession of the phallus (as it is she who "sought him"), she is also oddly fused with Yillah in the role of being the phallus. It seems this mix is what engenders anxiety in Taji. But it is important to note that this anxiety is coupled with invigorated "wild dreams" of desire. This scenario, therefore, begins to illustrate just how Hautia functions in terms of Taji's fantasy space. With her claims of knowledge about Yillah, Hautia acts as a spectral transmogrification of Yillah's desire—as a phantom surface over or before ("here") the abyss of Yillah's desire ("there") that still allures Taji. More specifically, Hautia might be seen to play the part of a requisite obstacle to Yillah, as a problem that acts, paradoxically, as a temporary fantasmatic solution to the more traumatic void left by Yillah's absence.

But the equation is imbalanced. After bantering with the resplendent queen, Taji carries this scenario to its end, explicitly desiring her and her "radiance." Yet, when he begins explicitly to place her in this fantasmatic role, she resists by mysteriously breaking into "a thousand constellations" and then disappearing from sight altogether (647). Within the narrative's terms, this resistance might merely stem from Hautia's enigmatic magical prowess, but in looking more closely at the dynamics of the scene's interactions, we see that such supernatural evasiveness may be a metaphoric enactment of a difference in the characters' relations to enjoyment itself.

Just prior to this episode, Taji recognizes Hautia as the incognito who appeared on Odo. Observing the queen's "fathomless" eye, he reflects: "But the same mysterious, evil-boding gaze was there, which long before had haunted me in Odo, ere Yillah fled.—Queen Hautia the incognito! Then the two wild currents met, and dashed me into foam" (646). The exact constitution of these "two wild currents" remains ambiguous: is it a combination of Hautia's attractive radiance and repulsive gaze, or of Yillah and Hautia proper? The action, however, soon illuminates that the foundational conflict at stake is the discord between Taji's and Hautia's schematics of desire, the tension in the final pages deriving from their failed attempts to bridge the gap between them.

Such difference is abruptly established with Taji's blunt command: "Yillah! Yillah!—tell me, queen!" (646). This, of course, is the same command cited in this chapter's epigraph—one Taji repeats in different forms at least three times. And it is Hautia's initial response that most aptly signals her role. After the first demand, Hautia "stood motionless; radiant and scentless: a dahlia on its stalk." When Taji pushes her to answer, she responds: "To all questions, Taji! I am mute.—Away!—damsels dance; reel round him; round and round!" (646).

This silence is loaded. A silence that can clearly be connected to a Lacanian notion of feminine jouissance. As noted, this type of enjoyment is an enigmatically supplemental one, but not in the simple sense of an exceptional portion of the phallic variety. As Alenka Zupančič explains: "Infinite [or, feminine] *jouissance* is not a *jouissance* so great or intense that words fail to express it. To use Jean-Claude Milner's logic, 'the infinite is that which says no to the exception to the finite.' 'Infinite' refers to the structure or topology of enjoyment and not to its quality (or quantity). Infinite *jouissance* is that which puts an end to 'exceptional enjoyment' in all meanings of the words."[100] Resonating with Copjec's claim that feminine enjoyment is that which is not susceptible to the "lure of transcendence," according to Zupančič, such a mode is impossible from within the phallic schematic—for it does not require the exception in the same way.

With regard to Hautia, we might read her silence as a mode of enjoyment that does not signify anything.[101] Put differently, it is not that she is keeping a piquant secret, but she is operating in relation to the lack (specifically of Yillah, but also in terms of the symbolic order in toto) in a way that language and phallic enjoyment cannot conceive. To borrow again from Zupančič, "the other [feminine] *jouissance* is the undetermined silence in which proceeds, in the finite, the articulation of the phallic *jouissance*."[102] This exact scenario can be seen at play in the novel, with Hautia's silence operating as the terrain on which Taji's desire is defined and articulated—even heightened.

Yet the scene is even more complex than this, as it appears that Hautia is attempting to interact with Taji from the perspective of her realm of enjoyment, believing, perhaps, that he shares her orientation. This becomes apparent when she initially answers his request for information about Yillah by in turn asking: "Is not thy voyage now ended?—take flowers! Damsels, give him wine to drink. After his weary hunt, be the wanderer happy" (646). Yet, happy how? In Taji's phallic mode, happiness clearly springs from the hunter's pursuit of the exception. Thus, Hautia implies that Taji may or should be able to "end" this quest and be "happy" in a different way altogether. It must be reiterated that Hautia operates in the phallic mode, pursuing Taji in an attempt to get him to "supplant [his] mourner's nightshade... with marriage roses" (646). But her experience of this mode is shown to be qualitatively different than Taji's. For she garners enjoyment not only from pursuing Taji but from capturing him—as figured in her playful claim: "Taji!—as a berry, that name is juicy in my mouth" (650). This consumption, however, is not totalizing. Instead of a monstrous siren or vampire, Hautia—again—seeks to bring Taji into her own system. The clear divide between the two can be seen in the exchange in which Taji implores: "Bring me that which I seek, and I will dive with thee, straight through the world, till we come up in oceans unknown." In clear contrast to this über-phallic proposition, Hautia retorts: "Nay, nay; but join hands, and I will take thee ... where Past shall be forgotten; where thou wilt soon learn to love the living, not the dead" (650).

Such a transition proves impossible. Dramatizing the ultimate impasse between the two, Melville moves the stakes toward death. Unable to conceive of Hautia's offer, a thwarted Taji threatens: "Oh vipress, I could slay thee!" (653). Pushed to this extreme, Hautia is forced to abandon her own quest and resigns: "Go, go,—and slay thyself: I may not make thee mine;—go,—dead to dead!—There is another cavern in the hill" (653). "Dead" here clearly takes on a fantasmatic resonance. That is, Hautia's mode does not require the dead, or the nonsubstantial object *a*, for desire to operate, while in Taji's system death (as transcendence) marks the sine qua non of fantasy and phallic enjoyment. When Taji rushes to the mysterious cavern and sees a deathly "white" figure that is "vaguely Yillah," he is, in turn, himself transformed into a "ghost," a "phantom's phantom" (653).

It is in this way that we might read the despairing end of the novel: as a radical enactment of the inner limit of fantasy. With all other wanderers returning to land, Taji, alone, "[seizes] the helm" with "eternity ... in his eye" and makes for the open sea, refusing to relinquish his quest for the lost Yillah. Fantasy, it seems, has given ground to drive—or at least closes with it. In this futile continuation of pursuit, we see hints of the impossible end or inside of fantasy: the death drive, the enjoyment of circular movements around the traumatic void itself. So, Taji hails the "realm of shades," and Melville ends the novel with the line: "And thus, pursuers and pursued flew on, over an endless sea" (654).

From this perspective, antebellum conceptions of the exotic Pacific and the figure of the native woman are perhaps more complex than contemporary approaches to the topic allow. In modifying our critical view of this scene of experience by considering sights of desire (in an imaginary/fantasmatic sense) along with the common frame of "sites of desire," we can more fully understand how Melville's work illuminates formative maritime fantasies of this era. In addition to imperative historical analyses of real colonial violence against—and resistance by—native women, as well as tangible ways native cultures' sexual practices and sailors' homoerotic and homosexual behavior complicated mainland coordinates, we might also attend to the way such extreme experiences test the internal bounds of Western structures of enjoyment.

· III ·

Ocean-States of Exception

· CHAPTER 5 ·

The *Crater* and the Master's Reign: Cooper's "Floating *Imperium*"

> *Force of law that is separate from the law, floating imperium, being-in-force [vigenza] without application, and, more generally, the idea of a sort of "degree zero" of the law—all these are fictions through which law attempts to encompass its own absence and to appropriate the state of exception.*
>
> —Giorgio Agamben, State of Exception

IN THIS AGE OF GUANTANAMO, inconsistencies within the American judicial-political landscape haunt the notion of democracy. Building on the work of Carl Schmitt, Giorgio Agamben avers that such contemporary juridical paradoxes correspond to the way that political power more generally instantiates and maintains itself via a "state of exception."[1] On the most basic level, this state marks "the original structure in which law encompasses living beings by means of its own suspension."[2] That is, it mirrors the way a sovereign exists in an ambiguous realm at once in and beyond positive law—being able to suspend the law in order to define it as such. As seen in the epigraph above, the traditional distinction between force of law and pure ideations of law mask the modus operandi of all legal functioning: a conceptually ambiguous state of exception where, in Agamben's terms, both anomie and *nomos* are linked in a "threshold of undecidability."[3]

According to Agamben, through a "voluntary creation of a permanent state of emergency," this state of exception has become the dominant paradigm of twentieth-century totalitarian and democratic governments alike.[4] And this loose teleological schematic is precisely where this chapter's antebellum concerns link to contemporary events. Though Agamben notes unequivocally the "enormous differences" as well as the "rivalry" between historical democratic and totalitarian systems, he suggests that the "unforeseen convergences" of these sociopolitical structures in the twentieth and twenty-first centuries warrants further assessment of their previous relations.[5] Thus, just because one cannot easily make definitive historiographical claims about a consistent similarity between them does not mean one cannot forward "historico-philosophical" claims about a possible "inner solidarity" of their operative structures.[6] In other words, the ambiguous modern synthesis between the two systems reveals shared elements that seem to extend into their respective pasts.

I would like to suggest that the antebellum era exists in an anxious realm that also, at times, reveals the homology between such social organizations: where the ideological structures at the onset of the modern capitalist world struggle to conceptually map contradictions related to liberal-democratic practices. Agamben's focus on historical juridical transitions and formations can be broadly situated within a previously discussed Marxist teleology that views the sixteenth- and seventeenth-century origins of capitalism as consolidating during the early nineteenth century. Casarino's oft-mentioned notion of the "crisis of modernity," therefore, might be broadened to encompass the tension-wrought developments within antebellum democratic institutions and their legal-ontological, or biopolitical, relation to subjects.

My final two chapters examine how antebellum maritime narratives illuminate fantasies that respond to the tumultuous transitions into the modern age of capitalism that Agamben interrogates. Placing Cooper and Melville even closer on the same stage, this chapter and the subsequent one act in concert to present how two of the authors' dystopian novels from the late 1840s and early 1950s—Cooper's *The Crater; or, Vulcan's Peak: A Tale of the Pacific* (1847) and Melville's *White-Jacket; or The World in a Man-of-War* (1850)—reveal shared but divergent attempts to delineate an apparent loss of the law within democratic structures. By examining Mark Woolston's doomed ideal community on Cooper's fantastic volcanic islands and White-Jacket's plight on a U.S. man-of-war, I portray how these maritime narratives negotiate early transitions into contemporary political formations. Specifically, I argue that Cooper and Melville represent different poles of a shared critique of developments within the Jacksonian nation-state. In this chapter, I situate Cooper's *The Crater* amid the Polk era, when Cooper's political thought is taking an increasingly antagonistic and admonitory tenor in regard to domestic politics. Using Lacan's notion of the master signifier (or *point de capiton*), I argue that Cooper's novel not only manifestly favors vesting power in constitutional law over Whig-backed congressional agency, but also, in so doing, fantasmatically defends the broader master signifier of the law and its political valences. In chapter 6, I explore how Melville's *White-Jacket* similarly laments a loss of the rule of law, but with more complex conclusions and ramifications. Instead of a jeremiad-like paean to lost originary national law, I claim that Melville's novel portrays how the loss of democratic rights within the *Neversink*'s martial structure reveals the bizarre and repugnant excesses that sustain a strange new manifestation of normative law.

As chapter 2 began to demonstrate, Cooper's maritime novels, much like those of his Leatherstocking series, are intricately concerned with the development of national "American conditions." There is, however, a distinct shift in Cooper's presentation of America during the latter part of his writing career. Whereas *The Pilot* constitutes a romantic and patriotic renarration of the country's revolutionary birth, *The Crater* provides an ominous warning of its potential demise. As the political content of this later novel attests, Cooper's public life and views take interesting and complex turns as the 1830s and especially the 1840s progress. Wayne Franklin explains that, by 1843 (the year Cooper published *Wyandotté*, a settlement novel illustrating the divisive effects of the American Revolution), "Cooper took less interest in national defense than in internal improvements."[7] Indeed, there is a clear shift between his seamlessly nationalistic *Notions of the Americans* (1828) and his critiques of Whig politics and American legislative practices in *A Letter to His Countrymen* (1834) and *The American Democrat* (1838). But even this political alignment seems to change in the 1840s. According to George Dekker, Cooper's public skirmishes with the Whig-based press in the 1830s were coupled with an apparent hardening of his Democratic positions. This can be seen in Cooper's support for Polk's defense of the Mexican–American War and the party's post-Jackson emphasis on executive power and expansionist policies. Yet, in Dekker's terms, Cooper's coupling of Manifest Destiny and Divine Providence leads him, by the late 1840s, to become "what his earliest writings explicitly condemned—a zealous and bigoted Christian missionary."[8] This formative shift in Cooper's political views yields a correlative shift in the way his work was popularly received. For example, Cooper's growing critique of egalitarian demagoguery and his involvement in what was known as the anti-rent controversy led the *American Whig Review* to embrace *The Redskins* (1846), the third novel in his *Littlepage Manuscripts* trilogy; conversely, the *Democratic Review*—a former ally against Whig interests—condemned Cooper in a review of *The Crater,* asserting: "Unless we have greatly mistaken his political philosophy, he is a monarchist; he is certainly in favor of a union of church and state, and would have the state subordinated to the church, and the people subordinated to the priesthood."[9]

In this multilayered context, Cooper's *The Crater* provides an interesting lens through which to explore the competing political formations that play out in a Crusoe-like maritime scene. Cutting across specific historical concerns and events is the central issue of constitutional law's relation to power and governance. And here the Lacanian conception of law and the role of the master signifier may be helpful in revisiting Cooper's novel and its political interventions. As mentioned, from a Lacanian perspective, the law is primarily a symbolic function and effect. While its positive content—its various historically and culturally determined ethical components—is undoubtedly important, Lacan's analysis interrogates the structural functions that undergird these constructions.[10] Accordingly, a Lacanian approach to the law considers not only the manifest content of legal history and its political developments, but also how such formations are erected and sustained via the central role of fantasy.

These two aspects of the law—the law as the agency of the Other in subject formation and the law as an established set of sociosymbolic mandates—overlap in the function of the master signifier. As discussed in previous chapters, based in part on Hegel's conception of the lacking master, the master signifier functions on two planes: in the castration of the subject and in the quilting of symbolic/ideological constructions.[11] The master signifier's latter function is associated with what Lacan calls the *point de capiton* (or "quilting point"). Žižek explains that if

> the *point de capiton* is a "nodal point," a kind of knot of meanings, this does not imply that it is simply the "richest" word, the word in which is condensed all the richness of meaning of the field it "quilts": the *point de capiton* is rather the word which, *as such,* on the level of the signifier itself, unifies a given field, constitutes its identity: it is, so speak, the word to which "things" themselves refer to recognize themselves in their unity.[12]

The master signifier is here a quilting point within an ideological field that functions, in essence, to stop the sliding of signifiers and thereby fix their meaning. In this important sense, a master signifier is not, in Žižek's terms, "a simple abbreviation that designates a series of markers but the name of the hidden ground of this series of markers that act as so many expressions-effects of this ground."[13] To say that this quilting point is hidden does not mean that the term or concept is itself necessarily obfuscated, like Benjamin's concealed hunchback chess player, but that its actual function as a place-holding nodal point is veiled.[14] This, then, is where fantasy comes into play—as the veil that screens the role of the master signifier (or, in other terms, as a veil over the fact that this signifier is, itself, divided or lacking).[15]

Linking the symbolic concept of the law to the functions of the master signifier and fantasy, we come full circle to Agamben's discussion of the state of exception and, thus, to a productive means for reconceiving Cooper's and Melville's critiques of antebellum politics. This series of relations is aptly summarized in Žižek's claim that

> the Master-Signifier is the privileged site at which fantasy intervenes, since the function of fantasy is precisely to fill in the void of the signifier-without-signified: that is to say, *fantasy is ultimately, at its most elementary, the stuff which fills the void of the Master-Signifier*: again, in the case of a Nation, all the mythic obscure narratives which tell us what the Nation is. In other words, sovereignty always ... involves the logic of the universal and its constitutive exception: the universal and unconditional rule of Law can be sustained only by a sovereign power which reserves for itself the right to proclaim a state of exception, that is, to suspend the rule of law(s) on behalf of the law itself.[16]

Considering these elements in the context of the nation, we see how the state of exception can be articulated in Lacanian terms as the power to intervene in the seemingly smooth facade of the law (sustained by fantasy) by manipulating the hidden or inaccessible function of the master signifier.[17] In turning to Cooper's and Melville's specific antebellum concerns, we might more closely attend to how they conceive of and represent the operation of the law in relation to power. Especially with Cooper, it will soon be clear that the function of the master signifier is paramount.

As noted, Cooper's *The Crater* clearly and repeatedly defines itself as political commentary. For example, the preface of the novel closes with the ominous proposition: "If those who now live in this republic, can see any grounds for a timely warning in the events here recorded, it may happen that the mercy of a divine Creator may still preserve and protect that which he has hitherto cherished and protected."[18] The events of the novel, commencing in the post–American Revolution 1790s, are thus directly linked to antebellum interests. Cooper's apprehension about contemporary politics is also seen when he comments on the potential strength of U.S. maritime labor (18) and the benefits of aggressive national imperialism (417), topics that resound with vested concerns of the antebellum Democratic Party. But it is a focus on the potential decline in moral and social order that most directly links the political landscapes of the two eras in the novel, where Cooper connects fictitious events in the eighteenth century to the ongoing shortcomings of the nineteenth.[19] Indeed, not only is the maritime action of the narrative catalyzed when the "war of the French Revolution . . . blazing in all the heat of its first fires" allows American merchant shipping to expand activity (16), but on a more formative level, the novel's resounding political and moral lesson is inextricably tied to the broader themes of national origin and democratic revolution. If, as I have argued, novels such as *The Pilot* seek to romantically renarrate the American Revolution in order to address social and economic concerns of the nineteenth century, then *The Crater*'s anxious conception of the legal and social implications of democratic revolutionary processes signal a vexed desire for a postrevolutionary system that can somehow hold against all past and future vicissitudes. In Lacanian terms, it signals a desire for a master signifier that can permanently quilt the social and economic fabric of the nation.

Such a focus on structural power relations pervades *The Crater*. In fact, in light of the prefatory admonition, the novel as a whole might be seen as an allegorical rise and fall of what Cooper views as the true master signifier of modernity: American democracy. Of central concern is what form this quilting point takes in Cooper's narrative. That is, how is it erected and maintained via fantasy? Though the specific answer to this question is not readily apparent at the novel's opening, the ground for it is subtly laid in the preface, where Cooper speaks to the inevitable problem of authenticity arising from the fact that the islands in the novel are unknown to geographers (being flagrantly fictional). Addressing the issue using the logic of empiricism, he cites the fact that 350 years before, the world had not realized that its record of continents was incomplete and, thus, suggests that though "much as is now known of the globe, a great deal still remains to be told" (3). While on the surface such a claim operates via a teleological progression of scientific knowledge, employing the term "told" signals an important shift in register. For he soon follows with the playful suggestion that the events of his narrative are "entitled to the most implicit credit" and then unravels the game with his assertion: "Whatever may be thought of the authenticity of its incidents, we hope this book will be found not to be totally without a moral. Truth is not absolutely necessary to the illustration of a principle, the imaginary sometimes doing that office quite as effectively as the actual" (4). Retroactively, then, we see that while the new knowledge to be "told" comes from the future, similar to knowledge being produced by developing disciplines of science, it here takes the explicit form of a "moral." That is to say, it comes in the form of a fixed "principle" communicated by a subject approximating a dictating master.

The ramifications of this opening frame play out on every level of the novel and, as we will see, shape its political vision. Indeed, the very form of the narrative reinforces this structure—with the "authority" for the "truths" of its content supposedly deriving from the journal of the recently deceased Mark Woolston, "the most distinguished" progenitor of a contemporary Pennsylvanian family (5). It is this conception of truth based on the words of a venerated dead father that, even more than Mark's model civic attributes, undergirds the novel's political message.

This is made abundantly clear when Mark and his trusty companion Bob Betts, a romantically cast natural sailor, find themselves delivered from a shipwreck in the Pacific onto an unknown volcanic island. The backstory commences in 1793, when a young Mark Woolston has his imagination fired by the sight of a "full-rigged ship" traveling up the Delaware (10). After convincing his father, Dr. Woolston, to approve, Mark signs on aboard the merchant ship *Rancocus* under the charge of a distant relative, Captain Crutchely. The tale of maritime initiation, in which Mark quickly demonstrates manly potential and becomes the second mate, is flanked by the romantic subplot of Mark's desire for Bridget Yardley, the daughter of his father's professional rival, to whom Mark proposes after returning from his first voyage. Despite parental disapproval, the two secretly marry, planning to reunite after Mark makes enough capital during a fourth voyage to "claim" his bride (not knowing of the large dowry Bridget has in store). And it is on this fateful journey, marked by irresponsible drunkenness on the part of Crutchely and the resentful second mate, Hillson, that the *Rancocus* runs upon a reef one night somewhere in the Pacific.

Cast away together on the island, Mark and Bob quickly interpret the events in terms of God's will. In so doing, they make it clear that Defoe's

Robinson Crusoe is a formidable pretext for their views, with Bob citing the novel several times, unequivocally stating that he deems it "the will of Providence" that he and Mark were to "Robinson Crusoe it" (58). Though contemporary scholars commonly note how Crusoe's brand of entrepreneurial individualism marks the literary birth of *homo economicus,* for Bob and Mark, at least, Defoe's novel is still primarily a spiritual conversion.[20] Cooper sows this theme by having Mark keep a Sunday Sabbath when building up his island "plantation" (85, 92–95) and later fall to his knees in prayer when a storm washes Bob and the newly completed *Neshamony* to sea (125).

But in a novel where the divine seemingly calls forth new lands from the depths of the sea, subtlety is a rare art. Cooper moves directly to his point, emphatically laying out a theory of "our probatory condition here on earth, and . . . the unknown and awful future to which it leads us" (138). Without parsing words, he argues that those dwelling "in the midst of civilization" do not "see around [them] the thousand proofs of the tendency of things to the fulfillment of the decrees announced to us ages ago by the pens of holy men" (140). Setting up a familiar Christian eschatological teleology, he goes on to claim that "the Ottoman power and Ottoman prejudices are melting away . . . under the heat of divine truth, which is clearing for itself a path that will lead to the fulfillment of its own predictions" (140). Casting Asiatic religions and cultures as a frozen plain being dissolved by Manifest Destiny–like divine "heat," Cooper thus erects a God who is progressively active in the material realm.

This activity is demonstrated with the miraculous earthquake that raises new fertile lands from the sea (bringing Mark "nearer to the arm of God" [167]) and, in turn, with the eradication of the entire island chain at the novel's close. But it is also apparent in Mark/Cooper's many cautionary asides about the real-world consequences of deviating from the will of God.[21] While it might be easy to stop here and dismiss the novel as a simple political allegory that cuts out human agency and the modern domains of scientific knowledge by positing that a divine presence ultimately intervenes in earthly events whenever it desires, pushing further one can see how this agency is constructed in a way that has complex political and ideological implications. These stem from the fact that such a God's relation to the world is in part mediated through Mark, the venerated founder of what becomes a thriving colony, as well as the civic law that Mark helps to establish.

This series of relations takes concrete alignment after the miraculous land-birthing earthquake, when Mark begins to survey and name the new territory. Though an ellipsis separates the acts of God and Mark's behavior, the novel's previous dogmatic metaphysical asides and the circumstances—the land seemingly thrown up for Mark to use and claim—clearly align the two. As such, amid Mark's exploration of new capes and channels we are told that "God was there ... as he is everywhere." Even further, Mark is shown daily to be "in the practice of communing in spirit, directly with his Creator" (173). In this sense, Franklin's observation that *The Crater* offers an implicit critique of antebellum society's fall from "American ideals" by contrasting modern social divisions with Mark's indomitable "godlike" voice seems apt.[22] We might, however, explore *how* Mark operates like a god in his developing island community and, moreover, how this community's downfall speaks to the ills of Cooper's age. In other words, we might qualify Mark's godlike status by conceiving of him as a master (in a Lacanian sense) aligned with a distant structural position of total agency that is filled out with the idea of God. As Mark begins to construct his island world, these increasingly vexed structural relations illuminate the aspects of American civics that Cooper so desperately seeks to address.

With this schematic in mind, the novel's drama on the crater and Vulcan's Peak might be broken into two simple movements: the development of the positive originary social and economic formations under Mark's tutelage, and the tale of their undoing. In terms of the former, from the moment Mark and Bob arrive on the mysterious crater, Mark views the land as a Virgilian middle landscape. In a twin act of possession ("his hills" [101]) and reformation (constructing a "plantation" [80]), Mark quickly molds the "whole hundred acres into a garden" (104). Besides applying neoclassical aesthetic paradigms to the landscape (a pure garden of flowers "absolutely free from weeds of every sort" within its bounds [152]), Mark establishes something of a Jeffersonian system of yeoman labor (of course, here on a palatial scale). Especially at first, Mark is able to sit on the summit of his crater, read his books, play his flute, and watch the growth of his "cultivation" (183). He deems it ill advised to grow more vegetables than he can consume (148); in fact, he regards it as "evil" for one to keep "more stock than is good for their owner" (151).

From the beginning, however, this yeomanized landscape includes important social divisions. In this regard, Bob Betts figures prominently as not only an ideal sailor but also an ideal citizen. When Cooper first introduces Bob aboard the *Rancocus,* he glorifies the sailor's sturdy build and maritime know-how as well as his loyalty—with Bob faithfully interpellating national identifications (looking down on sailors who were taken captive during the Revolutionary War) and being a "model of fidelity" to friends (23–24). In a clear departure from Tom Coffin, Bob's "fidelity" is soon folded into an explicit respect for both institutional authority and social distinction. This becomes apparent when Mark learns that Bob had seen distant breakers in advance of the shipwreck, but had demurely subordinated his concern in respect for the captain's decision to push on (saying: "It's going right in the wind's eye, Mr. Woolston, to go ag'in captain and dickey!" [41]). This respect for symbolic distinction is maintained even after the shipwreck, with Bob "insist[ing] on sleeping in the forecastle, though Mark had pressed him to take one of the cabin state-rooms" (72). Indeed, such distinction is maintained well after the shipboard roles had shifted to island-based relations, for even after the settlement's economy blooms, Bob is shown to turn down the "grant" of a large tract of property, feeling that he could not rightly claim it (330).[23] Tellingly, it is only after he has earned capital via whaling endeavors that Bob (buying the *Dragon* from Mark) is "elevated ... to a rank but a little below that of the 'gentlemen'" (374). And this "little" space is finally closed at the novel's end, with Bob selling his brig and justly amassing enough capital to ride as a "passenger" with Mark back to the colony, "having no scruples, now [that] he had become comparatively wealthy, about eating with his old shipmate, and otherwise associating with him" (498). Yet, even when Bob is a relative equal with Mark on the economic and, it seems, social plane, Cooper makes it clear that Bob remained "always ... a sort of humble companion" (454).

The benevolent and natural relation between Bob and Mark is echoed in the first part of the island's settlement in the way that Mark assumes authority. At first, the original hierarchical social balance is maintained after Bob returns to the island on the *Neshamony* with Bridget and her slaves Socrates and Dido, as well as the eager settlers Doctor Heaton, his wife, Anne, and their newly acquired indentured servants. With their arrival, Mark seamlessly transitions from viewing his island as a "plantation" to viewing it as a "colony" (202). In terms of leadership, the mysterious but seemingly natural relation between God's will (creation of islands) and Mark's possession (fancying himself an "Adam in the garden of Eden" [206]) is organically carried over into his role as "governor." When a "council" is called among the settlers "to devise a plan for their future government," Mark is "considered the head of the colony" based on his "experience" (220). In this regard, not only are "all his recommendations ... adopted" (220), but he is "unanimously chosen governor for life" (221). According to Cooper, such an arrangement is based on the fact that "the law [is] . . . the rule of right" and represents how "human society has little difficulty in establishing itself on just principles . . . when the wants are few and interests simple" (221–22).

Placing Mark in the unequivocal position of permanent master, Cooper casts the early colony as a naturally divided social landscape.[24] This is readily apparent in the way Mark divides the settlement in terms of space, spending long stints alone on the crater and moving the best of the immigrants ("forty select families") to the peak (320–21).[25] The initial division of labor is equally conservative in tenor, with the slaves Dido and Juno immediately assuming responsibility for menial tasks (222) and the colony contracting, "borrowing," and forcefully maintaining native labor (283, 290, 336–37).[26] Such practices may seem repugnant to modern audiences and surely would have been to many antebellum social reformers, but they are consistent with Cooper's broader sociopolitical vision. For example, in *The American Democrat* Cooper defends social stratification by appealing to the law, arguing that "equality of condition" is neither guaranteed by the constitution nor socially desirable.[27]

As noted, Cooper depicts the island's social division as directly stemming from Mark's original possession of the land—the "law of right" establishing a clear line of ownership where the "original possessors" and "discovers" are granted huge tracts of land before "general grants" are subsequently doled out to the population via a lottery (329–30). This brand of organic conservatism, of course, has vast legal and economic precedent in Western thought. And yet, for Cooper there seems to be more at stake than simple notions of possession. Though a natural hierarchy is maintained, the action of the novel suggests that such division puts the lower social stratum in position to raise themselves economically and socially. This is seen in Bob's rise in status, when middling settlers labor "in common" to improve the soil for agriculture (331), and in the way the slave Socrates voices pride when one of the colony's boats is named after his wife (226).

Such sentiments clearly align with popular views about political economy espoused throughout the eighteenth century and the early nineteenth. For instance, Henry Charles Carey's *Principles of Political Economy* (1837–40), the first two volumes of which Cooper had available in his study, optimistically builds on and modifies Adam Smith's well-known assertion that free trade benefits both owners and laborers, asserting that an increase of capital leads to "a constant diminution in the proportion required by both government and capitalist, attended by a constant increase in the proportion, and a rapid increase in the quality, retained by the labourer."[28] In other words, despite an economic division between high and low, the nature of economic growth creates "a constant tendency to approximation in the condition of the labourer and the capitalist."[29]

Socioeconomic visions such as Cooper's and Carey's do not simply promote sanguine conservative positions but contribute to specific antebellum land- and labor-rights controversies. This can be seen when Carey directly takes on David Ricardo's critique of rent practices, arguing that instead of a decline in labor productivity and profit (for both laborer and capitalist) as poorer soils are leased out, "labour is daily more productive ... [and] the labourer's power to accumulate capital is daily increasing."[30] Thus, for Carey, protection of rent practices and, more broadly, "perfect security of ... property" leads to greater prosperity for all parties.[31] Though not directly, Carey's polemic undoubtedly has a stake in the Anti-Rent War of 1839–46—a debate Cooper was quite interested in during the composition of *The Crater*. Centered on tracts of land along the Hudson River owned by the Van Rensselaer family since 1637, the controversy involved tenants who refused to pay back rent when Stephen Van Rensselaer died in 1839. Arguing that the patroon system that dictated their rental terms (what Cooper defines as a lifetime "durable lease") was antiquated, protesters resisted authorities and the courts until their cause finally won out in 1846.

As Robert Spiller notes, the Anti-Rent War catalyzed Cooper not so much because of specific rent concerns, but because the issue more broadly threatened the institution of private property. According to Spiller, Cooper held that the anti-renters "defied their contracts established in law" and thereby provided "evidence that the new America had lost sight of its principles."[32] More pointedly, in both the anti-rent controversy and in the novel, the specific alignment of moral principles, legal precedent, and property rights link to the symbolic position of a master figure. In both scenarios, Cooper appears to long for an arrangement in which a socioeconomic master (Stephen Van Rensselaer and Mark Woolston, respectively) acts as, metaphorically speaking, an ideological master signifier that quilts the legal and social planes. That is to say, for Cooper, the law's waning reign is directly linked to the master's loss of agency. Cooper also expressed this anxiety in his previous novel, *The Redskins; or, Indian and Injin* (1846), which explicitly takes on the anti-rent controversy. Near the opening of the novel, he applauds John Jay's earlier gubernatorial administration for "putting down" rent protests. And he laments: "This is not the age of John Jay's."[33]

This deterioration of the master's reign with respect to the law is dramatized vividly in the latter part of *The Crater*. From the moment Mark becomes governor, Cooper highlights the precarious state of his reign. At first this takes the form of apprehension about foreign threats to the colony, focused primarily on Waally, a hostile "Kannaka" chief from a nearby island chain. Thus the first step in becoming a colony is turning "the whole island into a second Gibraltar" (221). Although the outside threat is shown to be a valid one (when Waally's war canoes subsequently attack the colony), the colonists' anxiety registers less on military grounds and more on social ones, primarily in terms of protecting the settlers' females (203–4). Indeed, such social anxieties pervade all subsequent interactions with the natives, even after a military threat is quelled. This can be seen when Cooper lauds the way white shipwrecked sailors from the *Rancocus*, who had lived with Kannakas for some time, had "kept themselves free from [native] wives, and returned to their *colour*—that word being now more appropriate then *colours*, or ensign, unshackled by any embarrassing engagements" (279) as well as in later colony policies (including a "Navigation Act") formed to keep natives away from the crater and surrounding waters (345).

As the colony develops, the link between foreign and domestic threats closes even further, especially in terms of concern over emigration from America. At first, Mark keeps close control over the social construction of the colony, "selecting" 207 emigrants based on the criterion of "morals," "division among the various trades," and sexual economy—with "every man [being] married" (299). The colony's growth, however, becomes unchecked with the arrival of new colonists, leading to the creation of an outer harbor and settlements. This development quickly brings about significant changes in the colony, where Mark loses both political and social influence, and here Cooper most directly lays out his caustic social critique.

Though Mark's status as a master of the island is figured as naturally stemming from God's will, it exists on tenuous social ground. Much like the way the Lacanian master signifier acts to quilt an ideological field, Mark's position is maintained by and functions through its effects on the population. For example, Cooper describes how, in initially fortifying the peak, Mark "issued his orders with a show of authority" (222). The need for such a differentiating performance of power is reiterated in Mark's decision to begin to eat apart from the colonists, owing to his knowledge that "authority was best preserved by avoiding familiarity" (273), and in his conception of how such power retroactively allows him to maintain social "distinctions" in "tastes and qualities" among the colonists (347). His efforts include exercising influence over members of the council and encouraging Bob to resign and take up navigating tasks full-time, owing to his belief that the sailor was "out of his place in such a body, among men of . . . habits so much superior and more refined" (356).

In this light, the *Democratic Review*'s claim that *The Crater* outs Cooper as a monarchist is potentially on target in terms of the issue of localization of power. Yet, such an aspersion does not hold up when one considers Mark's political views, which reflect a distinctly anti-Whig tenor more than a pro-monarchy one. In terms of the salient issues of executive power and territorial expansion, Cooper's novel clearly leans toward Democratic sentiment.[34] Not only does he portray the need for a strong and totalizing commander in the character of Mark (aristocratic inflections aside), but he addresses obliquely popular attacks on executive power by including a qualifying aside when discussing the colonists' impassioned cries that Waally was a tyrant. Here, he suggests that "hatred of tyranny is innate in man, but it is necessary to distinguish between real oppression and those restraints which are wholesome, if not indispensable to human happiness" (252–53). When Mark subsequently lays out the "great principles" for his government, we see that the necessary restraints he has in mind look very much like those put forth by the old Jeffersonian lot. After decrying antebellum-era utopian projects as "modern absurdities on the subject of equality, and a community of interests" (299–300), Mark determines that his government should "protect all in their rights equally, but, that done, let every man pursue his road to happiness his own way; conceding no more of his natural rights than were necessary to the great ends of peace, security, and law" (325).[35] Cooper recontextualizes Mark's rule based on this "theory," suggesting that Mark held power only "for the greater good" and that he would gladly abnegate his position if another could more effectively fill it (325).

While such notions, coupled with the agricultural and horizontal growth of the colony, bespeak a broad alignment with Jackson- and Polk-era platforms of the Democratic Party, when one looks more closely at the way Cooper's ideal settlement crumbles, a political vision emerges that transcends antebellum party lines. This becomes apparent even before the downfall of Mark's reign begins. Building on minor criticisms of the deleterious effects of trade, and at a moment in the novel right before the colony develops into a whaling "state," Cooper emphatically describes how "trade, perhaps the most corrupt and corrupting influence of life—or, if second to anything in evil, second only to politics—is proclaimed to be the great means of humanizing, enlightening, liberalizing, and improving the human race!" (355). Trade is a problem, however, not only because the Christian church is "opposed" to most of its "practices" (355), but also because with it, "whole communities degenerate into masses of corruption, venality, and cupidity, when they set up the idol of commerce to worship in lieu of the ever-living God" (387). Cooper's qualm is thus more than an objection to qualitative changes in belief within an age of transition toward, in Jameson's terms, a "desacralization of the world."[36] Instead, it relates more specifically to the political and ideological fallout that comes from altering the formally sacred symbolic position that had determined such beliefs.

With an influx of new settlers, and systems of trade beginning to turn profits, Cooper ushers in the beginning of the end when a Nantucket man introduces whaling into the colony. At first Cooper lauds the way the whaling trade infuses the settlement with much-needed "interest" and "spirit" (358), but the activity effects important changes in both economic and symbolic alignments. In addition to generating a new locus of wealth, allowing middling men such as Bob to amass fortunes, the industry's requisite physical labor shifts the colony's fantasy coordinates. This transition is apparent in the way that brave Kannaka whalemen "rose greatly in the public estimation," forcing Mark himself to lead hunts in order to maintain his public image (368). Instead of controlling the colony's relations in absentia, from a distant seat of authority, Mark is pushed to act (literally, to perform) within the social fray—to maintain his power by attempting to embody the people's new conceptions of leadership. In this sense, Mark's role as master is already in a precarious state before the arrival of what Cooper deems the worst enemies of all: "religion, law, and the press" (430).

The closing events of the novel include ongoing external threats to the colony—such as pirate bands, acculturated "semi-savages," and the approaching naval wars of Europe. Nonetheless, the ostensibly internal dangers to Mark's rule, in the form of the above triad, are what prove most fatal. Religion plays the smallest part in this cabal, angering Mark primarily because settlers illegally admitted immigrants (here, priests of various sects) without his or the council's consent. The role of the press and the law, however, prove to be formative. After lamenting the effects of newfound wealth on the now "vain-glorious" colonists, Cooper portrays the infective influences of a printer and a lawyer. In what is the linchpin of his critique, Cooper argues that the lawyer taught the settlers that "they were wronged by their neighbors," thus using law not for "justice" but for "speculation and revenge" (431). In a similar manner, he suggests that the press (the "Crater Truth-Teller"), by taking up the topic of human rights, secured its own private ends by convincing the people "that they had hitherto been living under an unheard-of tyranny" (432).

The action of this dual-headed monster quickly undercuts Mark's power. The press is shown to have two operative effects: allowing a minority position underhandedly to yolk the public "we" to a "biased perspective," thereby acting as a sounding board for mobilizing public opinion on civic and legal issues, and more subtly engendering a cynical eye in its readers, with the newspaper's "dishonesty, selfishness, vulgarity, and lies" encouraging readers to question official public rhetoric. Accordingly, the "political effects" of the press are what most concern Cooper (435).

As with the case of whaling, when the paper begins promoting its theory of majority rule, Mark is forced to operate as an agent within the social discourse, as opposed to a distant and determining structural reference. Penning a series of defenses of the "fundamental law" that made him "ruler for life," Mark attacks the dangers associated with democratic popular rule (438). According to Mark, the central problem is not the tyranny over the minority, à la Tocqueville, but the structural concern that if the majority completely rules, "it has the right to set its dogmas above the commandments" (436).[37] In this way, Mark frames civic laws as ideally conditioned by a domain of higher principles, asserting that "the laws of God were nothing but the great principles which ought to govern human contact" and, therefore, "there was a power to which majorities should defer" (436). The previous claim that Mark would gladly give up his position "had there been another suited to such a station" is thus retroactively illuminating in terms of the real issue at hand: preserving the traditional and, in Cooper's view, just symbolic "station" of master. Though the rest of the novel's action finds this task defeated—with Mark replaced by a new governor after the press rallies a constitutional convention to limit a governor's term—contextualizing Mark's betrayed ideals with Cooper's broader political writings from the era not only reveals the way the novel's close rearticulates

Cooper's anti-Whig arguments, but also what may be the essence of his late political fantasy in toto.

With a public career in the 1830s marked by confrontations with prominent Whig critics; it is no wonder that Cooper's view of the media and public discourse is emphatically negative. In the opening of *A Letter to His Countrymen,* for example, Cooper cites the lamentable way Americans and members of the press engage "in the practice of quoting opinions of foreign nations, by way of helping to make up its own estimate of the degree of merit that belongs to its public men."[38] But even more problematic, for Cooper, is the way this lack of independent judgment extends to the public at large, creating a country of fickle-minded citizens. In this light, the offhand comment in *The Crater* that the American "Republican" should henceforth be referred to as American "Gossipian" relates to the danger of influence located in the press (28). As opposed to his earlier claim, in *Notions of the Americans,* that public opinion organically leads to truth (where the "precious grains of truth gradually get winnowed from the chaff... and become the mental alignments of the nation"),[39] in *The American Democrat,* Cooper casts the public as a mass "liable to popular impulses" and, therefore, "neither more or less than rabble" (91). This is only slightly more flattering than his comical depiction of the masses as monkey-like in *The Monikins* (1835). The crux of this issue, therefore, is the way that "cupidity and passions of men" threaten the "institutions" and "principles" of a country (the very factor that brings down Mark in *The Crater*) (9). In part, this problem relates to the social structures of modern democracies. For if, as Cooper attests, "democracies are necessarily controlled by publick opinion," then "the fraudulent and ambitious find a motive to mislead, and even to corrupt the common sentiment... to attain their ends" (63). And the press is unequivocally the means in this equation. Cooper goes even further with his polemic, however, citing how democracies like the one operating in the "confederated republick" of the United States are so "dependent on popular opinion" that they are "more liable to be influenced to their injury... through the management of foreign and hostile nations" (65). In fact, Cooper ventures so far as positing: "Whenever the government of the United States shall break up, it will probably be in consequence of a false direction having been given to publick opinion" (150).

Cooper's warning about Congress's and state institutions' power to define constitutional law and executive privilege is even more directly relevant to Mark's role of master. Cooper categorically asserts: "The legislature of this country, by the intention of the constitution, wields the highest authority under the least responsibility, and [therefore] ... is the power most to be distrusted" (23). Casting aside Whig attacks on the growing domain of the presidency by suggesting that there is greater danger that the president will "render the office less efficient than was intended" than "exercise an authority dangerous to the liberties of the country," Cooper instead emphasizes the fact that while the Constitution checks the acts of the executive, it does little to protect citizens from the actions of particular state governments (35, 16–17).

These ideas are stated in even more emphatic terms in Cooper's earlier *A Letter to His Countrymen,* wherein he references the dangerous effect of "disunion" or "revolution" that might stem from individual states lawfully "altering the characters of the respective constituencies" (314). To remedy this, Cooper suggests the creation of an impeachment procedure to hold legislative representatives in check and cites what he views as an egregious example of unconstitutional congressional activity when Congress passed a resolution declaring that President Jackson's dealings with the Bank of the United States were illegal (320). In terms of the latter issue, Cooper argues not only that such a resolution is in itself unconstitutional, but also that legislative members used foreign precedent to defend their actions (325). In addition, Cooper adds another wrinkle to his critique of how modern democracies allow alien forces to control the voting masses. Instead of focusing on the press, however, he argues that the "laborer is menaced" in that "he is discharged if he will not vote in conformity with the will of his employer" (337). While such a claim is spurious at best, Cooper's point is clear: manipulation of the ballot box and legislation via control of public opinion reduces the possibility of change (or, even more important given Cooper's views, the possibility of preventing change) in America to "reform as England has got reform, by tumults, and conflagrations, and threats of revolution" (337).

Coupling *The Crater*'s religious critique of what George Dekker calls "mobocracy" and Cooper's anti-Whig arguments of the 1830s and 1840s, we can see more clearly what is at stake in both forums.[40] *The Crater* does not offer only a religious critique of antebellum political economy or a partisan invective against Whig-like positions; in cutting across both at once, it illuminates a more formative political desire that might be seen to undergird all of Cooper's later social and political critiques.

All of the above concerns come to a head in a closing passage of *The Crater.* Through Mark, Cooper avers that "constitutions, or the fundamental law, ... were meant to be the expression of those just and general principles which should control human society, and as such should prevail over majorities" (436). Thus, for Cooper, it is not the Declaration of Independence (the revolutionary proclamation of freedom) that acts, in Fredrick Douglass's terms, as the "ring-bolt" for the subsequent direction of the country (a position also embraced by the anti-rent agitators), but the Constitution.[41] Again, in the context of *The American Democrat* and *A Letter to His Countrymen*, it is the Constitution's inability to prevent change or curb congressional power that is the problem. Mark's society and the antebellum political landscape are both in jeopardy because both leave open the possibility for alterations to the alignment of "general principles" and the law. On one level, this casts Cooper as a simple organic conservative, seeking to erase the constituent power of a growing population with a stabilizing constituted power. It seems that what Cooper desires most is to maintain the symbolic coordinates shaped in an originary state of exception. This is seen in *The Crater* with the law of right that follows the eruption of the islands, and in the United States with the constitutional ratification that follows the American Revolution.

But on another level, Cooper's vision is much more radical, critiquing *all* historical and earthly states of exception. This is hinted at in his novel *The Redskins*, where Cooper argues that land treaties from before the American Revolution should hold sway. The law of possession here trumps both the exception of the Revolution and the Constitution proper—the Constitution itself being "just" because it allows for "harmony" between state institutions and the general principle of property ownership (in the form of "the law of real estate").[42]

These issues culminate in *The Crater* when, in an aside, Cooper caustically argues: "Everything human is abused; and it would seem that the only period of tolerable condition is the transition state, when the new force is gathering to a head, and before the storm has time to break." Such teleological logic, as cynical as it is, aligns with the revolutionary thought of a Jefferson or a Paine, whereby periodic rebellion by constituent power is necessary in an ongoing struggle for freedom. But Cooper adds an essential turn: "In the mean time, the earth revolves; ... communities are formed and are dissolved; ... the whole, however, advancing slowly but unerringly towards the great consummation, which was designed from the beginning, and which is certain to arrive in the end. ... The supreme folly of the hour is to imagine that perfection will come before its stated time" (444). A Christian eschatological scenario such as this undercuts any historical change or agency—casting all "transitions" as either willed from above or inconsequential in light of a preestablished apocalypse. Yet, it is essential to see how this Christian narrative operates within *The Crater*.

By aligning Mark's reign and the "fundamental law" that supports it with divine agency, Cooper casts an otherworldly intervention as the structural source for an ideological quilting point in earthly time. He thus creates a fantasy wherein a preapocalyptic historical moment is transmogrified into and supported by an *a*historical one. In symbolic terms, such a fantasy of divine intervention acts as a means to "fill out" or screen off the void that constitutes Mark's reign (in its different forms) as a master or master signifier. Of course, such a fantasy has clear precedent in feudal narratives, but here it operates in relation to a pseudoconstitutional democracy with clear allegorical ties to America's antebellum republic. In this regard, Cooper would undoubtedly adhere to the letter of Paine's resounding claim that "in America THE LAW IS KING," but, it is important to note, without the irony.[43]

To close, we might safely locate "constitutional democracy" as the central concern and, hence, as the central ideological master signifier at stake in the work here discussed. By subordinating the horizon of material-world politics to the horizon of divine will and its "general principles," Cooper effectively stays any legitimate earthly revolution or significant alteration to the coordinates of civic precedent, for aligning the earthly master signifier of constitutional democracy with an idealized divine master seals off the sociosymbolic order from any bottom-up modifications. In short, it moves the state of exception out of the realm of history.

Yet, as we have seen, this rather simple political desire operates amid what is a complex bundle of anxieties relating to the shifting landscape of antebellum judicial and civic beliefs. Considering the formal and fantasmatic way that Cooper represents and addresses these anxieties may, therefore, be even more historically significant. As mentioned, contemporary scholars such as Žižek have productively recontextualized notions of democracy in light of the function of the master signifier.[44] For example, after summarizing democracy's well-known dual aspects of antagonist struggle (the uprising of constituent power in the form of "supernumerary" masses) and regulatory procedures (the imposition of constituted power), Žižek argues that the latter move, the democratic process of establishing hierarchical order, is itself a "defense" against the former, the democratic "violent intrusion of . . . egalitarian logic."[45] In more formal terms, Žižek asserts that "democracy" as a master signifier, as a concept that "quilts" the symbolic coordinates of modern capitalism's political world, works so well because its lack (which is, again, necessarily "filled out" by fantasy) is "directly inscribed into the social system, it is institutionalized in a set of procedures and regulations."[46]

It is precisely this sociopolitical manifestation of the lack of the master signifier that bothers Cooper. The problems he diagnoses within antebellum political and social formations seem to irk him because they reveal a correlative lack in symbolic coordinates themselves (the Constitution and the institutions of law based on it). *The Crater* may be a pivotal text because of the way its fanciful maritime setting allows us to glimpse how Cooper's cognizance of this symbolic lack allows him to repair it, as it were, with a fantasy of a totalizing symbolic arrangement. As such, Cooper's fantasmatic reign of law is undoubtedly also a reign of the master, a master he sees falling from grace as the nineteenth century pushes on. And this is a trend Melville seems to notice, too, but through a very different lens.

· CHAPTER 6 ·

The Sublime Abject of Democracy: Melville's "Floating *Imperium*"

But what relation can there be between exceptions?

—Maurice Blanchot, "Sade"

"AN ASYLUM FOR THE PERVERSE," "an asylum for all drunkards," "a sort of State Prison afloat."[1] Indeed, Melville fancies that the fictitious U.S. man-of-war *Neversink* is all of these. But more than an imperious and segmented floating caldron of vice, the ship, built of "parts of a Chinese puzzle" (164), houses a myriad of dark caverns and "inexplicable apartments" (127). Hastily written in the summer of 1849 (supposedly in about sixty days), *White-Jacket; or The World in a Man-of-War* is the second of two "jobs" Melville wrote after *Mardi*'s poor sales forced him to revert to standard maritime narratives.[2]

Part travelogue, part naval exposé, and loosely based on Melville's service on the USS *United States* from 1843 to 1844, *White-Jacket* may have been built to sell, but Melville intimates that it would do so despite controversy. In a letter to Lemuel Shaw, for instance, he suggests that the novel "will be sure to be attacked in some quarters."[3] And in a second letter that same day, Melville wrote Richard Henry Dana Jr. to enlist his public support for the project, admitting that "this man-of-war book . . . is in some parts rather man-of-*warish* in style—rather aggressive I fear."[4] While Melville no doubt is referencing the novel's polemical use of popular naval-reform rhetoric, I would like to suggest that it might be even more man-of-warish than Melville relayed, especially in terms of its implicit political and ideological ramifications.

Unhinging Melville's nice turn of phrase, we see that a central reason for the book's additional level of warishness is that its content exclusively depicts life on a naval frigate. Melville's narrator reiterates this strict aim by censoring himself when he begins to describe the port of Rio de Janeiro instead of adhering to his "one proper object, *the world in a man-of-war*"

(160). Though many critics note the novel's various historical and political contexts, Cesare Casarino's *Modernity at Sea* most aptly addresses the way the shipboard setting on the *Neversink* allows the novel to represent deep structures of an era in economic and social transition. Following Foucault, Casarino figures the nineteenth-century ship as a "heterotopia," a site that affects "the interference between representational and nonrepresentational practices."[5] In Casarino's view, the ship offers utopian experiential and representational possibilities—existing in "the historical moment when a tendentially global and increasingly unified world system comes into being [and thus] . . . the concept of heterotopia as well as the concept of space undergo . . . metamorphoses."[6] In this relatively open space of transitional rupture—a heterogeneous space where various representational, existential, economic, and social modes cut across each other—the *Neversink* acts, according to Casarino, as "a laboratory for modern epistemo-sexual experimentation."[7]

How representations of ship space illuminate crises in nineteenth-century conceptualizations of sexuality is undoubtedly an important line of inquiry, but I am interested in showing how the liminal space of Melville's *Neversink* also depicts a perhaps more disturbing metamorphosis within antebellum society. Reading central events in the novel in light of a Lacanian conception of perversion, I argue that White-Jacket's experiences expose a traumatic ontological shift toward what can be seen as a totalitarian realm. Unlike Cooper's anxious fear about the loss of an idealized law's agency, here it is the foundational locus of the democratic subject as such that is in jeopardy. Following Casarino and Otter's lead in viewing the *Neversink* as a zone of transitional crisis where various antebellum sociopolitical registers collide, I wish to trace how one of the most devastating aspects of this transition is a potential move from a traditional subject position sustained by fantasy ($S \lozenge a$) toward a form of totalitarian construction closer to perversion ($a \lozenge S$). By placing this shift within the context of antebellum debates about flogging, we will examine how Melville's man-of-war may dramatize a precarious consolidation of power that prefigures modern America's move toward a veritable state of exception, one that anticipates the perverse logic of modern totalitarian states.[8]

Perverse Measures/Martial Pleasures: The *Neversink* and the Modern Totalitarian State

Scholars throughout the twentieth century have interrogated the concept of totalitarianism. Reacting to the rise of Nazism and Stalinism, intellectuals from across the political spectrum turned their sights on this developing sociopolitical configuration. Hannah Arendt's *The Origins of Totalitarianism* (1951), for example, established benchmarks for this social structure that shaped most subsequent studies. Arendt argues that totalitarian movements "depend less on the structurelessness of a mass society than on the specific conditions of an atomized and individuated mass."[9] That is to say, the totalizing control that a totalitarian regime seeks is not effected by sheer centralized power, à la basic dictatorship, but through a centralization of power "and the occupation of the state machinery" to achieve a "total expansion into the population."[10] J. L. Talmon's subsequent *The Rise of Totalitarian Democracy* (1952) makes the important move of focusing on the way such totalitarian modes of power manifest in twentieth-century democracies, arguing that those democracies recognize "only one plane of existence, the political."[11]

This is, of course, the precise relation—the implicit and explicit way in which modern power systems extend into and control the "bare life" of their members—that Giorgio Agamben explores in his writings on the state of exception. By focusing on the corporeal and legal role of the *homo sacer* (sacred man), a figure in ancient Roman law who could be legally murdered but not sacrificed, Agamben extrapolates the broader thesis that "the inclusion of bare life in the political realm constitutes the original—if concealed—nucleus of sovereign power."[12] As mentioned in chapter 5, Agamben locates the zero level of such sovereign power in the "relation of the exception," or a "relation by which something is included [here, under law] solely through its exclusion."[13] Similar to Arendt and Talmon's view that totalitarianism effects a "total expansion into the population," Agamben argues that the "inner solidarity between democracy and totalitarianism" relates to the manner in which their modern manifestations transform politics into modes of biopolitics.[14]

This modern state of affairs, however, is not a product of spontaneous development. In a point central to this chapter's arguments, Agamben avers: "The contiguity between mass democracy and totalitarian states . . . does not have the form of a sudden transformation . . . ; before impetuously coming to light in our [twentieth] century, the river of biopolitics that gave *homo sacer* his life runs its course in a hidden but continuous fashion."[15] And this river, I hope to show, includes both the nineteenth-century sea and the martial zone of the *Neversink*.[16]

In considering Melville's antebellum naval system in light of Agamben's genealogy of juridical power, I am not necessarily concerned with supporting or fortifying the trajectory of his thesis. Instead, I view his historical master narrative, of sorts, as a convenient horizon for articulating the specific legal and ontological transitions that Melville's novel depicts. Consequently, I would like to emphasize Agamben's reference to the "hidden" nature of this "river of biopolitics," over and above his view that it is "continuous." Ian Baucom has taken issue with this latter aspect of Agamben's work, using Kant's conception of an "unjust enemy" to open up Agamben's rather rigid genealogy. Focusing on political discourse related to Atlantic imperial projects of the late sixteenth through the mid-seventeenth century, Baucom offers an alternate model for conceiving of modern states of exception, one based conceptually on the project of identifying the boundaries of international law via identifying those who, in Hobbes's terms, represent *homo homini lupus* (an "Enlightenment double of the man-who-is-a-wolf-to-man"). According to Baucom, in that era, those unjust enemies were linked to specific populations, such as the "native American of the 'new World' and the 'Caapmen,' 'Hottentoos,' and other indigenes of the South African Cape."[17] Therefore, he concludes, "looming into the present not through an unbroken intraconstitutional line of inheritance but from the legally free and empty zones of the imperial frontier, it is this figure, this *homo inimicus* (and not Agamben's *homo sacer*) that ... provide[s] the paradigm for our contemporaneity's global, war-making states of exception."[18] While not attempting to shift Agamben's historical grid, as Baucom does, my arguments add another fold to what is surely a discursive genealogy of modern juridical alignments. Moreover, since I examine what I view as one nineteenth-century site, or symptom, perhaps, of the becoming of modern legal and political alignments, the notion of genealogical origins is not as paramount as how citizens (such as Melville) fantasmatically negotiated the effects of distinct symbolic transitions that were under way.

Before exploring the specifics of Melville's novel, it is important to illustrate more generally how an imaginary nineteenth-century man-of-war relates to totalitarian political structures and, further, how these structures operate in terms of fantasy. Linking the concept of the state of exception to twentieth-century totalitarian–democratic movements, Agamben traces how modern biopolitical relations are built upon eighteenth- and nineteenth-century legal rationales for exceptions to and in written law. These primarily pertain to the ability of the sovereign to suspend law in times of emergency, and include France's *état du siège* (state of siege), England's martial law, and United States' constitutional ambiguity regarding executive privilege.[19] While Agamben addresses surrounding legal precedent and legislation in detail, he does not discuss the relevant site of nineteenth-century naval-ship space and the accompanying British and American versions of the Articles of War.

If one accepts Agamben's alignment of the relation of exception with modern totalitarian scenarios (an alignment, again, supported by traditional scholarship on totalitarianism), then the nineteenth-century naval vessel—cast off from the mainland and structured on every level by the Articles of War—clearly represents an early site where totalitarian arrangements might develop. Furthermore, the British and American versions of the articles contain interesting and, as we will see with the issue of flogging, vexed relations of exception built into their punitive martial statutes.

With Winston Churchill's famed description of the British naval tradition as "rum, sodomy, and the lash" in mind, coupled with the fact that the very first American naval mission ended in mutiny, the need for codified martial law to dictate naval standards of action and discipline seems clear.[20] Yet, within these rigid articles there are interesting paradoxes. The British Articles of War, which were adopted almost wholesale by the United States, were first established in 1661 and replaced in 1769 with an even more severe penal code. Unlike the British army's Mutiny Act, which required annual parliamentary renewal, the naval Articles of War constituted a more complex and divided legal ground. The articles themselves were a statute passed by Parliament that carefully delineated the legal procedures for dealing with serious infractions requiring a court-martial. As Markus Eder explains, however, these articles were supplemented by "The Printed Instructions" (or "Regulations and Instructions relating to His Majesty's Service at Sea"), "which were not a parliamentary statute but a set of regulations issued by the King in Council." These Printed Instructions affected two basic areas of discipline: "They permitted a ship's captain to summarily punish a mariner for minor offenses with a maximum of twelve lashes ... [and] roughly outlined the conduct of a naval court-martial."[21] In this arrangement, Parliament controlled the process of law pertaining to severe crimes, while the Crown possessed unmitigated power to dictate all relatively nongrave disciplinary measures. Such a formative gap between the parliamentary Articles of War and the Crown's Printed Instructions thus reveals an important tension at the heart of British martial law, one that seems to enact Agamben's notion of the mode of exception within the very fabric of legal coordinates.

This institutionalization of exception is even more pronounced in the United States' version of naval Articles of War. Although the British articles were primarily established to control officers—who ruled over masses of sailors from various nations—the early American republican government was more concerned with having, in Greg Dening's terms, "a morally upstanding military as much as a disciplined one."[22] In 1775, John Adams headed the task of writing the naval rules and regulations for the Continental Congress and decided to adopt the British articles, in his words, *totidem verbis*. In practice, however, Adams erected a thorny composite of various British standards. According to Dening, "Adams mixed the statuary Articles of 1661 with some those of 1749, together with the executive regulations of the British Admiralty, and added a number of inventions of his own."[23] Though one of Adams's goals seems to have been to suture the structural power gap within the British system, his changes included significant alterations and ramifications. First, Adams added a differentiation between officers and men, whereby he "limited by law the power of commanders to punish their officers, except by court martial."[24] As a consequence, the articles were now focused more squarely on the actions of common sailors. Second, he added flogging, which fell under the nebulous Printed Instructions domain in the British system, to the official law of the American articles. Such an act—placing all corporal punishment under the transparent control of legislatively conditioned law—would seem to at least superficially expunge the relation of exception from the letter of naval martial law. Yet Adams's moral vigilance (re)opened just such an exception in the very first article. Adams writes that it is a commander's duty to "guard against, and suppress, all dissolute and immoral practices, and to correct all such as are guilty of them, according to the usage of the sea service."[25] As Isaac Land notes, the concept of the "usage of the sea" references the long-standing military tradition of the "custom of the sea," an unwritten code that provided wide discretion to officers in overseeing official and unofficial disciplinary measures.[26] In referring to such a concept in the United States' articles, Adams thus locates a clear zone of exception within the law. While his articles collectively limit the punitive measures for all other minor offenses to twelve lashes, Adams's zeal to quell "immoral" shipboard activity inspires him to offer the "solution" that "unmentionable transgressions will be met with indescribable torments, at the captain's whim."[27]

In this historical and institutional context, it is clear that the rudimentary ground for a totalitarian mode of power is present in the nineteenth-century U.S. naval ship, where a perpetual and martial state of emergency allows the relation of exception to reign *in perpetuum*. I am interested in exploring how this potential sociopolitical relation manifests in Melville's fictional account of a man-of-war world. One level of this response is quite apparent. In his three late chapters on aspects of the American Articles of War, Melville, via his eponymous narrator, White-Jacket, condemns almost every aspect of nineteenth-century martial law, cynically recounting how the sailors, with hats in hand, listen to the articles read aloud by the captain's clerk, who imperiously repeats the refrain *"shall suffer death!"* (293). Building on a critique of how this spectacle was callously staged to enforce "reverence for the code," and more specifically how the articles dictated "whereby [he] lived, and moved, and had [his] being on board the ... ship," White-Jacket provides a multifaceted polemic against the articles themselves (292). His rather rudimentary attack focuses on the way supposedly free American citizens are "subject to ... cut-throat martial law" and how, "without a trial, you may, at a wink from the Captain, be condemned to the scourge" (294–95). In addition to decrying the foreign roots of this "Turkish code" that allows a Mohammed-like captain to command free men (297, 301)—going so far as to trace America's version of the articles to the despotic rule of Charles II (298)—Melville also addresses the inner paradoxes of the statutes, condemning the way they are predicated on an abeyance of the constitutional laws of the republic.

In his critique, White-Jacket notes the geographic basis for this exception, lamenting that his brother ashore can "call personally upon the President ... and express his disapprobation" while he, upon a naval frigate, is "liable at any time to be run up at the yard-arm" (294–95). Directly addressing how the captain "may almost be said to put off the citizen when he touches the quarterdeck" (301), White-Jacket appeals directly to legal tracts by Sir Matthew Hale and Blackstone, who emphasize the general unconstitutionality of martial law. In a line that in many ways evokes Agamben's argument, and that Cooper would salute, Hale is shown to write: "The

Martial Law, being based upon no settled principles, is, in truth and reality, no law, but something indulged rather than allowed as a law" (303).

Standard legal critiques of martial law such as these pervade the novel. It is, however, the way Melville dramatizes the effects of this sociopolitical space that reveals additional and potentially more important aspects of this strange world. On the one hand, White-Jacket's experiences demonstrate the lack of law within a martial state. To use Agamben's terms, life on the *Neversink* necessitates a veritable "ban" or exile from mainland constitutional citizenship. According to Agamben, the ban is an originary relation of civilization, whereby "law refers to life and includes it in itself by suspending it."[28] The ban, therefore, is the foundational structure of a relation of exception. In this situation, Agamben explains, law manifests as "being in force without signification."[29] That is to say, "what is at stake is a force of law without law (which should therefore be written: force-of-law)."[30] Much like Cooper's foreboding illustration of the diminishing agency of the law, Melville thus appears to warn about a dangerous loss of law within the modern antebellum nation-state.

On the other hand, however, White-Jacket's naval world reveals something very different from Cooper's apocalyptic islands. Instead of waning "general principles" leading to the decline of an idealized constitutional democracy, the world of the *Neversink* shows how the apparent loss of law within a martial state might in fact correspond to a repressed excess of law within the mainland sociosymbolic system itself. What I mean to suggest is that, in his narrative of life on a man-of-war, Melville illustrates a juridical–political system wherein what at first seems like a loss of law is shown to actually be a potentially new relation of law. As I will show, the subjugation that White-Jacket and his crew experience on the *Neversink* may stem from an anachronistic form of sovereign power (a relative dictatorship), but this power is portrayed unmistakably as both operating structurally and creating subordinate "slaves" in new ways.[31] A close consideration of these effects, which culminate in the issue of flogging, reveals what seems to be Melville's own warning about coming sociopolitical formations. Unlike Cooper's vision of rule by avaricious masses, to the detriment of law, Melville may suggest an even more troubling scenario: the reign of what can be called a perverse totalitarian logic.

Linking the concept of perversion with totalitarianism brings issues of desire and fantasy to bear on political and legal formations. Indeed, it is on the plane of fantasy that White-Jacket's critique of the *Neversink* may be most virulent—a plane that has been practically overlooked by scholars. As I have suggested in chapters 3 and 4, a Lacanian conception of enjoyment provides a critical lens through which to further explore the salient and subterranean levels of national experience pertaining to ideological formations, issues that are clearly central to Melville's *White-Jacket*. To understand the full import of Melville's narrative, we must consider more than traditional antebellum political and social formations alone, taking into consideration Žižek's point that "[a] nation exists only as long as its specific enjoyment continues to be materialized in certain social practices."[32] By temporarily entering and painstakingly studying the *Neversink*'s modes of social relation—relations that are inextricably shaped by the domain of politics—White-Jacket reveals a threatening shift toward not only totalitarian-like rule, but also attendant perverse formations of enjoyment and desire.

In a theoretical sense, the general relationship between these concepts can be discerned in Žižek's assertion that "at its most elementary . . . level, 'totalitarianism' is not simply a political force that aims at total control over social life, at rendering society totally transparent, but a short-circuit between messianic Otherness and a determinate political agent."[33] Put differently, at the heart of a totalitarian mode of existence is a reconfiguration of the relation between the subject ($) and the symbolic order (or the big Other, in Lacanese). It is important, however, to be as precise as possible with terminology here. By using the term "messianic Otherness," Žižek is referencing—and departing from—Jacques Derrida's contention that Democracy is predicated on a gap between "the messianic promise of 'democracy to come' and all of its positive incarnations."[34] While the nuances of this debate fall outside the scope of this chapter, reconceiving Derrida's conception of the founding exception of the law might be helpful in setting up the notion of perversion that I will use to explore Melville's novel. When discussing Benjamin's "Critique of Violence," Derrida describes the originary moment of law as follows: "The founding or revolutionary moment of law is, in law, an instance of non-law. But it is also the whole history of law. *This moment always takes place and never takes place in a presence*. It is the moment in which the foundation of law remains suspended in the void or over the abyss, suspended by a pure performative act that would not have to answer to or before anyone."[35] This postulate undoubtedly captures aspects of what Agamben refers to as the law's relation of exception, but it falls short of illuminating its own inherent implications in two pivotal areas. First, what Agamben's work adds is the point that this foundational "moment" when the law is "suspended" can and does occur *in* specific nonoriginary historical moments. More precisely, Agamben demonstrates how modern democratic systems are not only predicated on but also continually sustained by such suspensions of law. Second, and here we come back to the notion of fantasy, the reason that Derrida might be correct in suggesting that this "pure ... act" of legal suspension does not "have to answer to ... anyone" is not, as he seems to suggest, because it exists in some untimely hinterland, but because such an act exists in a relative structure of perversion, where there is an inversion of the normal places of subject and Other. That is to say, in this zone of exception where the law incorporates others by suspending itself, there is no one to answer to, because the law, the symbolic Other tout court, functions as a divided subject.[36]

As the specific aspects of this perverse structure are invaluable to my reading of *White-Jacket,* a brief overview is warranted. For the purpose of this discussion, we might break the concept down into two parts: Lacan's general conception of perversion and Žižek's understanding of the correlation between this mode and totalitarian political formations. Lacan states explicitly that perversion is "an inverted effect of phantasy. It is the subject who determines himself as object, in his encounter with the division of subjectivity." In doing so, "the sadist himself occupies the place of the object, but without knowing it, to the benefit of another, for whose *jouissance* he exercises his action."[37] This is why, in some cases, an executioner's "presence is reduced to being no more than the instrument."[38] With his jouissance "fixated," such a subject "freezes with the rigidity of an object, in view of having his division as a subject entirely reflected in the Other."[39] With an inversion of the normal fantasy structure (or, $a \lozenge \$$), perversion thus finds a subject (such as a masochist or a sadist) acting as if he or she is the direct instrument of "another will," or the object of an Other's desire.[40]

This notion, of course, builds on and departs from Freud's work on perversion.[41] As such, Lacan explicates sources of perversion using scenarios of childhood family drama. While the finer details of this saga are irrelevant, the basic plot is useful for setting up broader social conceptions of the relation. For Lacan, the perverse structure of acting as an object for an Other's will or desire links to how the child, in its desire for the mother's desire, at times "identifies with the imaginary object of her desire."[42] But there is more to it than merely attempting to fill the void in the mOther, as it were, by miming Mommy's object *a*. Though this perverse position is traditionally viewed as a refusal to relinquish the full enjoyment of the mother, Lacan makes clear that the pervert's ultimate aim is to invoke the absent Law (the father's separating injunction). According to Molly Anne Rothenberg and Dennis Foster, "Absent the intervention of the paternal function . . . , the only law that the pervert can bring into being is a set of rules and fantasy scenarios about limiting jouissance."[43] In these terms, perverts act in order to invoke what they feel is an absent law or limit, and garner enjoyment from what is imposed on them in the process. It is these two aspects of the perverse structure, the lack of paternal law (or, in other terms, the master signifier) and the way that the fantasizing subject casts him- or herself as the object of the Other's desire, that most directly relate to Žižek's conception of totalitarianism.

If Arendt portrays the historical ground for the way modern totalitarian systems seek to extend into all modes of social life, and if Agamben depicts how such a system of biopolitics is effected through a relation of exception, then Lacan's notion of perversion might be seen as a means to begin exploring how these arrangements operate in terms of fantasy. According to Žižek, modern totalitarian bureaucracy—a form of government familiarly outlined in Kafka's early twentieth-century novels and, I argue, glimpsed in Melville's *Neversink*—operates in an antithetical manner to traditional feudal states where the "irrational" master signifier (embodied in the Crown) reigns. As opposed to a situation where a centralized authority exerts too much power, totalitarian logic exists "where this unary point $[S_1]$ which 'quilts' the field of knowledge (S_2) is waning. In other words: when the bureaucratic knowledge loses its support of the Master-Signifier . . . and is 'left to itself,' it 'runs amok' and assumes the features of 'mischievous neutrality' proper to *superego*."[44]

To unpack this a bit: Žižek here moves the above-mentioned aspects of the perverse structure to the horizon of the sociopolitical realm, whereby modern totalitarian states replace the unary master with a totalitarian leader.[45] Whereas a master or master signifier functions as a single centralized ideological quilting point, a totalitarian leader, instead, "takes the shape of an object which embodies S_2, the chain of knowledge (the 'objective knowledge of the laws of history,' for example), assuming the 'responsibility' of carrying out the historical necessity in its cannibalistic cruelty."[46] Thus, the totalitarian agent is perverse in the way he or she acts as an object on behalf of the knowledge or ideological system that is cast in the place of the Other.[47]

While I will discuss the salient role of the superego below, it is here important to clarify its relation to this perverse political alignment. According to Lacan, the superego is an attendant aspect of the "schism as it occurs in the subject," resulting from one's relation to the symbolic order and especially the Law.[48] Though it can be seen as the obsessive imperative to enjoy, perhaps it is more helpful to view it here as the general "aggression that the subject turns back upon itself."[49] The superego's involvement in perverse and totalitarian logic becomes apparent when one considers the reason Lacan gives for its self-directed aggression: the fact that "the mediation of the Law is lacking."[50] In sum, while the prohibition effected by symbolic authority (qua Law) is always partially sustained by a superegotistical obscene supplement, where a subject maintains the Law with fantasy, in a perverse–totalitarian scenario—where there is no master signifier quilting the ideological field—what was before only an obscene supplement becomes the ruler of the land. Following the logic of the pervert, a totalitarian subject acts in accord with the Other's will in the guise of a specific system of knowledge (or, in the case of *White-Jacket*, systems of martial law and shipboard labor). And since the entire edifice is built upon a fantasmatic attempt to fill in for a lacking big Other (or master signifier), this process is shot through, as it were, with obscene and excessive enjoyment. In such a world, as we will see, the dominant mode is a bizarre and fickle law "impregnated with obscenity."[51]

In entering the *Neversink* with Melville—a world whose surface is the "unobstructed fabric" (87) of a diligently polished deck, but whose interior houses obscure "vaults of buried dead," gunpowder, and "unaccountable bachelor oddities" (125)—we see what it is like for an antebellum subject to move into a sociopolitical space that, while contemporaneous with and spawned from mainland life, exists in a distinct and unknown zone. Unlike Mark Woolston's maritime world of masterly origins and endings in *The Crater*, White-Jacket enters a bizarrely intricate and hermetic realm that is already complete and humming along. Thus the epigraph to this chapter, a quotation shamelessly out of context from Blanchot's argument, is meant to highlight the structural essence of White-Jacket's voyage: what happens when a subject (an "exception," or a divided being, in a Lacanian sense) enters a martial world ruled by a perverse state of exception?

The jacket. Why not begin where Melville does? In opening the novel, Melville meticulously describes the "outlandish garment of [his] own devising" that White-Jacket fashioned when the ship, toward the end of its three-year voyage, ran out of pea jackets (3). Such an odd commencement and even odder garment have fired scholars' hermeneutical engines for years, reading the jacket, as Samuel Otter points out, as "a marker of... class status, an emblem of Melville's textual production, the fabric of ideology, and... the surface of the human skin." In this sense, Otter is correct in saying that the jacket "protects, defines, differentiates, exposes, constricts, and liberates. Both ship and jacket overflow with meaning."[52] It is not relevant here to add another singular analogical reading of this jacket to the mix. Instead, let us pick up Otter's point of its functionality in the novel, specifically its role of differentiation. For if the novel is a pseudo-investigative report on conditions aboard an antebellum naval frigate, opening the novel with a chapter on the narrator's outlandish garb seems to foreground his separation from the broader man-of-war world, however slight this difference may be. Consequently, the jacket can be seen as a screen for fantasy, as ground for subjectivity in a precarious environment that, I argue, seeks to force him into a perverse structure of desire.

From this perspective, this "gleaming white" "strange-looking coat" might act as a fetish-object for the narrator (3–4), allowing him to partition himself off from the logic of the ship's space. As Rothenburg and Foster explain, the fetish object's primary goal is "to open a hole in the world of the mOther."[53] In a perverse scenario, the subject is immersed in a world structured by an Other and, thus, must open a space for his or her own desire, to effect the lack necessary for normal fantasy to operate. In a reverse scenario, here it is a normal castrated subject that, to maintain fantasy as such, must use a fetish object to pierce a hole in a totalizing and foreign world (as when White-Jacket constructs the coat by cutting a "slit" in the surface of a duck frock "as you would cut a leaf in the last new novel" [3]).

In yet another sense, the jacket, forced on White-Jacket by the conditions of the ship's cruise, might be seen as the object (a) that this world pushes him to occupy. As the narrator makes clear, the "metamorphosis" that the jacket yields, one that surpasses the fancies of Ovid, was a considerable "burden" to carry (3–4). This is not to say, however, that White-Jacket ever reduces himself to this object, as the inside of the garment is strewn with pockets and chambers that he alone constructed, and, of course, he does manage a final escape from its domain. Perhaps it is most useful to view the jacket as operating in an ambiguous zone between these two registers, a state that reflects White-Jacket's own shifting and precarious subject position while within the *Neversink* world.

If the jacket and its ground of "normal" subject experience act as an initial foil to the naval world it and the narrator are immersed in, then the early description of Jack Chase, the inimitable and "noble first Captain of the Top," bolsters this divide (13). Reigning from his "airy perch" above the decks, Chase is figured as a learned and erudite "gentleman," who, acting as "a bit of a dictator," "egotistically" tutors White-Jacket and the other top men's "manners" and "taste" so as to reflect well on himself (14–15). Going further than simply delineating Chase's romantic and aristocratic propensities, Melville shows how his relative cultural capital (highly inflected with class privilege, of course) allows him to resist the various power structures of the ship. For instance, even before he fully illuminates the disciplinary mechanisms of the *Neversink*, Melville recounts how Chase, being an advocate of "the Rights of Man . . . and the liberties of the world," jumps ship in South America to aid the Peruvian navy's revolutionary cause (17). On being recaptured by Captain Claret, Chase's apparent regal status aids in persuading the commander to accept him back into American service without punishment (19). This separation from and sway over the power system of the ship, as we will see, resurfaces again in the pivotal scene in which Chase helps dissuade Claret from flogging White-Jacket.

But these two baseline subject positions are situated in the labyrinthine universe of the *Neversink*. From the beginning, the ship's complex universe is cast in terms of a logically ordered system. Indeed, the early chapters dedicated to parsing out the "grand divisions" of the ship's multifarious labor positions and responsibilities invoke a strange Kafka-esque affinity between precisely atomized bureaucratic machinery and unruly vertiginous bedlam. For instance, after White-Jacket introduces his position as a "looser of the main royal" and expounds on the various categories of other sailors (such as the After-Guards' Men, the Waisters, and the Holders), he bewilderingly reports that these are only the principle divisions and that "the inferior allotments of duties are endless, and would require a German commentator to chronicle" (11). We thus begin to see how the ship is an organized whole, but one whose system extends into an "endless" microlevel. This idea is soon developed when White-Jacket attempts to share the overwhelming experience of entering this system. He suggests: "It is from this endless subdivision of duties in a man-of-war, that, upon first entering one, a sailor has need of a good memory, and the more of an Arithmetician he is, the better" (11). White-Jacket foregrounds not only the way this controlled world extends into a vanishing interior of particulars but also the foreign logic of the system, figuring its structure in terms of an abstruse mathematical formula. It is, therefore, a new numeric–symbolic schema that he must learn upon entering the ship, being assigned a "number of his mess," "his ship's number," his "watch-roll" number, "the number of his hammock," and the "number of [his] ... gun" (11). In fact, White-Jacket hyperbolizes that all of the knowledge he had acquired during "circumnavigations of the terraqueous globe" is "useless" in this new naval space, where "he must begin anew; he knows nothing; Greek and Hebrew could not help him, for the language he must learn has neither grammar nor lexicon" (12).

Hyperbole aside, White-Jacket undoubtedly shows that the ship does indeed have a grammar and a lexicon, but they remain innumerate in light of his previous learning and experience. It is in this hermeneutical context that we might situate the series of metaphors White-Jacket uses to represent the *Neversink*, conceiving of them as a chain of attempts to translate a systemic experience that allusively exceeds any single existing sociopolitical arrangement. But even more important, we begin to see how, to White-Jacket, the *Neversink* world exists as a closed and mysterious system of knowledge. Not only does he fail to understand the minute particulars of the bureaucratic organization of labor on the ship (the *"holders,"* for example, remaining nameless figures "pale as ghosts" that emerge from the dark interior only during gales [10–11]), but he also struggles with the more pressing task of discerning the symbolic center of the system's logic.[54] In other words, because he is unable to grasp the quantitative specifics of the system's parts, he fails in turn to conceive of its qualitative structural agency. In many ways resembling Žižek's notion of perverse totalitarian rule—where the lack of a totalizing master signifier is filled in with a totalizing system of knowledge—at the outset of the novel the *Neversink* appears as a monstrous and veritably headless institution. For even if it does not visibly lack a center, the multitudinal nature of the system makes any such potential master a strangely new and distant one.

This symbolic ambiguity is exacerbated when White-Jacket attempts to explain the system of authority that oversees activity within the divisions of the ship. Though he introduces this rule as "the omnipotent authority under which he lives," by looking past his rhetorical description of how authority is wielded and more closely at its structural aspects, it becomes apparent that the crew is living "through" or "in" a more totalitarian-like mode of authority, as opposed to "under" a singular centralized master (135). While this difference is manifestly present, the way White-Jacket unequivocally describes Captain Claret as "a Harry the eighth afloat" tends to elide the true relations of shipboard power (23). Here the portly and cantankerous

Claret rules in "almost a despotism" where his "word is law." Famously figuring the ship as "a bit of terra firma cut off from the main," Melville concludes that the *Neversink* is thus "a state in itself; and the captain is its king" (23). This assumption is precariously maintained throughout the narrative with the various ways Claret seemingly lords over the men: controlling labor and liberty time, forcing sailors to fight for his own amusement, indiscriminately flogging men, and even overseeing the announcement of the time of day.

But while there is a clear hierarchical order of power below Claret (extending from wardroom officers to the common "people" of the ship [24–29]), the exact parameters of his authority, especially the authority above him, are much more ambiguous. The main relation in question, of course, is that between himself and the imperious commodore. Yet, at pivotal moments, Melville reveals striking holes in the captain's domain of control. One such scene occurs in chapter 27, when Mad Jack, the lieutenant of the watch, a prototypical hardscrabble and patriotic natural sailor (33), countermands Claret's order to "*hard up* the helm" and "scud" before an oncoming gale, a command that Melville makes clear was recognized by all as dangerously "unwise" (110–11). The import of the event, however, comes from the fact that Claret neither reprimands nor punishes Mad Jack, responses called for by the Articles of War. Melville intimates that there are two potential reasons for this, both of which act to limn the zone of the captain's influence. On the one hand, the scene reveals that Claret's authority is not that of a pure dictator, whose "word is law," but that his rule is situated within, and conditioned by, a system of knowledge pertaining to the maritime world and nautical operations. On the other hand, Melville uses the events to highlight the fact that Claret was "in an uncertain equilibrio between soberness and its reverse" during the storm. The point, though, is not that Claret is an irresponsible or ineffective master, but that he is an incomplete one. For this observation is followed by the aside that "so exact and methodical in most things was the discipline of the frigate, that, to a certain extent, Captain Claret was exempted from personal interposition in many of its current events, and thereby, perhaps, was he lulled into security, under the enticing lee of his decanter" (111). In this important sense, Claret's rule is secondary to and conditioned by the system of discipline (which includes the physical and conceptual arrangement of labor) that regulates the ship.[55]

As mentioned, however, even within the given institutional power structure on the *Neversink* there is an indefinite arrangement of upper-level authority. While the captain is associated with laying down the law, White-Jacket explains that since the *Neversink* is a flagship, it has the honor of carrying a commodore. Though technically outranking the captain, the role of commodore is shown to be an odd and rather regal position with unspecified duties beyond the general notion of leading various groups of ships. In fact, White-Jacket's early depictions of the old war veteran in his stately epaulets are blatantly condescending: pondering if the taciturn commodore was "dumb," and observing that his own position on the topsails was preferable to a "supernumerary" office such as the commodore's that had "so little to do" (21–22). White-Jacket soon learns, however, that the commodore wields much more influence than he had assumed. Finding one of the commodore's many written notes in the scupper-hole, communiqués taken and couriered by the commodore's secretary, White-Jacket learns that the old man had ordered the lieutenant to serve pickles to the crew that day.

At the time, this information is a "revelation" to White-Jacket, offering proof that the commodore, along with the captain, "meddled immediately with the affairs of the ship" (22). He soon observes, however, that the commodore's authority more directly supersedes that of Claret's. In chapter 51, Jack Chase is haranguing the captain to allow a day's shore liberty when the commodore makes an unusual appearance on deck to discourse with the men. After a stately exchange, the commodore tentatively assents to Chase's request, responding: "I think we must let you go" (215). Considering Captain Claret's immediate and "stiff" order for Chase to return to duty, one can easily discern who the "we" connotes in the commodore's response.

Yet, the relationship between the captain and commodore is anything but a simple hierarchy. In the scene just described, for instance, White-Jacket avers that Claret treated Chase harshly because "he wanted to neutralize somewhat the effect of the commodore's condescension." Moreover, according to White-Jacket, Claret "had much rather the Commodore had been in his cabin" as "his presence, for the time, affected his own supremacy in his ship" (215). Instead of a vertical alignment, with the commodore pulling the strings behind the scenes (as the pickles note suggests), the power arrangement here appears much more fluid, contingent on notions of space and time. In fact, the perpetual tension between the two rather ambiguous zones of command might be seen to affect a second level of exception within the aforementioned martial exception initiated by the Articles of War.

Melville contextualizes this indefinite matrix of authority within broader historical transitions when he first introduces the commodore. According to White-Jacket, due to America's "certain vague, republican scruples . . . about creating great officers," the navy had no admirals (20). In lieu of such an official symbolic position, the commodore functioned in an ambiguous and liminal state. For while he oversaw small bands of vessels and was highly respected within the navy, a commodore's authority was not recognized by the federal government "above his captaincy" (21). In terms of the notion of perverse totalitarian structures, such a scenario corresponds almost to the letter with Žižek's contention that since "the Enlightenment wants to do without [the master's or master signifier's] . . . 'irrational' authority; thereupon, the Master appears in the guise of the 'totalitarian' Leader: excluded as S_1, he takes the shape of an object which embodies S_2."[56] That is, the commodore might be seen as a transmogrified and demoted admiral, a position that seeks to operate structurally in the same manner, but has to do so without recourse to the symbolic clout and ability incumbent to a master or master signifier. Thus, in terms of the *Neversink*'s system of command, White-Jacket is left in a state similar to the one he experienced with regard to the divisions of labor: sheer bewilderment. Besides the fact that the commodore and the captain vaguely share modes of power, the commodore himself exists in a tenuous position—appearing to rule in absentia, but with the contours of whom and how he rules remaining unknown. Ultimately, therefore, though the dignified commodore looms as an enigmatic personification of higher levels of bureaucratic power, the uncertainty surrounding his role calls attention to the agency of the system he operates within. And the ramifications of this are paramount for White-Jacket's experience as well as the novel's political message. It is in such an enclosed world, one seemingly run by a self-regulating and mysteriously totalizing system, that White-Jacket begins to see how control assumes the form of threatening and perverse structures. To recap: the *Neversink* can be viewed as a totalitarian martial bureaucracy, existing in a perpetual state of exception where its power structure is effected through a complex system that extends into the innermost fabric of its subjects' lives. As we have seen with the structure of labor on the ship and with the relationship between Claret and the commodore, this obscure system remains ambiguously self-generating and *a*centered, the absence of a coordinating master signifier resulting in a strange operational structure whose contours and logic designate the conceptual problem of the novel.

In this context, the narrative's self-proscribed goal of delineating the "world of a man-of-war" might be rearticulated as the task of grasping how this strange system affects its vast laboring crew. While the subsequent sections of the chapter will examine the two primary arenas of such influence—labor and corporal punishment—the logic that undergirds it can also be apprehended in the ship's broader superegotistical mode of monitoring and, in fact, orchestrating sailors' enjoyment.

As mentioned, it is well nigh a truism that power, however "pure" in its apparent relation to the law, is supported by a realm of excess.[57] According to Žižek, for example, "the notion of the obscene superego double-supplement of Power implies that there is no Power without violence. Power always has to rely on an obscene stain of violence."[58] In what is a very relevant example, Žižek claims that one of the primary reasons for the mutiny on HMS *Bounty* is that Captain Bligh's pedantic overzealousness was mixed with "an impeccable personal integrity" regarding martial punitive practices. As such, the crew paradoxically resisted Bligh's rule because he refused to allow them to practice any of the many debasing and violent rituals related to the aforementioned "usage of the sea." In Žižek's terms, Bligh was "blind to the structural function of the ritualized power relations among the sailors." By banning these rituals, rituals that "provided an ambiguous supplement to the public-legal power relations," Bligh severely delimited the sailors' level of (obscene) enjoyment as well as the efficacy of his rule.[59]

The concept of the superego is central to this topic. As discussed, the superego is the self-directed aggression that acts as an obscene supplement to symbolic authority. But in a perverse–totalitarian schema this relation is redoubled. Lacan's famous correction of Karamazov's dictum—where he shifts the premise "If God is dead, then everything is permitted" to "God is dead . . . Nothing is permitted anymore"[60]—may provide a helpful follow-up to my previous summation of the totalitarian superego. Lacan explains this paradox by arguing that "it's on the basis of the father's death that the prohibition of . . . *jouissance* is established in the first place."[61] On this simple scale, the death of the father (the father, Freud's primal father, God) shifts worldly dictates into symbolic injunctions that are integrated into the subject's constitution and unconscious (in part as the superego). Without God you may be free to behave as you like, but your unconscious will undercut your approach to and attainment of enjoyment.

This process is altered, however, in a totalitarian sociopolitical setting. A totalitarian regime lacks a totalizing symbolic center (effecting something like a perpetual state of exception), and this lack catalyzes the creation of systems of knowledge and laws to fill in for or invoke the totalizing function. Herein lies the difference between a normal supplemental superego and a totalitarian one. While the former acts as an internal appendage to normal law, attaching shadowy and obscene enjoyment to notions of limits and failures, the latter is moved to the center, institutionalized, as it were, as an external system shaped by strange and ruthless demands. And this externalization of the superego function has the effect of creating a perverse structure, where the enjoyment of subjects within it is controlled (and ultimately experienced) by the system itself. As *White-Jacket* portrays, to a subject immersed in the romantic ideological and ontological structures of antebellum America, such a system is repulsive on every level—threatening not only specific bourgeois and Enlightenment notions of liberty but also the very ground of individualism.

Within the *Neversink*'s shifting zone of competing registers, commands and controlled activities relating to sailors' enjoyment are shown to exist on a continuum between customary obscene "uses of the seas" rituals like those in Žižek's discussion of the *Bounty* and more explicit totalitarian orders. The difference, again, is that while the former are "supplementary" acts often performed beyond the supervision of official authority, the latter are literally commanded by the power structures—constituting a required duty and responsibility.

An early example of this is the roll that "grog" plays on the *Neversink*. As White-Jacket explains, in the American naval service, "the law allows one grill of spirits per day to every seaman" (53). Though this practice is voluntary (White-Jacket, himself, abstains) it is shown to operate in a rigorously systematized manner, merging with other daily functions. According to Melville, the grog is divided into two portions, or "tots," and dolled out before breakfast and dinner. In his words: "At the roll of the drum, the sailors assemble round a large tub . . . filled with the liquid; and, as their names are called off by a midshipman, they step up and regale themselves" (53). The experience of drinking spirits here becomes a regimented affair, a part and parcel of the itemized and imperious routine all sailors experience.

The grog system assumes additional import when Melville explains how the portions of liquor sustain many of the sailors throughout the day. In terms ripe with fantasmatic elements, he states: "To many of them, . . . the thought of their daily *tots* forms a perpetual perspective of ravishing landscapes, indefinitely receding in the distance. It is their great 'prospect in life.'

Take away their grog, and life possesses no further charm for them" (53). Life on the man-of-war, we should add. Grog, therefore, infuses a necessary level of enjoyment into many sailors' lives each morning and evening, functioning during laboring hours as a looming carrot at the end of a proverbial stick. And while the men are not ordered to partake, the martial procedures surrounding consumption all but signal this injunction.[62] Though White-Jacket notes that this desire for alcohol sometimes precedes sailors' immersion in man-of-war life—citing "several forlorn individuals" who joined the navy for its promise of a consistent supply of grog (53)—this desire is clearly rechanneled and controlled once aboard. Following Žižek's line of thought, one might suggest that the navy's official routine of ordering men to consider drinking at two specific times each day might unburden sailors of their potential (superegotistical) mainland battle to become sober.

There is, however, a clear dialectic within the contours of desire on the ship, ranging from extrastructural desire initiated by sailors to forms of desire shaped by the ship's mechanisms. In fact, the tension between these two modes can be seen as the primary antagonism in the novel, with members of the crew—White-Jacket foremost among them—struggling to maintain their seemingly independent desire (in other words, fantasy) in the face of a martial world bent on at least temporarily restructuring it.

Throughout the narrative, White-Jacket describes sailor-initiated events in terms that accent issues of desire and enjoyment. Sometimes manifesting in obscene and clandestine engagements and other times in more transparent activities that erupt within the routine of the ship, these practices convincingly reveal that the *Neversink*'s control of its men is not complete. In terms of grog, for instance, Melville follows up the above discussion by recounting how a group of sailors managed to purchase a bevy of illegally stowed bottles of eau de cologne from the purser's steward and secretly "regaled themselves" in a drunken "orgy" (55). Tension between this type of sailor-directed enjoyment and the ship's varying forms of authoritarian control can also be seen in the juxtaposition between the way old sailors of the topmasts "spin interminable yarns" (9) and the manner in which officers control sailors' forms of writing—searching for the poet-sailor Lemsford's box of works (which is later accidentally blown into the sea by a cannon [192]) as well as confiscating and running a nail through another sailor's document of naval abuses (43). This trajectory of force, however, is shown to work in the other direction as well. For example, White-Jacket recounts how when Captain Claret prohibited checkers, the crew responded by sending "an iron belaying-pin past his ears" one night; soon after "it was indirectly rumored that the checker-boards might be brought out again" (173).

In addition to asides about sailors' forceful resistance to infringements on their pleasure, White-Jacket frames potential separation from and rebellion against naval power in terms of the space of the *Neversink*.[63] A perfect example of this is his lurid and gothic depiction of the mysterious "subterranean parts" of the vessel. While many locations of the ship remain a mystery to White-Jacket, including the interiors of the captain's and commodore's chambers, his detailed account of the "inexplicable apartments" of the ship's deep interior suggest that they may, to some degree, remain unknown to the ship's authorities as well (128). These locked "vaults" and their stores of ammunitions, the domain of only the gunner and his minions, are unequivocally tied to potential armed rebellion when White-Jacket imagines that the selfsame gunner and his men were "intent upon laying a train of powder to blow up the ship" like "Guy Fawkes" at the Parliament building (128). In the same section, Melville links this caustic underground space to obscene desire. Here, he tells how the ship's yeoman, a small, old, goggle-eyed man, meticulously and obsessively maintained the stores of martial weapons. His excessive attachment to the duty included "poking into ... [the] furthest vaults and cellars, and counting over his great coils of ropes, as if they were all jolly puncheons of Old Port and Madeira" (125). The coupling of inner-ship spaces and strange personal enjoyment results in rumors of the yeoman's "unaccountable bachelor oddities," which makes it difficult for him to retain the help of an assistant (125). In fact, White-Jacket himself is shot through with fear at the prospect of being "immured all day in such a bottomless hole" when "the goggle-eyes" of the yeoman "fasten upon" him (125).

As Melville makes abundantly clear, however, all potential for subversive forms of enjoyment (regardless of aim) exist within an indomitable and multifarious system of control. The superegotistical nature of this disciplinary structure is even more apparent in the customary Fourth of July celebration than in the example of grog. According to White-Jacket, on this day all sailors' allowance of spirits is doubled. And if in harbor, "the whole ship is converted into a dram shop," with "relaxed discipline" permitting sailors to "reel about ... on all three decks, singing, howling, and fighting" (89). The violent nature of the melee is especially relevant, where "old and forgotten quarrels are revived" and "combatants ... fight out their hate" (89). Indeed, the structural necessity of this obscene supplement for regular discipline is highlighted when a sailor-run play that the crew performs in lieu of this drunken romp (as the ship is at sea) creates a "delirium of delight" that is broken only by an approaching storm (94). In other words, instead of a ritualized mode of perverse and bizarrely enjoyable violence bolstering the ship's normal routine, the play's use of imaginary structures (focused here on Jack Chase's heroic performance of Percy Royal-Mast) catalyzes a mode of desire that is out of step with and threatening to the ship's system.

By far the best example of a ritualized totalitarian-like use of enjoyment is Captain Claret's order in chapter 25 for all hands to *"skylark!"* Though White-Jacket calls the order "humane," considering the frigid weather and the captain's intent to force men to stay warm, the proceedings clearly take on a perverse superegotistical bearing. After the boatswain proclaims the general order, "the ship's company were electrified" as by an "exhilarating gas . . . , or an extra allowance of grog" (102). With the officers standing by, all discipline was "broken through, and perfect license allowed." In the "crazy carnival" that ensues, White-Jacket outlines how a "boisterous mirth" was coupled with modes of ritualized violence, with "sparring and wrestling," *"Kentucky bites,"* and "the *Indian hug.*" But the most salient aspect of the short scene is the account of how the skylarking crew responds to an "ugly-Tempered devil of a Portuguese" who refuses to partake in the physical antics (102). After the Portuguese sailor "swore that he would be the death of any man who laid violent hands upon his inviolable person," the crew jumps him and roughly carries him aloft. While in the grasp of the men, the sailor "recklessly" swings his belaying pin about in a defensive gesture, hitting another crew member in the head (103). According to White-Jacket, this injury promptly ends the skylarking session and sends the Portuguese sailor to the gangway the following day for a flogging. Though not stated, the clear message here—one White-Jacket picks up and develops with his own subsequent and traumatic brush with flogging—is that the multifarious system of the *Neversink* demands that all sailors abandon themselves to the desire of the authorities. Furthermore, we see that one of the purposes of such skylarking is a relative training session for realigning sailors' symbolic coordinates, where sailors are not only forced to enjoy, but in the process, forced to perversely enjoy being imposed upon.

To back up a bit, Melville makes a point of establishing the baseline for existence on the man-of-war as "the intolerable ennui of nothing to do"

(176). Geographically separated from mainland life in almost every way and immersed in a totalizing network of supervised around-the-clock labor-related activity, the crew is left with little entertainment when not at work. In White-Jacket's opinion, this is the reason why smuggling illicit goods is so pervasive. Yet, a striking symbolic divide accompanies this geographic one, not only severing the crew from mainland life proper, but also forcing them to operate in new ways in relation to subject constitution and enjoyment. In addition to their ritualized practices and directed activities, White-Jacket reveals that even sailors' elective free-time engagements are shaped by the ship's perverse logic. After presenting a series of violently sadistic "diversions ... licensed by authority"—such as single-stick ("rapping each other over the head with long poles") and hammer-and-anvil (a game of bodily croquet played on all fours)—he introduces the captain's favorite game, head-bumping (274–75). Here, "two negroes (whites will not answer) [butt] at each other like rams." Though the obscene nature of the event is apparent, White-Jacket emphasizes the fact that two particular black sailors were "repeatedly summoned" in order to tilt "for the benefit of the Captain's health" (275). This explicitly perverse arrangement (the sailors acting for the enjoyment of the captain) is heightened when Claret flogs the two men for continuing their match outside the bounds of the official contest, railing: "Rig the gratings, ... I'll teach you two men that, though I now and then permit you to *play*, I will have no *fighting*" (276). Thus, the sailors may battle and "play" for the amusement of the officers, but the moment this activity takes on a personal import the game is up.

From Labor to the Lash

It is important to loop back, in a way, and place all such superegotistical episodes in the context of White-Jacket's perceptions of the *Neversink*'s primary labor and disciplinary structures. While his experience of flogging marks the sine qua non of the novel's reform angle and will be explored at length below, it shares with his figuration of shipboard labor an abhorrence of any underlying perverse configurations and effects. Beyond the typical figuration of maritime laborers as lowly tools (the sailors' tendons like "hawsers" and topmen scurrying across rigging "like monkeys"), Melville emphasizes the relationship between these objectified laborers and the ship's broader systems of control. In an initial scene, for example, the sailors act in accordance with officers' broadcasted orders and the sound of a fife (mirroring naval scenes in Cooper's *The Pilot*).[64] What stands out in White-Jacket's account is the apparent eagerness and energy with which the men follow such commands. Moreover, and most important, each man is shown to expend this energy from and in a specific location. As White-Jacket avers in the sing-song manner in which labor orders and action are played out: "Where was White-Jacket then? White-Jacket was where he belonged. It was White-Jacket that loosed the main-royal" (7).

Though not in as direct a manner as the ship's obscene rituals, such labor relations portray a relatively perverse structure in the sense that sailors seemingly take pleasure (in at least some form) in acting out the will of the ship's command. Again, according to Lacan, the pervert "occupies the place of the object ... to the benefit of another, for whose *jouissance* he exercises his action."[65] While sailors are consistently represented as objects at the mercy of officers' control (with even their sleeping positions controlled by orders such as *"Sleepers ahoy! Stand by to slew round!"* [83]), the way White-Jacket presents the specific nature of the ship's "grand divisions" brings vague notions of desire into the picture, for once orders are cried, White-Jacket knows where to be. In his own words: "When the order is given to loose the main-royal, White-Jacket flies to obey it; and no one but him" (8). In this way, White-Jacket knows what the command wants, and views himself as the only means to answer it. This sentiment is bolstered in Melville's subsequent description of how "every man of a frigate's five-hundred-strong, knows his own special place, and is infallibly found there. He sees nothing else, attends nothing else, and will stay there till grim death or an epaulette orders him away" (8). Here again the fact that men are objectified and pigeonholed into divided mechanized labor is of less importance than the type of narrative (and, hence, fantasy) that sustains this division. In this case, even if sailors do not comprehend the ship's complete network of relations, each knows precisely how he fits into this Other's world: in a "special" place that it is his sole responsibility to fill.[66]

As the novel progresses, Melville begins to reveal the true nature of a system that casts men in such "special" places. The background for this is White-Jacket's aforementioned difference. Though fitting into his topmast role and adhering to the ship's authority, his jacket—signifying not only a distinct look but perhaps a distinct mode of (fantasmatic) existence—signals a potential resistance to the system. In a comical scene rich with significance, White-Jacket tells how one night he was almost toppled from the mast when sailors on the deck below took his white jacket for a ghost and lowered the halyards to test its corporeality. When the first lieutenant refuses to grant him black paint in order to fix his jacket, he questions how an officer could refuse, seeing that "but one dab of paint would make a man of a ghost" (78). Keeping in mind the way sailors conceive of themselves as special placeholders of the system's (or, big Other's) various needs, White-Jacket's comic spectral nature might be informative on two levels. In terms of his own identity, it gestures to the way he exceeds and resists total immersion in the *Neversink*'s apparatuses. Taking the ghostly metaphor seriously, we might view the scene as revealing the danger (for White-Jacket and the ship) of having a sailor among the networks of normal labor whose spectral nature acts as a symptom, as a shadow of something foreclosed by the reality of shipboard life. As Žižek notes, a "spectral apparition emerges to fill up the gap of what cannot be symbolized.... [It] conceals not social reality but what must be primordially repressed in order for social reality to emerge."[67] Thus, we might view this scene as depicting how White-Jacket's own subjectivity qua fantasy is one such element that must be "repressed" for the perverse structure of labor and social relations on the ship to emerge.[68]

On another level, we might read White-Jacket's spectralness as an "untimely" echo of not only the repressed loss of "normal" desiring subjectivity, but also of the true nature and end of the system of labor he is in. It should be remembered that the sailors who took White-Jacket as a specter fancied that he was the ghost of the recently drowned ship's cooper. Calling to mind Derrida's notion that a specter marks a presence that though "seem[ing] to be out front, [in] the future, comes back in advance from the past, from the back," and Lacan's well-known point that the return of the repressed comes from the future, White-Jacket may thus signal the fact that the sailors' "special" tasks may amount to a literal reduction of life (and loss of life) for an Other's access to enjoyment.[69]

This notion is indirectly reiterated when White-Jacket surmises that all the cumulative specialized labor contributes to the real purpose of the complex craft: naval warfare. As such, each man's various labor categories and responsibilities might ultimately end in "the bloody marks of red ink—a murderer's fluid" that records his death in the quarter-bill (70). The paradox of this can be seen in Melville's subsequent aside about the purser's notation of "D. D." in his book for dead sailors, connoting "Discharged, Dead" (344). While the inane coupling of these terms may seem an odd turn of phrase hatched by some seasick accountant, it unwittingly gestures toward important subterranean truths about the system at large. On one hand, the logical short circuit between death and discharging a sailor from service suggests a strange homology between such service and fatality. Put simply, it seems to speak to the fact that the *Neversink* produces reproducible, replaceable laboring bodies and functional actions out of masses of living men. On the other hand, this bizarre need to discharge the dead may bespeak an attempt (unconscious or otherwise) to occlude the excesses that the system garners from sailors' bodies and actions.[70]

We might, in this sense, link the potential anxiety in the purser's language to that which inspires the sailors' custom of running a sailmaker's needle through a dead man's nose before committing the body to the deep—a supplementary action associated with a fear of bodies loosening from their shrouds and returning to duty as haunting ghosts (339–40). The difference with the purser, however, is that he at times seeks to *use* these bodies after death. As White-Jacket alludes to in a short critique of the recently bygone system in which pursers could charge what they pleased for the sale of wares on vessels, pursers were known by the saying, "The Purser is a conjuror; he can make a dead man chew tobacco," meaning "the accounts of a dead man are sometimes subjected to post-mortem charges" (206). In this sense, for the purser at least, the true "special" function of a sailor is his ability to be converted into surplus value, or, in Lacanian terms, surplus enjoyment. Without pushing too far, the specific terms of this scenario are also quite relevant; in fact, they dramatize the scene of perversion par excellence. Here sailors are literally reduced to a pure means for the Other's (the purser's) enjoyment. Thus, unlike sliding a needle through a dead man's nose to stymie a ghostly return, the purser's symbolic refrain of "D. D." might represent an attempt to cover over not only that the dead are decidedly *not* discharged, but also that all living sailors in the service ultimately act as an objectified means for the system to cash in, as it were, on their lives.

Such an arrangement is subsequently portrayed in the gothic account of Dr. Cuticle's surgical antics. Like the purser, Cuticle operates in a mode that forces the common seaman to occupy the place of an object that acts for the benefit of Cuticle's own enjoyment. What's more, Cuticle himself exemplifies the dynamics of a perverse subject formation. With his "unsightly collection" of "morbid anatomy" and his interest in rare specimens of the human body, he appears to situate himself as a direct agent (like Lacan's executioner) of the Other's will—the Other, in Cuticle's case, being the demands of incomplete scientific knowledge (249). While the lengthy and grotesquely comic surgical scene is informative in many regards, most relevant to our concern is the explicit way an injured sailor is shown to act as an object of enjoyment for the medical staff.

After precipitously deciding that a wounded sailor's leg requires amputation (in the face of a series of contrary medical opinions), Cuticle performs the operation before a coterie of on-looking surgeons from various ships in the fleet. With a hanging human skeleton (standing in, perhaps, for the body of scientific knowledge Cuticle believes he is serving) at the foot of the amputation table, Cuticle eagerly performs the operation, commenting along the way on how the difficulty of the procedure—the wound being so near the vitals—makes it "an unusually beautiful one" (261). As the amputation progresses, with other surgeons taking turns manipulating the wound, Melville emphasizes the way the injured sailor shifts from a "pillar of life" to a fascinating writhing limb (259, 261). In fact, not only is this amputated limb slated to be the focus of the next day's examination—effectively replacing any lingering concern with the sailor's health—but when Cuticle learns of the sailor's death he callously and offhandedly adds the remaining parts of the dead body to the examination schedule as well (264).

It is important to remember, however, that not all sailors share White-Jacket's critical eye toward the effects of man-of-war life. In addition to the way in which many sailors seem to enjoy their station, some men, such as a fellow named Shakings, actually prefer the shipboard structures. Associating the *Neversink* with the New York penitentiary Sing Sing, where he was confined for years, Shakings is quite fond of the new martial "State Prison Afloat." In both scenarios he is "relieved from all anxieties about what he should eat or drink" and "never [feels] afraid of house-breakers" due to the "watchman" always on guard (175). Shakings's seemingly odd preference in some ways bears out Žižek's point that the "pacifying intervention of the external social law" has the potential positive effect of, on a political level, aligning the masses into a revolutionary ideological position, and on a personal level, enabling one "to elude the self-torture provoked by the obscene superegotistical 'law of conscience.'"[71] Here we clearly see the latter at the expense of the former and, what's more, are undoubtedly meant to scoff at Shakings's penal state of mind. Yet no matter where one falls on the spectrum of labor positions or attitudes about them, White-Jacket makes clear that this network of relations is not completely totalizing. Like a "Chinese Puzzle," he explains, "many pieces are hard to place, so there are some unfortunate fellows who can never slip into their proper angles, and thus the whole puzzle becomes a puzzle indeed" (164). As the primary events of the novel reveal, however, this puzzle has a strange will of its own and most decidedly wants all pieces to fit in their places. And if per chance an "unfortunate" piece is found in a gap, in the negative space still available for alternate subject positions, the end of the lash may find him, even if he is a ghost.

In coming to the topic of the lash, therefore, we come to the central topic of Melville's critique of the man-of-war world. Indeed, if the *Neversink* is an anomalous social structure that forces sailors' bodies and desires to take certain perverse forms, then being flogged by the cat-o'-nine-tails is the spectacular mise-en-scène of this process. Melville includes a number of chapters solely dedicated to careful analysis and condemnation of the Articles of War, and the majority of these legal qualms relate to the inveterate practice of flogging. Such arguments, as various scholars have shown, take up and capitalize on naval reform rhetoric popular in the 1840s, especially amid the congressional session of 1848–50, which ultimately led to an 1851 ban of all flogging on U.S. vessels.[72] The conceptual center of gravity of chapters 33 through 36, the sections focusing on contemporaneous flogging debates, is White-Jacket's series of loaded rhetorical questions: "Is it lawful for you to scourge a man that is a Roman? asks the intrepid Apostle, well knowing, as a Roman citizen, that it was not. And now, eighteen hundred years after, is it lawful for you, my countrymen, to scourge a man that is an American? to scourge him round the world in your frigates?" (142). Such a pointed address to American citizens, based on the Acts 22:25 passage in which Paul asks a centurion, "Is it lawful for you to scourge a man that is a Roman, and uncondemned?" negotiates a myriad of political and rhetorical levels.[73] Obliquely illuminating the relation of exception opened and sustained by the Articles of War by using popular religious scripts, Melville raises issues of citizenship (which, of course, has implicit racial implications), geopolitical identity, and constitutional law, but also timely notions of a Christian ethos that dominated antebellum politics and public life.

In this vein, scholars have productively situated Melville's presentation of flogging in various contexts, the most prevalent being those pertaining to legal reform rhetoric and racial discourses surrounding slavery. But focusing on such legal wrangling or racial discourse alone (and there is a fair share of it) may miss an important aspect of Melville's criticism of naval life. In terms of the law, Melville's various direct juridical polemics might be seen to operate based on a logical schematic of judging particular naval acts and legal structures (the Articles of War) against the ideal of constitutional (and Christian) law. Two simple benchmark cases might helpfully frame the terms of this debate, acting as relative poles on a continuum of maritime legal ideations during the era. The positive ideal might be the experiences of the *Hannah,* one of the first official ships of the U.S. Navy, whose foray ended in mutiny, but whose men were pardoned from flogging by pressure from a conscientious public. The negative pole might fittingly be the USS *Somers* case, whose three tragically hanged mutinous crewmen are referenced in chapter 70 of *White-Jacket.* In the former case, a public and legal consensus checks the claims of a captain; in the latter, shipboard authorities precipitously enforce their own verdict. While such a simple continuum of appropriate applications of republican constitutional law undoubtedly shapes the reform rhetoric of Melville and others, it also allows an important loose fish to sally through its nets. As I have argued throughout, *White-Jacket* includes not only a pointed attack on contradictions in the American navy, but also a portrayal of a terrifying and nebulous new sociopolitical formation.

Melville's rendering of flogging is the centerpiece of a broader portrayal of life in a martial state of exception. As such, in addition to notions of what is and is not an appropriate application of the Constitution, Melville's novel considers a salient and shadowy third component: the strange relations in this man-of-war world and their *effects* on its subjects. It is from this context that we should explore both the notions of flogging and the law in the novel. In a Lacanian sense, we should analyze the specific historical logic or rhetoric that shapes the parameters of Melville's critiques as well as what his depictions of the martial *Neversink* reveal about the way such concepts operate fantasmatically.

Such an approach shifts the way most seminal studies have approached the topic of flogging in *White-Jacket,* most notably those, such as Samuel Otter's *Melville's Anatomies,* that focus on antebellum racial politics. I would like to acknowledge the truly vital importance of the historical research presented in Otter's project and its contribution to continuing analysis of race, and also shift gears a bit to explore other symbolic and ideological issues at play below or in addition to those linked to antebellum conceptions of racial identity. Otter cogently builds on various scholars' discussions of the analogy between sailor and slave by rigorously comparing the two in narratives of the age. Locating Melville's flogging scenes within ex-slave and abolitionist tales about scourging, Otter foregrounds the issue of flesh and racialized pigments, ultimately arguing that in *White-Jacket,* "the collapsing of distance between sailor and slave threatens the narrator himself, ... and provokes a fantastic attempt at self-preservation" (77). While White-Jacket repeatedly and directly comments on the issue of slavery in relation to naval flogging, I suggest that in addition to reading these scenes—especially White-Jacket's brush with the lash—as a "fantastic" means to portray racial self-preservation, we should also contextualize them within a broader critique of the *Neversink*'s social network and its relation to the political import of fantasy and enjoyment.[74]

This entails modifying the way we view the novel's relation to antebellum reform rhetoric itself (Charles Anderson goes so far as definitively calling the novel "propaganda"). As Isaac Land delineates, naval-reform rhetoric in the early nineteenth century progressively used the figures of foreign or black sailors to garner legal protection for white maritime laborers. Thus, "advocates of naval reform eagerly promoted the binary opposition between good [white] sailors and sinful Others."[75] In such a schema—one Otter meticulously explores in his own way—using corporal punishment on white sailors thereby threatens their very whiteness, lumping them with the licentious racial and cultural others who supposedly require such immediate corrective disciplinary measures.[76] Yet, while depictions of flogging in *White-Jacket* directly relate to slavery and its narrative tropes, Melville most assuredly does not employ the racial binary forwarded by popular reform rhetoric. In fact, considering Land's point that shipboard racial segregation based on space and labor (in which black sailors were pigeonholed in specific locations and duties) followed broader legal segregations, such as the South Carolina's 1822 Negro Seaman Act, the novel might seem significantly to sidestep the topic of race.[77] Although Melville notes that "black slaves were frequently to be found regularly enlisted with the crew of an American frigate, their masters receiving their pay," and vividly portrays how the captain demeans two black sailors in the head-bumping game (378), he does little to distinguish their roles aboard the *Neversink*. Moreover, unlike popular naval-reform rhetoric, in the head-bumping fiasco Melville places the seat of perversion and aggression on the side of the captain and not the black sailors. This is all to say that we should take both Melville's noted use of and his *departure from* racialized reform rhetoric into consideration. Thus, scholars such as Wai Chee Dimock, who (following Anderson) suggest Melville used such reform rhetoric because of its popular appeal may be only partially correct—and may be overlooking the substantial social critique that uses and exceeds such discourse.[78] By glossing over race as a factor in scenes of flogging, Melville might be seen as shifting the focus of reform rhetoric, gesturing instead to the perverse structural issues at play within the martial institution itself. In other words, in lieu of the common binary of protect *us* and punish *them*, Melville offers a more direct critique of military networks of relation, one that begins to move beyond limited antebellum constructions of race.

A helpful schematic for highlighting the different registers of Melville's critique can be found in Žižek's distinctions among "subjective," "symbolic," and "systemic" forms of violence. According to Žižek, subjective violence is violence performed by a defined agent; symbolic violence is the "violence embedded in our language and its forms"; and systemic violence is the "often catastrophic consequences of the smooth functioning of our economic and political systems."[79] Using this schematic, studies that consider Melville's critique of martial flogging through the lens of race operate primarily on the subjective and symbolic levels—basing analysis on the imaginary level of skin color and the terror of being "marked." Starting, instead, with the symbolic level and its formations of fantasy and enjoyment—which, of course, include important historical considerations of legal and racial discourses—may reveal structural systemic violence perpetuated aboard the *Neversink*. But this difference in approach does not affect merely the relative horizon of violence one might assess; by implication, the horizon of violence assessed directly shapes the qualitative aspects of the rest of one's historical analysis. The difference in this case is between tracing anxiety about flogging to existing (antebellum) racial schematics predicated by a feudal model of power relations and tracing it to a strange new sociopolitical arrangement that is not yet fully formed or grasped.

Scholars such as Otter clearly see this new relation at play, citing, for example, the "sadism" apparent in Samuel Leech's account of flogging in *Thirty Years from Home* (1843).[80] Yet, instead of following the trajectory of Otter's important line of analysis, we might focus on the symbolic nature of the perverse relation that is central to such scenes. Indeed, other accounts of naval flogging from this era seem to home in on just such a relation. In the anonymously published *An Inquiry into the Nature and Effects of Flogging* (1824), for instance, a self-proclaimed sailor rails against the effects of corporal punishment in the Royal Navy. One of the most interesting aspects of the many accounts of such punishment, however, is his cognizance of the vividly apparent presence of desire in scenes of flogging. In one such scene, after explaining how "the crew are turned up to witness the infliction" whereby "an offender shall undergo the torture of the *lash*," he moves into a description of the lurid process of stripping and shaving the condemned's body so the boatswain's mate may have "fair play."[81] And the author goes further than simply using colloquial terms of enjoyment. In depicting the moments before the flogging, he writes: "The exclamation, 'where's the boatswain's mate?' is scarcely uttered, before the scourge of humanity in joyful anticipation exclaims, 'Here am I, Sir,' and immediately, with malignant satisfaction depicted in his countenance, cheerfully takes his station."[82]

While this account undoubtedly emphasizes the fact that flogging was viewed as a perverse scenario during the era in which Melville was writing, it limits the sadistic notion of enjoyment to the person wielding the lash. Melville furthers the sense of perversion by depicting how flogging scenes also push the witnessing crews and, most centrally, the luckless victims toward a perverse structure (having witnessed 163 floggings aboard the *United States,* Melville is a qualified judge).[83] The first detailed account of flogging in *White-Jacket* makes this readily apparent. White-Jacket describes the effect of being summoned to "witness punishment" on an average seaman:

> To the sensitive seaman that summons sounds like a doom. He knows the same law which impels it . . . that by that very law he also is liable at any time to be judged and condemned. And the inevitableness of his own presence at the scene; the strong arm that drags him in view of the scourge, and holds him there till all is over; forcing upon his loathing eye and soul the sufferings and groans of men who have familiarly consorted with him . . . all this conveys a terrible hint of the omnipotent authority under which he lives. Indeed, to such a man the naval summons to witness punishment carries a thrill. (135)

This "thrill" dons an emphatically negative connotation stemming from the double movement of identifying with and distancing oneself from a condemned sailor, and clearly registers on the level of perverse enjoyment. In fact, the dialectic between the imaginary scenario of witnessing a flogging and fantasizing about the "inevitableness" of "one's own presence" under the lash invokes Freud's "A Child Is Being Beaten," especially Freud's three phases of "beating-phantasies." Though only circumspectly, the position from which White-Jacket writes the scene just quoted might be located between the first two phases of Freud's schematic. In the first, a child fantasizes about his or her father beating another child; in the second, the child fantasizes that he or she is the one being beaten. As Freud makes clear, this move to the second phase, "a meeting-place between a sense of guilt and sexual love" is the "essence of masochism."[84] Instead of offering sophomoric diagnoses of White-Jacket's psychological state, it is more relevant to note the symbolic context of this fantasy scenario.

As Darian Leader explains, Lacan's work on Freud's beating-fantasy essay directly links the fantasized scenes in question to "the oedipal passage itself," whereby the father "is present ... not as an empirically based figure in the fantasy, but rather ... as the index of the imposition of the symbolic order."[85] That is to say, the beating fantasy represents a perverse fantasy in that it focuses on the will or desire of the Other—here in the guise of the father (or naval authorities, in White-Jacket's case)—in lieu of a missing and definitive law.

And it is in this context that both Melville's anxiously "thrilled" sailor and those luckless men being scourged should be placed: as unwitting participants in perverse fantasy alignments relating to the imposition of a symbolic network, for both the sailors commanded to watch floggings as well as those being disciplined are forced into this perverse scenario by the "legal" power of the ship's authorities. In simple materialist terms, the sailors' fantasies and desires are influenced by the structures of the perversely ordered world they are forcefully placed in.

Even here, in the *Neversink*'s most refined perverse structure, however, Melville shows how sailors do not all respond in a uniform manner. This becomes apparent in the varying and progressively disturbing effects of the lash in the above-mentioned flogging scene, when four sailors are scourged consecutively for brawling. The first, a man named John, depicts a heroically romantic resistance to the onslaught, standing still and simply bowing his head. In fact, his silence—not calling out and, thus, acknowledging or invoking the Other's existence—is shown to cause the crew to "[whisper] among themselves in applause of their ship-mate's nerve" (137). What's more, John walks from the gratings raring to fight again. The second man, Antone, is not as resilient. In his case, the blows cause him to "[surge] from side to side, pouring out a torrent of involuntary blasphemies." For a man "never before ... heard to curse," notes White-Jacket, such a response is significant (137). Though he does not openly submit, the lash clearly catalyzes his shift into a wretchedly obscene mode. Even though he calls afterward for the captain's life, his threat is ignored by the officers, who obviously recognize it as an empty and pathetic ploy to regain status. The third man, Mark, is shown to have only "cringed and coughed" during the punishment, but residual effects appear when he spends several days off duty afterward due to the "misery" of the "insult." According to White-Jacket, this bawdy, fighting sailor quickly "became silent and sullen for the rest of the cruise" (138). And the last man flogged is Peter. Here Melville paints a lucid picture of relative conversion, with the once brazen lad "imploring" the captain to spare him in "weeping entreaties and vows of contrition" (138). In so doing, Peter transforms the captain's will into God's will (the Other's will), a move that is reinforced when the captain retorts savagely that he "would not forgive God Almighty" (138). Peter's agonizing calls of *"My God! Oh! my God!"* during the flogging, therefore, depict an ambiguous mix of pleas to a now distant or nonexistent old master and to a new one invoked in and formed by the experience of the beating itself.

We thus see what is at stake in such flogging scenes. Despite the fact that all of the flogged sailors evince a semblance of outer resistance, Melville makes it clear that, through the lash, martial law seeks to alter the men's inner space—figuring it as hunting them "straight through to the other word, and out again at its other end" (296). Consequently, we see that flogging may here operate differently from traditional modes of punishment. Foucault's well-known *Discipline and Punish* is predicated on such a shift in disciplinary modes, when, in the eighteenth century, "the entire economy of punishment was redistributed."[86] In the modern world, according to Foucault, the spectacles of public execution and torture are replaced with theories of criminality that focus on assessing and controlling the bodies and psychological landscapes of citizens. This, of course, marks the birth of biopolitics proper, the origin of the prison's and the madhouse's reign. As Rebecca McLennan avers, in the antebellum United States, "the penal systems [and hence punishment itself] . . . constituted a separate and distinct species of involuntary servitude, and not one that is usefully confounded with that of chattel slavery."[87] In an age formed by republican ideologies based on "the rights of man," legal punishment needed to be unambiguously distinct from archaic and monarchical acts of disciplining power.[88] Yet, as we've seen, although *Neversink* is just such a type of modern disciplinary institution, it is one that—in the case of flogging—relies on an antiquated medium of public punishment. Considering this schism, we can see the way slavery analogies are quite appropriate.

While Melville at times links the spectacle of flogging to the traditional goal of "strik[ing] terror into ... beholders" (371), the intended effects of such a practice clearly exceed notions of coercion and deterrence and include a specific horizon of influence over the direct victims of the assault. It follows that flogging operates more in the mode of Foucault's notion of public execution (a political ritual portraying a sovereign's power over "those whom he ... reduce[s] to impotence") rather than torture (a procedure of "producing truth").[89] But when a martial institution is situated in an age dominated by modern conceptions of discipline, these two basic categories of punishment operate in a new way. In fact, flogging in *White-Jacket* seems to synthesize the older disciplinary modes, moving closer to what Foucault, paraphrasing Marx, refers to as modern institutional attempts to constitute "forces in order to obtain an efficient machine."[90] In the context of the totalitarian relation that I have been tracing, we can see how such discipline acts on both levels simultaneously. In one sense, flogging dramatizes a manifestation of the raw sovereign power that lies behind and within the state of exception sustained via the Articles of War. That is, it embodies the rarified moment when, as Agamben puts it, there is an "indistinction between violence and the law," whereby "violence passes over into law and law passes over into violence."[91] In another sense, it both effects and stages the qualitative way this sovereign power instantiates itself in and upon subjects. At the zero level, scourging is a direct means by which to force a subject to act as an object (object *a*) in relation to a sovereign Other.[92] As we see with White-Jacket's "thrill," the staged scene itself residually puts the crew one step closer to such a fantasy scenario: they garner obscene pleasure from watching another being beaten, envision (potentially) themselves as the one being flogged, and—if desiring to avoid this direct experience—thenceforth *act* as the authority of the ship wills it.[93]

Except, that is, for a few brave and romantic individuals who refuse to submit. In Melville's own words, "There was more than one noble man-of-war's-man who almost redeemed all the rest" (385). While the gallant Jack Chase is one such man and, as we will see, White-Jacket is another, "old Ushant" is named as a third (385). In many ways, Ushant's simple plight can be viewed as a romantic model for manhood that White-Jacket employs in his own struggles on the ship. Old Ushant is the captain of the forecastle and a veritable "Nester of the crew" (363). Having grown a "magnificent homeward-bounder," or a "wide, spreading beard," Ushant balks at the captain's order to cut it (353). In terms reminiscent of Bartleby's later "I prefer not to," Ushant time and again meets Claret's injunction to shave with a refrain of, "My beard is my own, Sir" (365–66). Moreover, instead of relenting, Ushant tells the Captain: "You may flog me, if you will; but, sir, in this one thing I can *not* obey you" (365). And get flogged he does, bearing it silently as he "stood as the Dying Gladiator dies" (366). Though Melville frames the beard as a "token of manhood," there is unquestionably a level of enjoyment at play here (368), which is emphasized when Melville figures Ushant subsequently sitting in irons spending "many hours in braiding his beard, and interweaving with it strips of red bunting" (366). In terms used in chapter 4, we might view this beard as not just a token of manhood qua independence, but as an embodiment of Ushant's symbolic phallus, which, again, means that he is a normalized castrated "male" subject in the game of fantasy.[94] This, in fact, may account for the reason Ushant's flogging scene is so brief, for there is little at stake on the level of fantasy. Ushant possesses his beard, his fantasizing identity, and being scourged can do little to alter that.

This is not so, however, with White-Jacket—not exactly, that is. For in the pivotal scene in chapter 67 where he is "arraigned at the mast" and threatened with flogging, he makes clear that his manhood is not an issue, writing: "I felt my man's manhood so bottomless within me, that no word, no blow, no scourge of Captain Claret could cut me deep enough for that" (280). In looking more closely at the short account of these events, we see that, unlike Ushant's heroic refusal to part with his localized and personal manhood/enjoyment, White-Jacket's motivations are tied to much grander issues. In fact, this brief conflict, which is headed off at the last minute by entreaties for mercy by the corporal of marines and Jack Chase, marks the most distinct and direct encounter between White-Jacket's interior system and the exterior martial structures of the *Neversink*. As such, the repercussions, though subtle, are profound.

Harking back to earlier discussions of the *Neversink*'s totalitarian alignment, the cause of White-Jacket's arraignment is his ignorance of the "particular station assigned him" during the order to "tack" or "wear" (277). As White-Jacket explains, he realized he should have known his "duty" (read: obligation to act for an Other) on this specific occasion, but saw that most other men on the ship were also unsure of their assigned tasks, seeming to "catch hold of the first rope that offered" (278). In this sense, White-Jacket is quite aware of the implicit (superego-like) impossibility of fully knowing the ship's logical system. Yet, when this enigmatic knowledge is used to judge him, the true potential violence of the scenario comes home.

After "the weather-lift on the main-yard" is not released, the officers refer to their "Station Bill" and find that the task was relegated to none other than White-Jacket. In a hurried scene colored by obscene immersion in mysterious bureaucratic machinery, White-Jacket bewilderingly and repeatedly asks a boatswain's mate what he is being summoned for before he is ushered to the mast by a flute's signal (278). While White-Jacket initially stands on the spar-deck and makes "a desperate swallow of [his] whole soul in [him]," his primary cause of anxiety appears to be the threat of, in Lacanian terms, the loss of his individuated fantasy structure. In other words, what is at stake is not just Claret taking something from White-Jacket (his enjoyment, his soul) but also the triumph of Claret's symbolic perspective. With honesty but an air of relished defiance, White-Jacket responds to the captain's leading question, "Why were you not at your station, Sir?" by asking: "What station do you mean, Sir?" Though his gap in knowledge is shown to lead to White-Jacket's potential flogging—with the two men going back and forth over the contention that he should have known his role—in this process White-Jacket reveals that the primary underlying conflict is, in fact, the gap between the *Neversink*'s knowledge, tout court, and his own conception of authority.

This appears first in the way White-Jacket refuses to tip his hat to the captain during the above scene. While the refusal alone gestures toward the issue of manhood, his rationale for omitting the courtesy points to another motivation. White-Jacket explains that he did not perform the gesture simply because it "was not obligatory upon [him] by the Articles of War" (279). The paradox of this logic—acknowledging, to the letter, the rule of the articles but not necessarily the authority they bestow on the captain—is borne out in the moments before the flogging. As they prepare for the punishment, White-Jacket pointedly laments that he was about to be scourged "for a crime of which [he] was utterly innocent" (280). Utterly innocent? While reasonable if read as a mere figure of speech, the statement becomes loaded with meaning if taken, as it seems to be used, as a straightforward claim. For it is clear that notions of innocence have no place in the logic of the *Neversink*'s justice. White-Jacket made this, as well as the fact that he should have known his assigned position, readily apparent just moments before. This logical slip, therefore, illuminates the way White-Jacket elides the gap opened in the Articles of War where the captain's domain of power resides. And here we see the inner truth of the fantasy-space in play.

White-Jacket's move of acknowledging the text of the articles (citing he was not therein required to tip his hat) but denying the captain's rule and the matrix of perversion it operates within is quite understandable, even expected, on a conceptual level. In an age that saw the Republic's revolutionary guard looming before them, notions of "liberty" were not taken lightly. Moreover, according to Peter Limbaugh, "liberty" to this revolutionary set was associated with historical examples of resistance to power, including the "Magna Carta, followed by the Peasants' Revolt of 1381, and the overthrow of Charles I in 1647."[95] With the words of Rousseau no doubt ringing in his ears—injunctions such as "the duty of obedience is owed only to legitimate powers"—White-Jacket has every reason in the world to conceive of himself as innocent.[96] Not only are such general notions of liberty commonplace, so too are critiques of the Articles of War pertaining to flogging. In fact, the same logical and legal arguments Melville provides on this matter are echoed in publications shown to be his source material.[97] To cite just one prominent example, John A. Lockwood's *United States Magazine and Democratic Review* article "Flogging in the Navy" (1849) closes with the complaint that the current articles did not establish any juridical tribunal other than the courts-martial, and, therefore, according to his argument, there was a desperate need for an intermediary institution "to serve as a court of appeal from the decision of the commander in the award of punishment."[98]

But the *Neversink*'s direct and impossible punitive hailing forces White-Jacket to do more than reason thusly. Following his pleas of innocence, he recounts how "there are times when wild thoughts enter a man's heart, when he seems almost irresponsible for his act and his deed" (280). In what is the height of paradox, White-Jacket uses this spot-on description of perverse logic to explain his determination to kill Claret and himself (throwing himself and Claret overboard) before being flogged. As White-Jacket explains, "Locking souls with him, I meant to drag Captain Claret from this earthly tribunal of his to that of Jehovah, and let Him decide between us" (280). Such a figuration reveals how this martial zone, this state of exception, creates perverse relations even in such a Cato-like romantic gesture. In an odd twist, we see how White-Jacket's imaginary act of outwardly avoiding a perverse–totalitarian scenario carries over into its opposite—where, by planning to kill Claret in order to preserve or, more specifically, invoke the Law, he replicates the perverse scene of acting for and on behalf of an Other (again, Jehovah).

In this short circuit, of sorts, between White-Jacket's passionate but reasonable legal objections to Claret's rule (knowing) and his mad, perverse rejection of it (potential doing) can be discerned the crux of his quandary. By acknowledging the exception opened by the articles, but not the rule that manifests there, White-Jacket refuses fully to act or exist in a state where the big Other of the Law is completely replaced with the random contingency of the will of an Other. Reminiscent of Cooper, Melville has White-Jacket keep such a state in ephemeral and theoretical abeyance—conceiving of it and even living under it to a degree, but always conceptually renarrating (and, hence, negating) it through a fantasmatic appeal to what he views as the distant and ideal Other of the Law.

It is, then, this remote and true Law that is ultimately at stake. And, it seems, White-Jacket can accept that martial structures are born of such Law only if they are kept at a safe distance (even, say, the width of a thin jacket). In turning this around a bit, the final lesson taught in *White-Jacket's* breathing panorama of the world of a man-of-war is a markedly modern one, even by our own standards. For we clearly see that White-Jacket can live in this perverse world, even join it and act perversely at times, so long as he perceives that a kernel of himself (for White-Jacket, no doubt, the soul) remains untouched. This notion might be seen, in Žižek's terms, as representing the "inherent transgression" implicit in ideology, or the fact that every ideological identification is sustained by an imagined "awareness that we are not fully identical to it."[99] In other words, for an ideological apparatus to function properly its subjects must maintain "an inner distance toward the ideological text."[100] This inner distance for White-Jacket takes the form of a fantasy of Law, whereby he can live in the fabric of the *Neversink*'s world so long as he conceives of its rule as being trumped at the zero level by a higher and just authority.

In this way, Melville's closing is remarkably poignant. In a short final chapter, he expands the man-of-war world metaphor into a global "world-frigate" (398). And like the *Neversink,* we are told that this ship "outwardly regarded ... is a lie," having "store-rooms of secrets ... slid[ing] along far under the surface" of its "oft-painted planks" and the sea (399). Moving toward specifics, he explains that the "Articles of War form [the] domineering code," under which "the people suffer many abuses" (398). But, alas, he implores, "whatever befall us, let us never train our murderous guns inbound" and ends with the resounding plea:

> Let us not mutiny with bloody spikes in our hands. Our Lord High Admiral will yet interpose; and though long ages should elapse, and leave our wrongs unredressed, yet, shipmates and world-mates! let us never forget, that,
>
> > Whoever afflict us, whatever surround,
> > Life is a voyage that's homeward-bound! (400).

An easy reading would disregard such sentiment as pandering to a nationalistic and sentimental public. Yet despite its saccharine and hyperbolic tenor, it adheres logically to the text at large. And in keeping with that text, what we find is a complex continuum of messages. Much like Cooper in form, Melville responds to the lack of political law by appealing to a heavenly one. This move is significant, for it eliminates recourse to democratic and constitutional authority, authority that is seemingly removed only by geography and that looms as a real possibility for salvation throughout the novel's action. At the same time, he figures the divine alternative of the Other, too, as being immediately inaccessible, casting it, in a Derridean sense, as a messianic arrival to come. In this way, while Melville's message may be less conservative religiously than Cooper's fire-and-brimstone vision of an Other realm closing with a fallen earthly one, it may ultimately be more conservative politically. What we are left with can be seen as the newly plowed ground for modern cynical ideology, for the warning seems concerned not only with a possible future martial totalitarian state at home and abroad, but also with the public's response to it. And here, at least on the surface, the solution is a practical one: "Each man must be his own savior" (400). Each man must save himself by keeping an inner distance from the structure of this state. Thus, the logic of the cynic takes the deck: an ideological position that sees very well the falsities of reality, the corruption and posturing of social systems and practices, but that does not fully renounce them.

Yet, if we push a bit, we can also glimpse a negated alternative. In almost the exact structural move that Melville employs in *Typee,* White-Jacket's imaginary attack on Claret might be seen as a fantasmatic other possibility.

One that, as in *Typee,* is frightfully repulsive and hence rejected, but that is seen nonetheless, even if only sideways. And this fantasy just might hold enough water to sink both the *Neversink* and the embattled "world-frigate." In Melville's terms, what is shown is that the indomitable present and its flawed structures might be changed, but only in the heat of a crisis that forces one to close the requisite space between himself/herself and the ideological world he/she inhabits. It is clear, however, that Melville does not deem this move positive in either ontic nor ontological terms. It requires violence and the casting of bodies into the cold deep, as well as, perhaps even more troubling, a requisite inversion of existing fantasy structures themselves.[101]

· EPILOGUE ·

Incomplete Sea

Yet the sea is not full; unto the place from whence the rivers come, thither they return again.

—Ecclesiastes 1:7

THE SEA IS NOT FULL. And it is hoped that, reciprocally, this book's own shortcomings and perhaps short shriftings might be seen as symptoms of an open process at work. I close with Melville's haunting fantasy of violence as a way to emphasize the contestatory and at times ambiguous political functions of maritime narratives in the antebellum era. Holding true to a Lacanian notion of the Janus-faced effect of fantasy—a pacifying means to structure reality via desire and, at the same time, a site where the unassimilable excesses of the process take form—these narratives do more than simply run the gamut of ideological and utopian impulses. Rather, they depict complex and tension-wrought processes of ideological construction that accompanied the age's transition into modern socioeconomic alignments.

As I have shown, using a Lacanian perspective to explore antebellum texts and contexts entails a shift methodologically from the predominant mode of historical materialism into something more akin to dialectical materialism. That is, this perspective not only acknowledges symbolic gaps and libidinal excesses within a reconstruction of historical reality, but also moves those impasses and surpluses into the very center of historical and textual analysis. In many ways, this approach follows from Joan Copjec's critique of the historicism of Foucault. Copjec refers to "historicism" as "the reduction of society to its indwelling network of relations of power and knowledge."[1] Focusing on the realm of negation beyond positive appearances, she argues that a Lacanian conception of the Real gestures toward aspects of society, such as desire, that historicism, through its coupling of "being and appearance," "wants to have nothing to do with."[2] Taking up this point more recently, Copjec uses the concept of an exotic force, a phenomenon that accounts for the way two objects in close proximity are pushed slightly away from each other, to suggest that psychoanalysis is an "exotic science." According to Copjec, such a discourse is "devoted to studying the exotic force that operates in the subject to push her from herself, opening a margin of separation between her and parts of herself she will never be able to assimilate."[3] This force, in Copjec's terms, has "ramifying consequences for the conception of the subject and her relations with others."[4] This same force, a force analogous to effects produced by the aforementioned function of the parallax gap, is also, therefore, a major aspect of any given historical reality.[5]

It is in this context that I would like to view the epigraph from Ecclesiastes. Although the sea is not full, in the biblical verse, because of something like the motion of circulation, the continual passage of water from the outside to the inside and vice versa, this action nonetheless renders sea space and the body of the ocean structurally incomplete. Indeed, Melville's oeuvre is marked by a figuration of the sea as a mysterious and incomplete space that is linked to a mysterious and incomplete space within the subject. In *Moby-Dick*, for instance, Melville famously has Narcissus plunge into the ungraspable "tormenting" image he saw in the fountain, the "same image . . . we ourselves see in all rivers and oceans."[6] Even more directly, he notes subsequently the "strange analogy" that connects the vacant symbolic space at the center of the ocean (which renders the ocean "masterless," "a mad battle steed that has lost its rider") and the inner structures of the self (where the "insular Tahiti" of the soul is "encompassed by all the horrors of the half known life").[7] By suggesting that historical analysis should center on the exotic force operating within the self and within social realities, I do not intend to frame the sea as a romantic or pure space of openness. Such a move, even if made with the best-intentioned élan of cultural utopianism or deconstruction, ignores the sedimented layers of oceanic history. As Ian Baucom poignantly writes in considering the *Zong* massacre, the mass killing of African slaves on the British slave ship *Zong* in 1781, the sea is, quite literally, "the unfolding of historical time"; or, in Derek Walcott's terms, "the sea is History."[8]

The concept of fantasy allows one to examine how this historical reality is constructed in relation to and in light of its own incompleteness—an incompleteness effected by the material and crisis-ridden process of socioeconomic development as well as by the exotic force within the human subject.⁹ And this, of course, has profound implications for historical and literary analysis, particularly analysis of maritime experience.

A significant ramification of using a Lacanian perspective to examine cultural and political maritime encounters is the way it adds a new and essential layer of meditation to how we commonly approach various contact zones. The contact-zone models that have developed in light of Mary Louise Pratt's original formulation, including subsequent calls for a comparative approach by scholars such as John Carlos Rowe, have generated rich contemporary scholarship on borders and hybridity.¹⁰ Yet, according to Copjec, "cultural 'hybridity' has the effect of underestimating the force of cultural attachments by which subjects are, precisely, 'gripped' and thus fails even to formulate the problem that needs to be addressed in dealing with the question of cross-cultural encounters."¹¹ Such sentiment falls in line with Slavoj Žižek's ongoing criticism of liberal-democratic multicultural perspectives on cultural analysis, where he argues for a critical perspective (one obviously inflected by Marxism) that recognizes "an antagonism that cuts diagonally across all particular groups."¹² My hope is that these chapters have illuminated some of what is at stake in these arguments for literary and historical analysis of nineteenth-century maritime texts.

By addressing the inner incompleteness or impossibility of the subject and his or her social structures (something like the "other limit," in Casarino's terms) as well as the outer sites of cultural, political, and geographic contact, we effectively move the contact zone into a new horizon of relations. Citing Ernesto Laclau's conception of antagonism, Žižek emphasizes the way *"external difference overlaps with internal difference."* By this he suggests that the "difference between beings and their Being is simultaneously a difference within beings themselves; that is to say, the difference between beings/entities and their Opening, their horizon of Meaning, always also cuts into the field of beings themselves."¹³ This schematic has significant conceptual and methodological implications for the contact-zone model of historical analysis. Most notably, it elevates the importance of considering the function of fantasy in any contact scenario—for, as I have shown, it is via fantasy that subjects and social systems address and structure their incompleteness. If the material reality of any social being is conditioned symbolically through the way his or her fantasy space addresses inner gaps, then such fantasy structures play an immensely formative role in addressing and defining outer borders and antagonisms. What this critical perspective reveals is that even if contemporary contact-zone models have moved past a notion of *tertia comparationis,* or neutral third terms of comparison, they are still perhaps limited by standard positivistic conceptions of encounter, transculturation, and hybridity.[14] In addition to revealing the way negative space permeates us, a psychoanalytic perspective allows us to explore how this space operates in a given historical reality, especially one marked by manifest cultural and social antagonism. Such an approach shifts the contact zone into a parallactic network of intertwining levels: on one plane, the relation between two or more cultural/symbolic systems, and on another plane, the relation between a given material social reality and that same social reality's own incompleteness (including the incompleteness of each human constituent).[15]

In addition to having implications for various interpretive models that seek to define the (spatial, symbolic) object of contemporary American Studies (transnationalism, postnationalism, hemispheric studies, and so on), *Antebellum at Sea* has a direct stake in recent scholarship on maritime topics. In varying ways, I have addressed this growing body of scholarship by working in its shadow, in the foreclosed spaces produced by standard historical analysis. For clarity's sake, I want to reiterate my esteem for much of this historical work. Studies on maritime themes by scholars such as Ian Baucom, Samuel Otter, Wai Chee Dimock, and many others have not only added to our knowledge of nineteenth-century maritime realities and writings, but have also, in the process, shifted critical attention to the importance of sea space and experience within the broader production of the modern world. As I mentioned in the Introduction, this gathering critical interest in sea-related themes, coalescing out of transnational and postcolonial paradigms, has inspired the tenuous creation of what the editors of a 2010 issue of *Publications of the Modern Language Association of America (PMLA)* dubbed "oceanic studies." Though this issue of *PMLA* includes short pieces from a myriad of promising studies addressing various aspects of the sea, I came away from the collection with a feeling of disappointment and concern.

My concern stems from the way prescriptive essays within the issue define the critical parameters of the field. For example, Patricia Yaeger's provocative editor's column includes the following discursive call to action: "The premise of the oceanic turn in literary studies is this: we have grown myopic about the role that seas and oceans play in creating ordinary histories and cultures. Although the sea has been an exciting, deadly catalyst for trade and exploration for millennia, by the nineteenth century . . . oceanic travel and ideas had become routine. It is the business of oceanic studies to disturb this routine."[16] Although figuring nineteenth-century oceanic travel as "routine" (an argument borrowed from Margaret Cohen) is perhaps problematic, a more subtle peril may be found in the directive to "disturb" such "routine" contemporary notions of the sea. At first, one cannot but wholeheartedly agree with Yaeger. And yet, might her suggestion effectively launch oceanic studies into the swamp of New Historicism? Her opening proposition to reconsider the role of the sea within the production of "ordinary histories" is laudable, but framing this reconsideration via a binary of new versus routine ideas might negate, or at least compromise, any suggested historical revision—promoting both a possible political reconception of sea experience and, at the same time, a romantic "make it new" call to historicists. While the former might entail broader historical and ideological concerns of modernity (of both land and sea), the latter might encourage the production of minor localized or thematic histories that leave these structuring histories in place.[17]

The significance of this difference can be seen in Hester Blum's essay "The Prospects of Oceanic Studies," in the same issue. Calling for a "reorientation of critical perspective," Blum suggests that "recent work in transnational studies has been dominated by attention to questions of empire, exchange, translation, and cosmopolitanism—critical frames not unique to the sea."[18] One could, of course, agree with the notion that such ideological criticism has yet to fully attend to the nuances of historical sea experience. But Blum goes on: "I would like to see a new model for oceanic studies, one whose prospect moves beyond methodologies and frameworks imported from existing discourses and takes the sea as a proprioceptive point of inquiry."[19] The historical, let alone the political, problems with such a suggestion should be apparent. Indeed, centering the sea within inquiry might yield productive new perspectives on historical realities. In fact, Russ Castronovo and Susan Gillman's *States of Emergency: The Object of American Studies* does just this, presenting essays that address spaces and objects (including the ocean) in an effort to "recalibrat[e] the metrics of time and space with which we study . . . particular American problems."[20] As opposed to this model, where oceanic space and experience exist within a dialectical relationship with specific social and political landscapes, Blum's brand of oceanic studies would constitute a distinct field of inquiry—a field based around an exceptional space that would, presumably, generate a new sphere of specialized knowledge. And because we start and end with this exceptional space, scholars need to check their political histories at the door. Such a notion not only faces the aforementioned limitations inherent in New Historicism, but also goes so far as to replicate the structural logic of New Criticism: calling for a "unique" sea to be analyzed, somehow, on its own terms.

What interests me most about the antebellum maritime narratives I have begun to trace is the manifold ways they *do* relate to broader "questions of empire, exchange, translation, and cosmopolitanism." But not in a reductive, zero-sum correlation. Perhaps one of the most important benefits of studying this era from a perspective that views social reality as an impossible and incomplete becoming is the way it opens up historical analysis to that which was politically and symbolically foreclosed by antebellum reality itself. This is more than just the popular mode of tracing what Theodor Adorno refers to as the *membra disjecta*, or "traces of the existing," in maritime narratives or of brushing history against the grain, as it were.[21] If we couple this latter move with Benjamin's proposition that "the realization of dream elements, in the course of waking up, is the paradigm of dialectical thinking," then what a Lacan-informed approach adds is a study of how historical "dream elements," themselves, contribute to the constitution of the world awake.[22]

By implication, we ourselves must begin to awake from the edicts of historicism that currently condition inquiry in most fields of American literary studies. To borrow Russ Castronovo's line: "History, we might say, is a discipline from which we are trying to awake."[23] In many ways following the Frankfurt School's model of historiography, a model that emerges with Marx and is taken up more recently in the work of Alain Badiou and Slavoj Žižek, I seek to carry through with a historical analysis that, as a premise, considers the " 'openness' of the past itself."[24] This approach is far from merely revisionist in nature; even with a historicist aim in sight, if one takes seriously the lessons of psychoanalysis, then the only way to begin adequately exploring the antebellum maritime world is to consider how America's historical socioeconomic and political realities are predicated on impossibility, antagonism, and failure.

Melville's *White-Jacket*, as well as any narrative here discussed, portrays this world as a concrete yet incomplete space set in motion by desire. Here, the sea, the romantic space that makes up the earthly width of the passage homeward—and, in *Moby-Dick* at least, the passage out—is shown to birth not only renegades and castaways, but also what will become the modern liberal–democratic cynic.[25] Yet, as I suggest in chapter 6, perhaps Melville gave this bold child of the future a sibling once, lost, of course, in that watery world. And apparently a bizarre child at that. With murderous propensities. Unsightly too. For, strangely, it had a needle through its nose.

Notes

Introduction

1. Alexander Slidell Mackenzie, *Case of the Somers' Mutiny: Defense of Alexander Slidell Mackenzie, Commander of the U.S. Brig Somers, before the Court Martial Held at the Navy Yard, Brooklyn* (New York: Tribune Office, 1843), 4.

2. Quoted in Michael Paul Rogin, *Subversive Genealogy: The Politics and Art of Herman Melville* (Berkeley: University of California Press, 1979), 6.

3. See Marcus Rediker, *Between the Devil and the Deep Blue Sea: Merchant Seamen, Pirates, and the Anglo-American Maritime World, 1700–1750* (Cambridge: Cambridge University Press, 1987), 64.

4. Benjamin Morrell, *A Narrative of Four Voyages to the South Seas, North and South Pacific Ocean, Chinese Sea, Ethiopic and Southern Atlantic Ocean, Indian and Antarctic Ocean. From the Year 1822 to 1832* (New York: J. & J. Harper, 1832), x–xi.

5. Richard Henry Dana Jr., *Two Years before the Mast and Other Voyages* (New York: Library of America, 2005), 18.

6. Herman Melville, *White-Jacket; or The World in a Man-of-War*, ed. Harrison Hayford et al. (Evanston, Ill.: Northwestern University Press, 2000), 77.

7. As Marcus Rediker discusses in *Between the Devil and the Deep Blue Sea*, though romantic accounts of the sea were developing in the eighteenth century, the "romance of the sea" and its vision of sailors being heralded by the ocean is in part a product of early twentieth-century American historians, such as Harvard's Samuel Eliot Morison (4–5).

8. Slavoj Žižek, *Looking Awry: An Introduction to Jacques Lacan through Popular Culture* (Cambridge, Mass.: MIT Press, 1992), 6.

9. As Peter Linebaugh and Marcus Rediker note in *The Many-Headed Hydra: Sailors, Slaves, Commoners, and the Hidden History of the Revolutionary Atlantic* (Boston: Beacon Press, 2000), in the early modern era, "beyond the line" did not merely reference sea space or ship space, but also colonial outposts in the Caribbean, where "outcasts of all nations" ("convicts, prostitutes, debtors, vagabonds, escaped slaves, and indentured servants, religious radicals, and political prisoners") "had migrated or been exiled to . . . new settlements" (158).

10. Cesare Casarino, *Modernity at Sea: Melville, Marx, Conrad in Crisis* (Minneapolis: University of Minnesota Press, 2002), 1. My use of Casarino's language

in the title of this volume is a gesture to what I hope is a deep homology between our projects, though they take very different forms.

11. This narrative function can be seen in terms of what Henri Lefebvre, in *The Production of Space,* trans. Donald Nicholson-Smith (Malden, Mass.: Blackwell Publishing, 1991), calls the "production" of "representations of space." See especially pages 40–46 for an explication of the difference between "representations of space" and "representational spaces."

12. Ralph Waldo Emerson, *The Journals and Miscellaneous Notebooks of Ralph Waldo Emerson,* vol. 4, ed. Alfred R. Ferguson (Cambridge, Mass.: Harvard University Press, 1964), 112.

13. I reference Adrian Johnston's "Slavoj Žižek's Hegelian Reformation: Giving a Hearing to *The Parallax View,*" *Diacritics* 37, no. 1 (Spring 2007): 13. He argues that abstractions "constituent to subjectivity as such" (fantasy among them) are inherently part of concrete reality. Thus, he writes: "To paraphrase Lacan, these abstractions have legs—or, as Žižek phrases it, they have 'effects in the Real.'"

14. Walter Benjamin, *The Arcades Project,* ed. Rolf Tiedmann, trans. Howard Eiland and Kevin McLaughlin (Cambridge, Mass.: Belknap Press of Harvard University Press, 1999), 389, 391.

15. Quoted in Jean Laplanche and J. B. Pontalis, *The Language of Psychoanalysis,* trans. Donald Nicholson-Smith (New York: Norton, 1974), 314.

16. Ibid.

17. See chapter 5 of Giorgio Agamben, *Stanzas: Word and Phantasm in Western Culture* (1993), for a discussion of Freud's inheritance of Medieval phantasmology.

18. Sigmund Freud, *The Interpretation of Dreams,* trans. Joyce Crick (Oxford: Oxford University Press, 1999), 81, 124.

19. Ibid., 320–21.

20. Sigmund Freud, "The Relation of the Poet to Day-Dreaming," in *Collected Papers,* vol. 4, trans. Joan Riviere (London: Hogarth Press and the Institute of Psycho-Analysis, 1948), 176.

21. Ibid., 183.

22. Sigmund Freud, "Formulations Regarding the Two Principles in Mental Functioning," in *Collected Papers,* vol. 4, trans. Joan Riviere (London: Hogarth Press and the Institute of Psycho-Analysis, 1948), 17.

23. Sigmund Freud, *Civilization and Its Discontents,* trans. and ed. James Stratchey (New York: Norton, 1989), 23–24.

24. Ibid., 30–31.

25. It is important to note to what extent the seeds of a Lacanian and what we might call a Žižekian model of fantasy are found in Freud's thought. According to Jacqueline Rose's *States of Fantasy* (Oxford: Clarendon Press, 1996), Freud's work directly linked fantasy to social configurations: "As early as 1897, . . . Freud links

fantasy to what makes group identifications possible and impossible at one and the same time.... Fantasy is not therefore antagonistic to social reality; it is its precondition" (3).

26. For early aims of revisiting Freud's work, see especially Jacques Lacan, "Discourse at Rome" (1953), published as "The Function and Field of Speech and Language in Psychoanalysis," in *Écrits*, trans. Bruce Fink (New York: Norton, 2006), 197–268, and *The Seminar of Jacques Lacan, Book I: Freud's Papers on Technique, 1953–1954*, ed. Jacques-Alain Miller, trans. Alan Sheridan (New York: Norton, 1991), hereafter cited as *Seminar I*. For comments on a relatively later approach to Freud, see Lacan, *The Seminar of Jacques Lacan, Book XVII: The Other Side of Psychoanalysis*, trans. Russell Grigg (New York: Norton, 2007), hereafter cited as *Seminar XVII*, where Lacan proposes to return to Freud in "a revival from the other direction" (12).

27. Jacques Lacan, "The Mirror Stage as Formative of the *I* Function as Revealed in Psychoanalytic Experience," in *Écrits*, trans. Bruce Fink (New York: Norton, 2006), 75.

28. Ibid., 76.

29. Jacques Lacan, *The Seminar of Jacques Lacan, Book XI: The Four Fundamental Concepts of Psychoanalysis*, ed. Jacques-Alain Miller, trans. Alan Sheridan (New York: Norton, 1998), 95–96, hereafter cited as *Seminar XI*.

30. This is why Lacan designates the subject with the cross-out or barred matheme $. For an excellent explication of this concept in relation to Lacan's notion of the gaze, see Todd McGowan's *The Real Gaze: Film Theory after Lacan* (Albany: State University of New York Press, 2007).

31. Lacan, *Seminar I*, 140.

32. Ibid., 174.

33. Yannis Stavrakakis, *Lacan and the Political* (New York: Routledge, 1999), 4.

34. Lacan, *Seminar I*, 66.

35. Jacques Lacan, *The Seminar of Jacques Lacan, Book XX: On Feminine Sexuality, the Limits of Love and Knowledge, 1972–1973*, ed. Jacques-Alain Miller, trans. Bruce Fink (New York: Norton, 1999), 93, hereafter cited as *Seminar XX*.

36. Ibid., 4.

37. Slavoj Žižek, *The Parallax View* (Cambridge, Mass.: MIT Press, 2006), 26.

38. Slavoj Žižek, *In Defense of Lost Causes* (New York: Verso, 2008), 127.

39. Žižek, *Parallax View*, 390.

40. Johnston, "Slavoj Žižek's Hegelian Reformation," 7.

41. Adrian Johnston, *Žižek's Ontology: A Transcendental Materialist Theory of Subjectivity* (Evanston, Ill.: Northwestern University Press, 2008), 163.

42. Žižek, *Parallax View*, 242. According to Žižek, "'ontological difference' is ultimately nothing but a rift in the ontic order" (*In Defense of Lost Causes*, 128).

43. Slavoj Žižek, *The Sublime Object of Ideology* (New York: Verso, 2002), 28.

44. Ibid., 21.

45. In "Slavoj Žižek's Hegelian Reformation," Adrian Johnston describes these relations in terms of causality, suggesting that with "the Lacanian-Žižekian subject-as-void, the emptied 'x' emerg[es] from the successive implosions of identification transpiring as moments of the process of subjectification to which the volatile not-All of being gives rise" (17). Thus, it is not simply that symbolic failures produce the Real, but that these planes themselves emerge from rifts in the ontic order of being, what Žižek dubs the "presymbolic X" (*Parallax View*, 390).

46. Lacan's formula for fantasy is $S \lozenge a$. Here, the barred S (interpellated subject) relates via a lozenge (the vectorial function of desire) to an *a* (object cause of desire).

47. Lacan, *Seminar XI*, 41.

48. Ibid., 60.

49. Žižek, *Sublime Object of Ideology*, 45.

50. Slavoj Žižek, *The Plague of Fantasies* (New York: Verso, 1997), 14. In *Lacan and the Political*, Stavrakakis reiterates that fantasy is a social phenomenon as opposed to merely the private thoughts of an individual, writing: "The domain of fantasy does not belong to the individual level; fantasy is a construction that attempts . . . to cover over the lack in the Other. As such it belongs initially to the social world; it is located on the objective side, the side of the Other, the lacking Other" (51). Gilles Deleuze and Félix Guattari share this view in *Anti-Oedipus: Capitalism and Schizophrenia*, trans. Robert Hurley, Mark Seem, and Helen Lane (Minneapolis: University of Minnesota Press, 1994). They claim that "the first error of [traditional] psychoanalysis is in acting as if things began with the child. This leads psychoanalysis to develop an absurd theory of fantasy" (275). Instead, fantasy should be contextualized within a broader social field; therefore, "every fantasy is a group fantasy" (280).

51. It is a well-known Lacanian truism that desire functions metonymically, shifting from one object to another. In *Seminar XVII*, Lacan explains this context by describing how the divided subject emerges (as a signifier) by "intervening in the already constituted field of the other signifiers" and, consequently, "something defined as a loss emerges. . . . This is what the letter to be read as object *a* designates" (15).

52. As Žižek makes clear in *The Plague of Fantasies*, in late Lacan, the conception of the object shifts from its role in intersubjective struggles of recognition to being, literally, "that [what] the subject itself 'is.'" In other words: "*objet petit a*, as the object of fantasy, is that 'something in me more than myself' on account of which I perceive myself as 'worthy of the Other's desire'" (8).

53. Žižek, *Parallax View*, 40.

54. Žižek, *Plague of Fantasies*, 7.

55. Ibid., 40.

56. Fredric Jameson, *The Political Unconscious: Narrative as a Socially Symbolic Act* (Ithaca, N.Y.: Cornell University Press, 1981), 79.

57. In Fredric Jameson, "Imaginary and Symbolic in Lacan," in *The Ideologies of Theory: Essays 1971–1986*, vol. 1 (Minneapolis: University of Minnesota Press, 1989), Jameson argues: "It is not terribly difficult to say what is meant by the Real in Lacan. It is simply History itself" (104).

58. Jameson, *Political Unconscious*, 82.

59. Žižek, *In Defense of Lost Causes*, 291.

60. Ibid. Žižek subsequently links the economic absent cause to the Lacanian Real (291) and translates this schematic into terms that consider class: "The social organization of production . . . is not just one among many levels of social organization, it is the site of 'contradiction,' of structural instability, of the central social antagonism ('there is no class relationship'), which, as such, spills over into all other levels" (295).

61. As Lauren Berlant notes in her discussion of genre, harnessing such potentially disruptive enjoyment does not always pose a problem for the status quo. In *The Female Complaint: The Unfinished Business of Sentimentality in American Culture* (Durham, N.C.: Duke University Press, 2008), she writes: "The power of a generic performance always involves moments of potential collapse. . . . But those blockages or surprises are usually *part* of the convention and not a transgression of it, or anything radical. They make its conventionality interesting and rich, even" (4). See also Clint Burnham's discussion of "consolidated deviance," in *The Jamesonian Unconscious: The Aesthetics of Marxist Theory* (Durham, N.C.: Duke University Press, 1995).

62. Slavoj Žižek, *Welcome to the Desert of the Real! Five Essays on September 11 and Related Dates* (New York: Verso, 2002), 18.

63. Slavoj Žižek, *The Metastases of Enjoyment: On Women and Causality* (New York: Verso, 2005), 175.

64. Žižek's use of examples goes much further than mere theoretical illustration, often acting to open up new conceptual understandings of reality and, in the process, dialectically recalibrating the original theoretical concepts themselves. This is why critiques of Žižek's method, such as Tim Dean's "Art as Symptom: Žižek and the Ethics of Psychoanalytic Criticism," (*Diacritics* 32, no. 2 [2002]), often miss their mark. For example, Dean argues that a central problem with Žižek's method is the way he "pumps up the concept of the real" (25), pushing this register into a zone of proximity with the Symbolic Order and thereby allowing him to generate a series of "examples that lend the real any number of . . . positive contents" (26). This perspective assumes that Žižek is using Lacan's early formulation of the Real (that which "resists symbolization absolutely" [*Seminar I*, 66]), as opposed to later ones, and dismisses the possibility of valid theoretical

innovation—innovation that Žižek clearly demonstrates subsequently in *The Parallax View.*

65. Fredric Jameson, *Valences of the Dialectic* (New York: Verso, 2009), 26–27.
66. Ibid., 26.
67. Ibid., 27.
68. For discussion of the spatial "interactive zigzagging" of insurrection, see Benedict Anderson, *Under Three Flags: Anarchism and the Anti-Colonial Imagination* (New York: Verso, 2005), 81–82.
69. I cite Jameson's example as a useful illustration of methodological aim. I do not intend to wade into the complex relationship between deconstruction (especially via Derrida) and dialectics or psychoanalysis. Many, including Žižek, have written a great deal on this latter topic; see especially Andrea Hurst's *Derrida vis-à-vis Lacan: Interweaving Deconstruction and Psychoanalysis* (New York: Fordham University Press, 2008).
70. As Lacan notes in "Kant with Sade," in *Écrits,* trans. Bruce Fink (New York: Norton, 2006), due to their function (the fact that they have no deeper meaning other than the way they structure desire/reality), fantasies cannot be interpreted via a traditional hermeneutical model. Thus, "[a] fantasy is, in effect, quite bothersome, since we do not know where to situate it due to the fact that it just sits there, complete in its nature as a fantasy, whose only reality is a *[de]* discourse and which expects nothing of your powers, asking you, rather, to square accounts with your own desires" (657–58).
71. There is, of course, much scholarship on the transition to capitalism in the eighteenth and nineteenth centuries; see, for example, Marx and Engel's *The German Ideology* (1845–46); Maurice Dobb, *Studies in the Development of Capitalism* (London: Routledge, 1947); Eric Hobsbawm, *The Age of Revolution, 1789–1848* (Cleveland: World, 1962); Perry Anderson, *Lineages of the Absolutist State* (London: NLB, 1974); Immanuel Wallerstein, *The Modern World-System II: Mercantilism and the Consolidation of the European World-Economy, 1600–1750* (New York: Academic Press, 1980); Charles Sellers, *The Market Revolution: Jacksonian America, 1815–1846* (New York: Oxford University Press, 1991); and Michael Hardt and Antonio Negri, *Empire* (Cambridge, Mass.: Harvard University Press, 2000).
72. Thomas Philbrick, *James Fenimore Cooper and the Development of American Sea Fiction* (Cambridge, Mass.: Harvard University Press, 1961), 2.
73. Alexis de Tocqueville, *Democracy in America,* trans. Arthur Goldhammer (New York: Library of America, 2004), 463.
74. Ibid., 465.
75. See especially Bruce A. Harvey, *American Geographics: U.S. Narratives and the Representation of the Non-European World, 1830–1865* (Stanford, Calif.: Stanford University Press, 2001), and Martin Brückner, *The Geographic Revolution in Early America: Maps, Literacy, and National Identity* (Chapel Hill: Published for

the Omohundro Institute of Early American History and Culture by University of North Carolina Press, 2006).

76. See Robert Sattelmeyer, "Thoreau and Melville's *Typee*," *American Literature* 52, no. 3 (November 1980): 462–68.

77. Carl Schmitt, *The Nomos of the Earth in the International Law of the Jus Publicum Europaeum*, trans. G. L. Ulmen (New York: Telos Press Publishing, 2006), 48–49. Schmitt claims this "new" *nomos* begins taking shape with the Monroe Doctrine but does not fully develop until the last decade of the nineteenth century (see part 4).

78. Fredric Jameson, "Cognitive Mapping," in *Marxism and Interpretation*, ed. Cary Nelson and Lawrence Grossberg (Urbana: University of Illinois Press, 1988), 349.

79. Jameson asserts that cognitive mapping is needed in our phase of late capitalism to allow for a conceptualization of self and space—a conceptualization that is necessary for utopian and revolutionary thought. Here, I am using the same function in more of an ideological role: in the development of early capitalism, both state power systems and the individuals within them needed to establish a similar sense of relative social-spatial ontology in a new global network of existence.

80. Gunnar Olsson, *Abysmal: A Critique of Cartographic Reason* (Chicago: University of Chicago Press, 2007), 7.

81. Edward W. Said, *Culture and Imperialism* (New York: Vintage Books, 1994), 71.

82. Edward W. Said, *Orientalism* (New York: Vintage Books, 1994), 87.

83. Charles Wilkes, *Narrative of the United States Exploring Expedition 1838, 1839, 1840, 1841, 1842*, vol. 1 (Philadelphia: 1850), xxix.

84. Ibid., xxx.

85. Herman Melville, "The Encantadas," in *The Piazza Tales*, ed. Harrison Hayford et al. (Evanston, Ill.: Northwestern University Press, 2000), 137.

86. A similar gap can be found in Royall Tyler's novel *The Algerine Captive, or, The Life and Adventures of Doctor Updike Underhill, Six Years a Prisoner Among the Algerines* (1797; New York: Modern Library, 2002). Here, the captivity narrative that constitutes the first half of the novel shifts abruptly into travelogue writing when the narrator attempts to describe life in Algiers.

87. Žižek, *Plague of Fantasies*, 20.

88. Edgar Allan Poe, "A Tale of the Ragged Mountains," in *The Complete Tales and Poems of Edgar Allan Poe* (New York: Vintage Books, 1975), 683.

89. I refer to the contemporary trends of Americanist scholarship that work against an inveterate tradition of "exceptionalism"—a nationalist view that rests on the assumption that "America" can be adequately defined by its spatial and ideological boundaries. See especially Winfried Fluck, Donald Pease, and John

Carlos Rowe, eds., *Re-Framing the Transnational Turn in American Studies* (Hanover, N.H.: Dartmouth College Press, 2011), the joint issue of the journals *Early American Studies* and *American Literary History* (45, no. 2 [2010]); Donald Pease, *The New American Exceptionalism* (Minneapolis: University of Minnesota Press, 2009); Russ Castronovo and Susan Gillman, eds., *States of Emergency: The Object of American Studies* (Chapel Hill: University of North Carolina Press, 2009); Laura Briggs, Gladys McCormick, and J. T. Way, "Transnationalism: A Category of Analysis," *American Quarterly* 60, no. 3 (September 2008): 625–48; Caroline F. Levander and Robert S. Levine, eds., *Hemispheric American Studies* (New Brunswick, N.J.: Rutgers University Press, 2008); the entire January 2003 issue of *PMLA*; David Noble, *Death of a Nation: American Culture and the End of Exceptionalism* (Minneapolis: University of Minnesota Press, 2002); John Carlos Rowe, *The New American Studies* (Minneapolis: University of Minnesota Press, 2002); Donald Pease and Robyn Wiegman, eds., *The Futures of American Studies* (Durham, N.C.: Duke University Press, 2002); and George Lipsitz, *American Studies in a Moment of Danger* (Minneapolis: University of Minnesota Press, 2001); as well as such foundational pieces as Janice Radway's address to the American Studies Association, "What's in a Name? Presidential Address to the American Studies Association, 20 November 1998," *American Quarterly* 15, no. 1 (1999): 1–32; José David Saldívar, *Border Matters: Remapping American Cultural Studies* (Berkeley: University of California Press, 1997); and Michael Denning, "'The Special American Conditions': Marxism and American Studies," *American Quarterly* 38, no. 3 (1986): 356–80.

90. See especially Russ Castronovo's *Necro Citizenship: Death, Eroticism, and the Public Sphere in the Nineteenth-Century United States* (Durham, N.C.: Duke University Press, 2001), David Kazanjian's *The Colonizing Trick: National Culture and Imperial Citizenship in Early America* (Minneapolis: University of Minnesota Press, 2003), and Christopher Castiglia's *Interior States: Institutional Consciousness and the Inner Life of Democracy in the Antebellum United States* (Durham, N.C.: Duke University Press, 2008).

91. Amy Kaplan, *The Anarchy of Empire in the Making of U.S. Culture* (Cambridge, Mass.: Harvard University Press, 2002), 46. In *The Novel and the Sea* (Princeton, N.J.: Princeton University Press, 2010), Margaret Cohen makes a similar point from a very different perspective, suggesting that "genres that travel across space ... must be able to address social and/or literary questions that are transportable, that can speak to divergent publics or a public defined in its diversity, dispersion, and heterogeneity" (168).

92. See Dana D. Nelson, *National Manhood: Capitalist Citizenship and the Imagined Fraternity of White Men* (Durham, N.C.: Duke University Press, 1998). Other recent considerations of masculinity and antebellum America include: Ami Pflugrad-Jackisch, *Brothers of a Vow: Secret Fraternal Orders and the Transformation*

of White Male Culture in Antebellum Virginia (Athens: University of Georgia Press, 2010); Peter Coviello, *Intimacy in America: Dreams of Affiliation in Antebellum Literature* (Minneapolis: University of Minnesota Press, 2005); David Green, *Men beyond Desire: Manhood, Sex, and Violation in American Literature* (New York: Palgrave Macmillan, 2005); Amy S. Greenburg, *Manifest Manhood and the Antebellum American Empire* (Cambridge: Cambridge University Press, 2005); and Mary Chapman and Glenn Handler, eds., *Sentimental Men: Masculinity and the Politics of Affect in American Culture* (Berkeley: University of California Press, 1999). For an excellent consideration of women and the nineteenth-century maritime experience, see Margaret S. Creighton and Lisa Norling, eds., *Iron Men, Wooden Women: Gender and Seafaring in the Atlantic World, 1700–1920* (Baltimore: Johns Hopkins University Press, 1996). There are also productive studies that consider gender from a non-heteronormative perspective, such as Lee Wallace's *Sexual Encounters: Pacific Texts, Modern Sexualities* (Ithaca, N.Y.: Cornell University Press, 2003).

93. See *PMLA* 125, no. 3 (May 2010). Though I focus on the antebellum United States, there are also many contemporary studies of maritime themes from other national and historical perspectives. These include Christopher Miller, *The French Atlantic Triangle: Literature and Culture of the Slave Trade* (Durham, N.C.: Duke University Press, 2008); Felicity Nussbaum, ed., *The Global Eighteenth Century* (Baltimore: Johns Hopkins University Press, 2003); Bernhard Klein, ed., *Fictions of the Sea: Critical Perspectives on the Ocean in British Literature and Culture* (Aldershot, U.K.: Ashgate, 2002); and Anna Neill, *British Discovery Literature and the Rise of Global Commerce* (Basingstoke, U.K.: Palgrave Macmillan, 2002).

94. I reference specifically foundational studies such as Samuel Otter's *Melville's Anatomies* (Berkeley: University of California Press, 1999) and Wai Chee Dimock's *Empire for Liberty: Melville and the Poetics of Individualism* (Princeton, N.J.: Princeton University Press, 1989) as well as Peter Linebaugh and Marcus Rediker's *The Many-Headed Hydra: Sailors, Slaves, Commoners, and the Hidden History of the Revolutionary Atlantic* (Boston: Beacon Press, 2000). Other relevant historical studies of maritime texts and contexts include: Daniel Heller-Roazen, *The Enemy of All: Piracy and the Law of Nations* (New York: Zone Books, 2009); Paul A. Gilje, *Liberty on the Waterfront: American Maritime Culture in the Age of Revolution* (Philadelphia: University of Pennsylvania Press, 2004); Philip Gould, *Barbaric Traffic: Commerce and Antislavery in the Eighteenth-Century Atlantic World* (Cambridge, Mass.: Harvard University Press, 2003); Vincent Carretta and Philip Gould, eds., *Genius in Bondage: Literature of the Early Black Atlantic* (Lexington: University of Kentucky Press, 2001); and Rediker, *Between the Devil and the Deep Blue Sea*.

95. Howard Eiland and Kevin McLaughlin, "Translators' Foreword," in Benjamin, *Arcades Project*, ix.

96. Benjamin, *Arcades Project*, 13.

97. Herman Melville, *Moby-Dick; or, The Whale*, ed. Harrison Hayford et al. (Evanston, Ill.: Northwestern University Press, 2001), 159.

98. Benjamin, *Arcades Project*, 389.

1. Fantasies of the Common Sailor

1. See the last chapter of Gilles Deleuze and Félix Guattari, *What Is Philosophy?*, trans. Hugh Tomlinson and Graham Burchell (New York: Columbia University Press, 1994), as well as the preface to Casarino, *Modernity at Sea*.

2. See especially Linebaugh and Rediker's analysis in *The Many-Headed Hydra*. In mentioning Francis Bacon, I primarily refer to his *An Advertisement Touching an Holy War* (1622).

3. For a comprehensive study of sailors' reading practices, see Harry R. Skallerup, *Books Afloat and Ashore: A History of Books, Libraries, and Reading among Seamen during the Age of Sail* (Hamden, Conn.: Archon Books, 1974). Hester Blum, in *The View from the Masthead: Maritime Imagination and Antebellum American Sea Narratives* (Chapel Hill: University of North Carolina Press, 2008), cogently extends this historical picture. For discussions of Barbary captivity narratives, see especially Blum's "Pirated Tars, Piratical Texts: Barbary Captivity and American Sea Narratives," *Early American Studies* 1, no. 2 (2003): 133–58; Paul Baepler, "The Barbary Captivity Narrative in American Culture," *Early American Literature* 39, no. 2 (2004): 217–46; Elizabeth Maddock Dillon, "Slaves in Algiers: Race, Republican Genealogies, and the Global Stage," *American Literary History* 16, no. 3 (2004): 407–36; and Robert J. Allison, *The Crescent Obscured: The United States and the Muslim World, 1176–1815* (New York: Oxford University Press, 1995).

4. *The Mariner's Library or Voyager's Companion* (Boston: Lilly, Wait, Colman and Holden, 1833), viii.

5. Emerson, *Journals and Miscellaneous Notebooks*, vol. 4, 103.

6. Margaret Cohen, "Traveling Genres," *New Literary History* 34, no. 3 (2003): 486.

7. Blum, *View from the Masthead*, 4.

8. Ibid., 5.

9. Cohen, *Novel and the Sea*, 12–13.

10. Ibid., 15, 2.

11. Ibid., 14.

12. Ibid., 57.

13. The problematics I reference can be seen in Cohen's account of the relation between ideology and maritime craft. Identifying craft as "one strand in the entangled, multivalent formation we call modern reason," she suggests: "With concerns of safety and knowledge paramount, craft eschewed ideology in favor of

pragmatism, and indeed, the writings of Dampier, Cook, and their colleagues on unfamiliar indigenous peoples were at moments remarkably sober and nonjudgmental. At the same time, the mariner utilized craft in the service of profit and conquest; . . . and as we shall see in sea adventure fiction, the heroism of the mariner was pressed into ideological and cultural work for nationalism and capitalism back on land" (*Novel and the Sea*, 58). Here, pragmatism is figured as being outside ideology, just as maritime labor is portrayed as somewhat exterior to the domains of nationalism and capitalism "back on land."

14. For more on this topic, see Brian P. Luskey's "Jumping Counters in White Collars: Manliness, Respectability, and Work in the Antebellum City," *Journal of the Early Republic* 26, no. 2 (2006): 173.

15. Michael Newbury, *Figuring Authorship in Antebellum America* (Stanford, Calif.: Stanford University Press, 1997), 10–12.

16. While there are many studies of the antebellum literary scene, see especially Newbury, *Figuring Authorship*; Perry Miller, *The Raven and the Whale: Poe, Melville, and the New York Literary Scene* (1956; repr., Baltimore: Johns Hopkins University Press, 1997); Jonathan Arac, *Commissioned Spirits: The Shaping of Social Motion in Dickens, Carlyle, Melville, and Hawthorne* (New York: Columbia University Press, 1989); Michael T. Gilmore, *American Romanticism and the Marketplace* (Chicago: University of Chicago Press, 1985); and John Evelev, "'Every One to His Trade': *Mardi*, Literary Form, and Professional Ideology," *American Literature* 75, no. 2 (2003): 305–33.

17. Linebaugh and Rediker, *Many-Headed Hydra*, 15–20.

18. Rediker, *Between the Devil and the Deep Blue Sea*, 80.

19. For antebellum magazine culture in relation to maritime themes, see Philbrick, *Cooper and the Development of American Sea Fiction*, especially chapter 3.

20. Statistic quoted in Myra C. Glenn, "Troubled Manhood in the Early Republic: The Life and Autobiography of Sailor Horace Lane," *Journal of the Early Republic* 26, no. 1 (2006): 63. See Blum, *View from the Masthead* for a detailed study of such sailor autobiographies.

21. See Horace Lane, *The Wandering Boy or Careless Sailor, and Result of Inconsideration* (Skaneateles, N.Y., 1839), and John Nicol, *The Life and Adventures of John Nicol, Mariner* (Ediburgh: Blackwood, 1822).

22. Olaudah Equiano's *The Interesting Narrative of the Life of Olaudah Equiano, or Gustavus Vassa, the African, Written by Himself* (1789; repr., New York: Penguin, 1995) is, therefore, a very relevant text, as it is both an ex-slave narrative and, at times, a naval maritime narrative. Although Equiano's authenticity was not challenged in his time—due in part, no doubt, to the published names of influential citizens who subscribed to the narrative—interestingly, and one might say paradoxically, modern scholars, such as Vincent Carretta, have questioned the veracity of his African birth (for example, see Carretta, "Crossing the Atlantic in Early

American Literary Studies," *Pedagogy* 2, no. 2 [2002]: 276–80). While ex-slave narratives may face similar structural limitations as maritime narratives in terms of otherness and narrative form, the fact that, presumably, an ex-slave narrative is written by one who was fully in the position of otherness avoids many of the symbolic tensions I am exploring in terms of representing common sailors. In Giorgio Agamben's terms, an ex-slave might be seen as a "witness" providing "testament" of harrowing experiences he/she is a "survivor" of; see Agamben, *Remnants of Auschwitz: The Witness and the Archive* (New York: Zone Books, 2002), 17. Though sea narratives can act in this mode, they more broadly present tales about foreign maritime experience and events (in the register of facts and the mode of adventure), as opposed to accounts of direct and immediate subjugation and violence. For an excellent historical discussion of personal narratives by various forms of subjugated antebellum groups, see Ann Fabian's *The Unvarnished Truth: Personal Narratives in Nineteenth-Century America* (Berkeley: University of California Press, 2000). For relevant studies of slave narratives and issues of authenticity, see especially John Sekora, "Black Message/White Envelope: Genre, Authenticity, and Authority in the Antebellum Slave Narrative," *Callaloo* 32 (Summer 1987): 482–515; James Olney, "'I Was Born': Slave Narratives, Their Status as Autobiography and as Literature," *Callaloo* 20 (1984): 46–73; and Jean Fagan Yellin, "Written by Herself: Harriet Jacobs' Slave Narrative," *American Literature* 53, no. 3 (1981): 479–86.

23. Antebellum maritime narratives thus inherit Enlightenment-era rhetorical assumptions predicated on the moral necessity of truth telling. For more on this topic, see especially Janet Gabler-Hover, *Truth in American Fiction: The Legacy of Rhetorical Idealism* (Athens: University of Georgia Press, 1990), and Ian Duncan, "Authenticity Effects: The Work of Fiction in Romantic Scotland," *South Atlantic Quarterly* 102, no. 1 (2003): 93–116. Although European audiences and critics had long suspected the veracity of travel narratives, as seen in the *Critical Review*'s 1770 claim that "because there have been lying travelers . . . the veracity of almost every traveler is suspected" (quoted. in George Dekker, *The Fictions of Romantic Tourism* [Stanford, Calif.: Stanford University Press, 2005], 6), readers of antebellum sea narratives may have had a vested interest in the accuracy of narratives' accounts.

24. James Fenimore Cooper, preface [1849] to *The Pilot: A Tale of the Sea*, ed. Kay Semour House, in *James Fenimore Cooper: Sea Tales: The Pilot, The Red Rover* (New York: Library of America, 1991), 5.

25. Ibid., 5–7.

26. James Fenimore Cooper, preface [1834] to *The Red Rover: A Tale*, ed. Thomas and Marianne Philbrick, in *James Fenimore Cooper: Sea Tales: The Pilot, The Red Rover* (New York: Library of America, 1991), 427.

27. Hershel Parker, *Herman Melville: A Biography*, vol. 1: *1819–1851* (Baltimore: Johns Hopkins University Press, 1996), 376.

28. Quoted in Walter E. Bezanson, "Herman Melville: Uncommon Common Sailor," in *Melville's Evermoving Dawn: Centennial Essays*, ed. John Bryant and Robert Milder (Kent, Ohio: Kent State University Press, 1997), 33.

29. Quoted in Parker, *Herman Melville*, 1:392.

30. Bezanson, "Herman Melville: Uncommon Common Sailor," 49. For more on the historical authenticity of Melville's claims in *Typee*, see Wilson Heflin, *Herman Melville's Whaling Years*, ed. Mary K. Bercaw Edwards and Thomas Farel Heffernan (Nashville: Vanderbilt University Press, 2004), esp. chapter 16.

31. Bezanson, "Herman Melville: Uncommon Common Sailor," 48.

32. Herman Melville, *Correspondence*, ed. Lynn Horth (Evanston, Ill.: Northwestern University Press and the Newbury Library, 1993), 23.

33. See Mary K. Bercaw Edwards, *Cannibal Old Me: Spoken Sources in Melville's Early Works* (Kent, Ohio: Kent State University Press, 2009), for a historical review of the oral sources that shape Melville's various discourses and, therefore, his presentation of maritime experience. John Samson's *White Lies: Melville's Narratives of Facts* (Ithaca, N.Y.: Cornell University Press, 1989) is also relevant, examining how Melville uses "facts" to level an ideological critique of antebellum realities.

34. Melville manifestly gestures toward a seaman's dark tan, but the racial implications are obvious. See Gwenda Morgan and Peter Ruston's "Visible Bodies: Power, Subordination and Identity in the Eighteenth-Century Atlantic World," *Journal of Social History* (Fall 2005): 42–44, for a discussion of race and class issues surrounding skin color and labor—specifically, how newspapers figured the sun-burned visages of seamen.

35. I am, of course, providing a rough gloss of Spivak's argument. By loosely equating antebellum common sailors with the colonial/postcolonial subaltern, I do not intend to equate levels or forms of oppression. Rather, following Spivak, I am interested in approaching this specific historical class (if we can use this term) in a manner that illuminates the politics of representation.

36. Casarino, *Modernity at Sea*, 120.

37. Ibid., 122.

38. By "heterogeneous," I am referring not merely to the crew's racial, national, and class composition, but also to the way, in Casarino's view, this mixture potentially forms "new worlds of corporeal praxis and affect" (*Modernity at Sea*, 108).

39. Rediker, *Between the Devil and the Deep Blue Sea*, 5.

40. Dana, *Two Years before the Mast*, 3; hereafter cited in the text by page number only.

41. Lacan, *Seminar XI*, 60. As Slavoj Žižek elucidates, the *objet petit a* "stands simultaneously for the imaginary fantasmatic lure/screen and for that which this lure is obfuscating, for the Void behind the lure" (*Parallax View*, 304).

42. This fantasy seems to gesture toward the late nineteenth and early twentieth-century notion of "vital contact." As Patrick Chura explains in "'Vital Contact': Eugene O'Neill and the Working Class," *Twentieth Century Literature* 49, no. 4 (Winter 2003): 520–46, by the early twentieth century, this term referred to "experimental interaction between genteel radicals and workers" (522). Citing Christine Stansell's work, Chura points out that such interactions were engendered by the belief that the upper class could "revivify themselves through contact with supposedly simpler, hardier, more spirited people" (522). Such sentiment can be seen in chapter 1 of *Two Years*, where Dana explains that his journey was "undertaken from a determination to cure, if possible, by a [*sic*] entire change of life, and by long absence of books and study, a weakness of the eyes" (5).

43. Blum, *View from the Masthead*, 87.

44. See Rediker, *Between the Devil and the Deep Blue Sea*, 57–60.

45. Greg Dening, *Bligh's Bad Language: Passion, Power and Theatre on the Bounty* (Cambridge: Cambridge University Press, 1992), 76.

46. The four positions align in the following way: $\frac{\text{agent}}{\text{truth}} \rightarrow \frac{\text{other}}{\text{product}}$

47. See Slavoj Žižek, "*Objet a* in Social Links," in *Jacques Lacan and the Other Side of Psycho-analysis: Reflections on Seminar XVII*, ed. Justin Clements and Russell Grigg (Durham, N.C.: Duke University Press, 2007), 107–128. Žižek notes "the historicity inscribed in Lacan's matrix of the four discourses," and explains that the master's discourse "stands not for the premodern master, but for the absolute monarchy, this first figure of modernity that effectively undermined the articulate network of feudal relations" (109). In *The Seminar of Jacques Lacan, Book VII: The Ethics of Psychoanalysis, 1959–1960*, ed. Jacques-Alain Miller, trans. Alan Sheridan (New York: Norton, 1992), hereafter cited as Lacan, *Seminar VII*, Lacan adds an earlier historical stage to this apparent teleological declension by discussing how Aristotle's classic Master is all-powerful, living apart from the labor of the slave; opposed to this is Hegel's master: "[a] cuckold of historical development" and a veritable "negation" of the classical position (11–12, 23).

48. Lacan's formula for the master's discourse is as follows: $\frac{S_1}{\$} \rightarrow \frac{S_2}{a}$

With S_1 representing a master signifier that addresses S_2 or knowledge, which is here in the position of other/slave. Through this interaction, S_2 produces and simultaneously loses a, or object a/jouissance, while $\$$, the truth of a divided subject, is hidden beneath the bar of S_1. Besides Lacan's *Seminar XVII*, for further explication see Justin Clemens and Russell Grigg, eds., *Jacques Lacan and the Other Side of Psychoanalysis: Reflections on Seminar XVII* (Durham, N.C.: Duke University Press, 2006), and Bruce Fink, *The Lacanian Subject: Between Language and Jouissance* (Princeton, N.J.: Princeton University Press, 1995).

49. Lacan, *Seminar XVII*, 21. For a discussion of how Lacan's figuration of the master's role breaks from Hegel's original conception, see Mladen Dolar, "Hegel as the Other Side of Psychoanalysis," in *Jacques Lacan and the Other Side of Psychoanalysis: Reflections on Seminar XVII*, ed. Justin Clemens and Russell Grigg (Durham, N.C.: Duke University Press, 2006).

50. Lacan, *Seminar XVII*, 31–32.

51. Ibid., 32.

52. The fantasmatic relation between master and slave is thus structurally homologous to the relation between the subject and the big Other (with the slave's knowledge acting, in part, to fill out this vacant space). According to Žižek: "The split between the subject's knowledge and the Other's knowledge ... is inherent in the subject himself: it is the split between what the subject knows and what the subject presupposes/imputes to the Other to know" (*Parallax View*, 353).

53. As Kevin Bruyneel suggests in *The Third Space of Sovereignty: The Postcolonial Politics of U.S.–Indigenous Relations* (Minneapolis: University of Minnesota Press, 2007), "Spivak's question is not about the vocal cords of the colonized; it is about the colonizer's eardrums. 'Can the subaltern speak?' really means, 'Are the colonizers deaf?' not 'Are the colonized mute?'" (217). Here, I am emphasizing the symbolic functions and formations that condition the colonizer's eardrums and, at the same time, expanding the definition of colonizer, locating it in discursive formations of discourse as well as in traditional institutions of power.

54. Lacan, *Seminar XVII*, 44. In Dominiek Hoens, "Toward New Perversion: Psychoanalysis," in *Jacques Lacan and the Other Side of Psycho-analysis: Reflections on Seminar XVII*, ed. Justin Clements and Russell Grigg (Durham, N.C.: Duke University Press, 2007), Hoens explains that the master's discourse seems to "[work] without a fantasmatic support" (93). He does so based on the double bar between the positions of the subject ($) and that of object *a*—the two poles of the Lacanian formula for fantasy. While this claim is sound, I argue that the discourse's formula as articulated in chapter 3 of Lacan's *Seminar XVII* suggests that the master does indeed have a fantasmatic connection to object *a*. Although Lacan states that "in its fundamental beginning the master's discourse excludes fantasy" as "that's what makes him ... completely blind," he also makes absolutely clear that it is, in fact, the master's discourse that "makes possible [the] ... articulation ... [of] fantasy, insofar as it is a relationship *a* has with the division of the subject—($ $\lozenge$ *a*)" (108). In the context of maritime narratives, the position of master (author/symbolic order) is relatively blind to its real desires and activities, but these elements are nonetheless there (existing beneath the bars) and at times mediated through the locus of S_2 (here, the sailor).

55. Lacan also refers to this concept as *plus-de-jouir* and *sens joui*. For a review of the concept, see Fink, *Lacanian Subject*, chapter 7, n. 28. See also Žižek, *Parallax*

View, 266–67, and *Sublime Object of Ideology*, 49–53, for discussions of the link between surplus enjoyment and surplus value.

56. It is in this sense that Žižek posits that "access to knowledge is . . . paid with the loss of enjoyment—enjoyment, in its stupidity, is possible only on the basis of certain non-knowledge" (*Sublime Object of Ideology*, 68).

57. Lacan, *Seminar XVII*, 50.

58. According to Fink, *Lacanian Subject*, this type of enjoyment (siphoned off, in a sense, from language) might be seen as a "symbolic *jouissance*"—where language and thought are potentially "*jouissance*-laden" (106). See especially Lacan's *Seminar XX* and his discussion of male sexuation for an explication of such "phallic enjoyment."

59. Edgar Allan Poe, "MS. Found in a Bottle," in *The Complete Tales and Poems of Edgar Allan Poe* (New York: Vintage Books, 1975), 119.

60. Ibid., 124.

61. Ibid., 122. As Poe's story predates Dana's narrative, I here merely refer to the desire that Dana articulates. Interestingly, D. H. Lawrence's 1923 *Studies in Classic American Literature* (New York: Penguin Books, 1977) figures Dana's desire in a similar context to that of Lacan's schematic of knowledge in the master–slave dialectic. Lawrence writes: "[Dana] must watch, he must know, he must conquer the sea in his consciousness. This is the poignant difference between him and the common sailor. . . . For the sea must be mastered by the human consciousness, in the great fight of the human soul for mastery over life and death, in KNOWLEDGE" (122).

62. Joseph Hart, *Miriam Coffin; or, The Whale-Fishermen* (Nantucket, Mass.: Mill Hill Press, 1995), 201.

63. Ibid., 203–4.

64. Ibid., 208.

65. Newbury, *Figuring Authorship*, 80–81.

66. Casarino, *Modernity at Sea*, 53.

67. Ibid., 54.

68. Mark Simpson, *Trafficking Subjects: The Politics of Mobility in Nineteenth-Century America* (Minneapolis: University of Minnesota Press, 2005), 30.

69. Melville, *Moby-Dick*, 242.

70. Ibid., 243.

71. Ibid., 242.

72. Fredric Jameson, *Marxism and Form: Twentieth-Century Dialectical Theories of Literature* (Princeton: Princeton University Press, 1974), 329.

73. Hester Blum, "Pirated Tars, Piratical Texts, Barbary Captivity, and American Sea Narratives," *Early American Studies: An Interdisciplinary Journal* 1, no. 2 (2003): 157. Though Blum is discussing eighteenth-century captivity narratives, this observation arguably extends to the greater genre of maritime narratives of the antebellum era. According to Margaret Cohen, "plain style" was "the language

of work at sea, and here, as in other aspects of work at sea, efficiency and economy were paramount. The observations recorded in the ship's log and carried over into retrospective voyage narratives, conveyed the maximum of accurate, precise information with the minimum effort and space"; as she notes, this rhetoric "extended to the spoken terminology of the sea" (*Novel and the Sea*, 42). In *White-Jacket*, Melville comically alludes to the specialized technical discourse of the sailor by noting its absence from the lexicon of classical rhetoric: "And Blair's lectures, University Edition—a fine treatise on rhetoric, but having nothing to say about nautical phrases, such as *'splicing the main-brace,' 'passing a gammoning,' 'puddinging the dolphin,'* and *'making a Carrick-bend'"* (168).

74. Margaret Fuller, *Summer on the Lakes, 1843* (Urbana: University of Illinois Press, 1991), 11–12.

75. *The Female Marine*, ed. Daniel A. Cohen (Amherst: University of Massachusetts Press, 1997), 72.

76. See Egan's review of the 1989 Naval Institute Press version of *Ned Myers* in *American Literature* 63, no. 2 (June 1991): 328–29.

77. James Fenimore Cooper, *Ned Myers; or, a Life before the Mast*, ed. Karen Lentz Madison and R. D. Madison (New York: AMS Press, 2009), iv; hereafter cited in the text by page number only.

78. Wayne Franklin, *James Fenimore Cooper: The Early Years* (New Haven, Conn.: Yale University Press, 2007), 71.

79. As Franklin makes clear in *Cooper: The Early Years*, Cooper also used other sailors as sources. In writing *The Pilot*, for example, he appeals to Commander Richard Dale for historical maritime details. More relevantly, he uses his distant cousin Benjamin Cooper, a navy sailor, who—according to Franklin—helped correct Cooper's nautical terminology in the pivotal chapter 5 action scene (403, 409).

80. See Blum's *View From the Masthead*, especially chapters 1 and 2, for an account of sailors' reading practices.

81. Lacan, *Seminar XI*, 198–99.

82. Thus, the university discourse entails: $\frac{S_2}{S_1} \to \frac{a}{\$}$

83. Lacan, *Seminar XVII*, 35.

84. Ibid., 149.

85. Such a relation can be rearticulated with Žižek's leading question: "Can the upper level of Lacan's formula of the discourse of the University—S_2 directed towards *a*—not also be read as standing for the university knowledge endeavoring [to] . . . integrate/domesticate/appropriate the excess that resists and rejects it?" (See Slavoj Žižek, "*Concesso non Dato*," in *Traversing the Fantasy: Critical Responses to Slavoj Žižek*, ed. Geoff Boucher, Jason Glynos, and Matthew Sharpe [Aldershot, U.K.: Ashgate, 2005], 227). In this sense, just as capitalism seeks to maintain itself while integrating and reappropriating excess in the form of surplus value,

maritime narratives might in part act as a means to integrate and control the excesses that resist the new domains of bureaucratic knowledge (in terms of both quantitative and qualitative aspects of knowledge and related elements of enjoyment) by fantasmatically locating this excess in the experiential knowledge of a common sailor's labor and adventures.

86. Hugh Egan, in his historical introduction "*Ned Myers*: The Book," in James Fenimore Cooper, *Ned Myers; or, a Life before the Mast*, ed. Karen Lentz Madison and R. D. Madison (New York: AMS Press, 2009), discusses the compositional and textual ambiguities of Cooper and Myers's collaboration, such as passages where Cooper appears to interject his own voice for that of Myers, as well as how Cooper supplements Myers's ostensible account with information from previous publications, especially his *History of the Navy of the United States of America* (Philadelphia: Lea & Blanchard, 1839). See also "Textual Commentary" section of this edition of *Ned Myers* for information on Cooper's revisions and emendations.

87. Egan, "*Ned Myers*: The Book," xxxvi–xxxvii.

88. Quoted in ibid., xli.

89. Using Lacan's mathemes, this ambiguous transition from the master's discourse to the university discourse can be seen to relocate the position of agency from a blind master (S_1) to that of (Cooper's) knowledge (S_2) and, in turn, shift the other/sailor from the bearer of knowledge (S_2) to an unmitigated a. The point, again, is that the exploited sailor always functioned as a means to approach object a, but in such a shift toward the university discourse, this role becomes even more apparent—so apparent as to complicate underlying fantasies.

90. Theodor Adorno, *Negative Dialectics*, trans. E. B. Ashton (New York: Continuum, 2003), 12. Adorno's notion of conceptual nonidentity can be correlated to his argument that "intellect's true concern is a negation of reification" (xvii).

91. Jean-Luc Nancy, *Being Singular Plural*, trans. Robert D. Richardson and Anne E. O'Byrne (Stanford, Calif.: Stanford University Press, 2000), xiii.

92. As Agamben makes clear in terms of the narratives of Holocaust witnesses, all testimony "contain[s] at its core an essential lacuna," and as such the "truth" of events is not "irreducible to the real elements that constitute it" (*Remnants of Auschwitz*, 12–13). Agamben demonstrates how, despite such lacunae, testimony may hold something "absent" within itself that moves toward this truth. In this context, by focusing on symbolic impasses in communicating the knowledge of the nineteenth-century common sailor, my own analysis does not attempt to merely deconstruct such narratives and their claims by illuminating and privileging the lacunae that Agamben observes. Instead, it seeks to focus on the way such lacunae function ideologically and fantasmatically in the antebellum world. It is my contention that such negative analysis (in the form of a traditional ideological critique) is required along with projects (such as Agamben's work) that explore the liberating and redeeming truths contained in narratives of subjugation and extreme experience.

93. Lacan, *Seminar XVII*, 149.
94. Melville, *Moby-Dick*, 99.

2. Tarrying with the National

1. See Rediker, *Between the Devil and the Deep Blue Sea*, for a discussion of seventeenth-century American ports and their maritime development. For information on the origination of the United States Navy, see especially Ian W. Toll, *Six Frigates: The Epic History of the Founding of the U.S. Navy* (New York: Norton, 2006), and Cooper, *History of the Navy of the United States of America*.
2. Wilkes, *Narrative of the United States Exploring Expedition*, xxix.
3. Tyler, *Algerine Captive*, 226.
4. Owen Chase, *Narrative of the Most Extraordinary and Distressing Shipwreck of the Whale-ship Essex*, ed. Nathaniel Philbrick (New York: Penguin Books, 2000), 15–16.
5. Federalist support for amassing a national navy can be found throughout the *Federalist Papers*; see especially nos. 11, 24, and 41. However, as Simon P. Newman discusses in "Wearing Their Hearts on Their Sleeves: Reading the Tattoos of Early American Seafarers," in *American Bodies: Cultural Histories of the Physique*, ed. Tim Armstrong (New York: New York University Press, 1996), eighteenth-century mariners were often at odds with the Federalists, who did little to protect American sailors from English impressment. In 1796, for example, sailors marched through the streets of Philadelphia wearing French colors and rallying for Jefferson's candidacy (24).
6. See Bruce Harvey, *American Geographics: U.S. National Narratives and the Representation of the Non-European World, 1830–1865* (Stanford, Calif.: Stanford University Press, 2001), 70.
7. Georg Lukács, *The Historical Novel*, trans. Hannah and Stanley Mitchell (Lincoln: University of Nebraska Press, 1983), 34–35.
8. On the idea of *homo economicus*, see Ian Watt, *The Rise of the Novel* (1957; repr., Berkeley: University of California Press, 2001), chapter 3.
9. Gerald J. Kennedy, " 'A Mania for Composition': Poe's Annus Mirabilis and the Violence of Nation-Building," *American Literary History* 17, no. 1 (2005): 1.
10. I use such wording ironically in light of the phrase "structures don't march in the streets," which "revolutionary" students wrote on Lacan's blackboard in 1968. Lacan agreed with the students' point, but from an antistructuralist position of the Real. For this exchange between Lacan and students, see Lacan, *Seminar XVII*, as well as the discussion of related theoretical concerns in Joan Copjec, introduction to *Read My Desire: Lacan against the Historicists* (Cambridge, Mass.: MIT Press, 1994).
11. Scholars of the nineteenth century have begun to take up time, itself, as a social and historical object of study. See especially Thomas M. Allen, *A Republic in*

Time: Temporality and Social Imagination in Nineteenth-Century America (Chapel Hill: University of North Carolina Press, 2008).

12. Radway, "What's in a Name? Presidential Address to the American Studies Association."

13. Homi K. Bhabha, "Anxious Nations, Nervous States," in *Supposing the Subject*, ed. Joan Copjec (New York: Verso, 1994), 203.

14. Ibid., 204.

15. Benedict Anderson, *Imagined Communities: Reflections on the Origin and Spread of Nationalism* (New York: Verso, 2006), 7, 24–26.

16. Slavoj Žižek, *Tarrying with the Negative: Kant, Hegel, and the Critique of Ideology* (Durham, N.C.: Duke University Press, 1993), 201.

17. Slavoj Žižek, "Eastern Europe's Republics of Gilead," *New Left Review* 183 (September–October 1990): 53.

18. Although American Studies scholars such as Lauren Berlant suggest this homology, arguing that "nations provoke fantasy," their analysis has tended to shy away from a Lacanian conception of fantasy—using, in the case of Berlant's earlier *The Anatomy of National Fantasy: Hawthorne, Utopia, and Everyday Life* (Chicago: University of Chicago Press, 1991), a more general notion of an imaginary creation of a "National Symbolic." Although Berlant's *The Female Complaint: The Unfinished Business of Sentimentality in American Culture* (Durham, N.C.: Duke University Press, 2008) includes what is perhaps a reductive portrayal of Žižekian fantasy as "disavowal," I fully acknowledge her book's claim that "a view of fantasy as an affective claim, a pulse that points toward what real ought to feel like, is a convention of women's intimate public and . . . is at the magnetizing core of all intimate publics" (267). Though not engaging the work of Žižek or Lacan, Christopher Castiglia's *Interior States: Institutional Consciousness and the Inner Life of Democracy in the Antebellum United States* (2008) includes an interesting consideration of many of these concerns.

19. Homi K. Bhabha, "Introduction: Narrating the Nation," in *Nation and Narration* (New York: Routledge, 1990), 5.

20. Bhabha, "Anxious Nations, Nervous States," 202.

21. Ibid., 207.

22. Ibid., 216. The type of historiography put forward here is in many ways related to a dialectical conception of history as redemption. As Marjorie Levinson explains in "Pre- and Post-Dialectical Materialisms: Modeling Praxis without Subjects and Objects," *Cultural Critique* 31 (Autumn 1995), "The Frankfurt School project of redemptive historiography can be read as the confessedly impossibilist attempt to realize the hopes of the present rather than wait for history to redeem them. In order to do that, the critic must shape her practice not to that present but to a future that is somehow (in some coded, partial, obscure, and un-self-conscious way) sealed up in contemporary material conditions" (113). We might

add the pole of the past to the equation as well. In Žižek's terms, one should consider the "'openness' of the past itself"; that is, the past "contains hidden, non-realized potentials, and the authentic future is the repetition/retrieval of *this* past" (Žižek, *In Defense of Lost Causes*, 141).

23. Lukács, *Historical Novel*, 32. Avrom Fleishman, *The English Historical Novel: Walter Scott to Virginia Woolf* (Baltimore: Johns Hopkins University Press, 1971), 38.

24. Fleishman, *English Historical Novel*, 38.

25. Walter Scott, preface [1831] to *The Pirate* (London: Thomas Nelson and Sons, 1905), v.

26. George Dekker, *The Fictions of Romantic Tourism* (Stanford, Calif.: Stanford University Press, 2005), 157.

27. Nicola Watson, *Revolution and the Form of the British Novel, 1790–1825* (Oxford: Clarendon Press, 1994), 127.

28. Ibid., 134.

29. Pierre Bourdieu, *The Field of Cultural Production*, ed. Randal Johnson (New York: Columbia University Press, 1999), 75.

30. Walter Scott, *The Pirate* (London: Thomas Nelson and Sons, 1905), 69; hereafter cited in the text by page number only.

31. Despite the island's hermetic appearance, its dependence on the wrecking system reveals its underlying economic connection to the outside world. That is, although the island adheres to the policy that "whatever was cast on [its] shores became [its] property" (109), its dependence on this distanced expropriation reveals its denied reliance on foreign/global economic systems. Cleveland's arrival, therefore, acts as, if not a "return of the repressed," then a manifestation of the real of their economic condition.

32. I will go on to figure this redefinition of self-perception in terms of a Lacanian shift in symbolic identification. For the correlation among nineteenth-century masculine identity, travel, and conceptions of honor, see Michael Nerlich's *Ideology of Adventure: Studies in Modern Consciousness, 1100–1750*, vol. 1, trans. Ruth Crowley (Minneapolis: University of Minnesota Press, 1987).

33. Žižek, *Sublime Object of Ideology*, 118.

34. Ibid., 110.

35. Ibid., 105. Lacan's notion that symbolic functions condition imaginary ones can be seen early in his seminars when he suggests: "The regulation of the imaginary depends on something which is located in a transcendent fashion . . . the transcendent . . . being nothing other than the symbolic connection between human beings" (Lacan, *Seminar I*, 140).

36. Bhabha, "Introduction: Narrating the Nation," 3.

37. This can also be seen in Norna's conversion, where, at the end of the narrative, the Norse-descended enchantress burns her magical laboratory (562),

changes her name back to Ulla, and takes up the Bible. The same can be said for Minna, who abruptly abandons her fantasies about ancient Norse pirate warriors for a fidelity to Cleveland's adoption of a British identity, whereby she, in Scott's terms, "learned to exchange the visions of old enthusiasm . . . for a truer and purer connection with the world" (564).

38. James Fenimore Cooper, *The Pilot: A Tale of the Sea*, ed. Kay Semour House, in *James Fenimore Cooper: Sea Tales* (New York: Library of America, 1991), 12; hereafter cited in the text by page number only.

39. I use the term "exergue" here in the spirit of Jacque Derrida's *Archive Fever: A Freudian Impression*, trans. Eric Prenowitz (Chicago: University of Chicago Press, 1996). In a metaphorical sense, Cooper's inclusion of the impressment theme at the outset of the novel can be seen to reveal the underside or "other-side" of labor within the romantic themes of nationalist activity he will present. Quite literally, however, whether it is Cooper's intent or not, this scene acts to present this political practice and problem (the military's lack of labor) as a pretext to the novel's events. Cooper himself, of course, saw firsthand the deleterious aspects of English impressment practices while aboard the American merchant vessel *Stirling* from 1806 to 1807.

40. H. Daniel Peck, "A Repossession of America: The Revolution in Cooper's Trilogy of Nautical Romances," *Studies in Romanticism* 15, no. 4 (Fall 1976): 590.

41. As mentioned in chapter 1, Cohen conceives of "know-how" as being located "on the deck, not the desk" ("Traveling Genres," 486) and includes "democratizing political implications" in its potentiality as "a universal human faculty" (487).

42. Cohen, "Traveling Genres," 488.

43. Franklin, *Cooper: The Early Years*, 412.

44. Susan Fenimore Cooper, *Household Edition of the Works of J. Fenimore Cooper* (New York and Cambridge, Mass.: Houghton Mifflin [Hurd and Mifflin], 1876–1884), xxii. Susan Cooper's passage read as follows: "With Long Tom Coffin, also, he was in later life less satisfied than most of his readers. As he looked back at the character, in the maturity of long experience, he saw it with a clearer view, a greater fullness of conception, a more complete finish of detail; he considered it, as it now appears, as only a sketch, and would gladly have wrought up the portrait of the old salt, a man after his own heart, to a finished picture, as he had done with Natty Bumppo. He felt that he had not done full justice to Long Tom. Of the two characters, he considered that of Boltrope better, perhaps, as a piece of workmanship, than that of the old Nantucket hero" (xxii).

45. See Philbrick, *Cooper and the Development of American Sea Fiction*, especially chapter 2, for a review of early nationalism and militarism in both Cooper's work and antebellum society.

46. Peck, "Repossession of America," 589.

47. Wayne Franklin, "Fathering the Son: The Cultural Origins of James Fenimore Cooper," *Resources for American Literary Study* 27, no. 2 (2001): 155.

48. For studies of Cooper's politics, see works such as Franklin, *Cooper: The Early Years*; George G. Dekker, *James Fenimore Cooper: The American Scott* (New York: Barnes and Noble, 1967); John P. McWilliams Jr., *Political Justice in a Republic: James Fenimore Cooper's America* (Berkeley: University of California Press, 1972); and James D. Wallace, *Early Cooper and His Audience* (New York: Columbia University Press, 1986).

49. Cooper can be seen to move from embracing the tenets of Federalism, promoted through his childhood relationship with John Jay, to supporting the Democratic-Republican DeWitt Clinton in the early 1820s, to adopting Jacksonian Democratic views, to focusing, later in his life, on the more conservative social side of his past.

50. Franklin, *Cooper: The Early Years*, 369.

51. Ibid., 241–43.

52. Such paradoxes in Cooper's thought infuse the novel in many ways—especially regarding issues of nationalism. For example, while *The Pilot* is a veritable national paean, its ambiguous figuration of American loyalists such as Colonel Howard and Alice Dunscombe may complicate binary lines of national identity. Such pseudo-sympathy with loyalists reveals Cooper's respect for elements of transatlantic European ties—which can be seen, as well, in the closing friendship between the American Captain Manual and the British Major Borroughcliffe (though Manual tragically dies after one of their congenial meetings on a "neutral" island).

53. James Fenimore Cooper, preface [1823] to *The Pilot: A Tale of the Sea*, ed. Kay Semour House, in *James Fenimore Cooper: Sea Tales* (New York: Library of America, 1991), 3–4.

54. According to Paul David Nelson, in "James Fenimore Cooper's Maritime Nationalism, 1820–1850," *Military Affairs* 41, no. 3 (October 1977): 129–32, Cooper avidly supported magazines' calls for nationalistic maritime material during and after the War of 1812. By 1820, he had published six anonymous articles in *The Literary and Scientific Repository, and Critical Review* (129). See also Philbrick, *Cooper and the Development of American Sea Fiction*, 42–47, for Cooper's early maritime nationalism.

55. Philbrick, *Cooper and the Development of American Sea Fiction*, 42.

56. Said, *Culture and Imperialism*, 63.

57. Quoted in Dekker, *Cooper: The American Scott*, 114.

58. Wallace, *Early Cooper and His Audience*, 118.

59. My reading is thus at odds with Cohen's claim in *The Novel and the Sea* that, in *The Pilot*, "crewmembers of the vessel are not just tools to be used by the master mariner, but part of the craft and essential to performance" (141). Consequently, I

do not share in her broader vision that nineteenth-century maritime labor was substantially less "dehumanizing" than industrial labor (with the "compleat capacity of craft" trumping the "degraded labor of industrial production") (144). Both claims, while perhaps sound on their own terms, can be seen to suffer from varying levels of myopia stemming from the desire to portray maritime labor (or "craft") as a historically exceptional mode of production. By way of example, the former statement interestingly casts naval officers as artisan masters, while the latter stands (if one accepts its premise) only if one cordons off notions of craft from the structures of power that condition such labor (structures sustained via various forms of violence, including impressment and corporal punishment sanctioned by the articles of war). See chapter 6 for a fuller discussion of oppression and maritime naval labor in terms of Melville's work.

60. Philbrick, *Cooper and the Development of American Sea Fiction*, 82–83.

61. Jameson, *Marxism and Form*, 416. In discussing the abandonment of the "great political and Utopian theories of the past," Jameson argues that "thought asphyxiates in our culture, with its absolute inability to imagine anything other than what it is." While I view Cooper as portraying a similar schematic in Coffin's inability to conceive of making it through the storm, I am not at all suggesting that Barnstable provides a revolutionary alternative, as his utopian vision is conditioned by the ideological notion of national "duty."

62. Philbrick, *Cooper and the Development of American Sea Fiction*, 81–83. Philbrick's point about the lack of lower-class threat to the Red Rover can also be seen in Cooper's later novel *The Crater*, where Bob Betts evinces similar natural propensities for nautical activity but always remains deferential to the genteel Mark Woolston.

63. Samuel Taylor Coleridge, *The Rime of the Ancient Mariner*, in *The Collected Works of Samuel Taylor Coleridge*, vol. 16: *Poetical Works: Part I*, ed. J. C. C. Mays (Princeton, N.J.: Princeton University Press, 2001), 381.

64. Cooper, preface [1849] to *The Pilot*, 7.

65. Linebaugh and Rediker, *Many-Headed Hydra*, 2.

66. Deleuze and Guattari, *Anti-Oedipus*, 277.

67. Dekker, *Cooper: The American Scott*, 120.

68. Stephen Railton, *Fenimore Cooper: A Study of His Life and Imagination* (Princeton, N.J.: Princeton University Press, 1978), 124.

69. Peck, "Repossession of America," 580.

70. James Fenimore Cooper, *Notions of the Americans: Picked Up by a Travelling Bachelor*, 2 vols. (1828; repr., New York: Frederick Ungar Publishing Co., 1963), 1:9.

71. Ibid., 2:64.

72. Ibid., 2:66.

73. Ibid., 2:68.

74. Ibid., 2:70.

75. James Fenimore Cooper, *History of the Navy of the United States of America* (1839; repr., Annapolis, Md.: Naval Institute Press, 2001), 41–42.

76. John C. McCloskey, "Cooper's Political Views in 'The Crater,'" *Modern Philology* 53, no. 2 (November 1955): 115.

77. John P. McWilliams, "Cooper and the Conservative Democrat," *American Quarterly* 22, no. 3 (Autumn 1970): 670.

78. Quoted in ibid., 672.

79. James Fenimore Cooper, *The American Democrat; or, Hints on the Social and Civic Relations of the United States* (1838; repr., New York: Alfred A. Knopf, 1931), viii.

80. Scott, *The Pirate*, 275.

81. Wai Chee Dimock, *Empire for Liberty: Melville and the Poetics of Individualism* (Princeton, N.J.: Princeton University Press, 1989), 3–4.

82. Cooper, *Notions of the Americans*, 2:79.

83. For example, even Barnstable and Griffith's scheme to wrangle away the women in Colonel Howard's charge ultimately corresponds to Captain Munson's mission to abduct British citizens.

84. Franklin, *Cooper: The Early Years*, 401.

85. Franklin notes, for example, how Cooper met with the Marquis de Lafayette during his visit to the United States in 1823 (*Cooper: The Early Years*, 370).

86. Wayne Franklin, introduction to *The Spy: A Tale of the Neutral Ground*, James Fenimore Cooper (New York: Penguin Books, 1997), xxix, xxviii.

87. Ibid., xxx. See also Wayne Fanklin's "'One More Scene': The Marketing Context of Cooper's 'Sixth' Leather-Stocking Tale," in *Leather-Stocking Redux; Or, Old Tales, New Essays*, ed. Jeffrey Walker (Brooklyn, N.Y.: AMS Press, 2011), 225–52.

88. See Melville, *Moby-Dick*, 354.

89. Cooper, *Notions of the Americans*, 2:62.

90. James Fenimore Cooper, *The Crater; or, Vulcan's Peak*, ed. Thomas Philbrick (1847; repr., Cambridge, Mass.: Belknap Press of Harvard University Press, 1962), 33.

91. Cooper, *Notions of the Americas*, 1:337.

92. David Kazanjian, "Mercantile Exchanges, Mercantilist Enclosures: Racial Capitalism in the Black Mariner Narratives of Venture Smith and John Jea," *New Centennial Review* 3, no. 1 (Spring 2003): 148.

93. As Isaac Land notes in "'Sinful Propensities': Piracy, Sodomy, and Empire in the Rhetoric of Naval Reform, 1770–1870," in *Discipline and the Other Body: Correction, Corporeality, Colonialism*, ed. Steven Pierce and Anupama Rao (Durham, N.C.: Duke University Press, 2006), eighteenth and nineteenth-century naval authorities were often suspicious of intimate relations between sailors. As I will discuss in chapter 6, one of John Adams's first rationales for naval corporal

punishment was to quell acts of sodomy. Though I do not intend to suggest that Coffin and Barnstable are anything but platonically connected, bonds between sailors, including *matelotage* (a form of marriage between two crew members), were popularly condemned by authorities (97).

94. Nelson, "Cooper's Maritime Nationalism," 129–30.

95. See Richard Kopley's introduction to Edgar Allan Poe, *The Narrative of Arthur Gordon Pym of Nantucket* (New York: Penguin Books, 1999), xxiii, for a brief discussion of the biblical significance of the name Ariel.

96. Peck, "Repossession of America," 597.

97. Philbrick, *Cooper and the Development of American Sea Fiction*, 56.

98. Casarino, *Modernity at Sea*, 2.

99. Ibid., 98.

100. James Fenimore Cooper, *The Red Rover: A Tale*, ed. Thomas and Marianne Philbrick, in *James Fenimore Cooper: Sea Tales* (New York: Library of America, 1991), 725.

101. Catherine Rottenberg, "*Passing*: Race, Identification, and Desire," *Criticism* 45, no. 4 (Fall 2003): 441–42.

102. Pease, *New American Exceptionalism*, 17.

3. Tattoos in *Typee*

1. See Ira Dye, "The Tattoos of Early American Seafarers, 1796–1818," *Proceedings of the American Philosophical Society* 133 (1989): 520–54.

2. Joseph Kabris was a shipwrecked French sailor who lived among the Marquesas in the late eighteenth century, and John Rutherford was an English deserter who lived with the Maori in and around 1820.

3. As Alex Calder, Jonathan Lamb, and Bridget Orr explain in "Introduction: Postcoloniality and the Pacific," *Voyages and Beaches: Pacific Encounters, 1769–1840*, ed. Calder, Lamb, and Orr (Honolulu: University of Hawai'i Press, 1999), 2: "Political history in Europe begins with the distinction between the civilizing contract and the savage state of nature; and depending on the bent of each political philosopher, either the benefits of contract are so plain as to make the alternative unthinkable (Thomas Hobbes, Edmund Burke), or civil society has entailed corruption on such a scale that the state of nature must be mourned as a lost paradise (Rousseau, Adam Ferguson)."

4. J. G. A. Pocock, "Nature and History, Self and Other: European Perceptions of World History in the Age of Encounter," in *Voyages and Beaches: Pacific Encounters, 1769–1840*, ed. Alex Calder, Jonathan Lamb, and Briget Orr (Honolulu: University of Hawai'i Press, 1999), 29.

5. Such an approach—here to be developed via a Lacanian perspective—attempts to come at these cultural issues from the opposite direction to the one

commonly taken by traditional anthropology. As Calder, Lamb, and Orr explain in "Introduction: Postcoloniality and the Pacific," the traditional approach enacts what Greg Dening calls "the zero point of ethnohistory," resulting in "the inescapable Eurocentricity of the anti-Eurocentric gesture." The ethos behind such methodology is thus the "expectation that weevil-like ideological impurities might be rattled out and discarded, leaving behind some portion of an original substance" (4, 15). Like Calder et al., I believe there is no getting rid of the weevils. Furthermore, my interest here is precisely to explore the way such insufferable weevils irreducibly appear in and shape antebellum maritime narratives.

    6. Herman Melville, *Typee: A Peep at Polynesian Life*, ed. Harrison Hayford et al. (Evanston, Ill.: Northwestern University Press, 2003), 218–19 (emphasis in the original); hereafter cited in the text by page number only.

    7. For clarity's sake, I use Melville's spelling of Taipi throughout the chapter. For biographical accounts of these events, see especially Charles Roberts Anderson, *Melville in the South Seas* (New York: Columbia University Press, in cooperation with the Modern Language Association of America, 1939); Hershel Parker, *Herman Melville: A Biography*, vol. 1: *1819–1851* (Baltimore: Johns Hopkins University Press, 1996); and Wilson Heflin, *Herman Melville's Whaling Years*, ed. Mary K. Bercaw Edwards and Thomas Farel Heffernan (Nashville: Vanderbilt University Press, 2004).

    8. In his account, Fernández de Quirós notes the practice of body marking, or "te patu tiki," meaning to "wrap in images." Quoted in Bronwen Douglas, "'Cureous Figures': European Voyagers and *Tatau*/Tattoo in Polynesia, 1595–1800," in *Tattoo: Bodies, Art, and Exchange in the Pacific and the West*, ed. Nicholas Thomas, Anna Cole, and Bronwen Douglas (Durham, N.C.: Duke University Press, 2005), 33.

    9. David Porter, *Journal of a Cruise Made to the Pacific Ocean by Captain David Porter in the United States Frigate* Essex, *in the Years 1812, 1813, and 1814* (Philadelphia: Bradford and Inskeep, 1815), microform, Early American Imprints, 2nd Series, no. 35674, 7.

    10. See T. Walter Herbert Jr., *Marquesan Encounters: Melville and the Meaning of Civilization* (Cambridge, Mass.: Harvard University Press, 1980), chapter 3.

    11. For more on Omai, see William Cummings, "Orientalism's Corporeal Dimension," *Journal of Colonialism and Colonial History* 4, no. 2 (2003).

    12. Robert Bogdan, *Freak Show: Presenting Human Oddities for Amusement and Profit* (Chicago: University of Chicago Press, 1988), 6.

    13. Rosemarie Garland Thompson, *Extraordinary Bodies: Figuring Physical Disability in American Culture and Literature* (New York: Columbia University Press, 1997), 63. Thompson equates these cultural others with domestic disabled "freaks," saying: "Hence, a nondisabled person of color billed as the 'Fiji Cannibal' was equivalent to a physically disabled, Euro-American called the 'Legless Wonder'" (63).

14. Bogdan, *Freak Show*, 241.

15. Samuel Otter, *Melville's Anatomies* (Berkeley: University of California Press, 1999), 269n17, includes the 1879 headline of a P. T. Barnum advertisement for Captain Costentenus: "Over 70,000,000 BLOOD-PRODUCING PUNCTURES."

16. Cassuto, for example, cites Melville's use of P. T. Barnum's Freak Show in an 1847 political satire. Leonard Cassuto, *The Inhuman Race: The Racial Grotesque in American Literature and Culture* (New York: Columbia University Press, 1997).

17. Ibid., 168.

18. Ibid., 7.

19. Otter, *Melville's Anatomies*, 3.

20. Ibid., 27.

21. I use the term "reterritorialization" in the spirit of Deleuze and Guattari's work in *Anti-Oedipus*. The notion that Langsdorff's recourse to race may be such a move is supported by Elena Gover, "'Speckled Bodies': Russian Voyages and Nuku Hivans, 1804," in *Tattoo: Bodies, Art, and Exchange in the Pacific and the West*, ed. Nicholas Thomas, Anna Cole, and Bronwen Douglas (Durham, N.C.: Duke University Press, 2005). Gover recounts how the man Langsdorff is describing, Mouwateie, is portrayed differently by three artists in Langsdorff's crew: Langsdorff, Tilesius, and Loewenstern (61–63).

22. See Jennifer Putzi, *Identifying Marks: Race, Gender, and the Marked Body in Nineteenth-Century America* (Athens: University of Georgia Press, 2006), 25.

23. According to Bronwen Douglas, "'Cureous Figures': European Voyagers and *Tatau*/Tattoo in Polynesia, 1595–1800," "During the late eighteenth century there was considerable flux in European ideas about and conventions for representing non-white people.... The modernist biological idea that race is phylogenetic and fundamentally differentiating began to challenge older, holistic beliefs about essential human similitude, while empirical naturalism supplanted long dominant neo-Classical values in art and aesthetics. Neo-Classicism had tied accuracy in depiction to an ideal of perfection, producing portraits that by more naturalistic standards are far from lifelike" (34). As Bernard Smith points out, in *Imagining the Pacific in the Wake of the Cook Voyages* (New Haven, Conn.: Yale University Press, 1992), "The exploration of the Pacific ... put an enormous pressure upon the classic as a standard. The analogy, the memory of Greece, could only be sustained if it continued to be identified with the vigor of the primitive" (221).

24. Otter, *Melville's Anatomies*, 39.

25. Similar scenes in which narrators respond to and judge Polynesian tattoos can be found in many antebellum-era narratives. Like Melville, Mary Davis Wallis, in *Life in Feejee, or, Five Years among the Cannibals* (1851; repr., Ridgewood, N.J.: Gregg Press, 1967), refers to the complexity of patterns in a negative way, writing: "An endless variety of tastes was displayed, which did not in my view add to their

beauty" (98). As Melville does, however, she later admires tattoos that are composed of "delicate parallel lines," referring to their bearers as "the handsomest race of men" (184–85). Charles Darwin, in *The Voyage of the Beagle* (1839; repr., Washington, D.C.: National Geographic Society, 2004), makes a related distinction between Tahitian tattoos, where "the ornaments follow the curvature of the body so gracefully, that they have a very elegant effect" (360), and the troubling way New Zealand facial tattoos, "[cover] the whole face, puzzle and mislead an unaccustomed eye" (374). In *Polynesian Researches: Hawaii* (1842; repr., Rutland, Vt.: Charles E. Tuttle, 1969), William Ellis likewise finds Hawaiian lip tattoos to be "rude" and distasteful, unlike "figures on the bodies of either the New Zealanders, Tahitians, or Marquesians, which are sometimes really beautiful" (203–4). A notable and quite relevant exception is David Porter, who records his observations of Typee tattoos in his *Journal of a Cruise to the Pacific Ocean*. Porter argues that "when the eye is once familiarized with men ornamented after this manner" there "may be discovered innumerable lines curved, straight, and irregular, drawn with the utmost correctness, taste and symmetry, and yet apparently without order or any determined plan" (14–15).

26. Cassuto, *Inhuman Race*, 6–7.

27. Bruce A. Harvey, *American Geographics: U.S. National Narratives and the Representation of the Non-European World, 1830–1865* (Stanford, Calif.: Stanford University Press, 2001), 68–69.

28. Herman Melville, *Omoo: A Narrative of Adventures in the South Seas,* ed. Harrison Hayford et al. (Evanston, Ill.: Northwestern University Press, 1999), 178, hereafter cited in the text by page number only. The early scene in *Typee* in which French colonial officials are embarrassed when the queen of Nukuheva lifts her skirt to show off her buttock tattoos is also quite relevant. Similar views about Pacific natives can also be found in, among other publications, Porter's *Journal of a Cruise Made to the Pacific,* where he warns his crew of the "treacherous" and dissimulating Marquesans (6); Poe, *The Narrative of Arthur Gordon Pym,* in which the fictitious Antarctic natives are "the most wicked, hypocritical, vindictive, bloodthirsty, and altogether fiendish race of men upon the face of the earth"; Wilkes, *Narrative of the United States Exploring Expedition,* when his instructions warn that "treachery is one of the invariable characteristics of savages and barbarians" (xxviii); Mary Davis Wallis, *Life in Feejee,* where she describes how in New Zealand "cannibalism is vanishing, or is practiced only in secret," as well as in her tale of the native Vernani's cruel and vicious revenge against his best friend: a capacity for "wickedness" that she did not previously see in his "appearance" (23, 38); and Mary Brewster's whaling journals, in which she describes "native habits" being "so permanently established that it is almost impossible to correct them, even those who have been taken when young, well educated—and under the best influences,

when left to themselves fall back into habits and customs of their race" (*"She Was a Sister Sailor": The Whaling Journals of Mary Brewster, 1845–1851*, ed. Joan Druett [Mystic, Conn.: Mystic Seaport Museum], 245).

29. In *Moby-Dick*, Melville playfully portrays racial difference as being a construct of the Imaginary when he writes, "as though a white man were anything more dignified than a whitewashed negro" (60). Yet, the social and political effects of racial fantasies are shown as well, when passengers by the docks jeeringly "marvelled" at Ishmael and Queequeg's apparent friendship.

30. Examples of the struggle with cultural and literal translation can be found in Ellis, *Polynesian Researches*, 31–32, where he describes how English missionaries helped the Americans produce the first Hawaiian spelling book in 1822, and in Wilkes's aforementioned mission instructions, which include a list of words provided by the War Department that he was to translate into "Indian vocabularies" (xxxi).

31. Anne D'Alleva, "Christian Skins: *Tatau* and the Evangelization of the Society Islands and Samoa," in *Tattoo: Bodies, Art, and Exchange in the Pacific and the West*, ed. Nicholas Brown, Anna Cole, and Bronwen Douglas (Durham, N.C.: Duke University Press, 2005), 94.

32. Ibid., 94–96. D'Alleva includes as an example an 1847 watercolor painting titled *Native Woman with letters 'Murderer' tattooed on her face—penalty for murdering her husband—Tahiti*, from the journal of Henry Byam Martin (99). Though she focuses on African experiences, Heidi Gengenbach, "Boundaries of Beauty: Tattooed Secrets of Women's History in Magude District, Southern Mozambique," *Journal of Women's History* 14, no. 4 (Winter 2003): 106–41, provides an interesting corollary to such accounts of colonial rule by exploring the potentially resistant aspects of tattooing in Mozambique.

33. Quoted in Otter, *Melville's Anatomies*, 38.

34. Ibid. Alfred Gell, in *Wrapped in Images: Tattooing in Polynesia* (Oxford: Clarendon Press, 1993), reiterates this traditional view that the tattoo is a form of a lure, claiming: "To view the tattoo is already to be in a position of seduction" (36).

35. Elizabeth Grosz, "Intolerable Ambiguity: Freaks as/at the Limit," in *Freakery: Cultural Spectacles of the Extraordinary Body*, ed. Rosemarie Garland Thompson (New York: New York University Press, 1996), 57.

36. Leslie Fielder, *Freaks: Myths and Images of the Secret Self* (New York: Simon and Schuster, 1978), 34.

37. T. Walter Herbert Jr., *Marquesan Encounters: Melville and the Meaning of Civilization* (Cambridge, Mass.: Harvard University Press, 1980), 170.

38. Tattoos in *Typee* should thus be distinguished from tattoos in novels such as *Moby-Dick*. Although Queequeg's tattoos are figured as "grotesque" and "twisted" "hieroglyphic marks" linked to a mysterious foreign cultural logic (crafted by "a

departed prophet and seer of his island"), the functional agency of this cultural logic is mitigated; consequently, so too are the effects that tattoos have on Western characters. The meaning and logic of the tattoos are removed one degree when Ishmael reveals that Queequeg, himself, could not "read" their "mysteries." Moreover, the distant logic of a former island prophet is conspicuously coded via Romantic-era tropes of knowledge—the tattoos representing "a complete theory of the heavens and the earth." As opposed to acting as a cultural threat, Queequeg's tattoos present an enticing "riddle," one that prompts Ahab, after "surveying poor Queequeg," to exclaim: "Oh, devilish tantalization of the gods!" (480–81).

39. Nicholas Thomas, introduction to *Tattoo: Bodies, Art, and Exchange in the Pacific and the West*, ed. Nicholas Thomas, Anna Cole, and Bronwen Douglas (Durham, N.C.: Duke University Press, 2005), 18.

40. See Joanna White, "Marks of Transgression: The Tattooing of Europeans in the Pacific Islands," in *Tattoo: Bodies, Art, and Exchange in the Pacific and the West*, ed. Nicholas Thomas, Anna Cole, and Bronwen Douglas (Durham, N.C.: Duke University Press, 2005), 72.

41. Thomas, introduction to *Tattoo*, 19–20.

42. Cummings, "Orientalism's Corporeal Dimension." See Newman, "Wearing Their Hearts on Their Sleeves," for a review of historical data on tattoo adaptations and practices of early-American sailors. For discussions of the tattoo and its multiform histories, see Robert Brain, *The Decorated Body* (New York: Harper & Row, 1979); Margo DeMello, *Bodies of Inscription: A Cultural History of the Modern Tattoo Community* (Durham, N.C.: Duke University Press, 2000); Ira Dye, "The Tattoos of Early American Seafarers, 1796–1818," *Proceedings of the American Philosophical Society* 133 (1989): 520–54; Alfred Gell, *Wrapping in Images: Tattooing in Polynesia* (Oxford: Clarendon Press, 1993); R. W. B. Scutt and Christopher Gotch, *Art, Sex, and Symbol: The Mystery of Tattooing* (New York: A. S. Barnes, 1974); W. D. Hambly, *The History of Tattooing and Its Significance: With Some Account of Other Forms of Corporal Marking* (London: H. F. & G. Witherby, 1925); Adrienne Kaeppler, "Hawaiian Tattoo: A Conjunction of Genealogy and Aesthetics," in *Marks of Civilization: Artistic Transformations of the Human Body*, ed. Arnold Rubin (Los Angeles: Museum of Cultural History, University of California, 1988); and Samuel M. Steward, *Bad Boys and Tough Tattoos: A Social History of the Tattoo with Gangs, Sailors, and Street-Corner Punks* (New York: Harrington Park Press, 1990).

43. Cassuto, *Inhuman Race*, 181.

44. Otter, *Melville's Anatomies*, 44–45.

45. To reiterate: I am suggesting that Tommo's response to the prospect of being facially tattooed may reveal how the culturally and ideologically charged issue of race may paradoxically act as a fantasmatic screen over other symbolic anxieties. Thus, in a traditional dialectical sense, shifting from a specific focus on

manifest racial issues (as important are they in their own right) to a broader symbolic inquiry allows a relative methodological "negation of a negation." According to Jean Hyppolite, in *Genesis and Structure of Hegel's Phenomenology of Spirit*, trans. Samuel Cherniak and John Heckman (Evanston, Ill.: Northwestern University Press, 1974), such a Hegelian move is "creative because the posited term had been isolated and thus was itself a kind of negation. From this it follows that the negation of a term allows the whole to be recaptured in each of its parts" (15). In this context, scholars who trace the symptom of tattoo anxiety to domestic conceptions of race (or other single positive historical constructs) and stop there may not fully attend to the implications inherent in Cassuto's aforementioned conception of "cultural grotesque" as a "liminal state between human and thing, becoming variables of both" (7). Such a frame for racial encounters, of course, comes close to Rey Chow's view, in *The Protestant Ethnic and the Spirit of Capitalism* (New York: Columbia University Press, 2002), that ethnicity is "an ontologically liminal phenomenon, something whose status is between subject and object." Consequently, according to Chow, "its representation . . . must involve a way of reading that is much more complex than the thematic approach" (51).

46. See Milton Stern, *The Fine Hammered Steel of Herman Melville* (Urbana: University of Illinois Press, 1957), and John Samson, "The Dynamics of History and Fiction in Melville's *Typee*," *American Quarterly* 36, no. 2 (Summer 1984): 276–90, as well as Samson's *White Lies: Melville's Narratives of Facts* (Ithaca, N.Y.: Cornell University Press, 1989).

47. Harvey, *American Geographics*, 85.

48. Ibid., 87.

49. Ibid., 88.

50. Ibid., 65.

51. Žižek, *Plague of Fantasies*, 13. For Althusser's notion of an epistemological break, see especially the introductory section of Louis Althusser, *For Marx*, trans. Ben Brewster (New York: Vintage Books, 1970). Gayatri Chakravorty Spivak espouses a similar view of historical change in *A Critique of Postcolonial Reason: Toward a History of the Vanishing Present* (Cambridge, Mass.: Harvard University Press, 1999), arguing that "the epistemic story of imperialism is the story of a series of interruptions, a repeated tearing of time that cannot be sutured" (208).

52. Žižek, *Plague of Fantasies*, 13.

53. According to T. Walter Herbert Jr., in the late eighteenth century the concept of Christian "millennialist improvement" coalesced with notions of empirical "historical advance" to form a modern understanding of "civilization" (*Marquesan Encounters*, 121). For contemporary studies of the development of modern indexical notions of time and evolution, see—in addition to seminal works by Michel Foucault and Johannes Fabian—Anne McClintock, *Imperial Leather: Race,*

Gender, and Sexuality in the Colonial Contest (New York: Routledge, 1995), especially the sections "Panoptical Time" (36–39) and "Anachronistic Space" (40–42).

54. Calder, Lamb, and Orr, "Introduction: Postcoloniality and the Pacific," 12.

55. A proper Žižekian reading might push this one step further and suggest that a formative underlying anxiety in this scenario stems from the antebellum era's move into the history-less zone of modern capitalism—and that the threat from the Typees (in part) represents a fantasy displacement, where the potential modern loss of history is precipitated by an agency belonging to a foreign people/realm (other) that is loosely associated with a distant past (thus, history is not lost by us but stolen by them). While such a reading may be valid, it overlooks two interlocking points: the fact that this crisis of history may not have fully erupted in Melville's moment and, therefore, the very real agency that the Typees have to disrupt Western symbolic coordinates.

56. Jacques-Alain Miller, "On Shame," in *Reflections on* Seminar XVII: *Jacques Lacan and the Other Side of Psychoanalysis*, ed. Justin Clemens and Russell Grigg (Durham, N.C.: Duke University Press, 2006), 13. See chapters 5 and 6 of this volume for my discussion of antebellum responses to an apparent waning of the master signifier in the political field.

57. Ibid., 18.

58. For a more thorough explication of Lacan's master's discourse, see chapter 1.

59. Miller, "On Shame," 20. Though Miller focuses on *Seminar XVII*, such sentiment can be seen across Lacan's later work. See, for example, Lacan, *Seminar XX*, and Lacan's assertion that "every dimension of being is produced in the wake of the master's discourse," and, thus, "Place as a function is created by discourse itself" (32–33).

60. Miller, "On Shame," 19.

61. Ibid.

62. Herman Melville, *Mardi and a Voyage Thither*, ed. Harrison Hayford et al. (Evanston, Ill.: Northwestern University Press, 1998), 206.

63. Melville returns to this link between a haunting and ghostly agency and the possession of mysterious tattoos in his 1855 *Israel Potter, His Fifty Years of Exile*, ed. Harrison Hayford et al. (Evanston, Ill.: Northwestern University Press, 2000). Interestingly, he here figures the Scottish captain John Paul Jones as the bearer of this nexus. While secretly watching him one night, Israel spies Jones staring into a mirror with "savage satisfaction" and studying his "mysterious tattooings," composed of "large twisting ciphers covering the whole inside of the [right] arm." Israel goes on to associate these "labyrinthine" marks with "thorough-bred savages" and the "hidden power" of a "prophetical ghost" "haunting an ambuscade" (62–63). In *Mardi*, the anxiety about a foreign sky of tattoos can also be read in terms of Lacan's discussion the "lamella" in *Seminar XI*. As Žižek notes in *How to Read*

Lacan (London: Granta Books, 2006), the lamella is "an entity of pure surface, without the density of a substance, an infinitely plastic object that can incessantly change its form." In relation to the death drive, such an object represents a ghost-like "undead" "insistence," an "uncanny excess of life" (62). Thus, Tammahamma-ha's spectral tattoos relate to a cultural other and symbolic Other, and also to the way such concepts erupt as a traumatizing and excessive lack in Taji's own world.

64. Though it may seem counterintuitive to bring Derrida's work—however tangentially—into a Lacanian analysis, his notion of the visor effect helpfully illuminates relationships at play in this scenario. For a well-known example of the antagonism between Derrida and Lacan, see especially John P. Muller and William J. Richardson, eds., *The Purloined Poe: Lacan, Derrida, and Psychoanalytic Reading* (Baltimore: Johns Hopkins University Press, 1988); for a more recent consideration of the complex intersections of their thought, see Andrea Hurst, *Derrida vis-à-vis Lacan: Interweaving Deconstruction and Psychoanalysis* (New York: Fordham University Press, 2008).

65. Jacques Derrida, *Specters of Marx: The State of the Debt, the Work of Mourning, and the New International*, trans. Peggy Kamuf (New York: Routledge, 1994), 6–7.

66. See Slavoj Žižek's Lacanian critique of "Messianic Otherness" in *For They Know Not What They Do: Enjoyment as a Political Factor* (New York: Verso, 2008), especially xxvii–xxix. Derrida, *Specters of Marx*, 7.

67. See the Books of Samuel in the Old Testament for an account of the Hebrew king Saul's fall to the invading Philistines. There is also an interesting moment early in *Typee* when Tommo describes the gaze of a ranking Typee that evinces elements of the visor effect without the metaphor of a special or material screen; instead, the cultural difference of the native engenders such an obstacle. Melville writes: "One of them in particular, who appeared to be the highest in rank, placed himself directly facing me; looking at me with a rigidity of aspect under which I absolutely quailed. He never once opened his lips, but maintained his severe expression of countenance, without turning his face aside for a moment. Never before had I been subjected to so strange and steady a glace; it revealed nothing of the mind of the savage, but it appeared to be reading my own" (71).

68. Herbert, *Marquesan Encounters*, 135.

69. Slavoj Žižek, "The Real of Sexual Difference," *Reading Seminar XX: Lacan's Major Work on Love, Knowledge, and Feminine Sexuality*, ed. Suzanne Barnard and Bruce Fink (Albany: State University of New York Press, 2002), 70.

70. Coincidentally, Lacan uses the trope of the tattoo in *Seminar XI* to describe the barring of the subject by/through language, writing: "The subject . . . is marked off by the single stroke, and first he marks himself as a tatoo *[sic]*, the first of the signifiers" (141).

71. Slavoj Žižek, "Ideology I: No Man Is an Island . . . ," Lacan.com (www.lacan.com/zizwhiteriot.html), accessed January 17, 2011. The rest of the passage reads: "Subjects are literally holes, gaps, in the positive order of being: they dwell only in the interstices of being, in those places where the job of creation is not done to the end. . . . Far from being the Crown of Creation, a subject bears witness to the fact that there are spots of unfinished reality in the order of things: the objective correlate of a subject is a proto-real spectral object–stain which is not yet fully actualized as part of positive reality."

72. Fink, *Lacanian Subject*, 62.

73. Žižek, "*Concesso non Dato*," 234.

74. I am here using a simplified version of the Lacanian concept of traversing the fantasy. Claiming that Tommo renegotiates the Typee as object *a* is not to suggest that he simply rids himself of this element (the extra X that inculcates them) within his fantasy space. Rather, the object *a* also should be seen as a locus for the Other's desire for oneself; thus, by prospectively moving closer to the Typee, Tommo recognizes his illusory overinvestment of the natives (the common "that's not it" refrain) and also experiences a more radical reorientation of the way he views the world. That is, by shifting his perspective on the Typee, Tommo may be exposed to the more foundational aspects of fantasy that undergird his own "reality."

75. Slavoj Žižek, *The Ticklish Subject: The Absent Center of Political Ontology* (New York: Verso, 2000), 18. I am suggesting that the threat of the Typees' tattooing him reveals the agency of others per se, and also how this outside threat exists in relation to Tommo's own symbolic constructs and their demands. Paradoxically, the apparently free and natural choice of home and mother may not only be imposed by the Typees' injunction to choose, but this foreign injunction may also mask the way it is dually instituted by his own symbolic order's demands.

76. See Walter Benjamin, "Theses on the Philosophy of History," in *Illuminations*, ed. Hannah Arendt (New York: Schocken Books, 1968), especially Theses XVII and XVIII.

77. The meaning of "Tommo" is quoted in Samson, "The Dynamics of History and Fiction in Melville's *Typee*," 281.

4. Melville's "Porno-Tropics"

1. Quoted in Parker, *Herman Melville: A Biography*, 531. The reviewer was George Washington Peck, writing in the *American Review*.

2. Melville, *Moby-Dick*, 7.

3. Quoted in Parker, *Herman Melville*, 464.

4. A wealth of contemporary book-length works explore sexuality and the colonial Pacific. See especially, in addition to McClintock, *Imperial Leather*, Francis

Barker et al., eds., *Europe and Its Others: Proceedings of the Essex Conference on the Sociology of Literature, July 1984*, vol. 2 (Colchester, U.K.: University of Essex, 1985); Rudi C. Bleys, *The Geography of Perversion: Male-to-Male Sexual Behaviour Outside the West and the Ethnographic Imagination, 1750–1918* (New York: New York University Press, 1995); Ann Laura Stoler, *Race and the Education of Desire: Foucault's History of Sexuality and the Colonial Order of Things* (Durham, N.C.: Duke University Press, 1995); Lenore Manderson and Margaret Jolly, eds., *Sites of Desire/Economies of Pleasure: Sexualities in Asia and the Pacific* (Chicago: University of Chicago Press, 1997); Lee Wallace, *Sexual Encounters: Pacific Texts, Modern Sexualities* (Ithaca, N.Y.: Cornell University Press, 2003); and Patty O'Brien, *The Pacific Muse: Exotic Femininity and the Colonial Pacific* (Seattle: University of Washington Press, 2006).

5. Lenore Manderson and Margaret Jolly, introduction to *Sites of Desire/Economies of Pleasure: Sexualities in Asia and the Pacific* (Chicago: University of Chicago Press, 1997), 1.

6. Lee Wallace, *Sexual Encounters: Pacific Texts, Modern Sexualities* (Ithaca, N.Y.: Cornell University Press, 2003), 17.

7. Ibid., 19.

8. According to Peter Hulme, "Polytropic Man: Tropes of Sexuality and Mobility in Early Colonial Discourse," in *Europe and Its Others: Proceedings of the Essex Conference on the Sociology of Literature, July 1984*, vol. 2, ed. Francis Barker et al. (Colchester, U.K.: University of Essex, 1985), the figure of the polytropic man "comes from the epithet applied to Odysseus in the first line of the *Odyssey*" (20). For my purposes in this chapter, this figure should also be linked to what Lacan refers to in *Seminar VII* as the "man of pleasure"—a subject who attempts (and must ultimately fail) to experience the eighteenth-century "naturalist liberation of desire" (3–4).

9. Margaret S. Creighton and Lisa Norling, introduction to *Iron Men, Wooden Women: Gender and Seafaring in the Atlantic World, 1700–1920*, ed. Creighton and Norling (Baltimore: Johns Hopkins University Press, 1996), ix.

10. As Peter Linebaugh and Marcus Rediker note, Bonny and Read's popularity landed them on the cover page of *A General History of the Pyrates* (1724); see Linebaugh and Rediker, *Many-Headed Hydra*, 167. For more on eighteenth-century female pirates, see also Rediker's "Liberty beneath the Jolly Roger: The Lives of Anne Bonny and Mary Read, Pirates," in *Iron Men, Wooden Women: Gender and Seafaring in the Atlantic World, 1700–1920*, ed. Margaret S. Creighton and Lisa Norling (Baltimore: Johns Hopkins University Press, 1996), as well as Dianne Dugaw, *Warrior Women and Popular Balladry, 1650–1850* (Cambridge: Cambridge University Press, 1989), and Jo Stanley, ed., *Bold in Her Breeches: Women Pirates across the Ages* (London: Pandora, 1995).

11. See Dianne Dugaw, "Female Sailors Bold: Transvestite Heroines and the Markers of Gender and Class" in *Iron Men, Wooden Women: Gender and Seafaring*

in the Atlantic World, 1700–1920, ed. Margaret S. Creighton and Lisa Norling (Baltimore: Johns Hopkins University Press, 1996).

12. Although the nineteenth-century ideological transition that Dianne Dugaw discusses frames traditional domestic plots and spaces as intentionally conservative and apolitical, Amy Kaplan and other scholars have convincingly linked such domestic spheres and concerns directly to imperial projects.

13. Catharine Maria Sedgwick, "Modern Chivalry," in *Tales and Sketches by Miss Sedgwick* (Philadelphia: Carey, Lea, and Blanchard, 1835), 121.

14. Haskell Springer, "The Captain's Wife at Sea," in *Iron Men, Wooden Women: Gender and Seafaring in the Atlantic World, 1700–1920*, ed. Margaret S. Creighton and Lisa Norling (Baltimore: Johns Hopkins University Press, 1996), 93. The journals I mention are: Abby Jane Morrell's *Narrative of a Voyage to the Ethiopic and South Atlantic Ocean, India Ocean, Chinese Sea, North and South Pacific, in the Years 1829, 1830, 1831,* Eliza Azelia Williams's *The Voyage of the Florida, 1858–1861,* Mary Brewster's *The Whaling Journals of Mary Brewster, 1845–1851,* and Mary Davis Wallis's *Life in Feejee; or, Five Years among the Cannibals.* For more on antebellum wives at sea, see Joan Druett, *Petticoat Whalers: Whaling Wives at Sea, 1820–1920* (Auckland: Collins, 1991); Linda Grant De Pauw, *Seafaring Women* (Boston: Houghton Mifflin, 1982); Fred B. Duncan, *Deepwater Family* (New York: Pantheon, 1969); and Julia C. Bonham, "Feminist and Victorian: The Paradox of the American Seafaring Woman of the Nineteenth Century," *American Neptune* 37 (July 1977): 203–18.

15. Springer, "Captain's Wife at Sea," 94.

16. Hart, *Miriam Coffin*, 317.

17. Ibid., 318.

18. McClintock, *Imperial Leather*, 214.

19. Wallace, *Sexual Encounters*, 22.

20. Ibid., 24.

21. Suzanne Barnard, introduction to *Reading* Seminar XX: *Lacan's Major Work on Love, Knowledge, and Feminine Sexuality,* ed. Suzanne Barnard and Bruce Fink (Albany: State University of New York Press, 2002), 1. The first complete English translation of *Seminar XX* (Norton) was published in 1998.

22. Renata Salecl, introduction to *Sexuation,* ed. Salecl (Durham, N.C.: Duke University Press, 2000), 2.

23. In addition to Lacan's *Seminar XX* and *Seminar XVII,* as well as seminal sections of *Écrits,* see also secondary explications of sexuation, such as Joan Copjec, *Read My Desire: Lacan against the Historicists* (Cambridge, Mass.: MIT Press, 1994) and *Imagine There's No Woman: Ethics and Sublimation* (Cambridge, Mass.: MIT Press, 2002); Slavoj Žižek, *The Metastases of Enjoyment: On Women and Causality* (London: Verso, 1994); Bruce Fink, *The Lacanian Subject: Between Language and Jouissance* (Princeton, N.J.: Princeton University Press, 1995) and *Lacan to the*

Letter: Reading Écrits *Closely* (Minneapolis: University of Minnesota Press, 2004); Bruce Fink and Suzanne Barnard, eds., *Reading Seminar XX* (Albany: State University of New York Press, 2002); Salecl, *Sexuation;* and Frances L. Restuccia, *Amorous Acts: Lacanian Ethics in Modernism, Film, and Queer Theory* (Stanford, Calif.: Stanford University Press, 2006).

24. Lacan, *Seminar XX*, 9.
25. Ibid., 32.
26. Ibid., 35.
27. Fink, *Lacan to the Letter*, 149.
28. See Lacan, *Seminar XVII*, 44.
29. Fink, *Lacan to the Letter*, 156.
30. Lacan, *Seminar XVII*, 48.
31. Jacques Lacan, "The Subversion of the Subject and the Dialectic of Desire in the Freudian Unconscious," in *Écrits*, trans. Bruce Fink (New York: Norton, 2006), 693–94.
32. I use the masculine pronoun here strictly in terms of Lacan's symbolic schema. Again, technically, a biological woman can be sexuated as a male.
33. Lacan, *Seminar XX*, 86. Of this Lacan also writes: "This . . . [barred subject] never deals with anything by way of a partner but object *a* inscribed on the other side of the bar. He is unable to attain his sexual partner, who is the Other, except inasmuch as his partner is the cause of his desire" (ibid., 80). This is because, in Joan Copjec's terms, the positions of male and female merely "qualify the mode of the failure of our knowledge" (*Read My Desire*, 212).
34. In "Subversion of the Subject and the Dialectic of Desire," Lacan writes: "The shift of $(-\varphi)$ (lowercase phi) as phallic image from one side to the other of the equation between imaginary and the symbolic renders it positive . . . , even if it fills a lack. Although it props up (-1), it becomes Φ (capital phi) there, the symbolic phallus that cannot be negativized, the signifier of jouissance" (697).
35. Fink, *Lacan to the Letter*, 139.
36. Salecl, introduction to *Sexuation*, 7.
37. McClintock, *Imperial Leather*, 193.
38. See especially Judith Butler, *Gender Trouble: Feminism and the Subversion of Identity* (New York: Routledge, 1999) and *Bodies That Matter: On the Discursive Limits of "Sex"* (New York: Routledge, 1993); Luce Irigaray, *This Sex Which Is Not One*, trans. Catherine Porter with Carolyn Burke (Ithaca, N.Y.: Cornell University Press, 1985) and "Any Theory of the 'Subject' Has Always Been Appropriated by the Masculine," in *Speculum of the Other Woman*, trans. Gillian C. Gill (Ithaca, N.Y.: Cornell University Press, 1985); Monique Wittig, "One Is Not Born a Woman," *Feminist Issues* 1, no. 2 (Winter 1981); Jane Gallop, *Reading Lacan* (Ithaca, N.Y.: Cornell University Press, 1985) and *The Daughter's Seduction: Feminism and Psychoanalysis* (Ithaca, N.Y.: Cornell University Press, 1982). For a brief overview of the rela-

tions between feminism and various psychoanalytical approaches to gender, see the section "A Holy Trinity?" in Jolly and Manderson's introduction to *Sites of Desire/Economies of Pleasure*.

39. Lacan, *Seminar XX*, 72.

40. Ibid., 8.

41. For his graphic account of the relation between the two sexes, see Lacan, *Seminar XX*, chapter 7.

42. Ibid., 73.

43. Miller, "On Semblances in the Relation between the Sexes," 17. In *Gender Trouble*, Judith Butler also discusses this point, writing: "By claiming that the Other that lacks the Phallus is the one who *is* the Phallus, Lacan clearly suggests that power is wielded by this feminine position of not-having, that the masculine subject who 'has' the Phallus requires the Other to confirm and, hence, be the Phallus in its 'extended' sense" (56).

44. We might thus push against Judith Butler's otherwise astute critique of the pervasive role of lack in Lacan. Butler censures what she deems "a romanticism or, indeed, a religious idealization of 'failure,' humility and limitation before the Law, which makes the Lacanian narrative ideologically suspect." In fact, she goes so far as to refer to Lacanian theory as a "kind of 'slave morality' " that establishes "the paternal law as the inevitable and unknowable authority before which the sexed subject is bound to fail" (*Gender Trouble*, 72–73). In "The Real of Sexual Difference," in *Reading Seminar XX: Lacan's Major Work on Love, Knowledge, and Feminine Sexuality*, ed. Suzanne Barnard and Bruce Fink (Albany: State University of New York Press, 2002), Slavoj Žižek addresses Butler's point, arguing that the claim that Lacan creates a transcendental big Other (or "Law") misses Lacan's point that "there is no a priori formal structural scheme exempted from historical contingences" (71–73). Žižek also considers Butler's reading of Lacan in terms of sexual difference in *The Ticklish Subject: The Absent Centre of Political Ontology* (New York: Verso, 2000), 273–79.

45. E.D.E.N. Southworth, *The Deserted Wife* (New York: D. Appleton & Co., 1850), 10; hereafter cited in the text by page number only.

46. Copjec, *Imagine There's No Woman*, 9.

47. Slavoj Žižek, "Forward to the Second Edition: Enjoyment within the Limits of Reason Alone," in *For They Know Not What They Do: Enjoyment as a Political Factor* (New York: Verso, 2008), xxvii.

48. Among many other studies that discuss the role of Edenic paradigms for viewing Pacific women, see: Pocock, "Nature and History, Self and Other"; Vladimir Kapor, "Shifting Edenic Codes: On Two Exotic Visions of the Golden Age in the Late Eighteenth Century," *Eighteenth-Century Studies* 41, no. 2 (2008): 217–30; O'Brien, *Pacific Muse*; Barker et al., eds., *Europe and Its Others*; and Herbert, *Marquesan Encounters*. See also relevant eighteenth-century texts, such as Denis

Diderot, *Supplément au Voyage de Bougainville* (1772), and Jean-Jacques Rousseau, *Émile* (1762).

49. See Raymond W. Stedman's *Shadows of the Indians: Stereotypes in American Culture* (Norman: University of Oklahoma Press, 1982).

50. O'Brien, *Pacific Muse*, 30.

51. Fink, *Lacan to the Letter*, 119. Besides its ties to Freud, Lacan's notion of the Other's desire also clearly relates to Alexandre Kojève's readings of Hegel and the concept of "recognition." See especially Kojève, *Introduction to the Reading of Hegel: Lectures on the Phenomenology of Spirit,* assembled by Raymond Queneau, ed. Allan Bloom, trans. James H. Nichols Jr. (Ithaca, N.Y.: Cornell University Press, 1980).

52. Quoted in O'Brien, *Pacific Muse*, 64.

53. See, especially, Ann Laura Stoler, *Race and the Education of Desire: Foucault's History of Sexuality and the Colonial Order of Things* (Durham, N.C.: Duke University Press, 1995), and Sharon Tiffany and Kathleen Adam, *The Wild Woman: An Inquiry into the Anthropology of an Idea* (Cambridge, Mass.: Schenkman Publishing, 1985).

54. For more on Baartman, see especially Anne Fausto-Sterling, "Gender, Race, and Nation: The Comparative Anatomy of 'Hottentot' Women in Europe, 1815–1817," in *Deviant Bodies: Critical Perspectives on Difference in Science and Popular Culture,* ed. Jennifer Terry and Jacqueline Urla (Bloomington: Indiana University Press, 1995); Rachel Holmes, *African Queen: The Real Life of the Hottentot Venus* (New York: Random House, 2007); and Priscilla Netto, "Reclaiming the Body of the 'Hottentot': The Vision and Visuality of the Body Speaking with Vengeance in Venus Hottentot 2000," *European Journal of Women's Studies* 12, no. 2 (2005): 149–63.

55. David L. Eng, *Racial Castration: Managing Masculinity in Asian America* (Durham, N.C.: Duke University Press, 2001), 8–9.

56. On Lacan's idea that "truth has the structure of a fiction," see Žižek, *How to Read Lacan*, 32–33, and *Parallax View*, 30.

57. O'Brien, *Pacific Muse*, 22.

58. Karl Marx, *Capital: A Critique of Political Economy*, vol. 1, trans. Ben Fowkes (New York: Penguin, 1990), 164. Žižek provides an helpful reading of Marx's views in *The Sublime Object,* pointing out that "with the advent of bourgeois society, the relations of domination and servitude [seen in the Feudal era] are *repressed*. . . . [T]he repressed truth—that of the perseverance of domination and servitude—emerges in a symptom which subverts the ideological appearance of equality, freedom, so on. This symptom, the point of emergence of the truth about social relations, is precisely the 'social relations between things' " (26).

59. O'Brien, *Pacific Muse*, 70.

60. I use here the manuscripts of Cook's own journals, made available by the Hakluyt Society. While it is John Hawkesworth's version (1773, vols. 1–3) that was

first published, the originals allow for a potentially more accurate view of Cook's representation of Pacific encounters.

61. James Cook, *The Journals*, ed. Philip Edwards (New York: Penguin, 2003), 376–77; hereafter cited in the text by page number only.

62. Cook's ethical fantasies in this way resemble the notions of natural law that condition Melville's thought in *Typee*; for more on this topic, see Bruce Harvey, *American Geographics*. Cook appears to establish an implicit divide between black native women and natives with other racial markings, where the former are not bound by shame because they are not "true women." For more on this concept, see Kelvin Santiago-Valles, "'Race,' Labor, 'Women's Proper Place' and the Birth of Nations: Notes on Historicizing the Coloniality of Power," *CR: The New Centennial Review* 3, no. 3 (Fall 2003): 47–69.

63. See especially pages 370 and 452.

64. Edward Robarts, *The Marquesan Journal of Edward Robarts, 1797–1824*, ed. Greg Dening (Honolulu: University Press of Hawai'i, 1974), 86; hereafter cited in the text by page number only.

65. See pages 87 and 91, where Robarts describes the songs of women.

66. Todd McGowan, *The Real Gaze: Film Theory after Lacan* (Albany: State University of New York Press, 2007), 5–6.

67. Porter, *Journal of a Cruise*, 5–6.

68. Ibid., 10.

69. Ibid., 13, 16.

70. Ibid., 14.

71. Wilkes, *Narrative of the United States Exploring Expedition*, 18.

72. Ibid., 22.

73. Ibid., 93–94.

74. Wallis, *Life in Feejee*, 96.

75. Ibid., 26.

76. Ibid., 184.

77. Ellis, *Polynesian Researches*, 2.

78. Ibid., 87.

79. See Wilkes, *Narrative of the United States Exploring Expedition*, 79, and Wallis, *Life in Feejee*, 63, 85.

80. To reiterate earlier claims: my approach shares with projects like Lee Wallace's an aim of tracing the disruptive effect of Polynesian sexuality. But by framing such sexuality in the context of a Lacanian notion of sexuated fantasies, this disruption shifts from ontologically and empirically positive terms of affect to something approaching a negative affect. The stakes of this move can be articulated using Copjec's critique of Butler's work. Copjec refers to Butler's argument as being delimitedly Aristotelian: "that is, it conceives the universe as a positive, finite term ('normative and exclusionary') that finds its limit in another positive,

finite term" (*Read My Desire*, 222–23). As my reading of Melville will show, these novels do not outline the clear existence of feminine jouissance so much as acknowledge the limit of phallic jouissance in a way that would allow this as a negative postulate.

81. Lacan, *Seminar XX*, 10.
82. Copjec, *Read My Desire*, 226.
83. The effect of these women on Tommo is homologous to Žižek's discussion of the case of Harpo Marx. In "The Thing from Inner Space," in *Sexuation*, ed. Renata Salecl (Durham: Duke University Press, 2000), Žižek suggests that Marx's "absolute undecidabilty—or, rather incommensurability—makes him a monstrous Thing, an Other *qua* Thing, not an intersubjective partner, but a thoroughly *in-human* partner" (217).
84. Melville, *Correspondence*, 106.
85. Quoted in Parker, *Herman Melville*, 628.
86. Melville, *Mardi*, 8; hereafter cited in the text by page number only.
87. In "On Semblances in the Relation between the Sexes," Jacques-Alain Miller writes: "The fact that Woman does not exist does not mean that the place of woman does not exist, but rather that this place remains essentially empty. The fact that this place remains empty does not mean that we cannot find something there. But in it, we find only masks, masks of nothingness, which are sufficient to justify the connection between women and semblances" (14). Žižek provides a more precise articulation of this in *How to Read Lacan*, asserting: "Fantasy itself is for Lacan a semblance: it is not primarily the mask that conceals the Real beneath, but, rather, the fantasy of what is hidden behind the mask. So, for instance, the fundamental male fantasy of a woman is not her seductive appearance, but the idea that this dazzling appearance conceals some imponderable mystery" (114).
88. See Lacan, *Seminar I*, chapters 10 ("The Two Narcissisms") and 11 ("Ego-Ideal and Ideal Ego").
89. Lacan, *Seminar I*, 142.
90. Lorenzo Chiesa, *Subjectivity and Otherness: A Philosophical Reading of Lacan* (Cambridge, Mass.: MIT Press, 2007), 24.
91. Sigmund Freud, "Mourning and Melancholia," in *Collected Papers*, vol.4, trans. Joan Riviere (London: Hogarth Press and the Institute of Psycho-Analysis, 1948), 154–55.
92. Ibid., 155. In Žižek's terms: "Melancholy occurs when we finally get the desired object, but are disappointed with it" (*How to Read Lacan*, 68).
93. Giorgio Agamben, *Stanzas: Word and Phantasm in Western Culture*, trans. Ronald L. Martinez (Minneapolis: University of Minnesota Press, 1993), 20.
94. Žižek, *Plague of Fantasies*, 13.
95. McGowan, *Real Gaze*, 6.

96. In "Melancholy and the Act," *Critical Inquiry* 26, no. 4 (Summer 2000), Žižek defines this process by explaining how "anamorphosis undermines the distinction between objective reality and its distorted subjective perception; in it, the subjective distortion is reflected back into the perceived object itself, and, in this precise sense, the gaze itself acquires a supposedly objective existence" (659).
97. Lacan, *Seminar XX*, 4.
98. Ibid., 111.
99. Ibid., 126.
100. Alenka Zupančič, "The Case of the Perforated Sheet," in *Sexuation*, ed. Renata Salecl (Durham: Duke University Press, 2000), 296.
101. This silent enjoyment might be seen to exemplify Lacan's point that "there is a jouissance that is hers *(à elle)*, that belongs to that 'she' *(elle)* that doesn't exist and doesn't signify anything" (*Seminar XX*, 74).
102. Zupančič, "Case of the Perforated Sheet," 290.

5. *The Crater* and the Master's Reign

1. See especially Carl Schmitt, *Political Theology: Four Chapters on the Concept of Sovereignty* (Chicago: University of Chicago Press, 1985).
2. Giorgio Agamben, *State of Exception*, trans. Kevin Attell (Chicago: University of Chicago Press, 2005), 3.
3. Ibid., 86.
4. Ibid., 2.
5. Giorgio Agamben, *Homo Sacer: Sovereign Power and Bare Life*, trans. Daniel Heller-Roazen, ed. Werner Hamacher and David E. Wellbery (Stanford, Calif.: Stanford University Press, 1998), 10.
6. Ibid.
7. Wayne Franklin, *The New World of James Fenimore Cooper* (Chicago: University of Chicago Press, 1982), 183.
8. Dekker, *Cooper: The American Scott*, 247.
9. Quoted in George G. Dekker and John P. McWilliams, *James Fenimore Cooper: The Critical Heritage* (Boston: Routledge & Kegan Paul, 1973), 25.
10. Lacan writes, "The question of ethics is to be articulated from the point of view of the location of man in relation to the real" (*Seminar VII*, 11).
11. See chapter 1 for a discussion of Lacan's use of Hegel's "master."
12. Žižek, *Sublime Object of Ideology*, 95–96. While I employ Slavoj Žižek's and Russell Grigg's translation of Lacan's term *le point de capiton* as "quilting point," Bruce Fink argues that a more appropriate rendering is "button tie." See chapter 3 of Fink, *Lacan to the Letter*, for an explication of this concept as it appears in *Écrits*.

13. Slavoj Žižek, *Interrogating the Real*, ed. Rex Butler and Scott Stephens (New York: Continuum, 2005), 202.

14. I refer to the first of Benjamin's "Theses on the Philosophy of History," where a supposedly automatized chess machine is controlled by a small hunchback hidden inside the apparatus.

15. This is apparent in Lacan, *Seminar VII*, where Lacan correlates symbolic castration with both fantasy and, what is quite relevant for this chapter's concerns, the law. After claiming that castration is "the only cause of desire," he asserts that "fantasy dominates the entire reality of desire, that is to say, the law" (129).

16. Žižek, *Parallax View*, 373.

17. Focusing on Cooper's concerns with the law and democracy in terms of a Lacanian notion of the master signifier is indirectly relevant to the contemporary political landscape of the Left. As opposed to projects that seek to construct new spaces or forms of democratization, Žižek emphatically and repeatedly views "democracy" as the "true Master-Signifier" of capitalism (*Parallax View*, 320). As such, he posits that the most appropriate anticapitalist task is "undermining the fetishist status of Democracy as our Master-Signifier" ("*Concesso non Dato*," 222). In this context, I seek not merely to explore how the master signifier of democracy operated in Cooper's age, but to contribute to a broader critique of our contemporary political-ideological conception of democracy by illuminating specific historical sites where its previous construction was in crisis.

18. James Fenimore Cooper, *The Crater; or, Vulcan's Peak*, 6; hereafter cited in the text by page number only.

19. See chapter 2 of *The Crater*, where Cooper goes on at length about the decline of moral standards from the year 1796 to 1847 (27).

20. See especially Watt, *Rise of the Novel*.

21. In addition to the preface's warning, see also when Cooper wonders if "much of what Mark and Bridget . . . suffered" was a "consequence of acting directly in the face of the wishes and injunctions of their parents"; when Mark surmises if the *Rancocus*'s "offense" of trading in sandalwood used for pagan idols effected divine punishment in the form of the shipwreck (33); and later when Cooper directly states: "There is much reason to believe that a portion of our transgressions is to meet with its punishment here on earth" (281).

22. Franklin, *New World of James Fenimore Cooper*, 193.

23. Though Cooper gives specific economic logic for Bob's refusal based on the notion of "original possession," Bob's decision also clearly aligns with his desire to maintain social and class boundaries.

24. This natural division departs from many seventeenth- and eighteenth-century views about natural society and the ideal development of civics. Though Hobbes's *Leviathan* calls for a singular ruler to provide social order, this need springs from the caveat that natural human relations are selfish and base—a far cry from Coo-

per's spontaneously harmonious miniature settlement. *The Crater*'s settlement, however, also departs from Rousseau's view that the social contract develops through a relatively balanced exchange, whereby each member "puts into the community his person and all his powers under the supreme direction of the general will," as well as Paine's vision of a "natural liberty" where, in the first parliament, "every man, by natural right, will have a seat." See Jean-Jacques Rousseau, *The Social Contract*, trans. Maurice Cranston (New York: Penguin, 1968), 61, and Thomas Paine, *Common Sense* (New York: Signet Classics, 2003), 6.

25. There is also an apparent racial component to spatial division. In addition to the settlement's avid attempts to defend against native intrusion, Cooper notes how, in the early settlement, "all the blacks remained at the Reef" while the primary settlers worked and lived by the lush peak (229).

26. Although Cooper has the colonists reject the call of some to "make slaves" of the Kannakas, he shows how they take young native men "hostage" to work at sea and to ensure the compliance of their parents (336). More generally, the settlers make the natives "into a sort of Irish" by motivating the "wild beings" to work merely for the right of viewing the blasts used to loosen rock (342).

27. Cooper, *American Democrat*, 42–43; hereafter cited in the text by page number only.

28. H. C. Carey, *Principles of Political Economy*, 3 vols. (Philadelphia: Carey, Lea & Blanchard, 1838), 2:463.

29. Ibid., 2:464. Carey builds on the work of Alexander Hamilton and Adam Smith to establish the American School of economics—a system advocating tariff protections and government support for physical and financial infrastructure. While Cooper would not have agreed with the broader platform of the "American System" theories of the time, as we will see, his notions of property and rent rights clearly align with those of Carey. And, of course, Cooper begins to gravitate toward the politics of Clay and Webster in the 1850s. For more on Carey and the American School, see especially Lewis Henry Haney, *A History of Economic Thought: A Critical Account of the Origin and Development of the Economic Theories of the Leading Thinkers in the Leading Nations*, rev. ed. (New York: Macmillan, 1920); Abraham David Hannath, *Henry Charles Carey: A Study in American Economic Thought* (Baltimore: Johns Hopkins University Press, 1931); and Roger Blackhouse, *Early Histories of Economic Thought, 1824–1914* (London: Routledge, 2000).

30. Carey, *Principles of Political Economy*, 1:212. See David Ricardo, *On the Principles of Political Economy and Taxation* (London: John Murray, 1817).

31. Carey, *Principles of Political Economy*, 2:465.

32. Robert E. Spiller, *James Fenimore Cooper* (Minneapolis: University of Minnesota Press, 1965), 37.

33. James Fenimore Cooper, *The Redskins; or, Indian and Injun: Being the Conclusion of the Littlepage Manuscripts*, vol. 1 (New York: Burgess and Stringer, 1846), 27.

34. In addition to suggesting support for territorial expansion through the action of the novel, Cooper offers direct praise of American military campaigns to extend the domains of the country; see especially *The Crater*, 296–97 and 417.

35. McCloskey, in "Cooper's Political Views in 'The Crater,'" latches on to the first passage (antebellum-era utopian projects decried as "modern absurdities on the subject of equality, and a community of interests") in his cold war reading of the novel, framing Cooper's real political target as the "extreme growth of the leveling movement" (115). It should go without saying that such an attempt to cast Cooper as an early enemy of communism is an inane and reductive proposition. That said, Thomas Philbrick's introduction to the 1962 Harvard edition of *The Crater* holds that the novel is in part a response to the growth of Fourierism in the 1840s.

36. Jameson, "Cognitive Mapping," 349.

37. For Tocqueville on tyranny over the minority, see especially *Democracy in America*, vol. 1, part 2, chapter 7.

38. James Fenimore Cooper, *A Letter to His Countrymen*, in *The American Democrat and Other Writings*, ed. Bradley J. Birzer and John Willson (Washington, D.C.: Regnery Publishing, Inc., 2000), 269; hereafter cited in the text by page number only.

39. Cooper, *Notions of the Americans*, quoted in Dekker, *Cooper: the American Scott*, 21.

40. Dekker, *Cooper: The American Scott*, 248.

41. Frederick Douglass, "What to the Slave Is the Fourth of July?," in *The Oxford Frederick Douglass Reader*, ed. William L. Andrews (Oxford: Oxford University Press, 1996), 112.

42. Cooper, *The Redskins*, v–vi.

43. Paine, *Common Sense*, 38.

44. See Slavoj Žižek, "Robespierre, or the 'Divine Violence' of Terror," introduction to Maximilien Robespierre, *Virtue and Terror*, text selected and annotated by Jean Ducange, trans. John Howe (New York: Verso, 2007). In addition see, especially, Žižek, *Parallax View*, 320, and "Concesso Non Dato," 222. Jacques-Alain Miller also articulates this claim in *Le Neveu de Lacan: Satire* (Lagrasse: Verdier, 2003), 270.

45. Žižek, "Robespierre, or the 'Divine Violence' of Terror," xxxii.

46. Ibid., xxxiii.

6. The Sublime Abject of Democracy

1. Melville, *White-Jacket*, 74, 54, 175; hereafter cited in the text by page number only.

2. See the oft-quoted passage in a letter of October 6, 1849, to Lemuel Shaw in which Melville laments that "no reputation that is gratifying to me, can possibly be achieved by either of these books [namely, *Redburn* and *White-Jacket*]. They are two *jobs*, which I have done for money—being forced to it, as other men are to sawing wood" (Melville, *Correspondence*, 138).

3. Ibid.

4. Ibid., 140.

5. Casarino, *Modernity at Sea*, 12.

6. Ibid., 28.

7. Ibid., 38.

8. C. R. L. James's seminal *Mariners, Renegades, and Castaways* (Hanover, N.H.: Dartmouth College, 1953) also considers Melville's work in the context of twentieth-century totalitarianism, though with a different approach and conclusion. For other political readings of *White-Jacket*, see especially Charles Anderson, *Melville in the South Seas* (New York: Columbia University Press in cooperation with Modern Language Association of America, 1939); Richard Manley Blau, *The Body Impolitic: A Reading of Four Novels by Herman Melville* (Amsterdam: Rodopi, 1979); Michael Paul Rogin, *Subversive Genealogy: The Politics and Art of Herman Melville* (New York: Alfred A. Knopf, 1979); and John Samson, *White Lies: Melville's Narratives of Facts* (Ithaca, N.Y.: Cornell University Press, 1989).

9. Hannah Arendt, *The Origins of Totalitarianism* (New York: Harcourt, Brace and Company, 1951), 312.

10. Ibid., 318. While there are many studies of totalitarianism from this era, see especially Carl J. Friedrich, ed., *Totalitarianism: Proceedings of a Conference Held at the American Academy of Arts and Sciences, March 1953* (Cambridge, Mass.: Harvard University Press, 1954).

11. J. L. Talmon, *The Rise of Totalitarian Democracy* (Boston: Beacon Press, 1952), 2.

12. Agamben, *Homo Sacer*, 6.

13. Ibid., 18.

14. Ibid., 10, 120.

15. Ibid., 121.

16. As Agamben notes, Alexis de Tocqueville's forebodings about democracy's dangers in many ways testify to the early formations of what will become totalitarian modes (*Homo Sacer*, 10). In terms of Melville's antebellum man-of-war, I will show how the martial structures there reveal the inner workings of what Amy Kaplan calls the "ambiguous spaces that were not quite foreign nor domestic" within the nineteenth century's nation- and empire-building processes (*Anarchy of Empire*, 15). At the time I was completing this manuscript, William V. Spanos's *The Exceptionalist State and the State of Exception: Herman Melville's* Billy Bud, Sailor

was published (Baltimore: Johns Hopkins University Press, 2011). Although Spanos shares my interest in conceiving of Melville's work as a telling prehistory to contemporary political formations, our projects focus on very different sites and conceptual modalities of antebellum states of exception.

17. Ian Baucom, "Cicero's Ghost: The Atlantic, the Enemy, and the Laws of War," in *States of Emergency: The Object of American Studies,* ed. Russ Castronovo and Susan Gillman (Chapel Hill: University of North Carolina Press, 2009), 126. See also Daniel Heller-Roazen's *The Enemy of All: Piracy and the Law of Nations* (2009), which provides a valuable comparative approach to this topic and traces the shifting register of the "pirate" in relation to Cicero's notion of "the enemy of all."

18. Baucom, "Cicero's Ghost," 141.

19. Agamben, *State of Exception*, 11–21.

20. In Dening, *Mr. Bligh's Bad Language,* Dening explains that the crew of the *Hannah* mutinied after their expectations for prize money were not met (151–52).

21. Markus Eder, *Crime and Punishment in the Royal Navy of the Seven Years' War, 1755–1765* (Burlington, Vt.: Ashgate, 2004), 41.

22. Dening, *Mr. Bligh's Bad Language,* 149–50.

23. Ibid., 150.

24. Ibid.

25. From Article 1 of the "Rules and Regulations for the Government of the United States Navy," in *The public and general Statutes passed by the Congress of the United States of America, from 1789 to 1827 inclusive, whether expired, repealed, or in force; arranged in chronological order, with marginal references, and a copious index. To which is added the Constitution of the United States, and an appendix,* vol. 1, published under the inspection of Joseph Story (Boston: Wells and Lilly, 1827), 761.

26. Land, " 'Sinful Propensities,' " 95.

27. Quoted in ibid., 96.

28. Agamben, *Homo Sacer*, 28.

29. Ibid., 51.

30. Agamben, *State of Exception*, 39.

31. I refer to White-Jacket's well-known declaration (reminiscent of Rousseau's "Man was born free, and he is everywhere in chains" [*Social Contract,* 49]): "I was not born a serf, and will not live a slave!" (Melville, *White-Jacket,* 295).

32. Žižek, "Eastern Europe's Republics of Gilead," 53.

33. Žižek, "The Real of Sexual Difference," 66.

34. Ibid.

35. Jacques Derrida, "Force of Law: The 'Mystical Foundation of Authority,' " in *Deconstruction and the Possibility of Justice,* ed. Drucilla Cornell, Michael Rosenfeld, and David Gray Carlson (New York: Routledge, 1992), 36.

36. This is not to suggest that in such a scenario the Law, acting as a relatively divided subject, necessarily operates in a totalizing manner. According to Žižek, such Benjaminian "divine violence" also allows for a revolutionary subject to take on the "heroic assumption of the solitude of a sovereign decision. It is a decision (to kill, to risk or lose one's own life) made in absolute solitude, not covered by the big Other" (Žižek, "Robespierre, or the 'Divine Violence' of Terror," xi).

37. Lacan, *Seminar XI*, 185.

38. Jacques Lacan, "Kant with Sade," in *Écrits*, trans. Bruce Fink (New York: Norton, 2006), 652–53.

39. Ibid., 653.

40. Lacan, *Seminar XI*, 185.

41. Without intending to simplify Freud's thought on this matter, one can say that he sees perversion as a relatively natural state of childhood sexuality. In "The Archaic Features and Infantilism of Dreams," in *Introductory Lectures on Psychoanalysis*, trans. and ed. James Strachey (New York: Norton, 1966), for example, Freud makes the now well-known point that children are generally polymorphous sexual beings and that the "barriers" required for proper socially sanctioned genital sex occur with "education" (258). In this sense, Freud views adult perversion "as nothing else than a magnified infantile sexuality split up into its separate impulses" (Freud, "The Sexual Life of Human Beings," in *Introductory Lectures on Psychoanalysis*, trans. and ed. James Strachey [New York: Norton, 1966], 385). While in his discussions, these perversions fall into the general categories of libidinal object replacement or displacement scenarios, he does gesture toward the type of fantasy inversion that Lacan discusses (ibid., 378–79). For instance, Freud suggests that in the narcissistic scenario, a subject "can . . . leave [libidinal] objects and set the subject's own ego in their place" ("The Libido Theory and Narcissism," in *Introductory Lectures on Psychoanalysis*, trans. and ed. James Strachey [New York: Norton, 1966], 517). Of course, Freud discusses these and related issues in various other works; see especially "The Economic Problem in Masochism," in Freud, *Collected Papers*, trans. Joan Riviere, vol. 2 (London: Hogarth Press and the Institute of Psycho-Analysis, 1948).

42. Jacques Lacan, "On a Question Prior to Any Possible Treatment of Psychosis," *Écrits*, trans. Bruce Fink (New York: Norton, 2006), 463.

43. Molly Anne Rothenberg and Dennis Foster, introduction to *Perversion and the Social Relation*, ed. Molly Anne Rothenberg, Dennis Foster, and Slavoj Žižek (Durham, N.C.: Duke University Press, 2003), 5.

44. Žižek, *For They Know Not What They Do: Enjoyment as a Political Factor* (New York: Verso, 2008), 236.

45. Ibid., 235.

46. Ibid.

47. It is in this sense that Žižek describes the totalitarian subject as S_2. This subject "would thus be the semblance of a neutral 'objective' knowledge, under which the obscene object-agent of a superegotistical Will hides" (ibid., 235).

48. Lacan, *Seminar I*, 196.

49. Lacan, *Seminar VII*, 194.

50. Ibid.

51. Žižek, *For They Know Not What They Do*, 237.

52. Otter, *Melville's Anatomies*, 52.

53. Rothenberg and Foster, introduction to *Perversion and the Social Relation*, 5–6.

54. Melville comically demonstrates this point in chapter 31, when he laments that there was no "*Hand-book of the Neversink*, so that the tourist might have a reliable guide" (127). Comparing Melville's description of the *Neversink* with Dana Jr.'s schematic of life on the merchant ship the *Pilgrim* illuminates the bizarre quality of the naval frigate's arrangement. Though both include multiple and clear hierarchical divisions, the *Pilgrim* acts as a transparent and knowable system, whereas the *Neversink* remains ambiguously foreign and indefinite.

55. By way of comparison, Claret's imperious but incomplete reign might be placed next to that of the captain of the Atlantic liner *Southampton*, a vessel Melville boarded in October 1849 to take proofs of *White-Jacket* to England. In his journal, Melville recounts how he and his German scholar friend Mr. Adler comically "put the Captain in the Chair [presumably in a mock legal scene], & argued the question 'which was best, a monarchy or a republic?'" (Herman Melville, *Journals*, ed. Howard Horsford et al. [Evanston, Ill.: Northwestern University Press and the Newbury Library, 1989], 10).

56. Žižek, *For They Know Not What They Do*, 235.

57. While scholars such as Foucault and Jameson discuss this point, for a Lacanian approach to relevant issues see especially Žižek, *Parallax View*, 306–8 and 370–73.

58. Ibid., 338. The notion of excess that sustains the law (via superego) should be differentiated from forms of release-valve deviance, or a zone or mode of rebellious activity ultimately controlled by a power system; as opposed to the latter, the type of excess at stake here is an internal component of legal power apparatuses.

59. Žižek, *Interrogating the Real*, 253. See Dening, *Mr. Bligh's Bad Language*, for a more substantial analysis of the relation between Bligh's approach to discipline and the infamous mutiny.

60. Lacan, *Seminar XVII*, 119–20.

61. Ibid., 120.

62. White-Jacket later emphasizes the subterranean issues of power and enjoyment that infuse the control of consumption. In chapter 91, for instance, he refus-

es to smoke altogether rather than do it in the restricted manner the rules allow, claiming he would "abandon the luxury rather than enslave it to a time and place" (387).

63. See, for example, chapter 74's discussion of how "dissatisfied" British seamen often "spiked" the guns of their ships (313).

64. Melville later notes how, in the navy, sailors are not allowed to sing out while they work, laboring instead only to the sound of a fife (58). Thus, instead of framing their work with their own voices, sailors must labor to the official herald and call of the officers' instruments.

65. Lacan, *Seminar XI*, 185.

66. This is dramatized in the hyperbolic way Melville figures sailors' mental and physical attributes taking on the characteristics of their specific stations. See especially chapter 12's comic–materialist discussion of how a particular ship space and activity shape one's personality (44–49).

67. Žižek, *Interrogating the Real*, 85.

68. Sailors' anxiety about the dead coming back to haunt the present can be seen as well in chapter 80's discourse between two old sailors stitching up the body bag of a deceased fore-top-man. Here, they surmise how "corpses is cunning" and recount how "You think [the bodies] sink deep, but they comes up agin as soon as you sails over 'em.... [T]hey ar'n't dead yet" (339).

69. Derrida, *Specters of Marx*, 10.

70. As White-Jacket notes, the fact that only a man-of-war carries life buoys for its crew's protection (attended by two around-the-clock sentinels) may be a materialized example of an "empty gesture." As we see with the cooper's death on account of a flawed buoy design, the apparatus and its routine (the sentinels pacing up and down the decks) appear to function only symbolically, as a means to assuage sailors' anxieties about the truth of the underlying system: that they may very well die.

71. Žižek, *For They Know Not What They Do*, 240–41.

72. While I will discuss Samuel Otter and Wai Chee Dimock's work within this context, see also Myra C. Glen's "The Naval Reform Campaign against Flogging: A Case Study in Changing Attitudes toward Corporal Punishment, 1830–50," *American Quarterly* 35 (1983): 408–25, and *Campaigns against Corporal Punishment: Prisoners, Sailors, Women, and Children in Antebellum America* (Albany: State University of New York Press, 1984), as well as Collamer M. Abbott, "*White-Jacket* and the Campaign against Flogging in the Navy," *Melville Society Extracts* 89 (1992): 24–25; Anderson, *Melville in the South Seas*, chapter 16 ("*White-Jacket* as Propaganda"); and Sampson, *White Lies*.

73. Quoted in Land, "'Sinful Propensities,'" 98.

74. For White-Jacket's comments on flogging, see especially pages 138, 141, 144, and 277.

75. Land, "'Sinful Propensities,'" 100.

76. According to Land, "By equating flogging with atrocity narratives of confinement, rape, and torture, the advocates of naval reform dismissed the 'customs of the sea,' insisting that an insult to white bodies in one place was an insult to white bodies everywhere" ("'Sinful Propensities,'" 102–3). It should be noted that this is the very argument Richard Henry Dana Jr. puts forth at the close of *Two Years before the Mast*, but toward a different end. He defends the practice of flogging in part because "more than three-fourths of the seamen in our merchant vessels are foreigners. They are from all parts of the world. A great many from the north of Europe, besides Frenchmen, Spaniards, Portuguese, Italians, men from all parts of the Mediterranean, together with Lascars, Negroes, and, perhaps worst of all, the off-casts of British men-of-war, and men from our own country who have gone to sea because they could not be permitted to live on land" (353–54).

77. See Land, "'Sinful Propensities,'" 108.

78. See Dimock, *Empire for Liberty*, 100.

79. Slavoj Žižek, *Violence: Six Sideways Reflections* (New York: Picador, 2008), 1–2.

80. Otter, *Melville's Anatomies*, 68.

81. *An Inquiry into the Nature and Effects of Flogging: The Manner of Inflicting It at Sea; and the Alleged Necessity for Allowing Seamen to Be Flogged at Discretion in the Royal Navy and the Merchant Service* (London: Hunt and Clarke, 1826), Goldsmiths'-Kress Library of Economic Literature, no. 25066, 9–10.

82. Ibid.

83. Statistic quoted in Dening, *Mr. Bligh's Bad Language*, 154.

84. Sigmund Freud, "A Child Is Being Beaten," in *Collected Papers*, vol. 2, ed. Ernest Jones, trans. Joan Riviere (London: Hogarth Press and the Institute of Psycho-Analysis, 1948), 184.

85. Darian Leader, "Beating Fantasies and Sexuality," in *Sexuation*, ed. Renata Salecl (Durham, N.C.: Duke University Press, 2000), 113.

86. Michel Foucault, *Discipline and Punish: The Birth of the Prison*, trans. Alan Sheridan (New York: Vintage Books, 1995), 7.

87. Rebecca M. McLennan, *The Crisis of Imprisonment: Protest, Politics, and the Making of the American Penal State, 1776–1941* (Cambridge: Cambridge University Press, 2008), 9.

88. McLennan cites Benjamin Rush's and Thomas Jefferson's protests against all corporal punishment (except in cases of murder and, tellingly, those occurring in the military service) (ibid., 19–20). For other studies of the early republic's conceptions of punishment, see David J. Rothman, *Discovery of the Asylum: Social Order and Disorder in the New Republic* (Boston: Little, Brown, 1971), and Lawrence Friedman, *Crime and Punishment in American History* (New York: Basic Books, 1993).

89. Foucault, *Discipline and Punish*, 50, 39.

90. Ibid., 164. A historically plausible reason why flogging was employed in an age when punishment often took the form of institutionalized involuntary servitude may be the fact that sailors were *already* in a penal-like contract of labor. Furthermore, many sailors had few possessions to confiscate. Thus, with the same logic Foucault attributes to feudal punishment—that is, "the body [is] . . . in most cases the only property accessible"(25)—the only "liberty" to attack is that of the body's integrity. For other studies that consider themes of punishment or flagellation and the development of modernity, see, for example, Niklaus Largier, *In Praise of the Whip: A Cultural History of Arousal*, trans. Graham Harman (New York: Zone Books, 2007); Diana Paton, *No Bond but the Law: Punishment, Race, and Gender in Jamaican State Formation, 1780–1870* (Durham, N.C.: Duke University Press, 2004); and Louis Masur, *Rites of Execution: Capital Punishment and the Transformation of American Culture, 1776–1865* (New York: Oxford University Press, 1991).

91. Agamben, *Homer Sacer*, 32.

92. In these terms, it may not be going too far to categorize such flogging practice as a "rape in fantasy" (see Žižek, *Parallax View*, 69). Instead of Žižek's schematic, however, where one's fantasy is forced out and then ruthlessly abandoned ("thrown upon the victim"), here the ship's own fantasy structures (linked to systems of power) are forced on the sailors' bodies and minds. Judith Butler's reading of Foucault in *Gender Trouble* is worth repeating here. Emphasizing the point that Foucault's analysis in *Discipline and Punish* is not predicated on traditional ideations of inside/outside, Butler explains that "the strategy has been not to enforce a repression of [prisoners'] . . . desires, but to compel their bodies to signify the prohibitive law as their very essence. . . . That law is not literally internalized, but incorporated" (171).

93. Another way of articulating the effect of flogging is through Benjamin's notion of the "lawmaking" and "law-preserving" functions of violence; see Walter Benjamin, "Critique of Violence," in *Selected Writings, vol. 1: 1913–1926*, ed. Marcus Bullock and Michael W. Jennings (Cambridge, Mass.: Belknap Press of Harvard University Press, 2003). He describes the former as referring to "all violence used for natural ends," which might include forms of violence that function to instantiate the law itself (240). The latter form, according to Benjamin, is "use of violence as a means for the state," or, in other terms, "the subordination of citizens to laws" (241). We see flogging operating on both levels at once. Here, it acts as a law-preserving (military) violence in that it sustains the legal authority of the commanders. But it also acts concomitantly as a necessary lawmaking violence where, in a martial state of exception's perforated border between violence and law, such acts literally cut into normal fantasy-structures of the Law (perhaps approaching a mode of "divine violence"), forcing subjects into new perverse coordinates.

94. In this sense, Ushant bravely performs Lacan's famous ethical injunction never to "yield with regard to your desire" (quoted in Žižek, *In Defense of Lost Causes*, 5).

95. Peter Linebaugh, *The Magna Carta Manifesto* (Berkeley: University of California Press, 2008), 127.

96. Rousseau, *Social Contract*, 53.

97. See Parker, *Herman Melville*, 1:653.

98. John A. Lockwood, "Flogging in the Navy," *United States Magazine and Democratic Review* 25, no. 134 (Aug. 1849): 115.

99. Žižek, *Plague of Fantasies*, 21.

100. Žižek, *Ticklish Subject*, 14.

101. We might link Melville's nightmarish fantasy of a liberating totalitarian violence with a broader antebellum shift during the 1840s and 1850s toward imagining such structures of political action. See, for example, Michael Ziser's argument, in "Emersonian Terrorism: John Brown, Islam, and Postsecular Violence," *American Literature* 82, no. 2 (June 2012): 333–60, that, in the 1850s, Ralph Waldo Emerson "reformulate[d] his beliefs into a properly postsecular recognition of the formal necessity of a new kind of religious orthodoxy and violence to effect political change within a modern liberal state" (336). The radical thought that Ziser and others have noted in Emerson's work during the 1850s is characterized by a new emphasis on the relationship between the individual and what we might call cosmic power. This informs Emerson's claim, from his essay "Courage," that "If you accept your thoughts as inspirations from the Supreme Intelligence, obey them when they prescribe difficult duties" (qtd. in Ziser, "Emersonian Terrorism," 351). Might Melville's own fantasy reveal or perhaps anticipate a similar model of ethical and political action?

Epilogue

1. Copjec, *Read My Desire*, 6.
2. Ibid., 14.
3. Joan Copjec, "Islam and the Exotic Science," *UMBR(a): A Journal of the Unconscious* (2009): 8.
4. Ibid.
5. In *The Parallax View*, Žižek asserts that dialectical materialism, as opposed to historical materialism, "introduces topics like the death drive, the 'inhuman' core of the human, which reach over the horizon of the collective *praxis* of humanity; the gap is thus asserted as inherent to humanity itself, as the gap between humanity and its *own* excess" (5). Thus, "a parallax gap [is] at the very core of psychoanalytic experience" (19).

6. Melville, *Moby-Dick*, 5.
7. Ibid., 274.
8. Ian Baucom, *Specters of the Atlantic: Finance Capital, Slavery, and the Philosophy of History* (Durham, N.C.: Duke University Press, 2005), 312. Walcott quoted in ibid., 309.
9. This interpretative approach is thus similar to Adorno's mode of negative dialectics. In *Late Marxism: Adorno, or the Persistence of the Dialectic* (New York: Verso, 2007), Frederic Jameson explains Adorno's conceptual move: "Interpretation as such—the reading of the particular in the light of the absent universal—is dialectically transformed and 'sublated': producing a new mode of interpretation in which the particular is read, not in the light of the universal, but rather in the light of the very contradiction between universal and particular in the first place" (32). A Lacanian approach takes this one step further, moving this interpretative and conceptual gap into the ideological fabric of reality itself. In other words, Adorno's method of "turning a text inside out and making it into a symptom of the very problem of interpretation" is carried over into the sociopolitical realm at large (32). It is in this context that Žižek notes the limitation of Adorno's approach. In *The Metastases of Enjoyment: On Women and Causality* (New York: Verso, 2005), Žižek argues that, "at the point where, according to Adorno, psychoanalysis reaches its limit and witnesses the demolition of its 'object' (the psychological individual), *at this very point the 'agency of the letter' emerges as such in 'historical reality' itself*" (20–21, emphasis in the original).
10. In Mary Louise Pratt, *Imperial Eyes: Travel Writing and Transculturation* (New York: Routledge, 1992), she defines contact zones as "social spaces where cultures meet, clash, and grapple with each other, often in contexts of highly asymmetrical relations of power" (584). John Carlos Rowe, in *The New American Studies* (Minneapolis: University of Minnesota Press, 2002), proposes the construction of "a new comparative U.S. cultures curriculum and canon around an elaborated and developed theory of the contact zone" (12).
11. Copjec, "Islam and the Exotic Science," 9.
12. Žižek, *Parallax View*, 9. Žižek uses this logic in *In Defense of Lost Causes*, where he cautions against the production of a "multitude of local fictions." "It all depends," he suggests, "on how these fictions relate to the underlying Real of capitalism—do they just *supplement* its imaginary multitude, as the postmodern 'local narratives' do, or do they *disturb* its functioning?" (33).
13. Žižek, *Parallax View*, 24. The connection between external and internal difference is, in this way, parallactic in nature. In "Slavoj Žižek's Hegelian Reformation," Adrian Johnston describes Žižek's conception of this relation as follows: "The 'true' reality of material being (as substance) passes into the 'false' illusions of

more-than-material nonbeing (as subject). But through a movement of reciprocal dialectical modification, these illusions then pass back into their respective reality, becoming integral parts of it; and, at this stage, they no longer can be called illusions in the quotidian sense of the word" (14). Žižek's own discussion of the relationship between economy and politics is a useful correlative. He suggests: "If, for Lacan, there is no sexual relationship, then, for Marxism proper, there is *no relationship between economy and politics,* no 'meta-language' enabling us to grasp the two levels from the same neutral standpoint, although—or, rather, *because*—these two levels are inextricably intertwined" (*Parallax View,* 320, emphasis in the original).

14. Contemporary scholars associated with American Studies have offered innovative methods and metrics for analyzing the vast array of interfaces and antagonisms that accompany the development of modernity. For example, David Kazajian, in *The Colonizing Trick: National Culture and Imperial Citizenship in Early America* (Minneapolis: University of Minnesota Press, 2003), offers the "flashpoint" as a conceptual model that enables "a comparative study of multiple (rather than binary) racial formations and the global (rather than simply national or domestic) systems in which they emerged" (5). More recently, Russ Castronovo and Susan Gillman set up their edited volume *States of Emergency: The Object of American Studies* (Chapel Hill: University of North Carolina Press, 2009) as a collection that uses Walter Benjamin's notion of the "state of emergency" to shift analysis into "transtemporal sites of comparison" (7).

15. There are, of course, examples of traditional historical studies that approach the type of analysis I am suggesting. See, for example, Kevin Bruyneel, *The Third Space of Sovereignty* (Minneapolis: University of Minnesota Press, 2007), in which he demonstrates how American indigenous peoples "speak against and across the boundaries of colonial rule by articulating and fighting for a third space: a space of sovereignty and/or citizenship that is inassimilable to the modern liberal democratic settler-state and nation" (217).

16. Patricia Yaeger, "Editor's Column: Sea Trash, Dark Pools, and the Tragedy of the Commons," *PMLA* 125, no. 3 (May 2010): 524.

17. Although there are interesting aspects of Yaeger's conception of "ecocriticism$," a "prosthetic term that insists on the imbroglio of markets and nature," it can be seen to utilize and reproduce the structural logic of the traditional contact-zone model just discussed. In so doing, it displaces inner gaps within "capitalism" onto outer gaps between "markets and nature." Although Yaeger comes close to productively aligning the two planes, suggesting that "the ocean as *oikos* or home rolls under, beneath, and inside the edicts of states and free market capitalism," her formulation casts the sea as a veritable big Other—a potential problem for many ecocritical approaches ("Editor's Column," 529).

18. Hester Blum, "The Prospects of Oceanic Studies," *PMLA* 125, no. 3 (May 2010): 671.

19. Ibid.

20. Castronovo and Gillman, *States of Emergency*, 5. According to Castronovo and Gillman, "We need transtemporal sites of comparison, such as those defined by oceans as well as by land, if we are to make visible both the global and the local routes that bring the objects of American studies—race, slavery, immigration, the state—into circulation" (7).

21. Theodor Adorno, *Aesthetic Theory*, ed. Gretel Adorno and Rolf Tiedemann, trans. Robert Hullot-Kentor (Minneapolis: University of Minnesota Press, 1997), 7.

22. Benjamin, *Arcades Project*, 13.

23. Russ Castronovo, "Disciplinary Panic: A Response to Ed White and Michael Drexler," *Early American Literature* 45, no. 2 (2010): 485.

24. Žižek, *In Defense of Lost Causes*, 141. Žižek's broader point is: "The past itself is not simply 'what there was,' it contains hidden, non-realized potentials, and the authentic future is the repetition/retrieval of *this* past, not of the past as it was, but of those elements in the past which the past itself, in its reality, betrayed, stifled, failed to realize" (141). This, of course, follows from the Adorno–Horkheimer position that "what is at stake is not conservation of the past but the fulfillment of past hopes"; Max Horkheimer and Theodor Adorno, *Dialectic of Enlightenment: Philosophical Fragments*, ed. Gunzelin Schmid Noerr, trans. Edmund Jephcott (Stanford, Calif.: Stanford University Press, 2002), xvii. It also can be seen in Marx's early thoughts on historical analysis, depicted in a well-known letter to Arnold Ruge in September 1843; see Ludwig Feuerbach, Karl Marx, and Friedrich Engels, *German Socialist Philosophy*, ed. Wolfgang Schirmacher (New York: Continuum Publishing, 1997). Here, Marx argues for a *"ruthless criticism of all that exists"* (87), wherein he suggests that "it will become evident that it is not a question of drawing a great mental dividing line between past and future, but of *realizing* the thoughts of the past" (89). While at times a valid critique, the pejorative charge of "presentism" is, from the above perspective, often leveled from a defensive and ideological position. Gianni Vattimo and Santiago Zabala, in *Hermeneutic Communism: From Heidegger to Marx* (New York: Columbia University Press, 2011), provide a helpful conceptual schematic that might be useful for conceiving of these competing ideological notions of historical analysis. In their terms, there is a clear divide between what they call a "politics of description" and "interpretation." Description is a mode that we might associate with traditional historicism, which is "functional for the continued existence of a society of domination, which pursues its truth in the form of imposition (violence), conservation (realism), and triumph (history)" (12). According to Vattimo and Zabala, "unlike description, for which

reality must be imposed, interpretation instead must make a new contribution to reality" (4). The type of historicism I am forwarding might thus be seen as a practice of interpretation.

25. See, for example: "The world's a ship on its passage out, and not a voyage complete; and the pulpit is its prow" (Melville, *Moby-Dick,* 40). Or Ahab's line to the *Bachelor*'s captain: "Thou art a full ship and homeward bound, thou sayst; well, then, call me an empty ship, and outward-bound" (495).

Index

Abbott, Collamer M., 297n.72
abstractions as part of concrete reality, Johnston on, 248n.13
Acushnet (whaler), 99
Adam, Kathleen, 286n.53
Adams, John, 202–3, 271n.93
Adorno, Theodor, 244, 303n.21, 303n.24; Cohen's critique of, 28; negative dialectics of, 54, 301n.9; notion of conceptual nonidentity, 264n.90
Adventures of Louisa Baker, The (Coverly), 46, 126
aesthetics, Polynesian tattoos' qualitative aspects troubling Western conventions of, 101–2
African Americans, bifurcation of desire-to-be and identification of, 92. *See also* race; slavery
Agamben, Giorgio, 179, 203, 205–6, 207, 248n.17, 258n.22, 288n.93, 289n.2, 289n.5; on contiguity between mass democracy and totalitarian states, 199–201; on flogging as moment of indistinction between violence and law, 232; on force of law without law, 204; on lacunae at core of testimony, 264n.92; on melancholia, 164; on originary moment of law, 206; on state of exception, 175–76, 199, 200–201; on Tocqueville, 293n.16

agency: Cooper's anxiety over master's loss of, and waning reign of law, 186–88, 189, 190, 195; of cultural other, vulnerability of the West's symbolic schemas and, 114–16, 279n.55; female, dangerous effect in marketplace of, 127; master's discourse and, 41; narratives involving translation and transcription and, 44, 54; of native women in Melville's *Mardi*, 158; of native women in Melville's *Typee*, 152, 154–55; of tattoo, invasive, 108, 110, 112; university discourse and, 40
aggressive-grotesque in *Typee*, reframing, 99–109
Algerine Captive, or, The Life and Adventures of Doctor Updike Underhill, Six Years a Prisoner among the Algerines, The (Tyler), 58, 253n.86
Allen, Thomas M., 265n.11
Allison, Robert J., 256n.3
Althusser, Louis, 111, 278n.51
American Board of Commissioners for Foreign Missions, 100
American Democrat, The (Cooper), 84, 177, 185, 191, 193
American exceptionalism, 59, 253n.89
American Jurist (periodical), 103

American Monthly Magazine, 30
American Revolution, 180; Cooper's ambivalence about, 73, 74, 75; renarration of, in Cooper's *The Pilot*, 180; U.S. marine forces during, Cooper on, 83, 84
American School of economics, 291n.29
American Studies, 17, 59–60, 242, 302n.14
American Whig Review, review of Cooper's *Redskins*, 177
Anderson, Benedict, 59, 60, 252n.68, 266n.15
Anderson, Charles Roberts, 227, 273n.7, 293n.8
Anderson, Perry, 252n.71
antebellum era: economic landscape of, 2, 4; political relationship among fantasy, desire, and maritime experience in, 2; transitions into modern age of capitalism, 17, 112, 176
anthropology, traditional methodology of, 273n.5
Antigone and Oedipus, 113, 114
Anti-Rent War of 1839–46, 177, 186–87
anxiety: about ability to label and control bodies, 101–3, 107–8; affixed to national identity, Bhabha on, 61; about foreign sailors in American merchant service, 88–89; about issue of authenticity, 26, 30–39, 42, 44; over loss of identity, tattoos in *Typee* as cause of, 101, 106, 110, 112–21; over master's loss of agency and waning reign of law, 186–88, 189, 190, 195; racial, 106, 108; tattoo, 277n.45; threat posed by feminine excess, 153, 154–55; Western, about facial disfigurement by tattoo, 98, 99, 100, 101–3, 106–8, 110–11
Arac, Jonathan, 257n.16
Arcades Project, The (Benjamin), 21
Arendt, Hannah, 199, 207, 293n.9
Aristotle, classic Master of, 260n.47
Articles of War, 201–4; British Printed Instructions on naval discipline under, 201–2; critiques of, pertaining to flogging, 235; institutionalization of exception under, 201–4, 212, 213, 232; Melville's analysis and condemnation of, in *White-Jacket*, 203–4, 225–26, 234–35, 236; naval vessel structured by, 201; United States' version of naval, 201, 202–3
Athenaeum, The, review of *Ned Myers*, 53
authenticity, issue of, 19, 26, 30–39, 42, 44; addressed in preface to Cooper's *The Crater*, 180–81; as antebellum fantasy, 34–35, 36; consciousness of desires surrounding, 43; Cooper's focus on realism, 31–32; in Cooper's *Ned Myers*, 48; in ex-slave narratives, 257n.22; with Melville's *Typee*, 32–34, 99; in travel narratives, 258n.23
author: antebellum authorship, competing rhetorical paradigms of labor and, 29; as authentic sailor, 26, 30–39; developing notion of celebrity and, 44; sailor and, dichotomy between positions of, 32–33; sailor and, structural relations between, 25–26
authority aboard *Neversink* in Melville's *White-Jacket*, system of, 211–15; commodore, role of, 213–15;

INDEX 307

superego in perverse and totalitarian logic of, 208, 215–20
autobiography, maritime texts constructed within paradigm of, 30, 31, 47

Baartman, South African "Hottentot Venus" Saartjie, 137, 286n.54
Bacon, Francis, 26, 256n.2
Badiou, Alain, 244
Baepler, Paul, 256n.3
Banks, Joseph, 97, 137
Barbary piracy narratives, 27, 256n.3
Barker, Francis, 282n.4, 285n.48
Barnard, Suzanne, 129, 283n.21, 284n.23
Barnum, P. T., 274nn.15–16
Baucom, Ian, 18, 200, 242, 294n.17, 301n.8; on *Zong* massacre (1781), 240
beating fantasy, Freud's phases of, 229–30
Benjamin, Walter, 179, 205, 248n.14, 281n.76, 290n.14, 302n.14; on dialectical method, 5; dream interpretation model, 17, 21, 244; on "lawmaking" and "law-preserving" functions of violence, 299n.93
Berlant, Lauren, 251n.61, 266n.18
Bezanson, Walter E., 33, 34, 259n.28
Bhabha, Homi K., 59, 60–61, 64, 71, 266n.13, 266nn.19–22
big Other, 65–66, 118, 261n.52; absent sociosymbolic, in prison scene in Melville's *Omoo*, 156; as divided or barred Other, 131, 284n.33; fantasy as screen concealing lack of symbolic order's, 65–66; sailors as special placeholders of maritime system's needs, 221, 222, 223–24, 233–34, 297n.66; symbolic order and, 65–66, 130–31, 135; undefined,

in scene of dancing girls in Melville's *Typee*, 155
biopolitics, 199, 200, 201, 207, 231
Blackhouse, Roger, 291n.29
blackness, association of tattooing and, 101
black sailors, 89, 220, 227–28
Blackstone, 203
Blanchot, Maurice, 197, 208
Blau, Richard Manley, 293n.8
Bleys, Rudi C., 282n.4
Blum, Hester, 18, 46, 256n.2, 257n.20, 262n.73, 263n.80, 303n.18; analysis of *Two Years*, 38–39; on maritime labor, 27–28; on oceanic studies, 243–44
body marking, practice of, 273n.8. *See also* tattoo(s); tattoos in *Typee*
Bogdan, Robert, 100, 109, 273n.12
Bonham, Julia C., 283n.14
Bonny, Anne, 125, 282n.10
"Borromean knot," Lacan's notion of, 118
Bounty, HMS, mutiny on, 215, 216
Bourdieu, Pierre, 63, 267n.29
bourgeois society, Marx on human relations in, 139, 286n.58
Brain, Robert, 277n.42
Bread and Cheese Club, New York's, 74–75
Brewster, Mary, 126, 275n.28, 283n.14
Briggs, Laura, 254n.89
Brückner, Martin, 252n.75
Bruyneel, Kevin, 261n.53, 302n.15
bureaucracy: division of labor aboard *Neversink* in Melville's *White-Jacket*, 210, 211, 214, 234; systems of knowledge and, 52, 264n.85; totalitarian, 207, 214
"Burial at Sea, A" (Leggett), 30
Burke, Edmund, 272n.3

308 INDEX

Burnham, Clint, 251n.61
Butler, Judith, 284n.38, 285nn.43–44, 287n.80, 299n.92

Caduveo Indians of Brazil, facial tattoos of, 109
Calder, Alex, 112, 272n.3, 273n.5
cannibalism, 110, 113
capital: American seamen as social group within symbolic matrix and structure of, 35; other limit of, 91, 241; outer limit of, 91; shift from classical (market) to monopoly or imperial, 14–15; social rank changed through, in Cooper's *The Crater*, 184, 185–86; symbolic, 63, 68, 70
capitalism: cognitive mapping needed in development of, 15, 253n.79; consolidation during early nineteenth century, 176; "democracy" as "true master-signifier" of, Žižek on, 194–95, 290n.17; surplus value in, 41, 129, 263n.85; tumultuous transitions into the modern age of, 17, 112, 176, 252n.71; Žižek on history lost with growth of, 112, 279n.55
capitalist–proletariat dialectic, 40
Carey, Henry Charles, 185–86, 291nn.28–29
Carib women, sexual violence against, 139. *See also* women, native
Carretta, Vincent, 255n.94, 257n.22
Casarino, Cesare, 18, 35, 247n.10, 259n.38; crisis of modernity, notion of, 4, 176; on Melville's *White-Jacket*, 44, 198; on "outer limit" and "other limit" of capital, 91, 241
Cassuto, Leonard, 100, 274n.16; notion of grotesque, 101, 103, 278n.45; on tattoo "as basis for a wild story," 108

Castiglia, Christopher, 17, 254n.90, 266n.18
castration. *See* symbolic castration, Lacanian notion of
Castronovo, Russ, 17, 243, 244, 254n.89, 254n.90, 302n.14, 303n.20, 303n.23
celebrity, developing notion of, 44
Chapman, Mary, 255n.92
Charles and Henry (whaler), 99
Charles I, overthrow of (1647), 235
Chase, Owen, 58, 265n.4
Chiesa, Lorenzo, 162, 288n.90
"Child Is Being Beaten, A" (Freud), 229–30
Chow, Rey, 278n.45
Chura, Patrick, 260n.42
Churchill, Winston, 201
Cicero, 294n.17
citizenship: Bob in Cooper's *The Crater* as ideal citizen, 183–84; martial law and ban from, 203, 204
Civilization and Its Discontents (Freud), 6
"civilization" and "progress," development of competing notions of, 112
civilizing contract and savage state of nature, distinction between, 272n.3
Clarke, James Freeman, 46
class: antebellum authors' competing rhetorical paradigms of labor, 29; class divide in "Town-Ho's Story" in Melville's *Moby-Dick*, 45; commercial, Cooper's anxiety about rise of, 82–84; Cooper's class angst, 74; Cooper's *Ned Myers* and issues pertaining to fantasies of class experience, 48; in Cooper's *The Pilot*, 76–77, 81–84, 89; Dana's foregrounding of issue of, in *Two Years before the Mast*, 36–39; gap

between class identities, 34; gap between subaltern subjectivities and discourses used to represent them, 34–35; in *Moby-Dick*, representation and, 35; in Scott's *The Pirate*, 84; skin color and labor and, issues surrounding, 34, 259n.34; social behavior and, 82; "vital contact" between upper and lower, notion of, 260n.42. *See also* labor, maritime

Clemens, Justin, 260n.48

Clinton, DeWitt, 74–75, 269n.49

cognitive mapping, 15, 253n.79

Cohen, Margaret, 18, 27, 243, 254n.91, 256n.6; on plain style, 262n.73; on relation between ideology and maritime craft, 28–29, 256n.13; view of nineteenth-century maritime labor, 73, 256n.13, 268n.41, 269n.59

Coleridge, Samuel Taylor, 25, 81, 270n.63

colonial/postcolonial subaltern, 34–35, 259n.35, 261n.53

common sailor, fantasies of, 25–55; author as authentic sailor, 26, 30–39; autobiographical work, 30, 31, 47; changing presentation of sailors, 26; sailor's experiential knowledge, 26–29, 39–43, 52, 264n.85; sailor's schizophrenic-like movement across international waters, 47; telling yarns, 44–55

common sailors: black, 89, 220, 227–28; colonial/postcolonial subaltern and, 259n.35; Cooper's depiction of, in *The Pilot*, 76–77, 81–84; cross-dressing, 46, 125–26; foreigners as, anxiety about, 88–89; ideal nationalistic, 85–86; ideal sailor, Coffin in Cooper's *The Pilot* as, 77–81; impressment of, 73, 265n.5, 268n.39; intimate relations between, naval corporal punishment and suspicion of, 271n.93; invested with type of object *a*, 37, 38–39, 42–43; with tattoos, 107, 277n.42

conceptual nonidentity, Adorno's notion of, 264n.90

Congress, Cooper's warning about power of, 191–92

Constitution, Cooper on, 193

Constitution, USS, 126

constitutional democracy, 194

consumption, subterranean issues of power and enjoyment infusing control of, in Melville's *White-Jacket*, 217, 296n.62

contact-zone models, 124, 241–42, 301n.10, 302n.17

Cook, James, 97, 100, 107, 286n.60, 287nn.61–62; influence on views about the Pacific, 140, 148; perceptions conditioned by fantasy of phallic economy, 142; portrayal of native women, 140–42, 287n.62

Cooper, Benjamin, 263n.79

Cooper, James Fenimore, 26, 57, 258nn.24–26, 263n.77, 268n.38, 270n.70, 271n.75, 271n.79, 271n.90, 272n.100, 290n.18, 291n.33, 292n.38; ambivalence about American Revolution, 73, 74, 75; anonymous magazine articles by, 269n.54; anxiety about rise of commercial class, 82–84; anxiety over master's loss of agency and waning reign of the law, 186–88, 189, 190, 195; condemnation for inspiring mutiny attempt on USS *Somers*, 2; coupling of Manifest Destiny and Divine

Cooper, James Fenimore (*continued*)
Providence, 177–78, 182–83; as Democrat, 188; encounter with English impressment, 268n.39; focus on realism, 31–32, 76, 81–82; illustration of diminishing agency of law, 204; maritime experience of, 48–49; meeting with Marquis de Lafayette, 271n.85; as monarchist, criticism of, 188; patriotism of, 75; political identity in 1820s, 74–75; politics of, 84, 86, 87, 188, 190–94, 195, 269nn.48–49, 269n.52; politics of, shift in, 177–78; on pursuit of profit, 88–89; sailors used as sources by, 263n.79; shift in presentation of America during latter part of writing career, 177, 179–80; social and economic views of, 74–75, 185–86; sociopolitical vision of, 185; support for territorial expansion, 292n.34; on trade as corrupting influence, 189. See also *Crater; or, Vulcan's Peak: A Tale of the Pacific, The* (Cooper); *Ned Myers; or, a Life before the Mast* (Cooper); *Pilot: A Tale of the Sea, The* (Cooper)

Cooper, Susan Fenimore, 73, 268n.44

"Cooper's Political Views in 'The Crater'" (McCloskey), 292n.35

Copjec, Joan, 170, 283n.23, 300n.3; critique of Butler's work, 287n.80; critique of historicism of Foucault, 239–40; on cultural hybridity, 241; on exotic force, 239–40; on feminine jouissance, 134–35; on Lacanian woman and "failure of the limit" of symbolic order, 152

corporal punishment, 298n.88; Dana's defense of, in *Two Years before the Mast*, 89, 298n.76; suspicion of intimate relations between sailors and, 271n.93; tattoo used as means of, 105, 276n.32. *See also* flogging

Costentenus, Captain, 101, 274n.15

"Courage" (Emerson), 300n.101

Court-martial, 1–2, 201, 235

Coverly, Nathaniel, Jr., 126

Coviello, Peter, 255n.92

craft, relation between ideology and maritime, 28–29, 256n.13

Crater; or, Vulcan's Peak: A Tale of the Pacific, The (Cooper), 19, 20, 88, 176–96, 270n.62; backstory of, 181; Christian eschatological scenario in, 182, 193–94; colony in, development of, 184–85, 187–90; colony in, external and internal threats to, 187, 189–91; compared to Melville's *White-Jacket*, 208; division of labor in, 185, 291n.26; law "of right" in, 185–86, 193; Manifest Destiny and Divine Providence coupled in, 177–78, 182–83; master figure in, 183, 186–88, 195; master figure in, undercutting of power of, 189, 190; miraculous land-birthing earthquake in, 182–83; problem of authenticity addressed in preface to, 180–81; social divisions in, 183–88, 290nn.23–24, 291n.25; as warning of America's potential demise, 177, 179–80, 183; whaling introduced into colony, 189; yeomanized landscape created in, 183

Creighton, Margaret S., 125, 255n.92, 282n.9

criminality, theories of, 231

"Critique of Violence" (Benjamin), 205

Cromwell, Samuel, 1
cross-cultural encounters, 241; from Lacanian perspective, scenes of, 19–20; mediated by symbolic systems of the West, 98. *See also* Pacific; Pacific islands, European eroticization of native women of; tattoos in *Typee*; *Typee* (Melville)
cross-dressing sailors, 46, 125–26
"cultural grotesque": Cassuto's conception of, 101, 103, 278n.45; of Melville, rethinking, 97–121. *See also* tattoos in *Typee*
cultural hybridity, Copjec on, 241
Cummings, William, 107, 273n.11
Cummins, Maria, 18
Cuneo, Michele de, 139
cynic, logic of, 237, 245

Dale, Richard, 263n.79
D'Alleva, Anne, 105, 276nn.31–32
Dana, Richard Henry, Jr., 1, 4, 11, 19, 26, 31, 42, 43, 197, 247n.5; challenge to romantic conceptions of sea experience, 3; defense of corporal punishment at sea due to foreign seamen on vessels, 89, 298n.76; desire to know the sea, 262n.61; foregrounding of issue of class in *Two Years before the Mast*, 36–39; life on Melville's *Neversink* compared to *Pilgrim*, 296n.54. *See also Two Years before the Mast* (Dana)
Darwin, Charles, 275n.25
daydreams, Freud on, 5–6
Dean, Tim, 251n.64
death: discharge of dead sailors in Melville's *White-Jacket*, 222–23, 297n.68, 297n.70; Miller's "zone between-two-deaths," 114, 117, 120;

prohibition of jouissance on basis of father's, Lacan on, 215; second, 113, 114, 115; shame-induced, 113; as sine qua non of fantasy and phallic enjoyment, 171
Death of a Nation: American Culture and the End of Exceptionalism (Noble), 59
Declaration of Independence, 193
deconstruction and dialectic, distinction between, 12, 252n.69
Defoe, Daniel, 181–82
Dekker, George G., 192, 258n.23, 267n.26, 269n.48, 289n.9; on Cooper's anxiety about rise of commercial class, 82–83; on Cooper's political alignment, 177; on Scott, 62
Deleuze, Gilles, 25, 82, 250n.50, 256n.1, 274n.21
DeMello, Margo, 277n.42
democracy(ies): apparent loss of law within democratic structures, 20–21, 176–77 (see also *Crater; or Vulcan's Peak: A Tale of the Pacific, The* [Cooper]; *White-Jacket; or The World in a Man-of-War* [Melville]); constitutional, 194; Cooper's *The Crater* as allegorical rise and fall of American, 180; Derrida on, 205; as master signifier, 180, 194–95, 290n.17; social structures of modern, Cooper on, 191–92; state of exception as dominant paradigm of twentieth-century, 175–76; Tocqueville's foreboding about, 293n.16; totalitarian modes of power manifest in, 199–201, 203
Democracy in America (Tocqueville), 13–14
Democratic Party, 180, 188

Democratic Review, on Cooper's *The Crater,* 177–78, 188
Dening, Greg, 39, 260n.45, 273n.5; on mutiny aboard *Hannah,* 294n.20, 296n.59; on U.S. version of Articles of War, 202
Denning, Michael, 254n.89
De Pauw, Linda Grant, 283n.14
Derrida, Jacques, 268n.39, 280nn.64–65, 294n.35; on democracy, 205; "Messianic Otherness," concept of, 116; on originary moment of law, 205–6; specter, notion of, 222; visor effect, notion of, 115–16, 280n.64, 280n.67
Deserted Wife, The (Southworth), 134–36
desire: condoned and respectable, anxious play between, 137; dialectic between extrastructural, and desires shaped by ship's authoritarian control in Melville's *White-Jacket,* 217–20; distinction between identification and "desire-to-be," 92–93; excessive feminine, notion of, 127–28; fantasy and, 3–4, 11; fantasy and, Lacanian notion of, 9–10; female, acknowledgement of, 143, 145, 146; from Lacanian psychoanalytic perspective, 3; melancholic loss of, 164; of native woman, problem of, 149, 150–72; object of (object *a*), 37, 38–39; Other's desire, Lacan's notion of, 137, 286n.51; perverse enjoyment and, 219; in scenes of flogging, 228–29. *See also* feminine enjoyment/jouissance; women, native
dialectic(s): capitalist–proletariat, 40; distinction between deconstruction and, 12, 252n.69; Hercules–Hydra, 82; between ideal ego and ego-ideal, 162–63; master–slave, 40, 41; negative, 54, 301n.9
dialectical materialism, 300n.5; analysis based on, 13; shift methodologically from historical materialism to, 239; Žižek's development of new, 8–9
Diderot, Denis, 137, 286n.48
Dillon, Elizabeth Maddock, 256n.3
Dimock, Wai Chee, 18, 85, 227, 242, 255n.94, 271n.81
Discipline and Punish (Foucault), 231, 299n.92
discourses, Lacanian, 39–43, 50, 51–52, 53, 113, 260nn.47–48, 279n.59. *See also* master's discourse; university discourse
divided subject, 39; law as, in zone of exception, 206, 295n.36
Divine Providence, Cooper's coupling of Manifest Destiny and, 177–78, 182–83
Dobb, Maurice, 252n.71
Dolar, Mladen, 261n.49
Dolphin (ship), 139
domesticity, norms of female, 125, 126
Douglas, Bronwen, 273n.8, 274n.23
Douglass, Frederick, 193, 292n.41
Dowie, Menie Muriel, 125–26
down-classing projects, foundational assumption in, 37
dreams: Benjamin's dream interpretation model, 17, 21, 244; Freud on fantasy and, 5–6
Druett, Joan, 283n.14
Dugaw, Dianne, 125–26, 282nn.10–11, 283n.12
Duncan, Fred B., 283n.14
Duncan, Ian, 258n.23
Duyckinck, Evert, 30–31

D'Wolf, Captain John, 33
Dye, Ira, 272n.1, 277n.42
"Dynamics of History and Fiction in Melville's Typee, The" (Samson), 110

Ecclesiastes, 239, 240
ecocriticism$, Yaeger's conception of, 302n.17
economics, American School of, 291n.29
economy, Žižek on politics and, 11, 302n.13
Écrits (Lacan), 249nn.26–27, 252n.70, 283n.23, 284n.31, 289n.12, 295n.38, 295n.42
Edenic paradigms for Pacific women, 137, 285n.48
Eder, Markus, 201, 294n.21
Edwards, Mary K. Bercaw, 259n.30, 259n.33, 273n.7
Egan, Hugh, 48, 53, 263n.76, 264n.86
ego-ideal, dialectic between functions of ideal ego and, 162–63
Eiland, Howard, 21, 255n.95
Ellis, William, 106, 275n.25, 276n.30; missionary experiences on Society and Sandwich Islands, 147–49
Emerson, Ralph Waldo, 4, 14, 27, 248n.12, 300n.101
empirical naturalism, 274n.23
Encantadas, or Enchanted Isles, The (Melville), 16, 17
Encore (Lacan), 166–67
Eng, David L., 137–38, 286n.55
Engels, Friedrich, 252n.71, 303n.24
Enlightenment era, 97–98, 102, 125, 138, 214, 215, 258n.23
epistemological break, Althusser's notion of, 111, 278n.51
Equiano, Olaudah, 257n.22
Essex (frigate), 99

ethics, Lacan on, 289n.10
ethnicity, as ontologically liminal phenomenon, 278n.45
ethnographic work, incorporation of Polynesians through, 109
Evelev, John, 257n.16
exception, state of. *See* state of exception
excess, notion of, 296n.58. *See also* feminine enjoyment/jouissance; women, native
exotic force, concept of, 239–41
experiences "beyond the line," 4, 39, 247n.9
experiential knowledge of sailor, 26–29, 39–43, 52, 264n.85
ex-slave narratives, 257n.22

Fabian, Ann, 258n.22
Fabian, Johannes, 278n.53
face (subjectivity/identity), Tommo's fear of losing foundational fantasy of, 112–13
fantasme, French, 5
fantasy(ies): antebellum maritime narratives and, 13–21; central paradox of, 37; about class and labor experience, foundational, 26; cultural encounters structured by, 161; desire and, 3–4, 9–10, 11; dual nature of, 11; entering sociosymbolic order via, 66; experiences "beyond the line," 4, 39, 247n.9; of experiential transformation, 46–47; Freud on dreams and, 5–6; Freud's phases of "beating-phantasies," 229–30; function in any contact scenario, 241–42; inner limit of, 171; inverted effect of, perversion as, 206; jacket in Melville's *White-Jacket* as screen

fantasy(ies) (*continued*)
for, 209, 222; Lacanian view of, 5, 6–10, 12, 15, 36, 117–18, 252n.70; Lacanian view of, Janus-faced effect, 239; Lacanian view of, Žižek's modifications of, 5, 8–12; Lacan's formula for, 250n.46; linked to social configurations, Freud's work on, 248n.25; narratives involving translation and transcription as, 54; psychoanalytic view of, 5–6; as screen concealing lack of symbolic order's big Other, 65–66; of separation between the positions of editor and narrator, 52; social function of, 3–4; as social phenomenon, 250n.50; "traversing the fantasy," Lacan's notion of, 119–20, 138, 281n.74; as veil that screens role of master signifier, 179. *See also* phallic fantasy

Fatu Hiva, 99

Fausto-Sterling, Anne, 286n.54

Federalism, Cooper's roots in, 74, 84

Federalist Papers, support for national navy in, 265n.5

female agency, dangerous effect in marketplace of, 127

Female Complaint: The Unfinished Business of Sentimentality in American Culture, The (Berlant), 251n.61

female desire, acknowledgement of, 143, 145, 146

Female Marine, The (anonymous trilogy), 46, 126

feminine enjoyment/jouissance, 20, 288n.80; Copjec on, 134–35; male-oriented fantasies about female excess as defense against traumatizing form of, 128; in Melville's *Mardi*, 149, 150, 158–72; in Melville's *Omoo*, 149, 155–58; in Melville's *Typee*, 149, 150–55; silence connected to Lacanian notion of, 170, 289n.101; state of being not-whole or not-all within symbolic limits, 152, 153, 154; Wallis's relative notion of, 146–47

feminine structure of sexuation, 132–33; central paradox of, 133; in Southworth's *The Deserted Wife*, 134

Ferguson, Adam, 272n.3

fetish object, jacket in Melville's *White-Jacket* as, 209

Feuerbach, Ludwig, 303n.24

Fielder, Leslie, 106, 276n.36

Fink, Bruce, 119, 260n.48, 283n.23; on effect of language and knowledge on jouissance, 130; on phallic signifier, 131; rendering of Lacan's term *le point de capiton*, 289n.12; on symbolic jouissance, 262n.58; on Western fantasy of potential harmony between sexes, 129

"flashpoint" as conceptual model, 302n.14

Flea, James, 71–72

Fleishman, Avrom, 62, 267n.23

flogging, 201, 298n.76, 299nn.92–93; altering men's inner space through, 231; ban on (1851), 225; critiques of Articles of War pertaining to, 235; debates over, 225–26; desire in scene of, 228–29; as different from traditional modes of punishment, 231–32; different responses to, 230–31; historically plausible reason for use of, 299n.90; as law-preserving and lawmaking violence, 299n.93; Melville's presentation of, in *White-Jacket*,

219, 225–35; naval summons to witness, 229, 230; as perverse scenario, 229–31; as public punishment, 231, 232; slavery in relation to naval, 227–28, 232; in U.S. version of Articles of War, 202–3
"Flogging in the Navy" (Lockwood), 235
Fluck, Winfried, 253n.89
"Formulations Regarding the Two Principles in Mental Functioning" (Freud), 6
For They Know Not What They Do: Enjoyment as a Political Factor (Žižek), 280n.66, 285n.47, 295n.44, 296n.51, 296n.56, 299n.71
Foster, Dennis, 207, 209, 295n.43
Foucault, Michel, 278n.53, 298n.86; Butler's reading of, 299n.92; Copjec's critique of historicism of, 239–40; on logic of feudal punishment, 299n.90; on shift in disciplinary modes, 231, 232
Fourierism, 292n.35
Frankfurt School model of historiography, 244, 266n.22
Franklin, Wayne, 73, 263nn.78–79, 269n.47, 271n.85, 271nn.86–87, 289n.7; on Cooper's maritime experience, 48–49, 263n.78; on Cooper's politics, 74–75, 86, 87, 177; on Cooper's *The Crater*, 183
freaks and freak shows: broader mechanisms making tattooed person into freak, in antebellum America, 106–8; cultural others equated with domestic disabled "freaks" in, 273n.13; P. T. Barnum and, 274nn.15–16; safety of domestic freak show, 106; tattoo transference and refracted freaks, 100–109

Freud, Sigmund, 119, 248nn.17–25, 286n.51, 288n.91, 298n.84; on dreams and fantasy, 5–6; Lacan's return to, 249n.26; melancholy for, 164; on narcissism, 295n.41; on perversion, 206, 295n.41; phallus associated with physical penis by, 131; phases of "beating-phantasies," 229–30; race and sexuality in *Totem and Taboo*, 137–38; seeds of Lacanian and Žižekian model of fantasy in, 248n.25
Friedrich, Carl J., 293n.10
Fuller, Margaret, 46, 263n.74

Gabler-Hover, Janet, 258n.23
Gallop, Jane, 284n.38
Gansevoort, Guert, 2
gaze: imperial, 145; Lacanian, 144–45; Lacanian, of Hautia in Melville's *Mardi*, 166, 169; objective existence of, Žižek on, 289n.96
Gell, Alfred, 276n.34, 277n.42
gender: in antebellum America, issues of, 18; Enlightenment notions of, 125; fantasies of experiential transformation, 46–47; within maritime romances, 127–28; norms of female domesticity, 125, 126; reversal, in prison scene in Melville's *Omoo*, 157; role in antebellum maritime narratives, 125–36. *See also* women; women, native
Gender Trouble (Butler), 299n.92
General History of Pyrates, A, 282n.10
Gengenbach, Heidi, 276n.32
Gilje, Paul A., 255n.94

Gillman, Susan, 243, 254n.89, 302n.14, 303n.20
Gilmore, Michael T., 257n.16
Glenn, Myra C., 257n.20, 297n.72
global market, capital's move into, 14–15
global network, gap between "lived experience and structure" in new, 14–16
Gotch, Christopher, 277n.42
Gould, Philip, 255n.94
Gover, Elena, 274n.21
governments, state of exception as dominant paradigm of twentieth-century totalitarian and democratic, 175–76. See also democracy(ies); state of exception; totalitarianism/totalitarian state
Gow, John, 71–72
Green, David, 255n.92
Greenburg, Amy S., 255n.92
Grigg, Russell, 260n.48
grog system in Melville's *White-Jacket*, 216–19
Grosz, Elizabeth, 106, 276n.35
grotesque, Cassuto's notion of, 101, 103, 278n.45. See also tattoo(s); tattoos in *Typee*
Guattari, Félix, 25, 82, 250n.50, 256n.1, 274n.21

Hale, Sir Matthew, 203–4
Hambly, W. D., 277n.42
Hamilton, Alexander, 291n.29
Handler, Glenn, 255n.92
Handy, Willowdean Chatterson, 109
Haney, Lewis Henry, 291n.29
Hannah (ship), pardon of mutinous men from flogging on, 226
Hannath, Abraham David, 291n.29
Hardt, Michael, 252n.71

Harper's New Monthly Magazine, 45
Hart, Joseph C., 43, 127, 262n.62
Harvey, Bruce A., 59, 103, 110–11, 112, 252n.75, 265n.6, 275n.27, 287n.62
Hawkesworth, John, 286n.60
Heflin, Wilson, 259n.30, 273n.7
Hegel, G. W. F., 8, 40, 178, 260n.47, 261n.49, 286n.51
Heller-Roazen, Daniel, 255n.94, 294n.17
Herbert, T. Walter, Jr., 107, 117, 273n.10, 276n.37, 278n.53
Hercules–Hydra dialectic, 82
"Herman Melville: Uncommon Common Sailor" (Bezanson), 33
heroism: creation of national heroes, 92–93; new criterion for, in Cooper's *The Pilot*, 80
heterotopia, *Neversink* in Melville's *White-Jacket* as, 198
Hinaereeremonoi, tale of, 106
historical break, 111–13; induced by tattoo in *Typee*, 111, 112–13
Historical Novel, The (Lukács), 62
historical romance genre, 59, 75. See also *Pilot: A Tale of the Sea, The* (Cooper); *Pirate, The* (Scott)
historicism: competing ideological notions of, 303n.24; of Foucault, Copjec's critique of, 239–40; New Historicism, 243, 244; waking from edicts of, 244
history: Frankfurt School model of historiography, 244, 266n.22; hidden, nonrealized potentials of the past, Žižek on, 267n.22, 303n.24; historical break, 111–13; modern notion of, 112–13; potential modern loss of, 279n.55; as redemption, dialectical conception of, 266n.22
History of the Navy of the United States of America (Cooper), 83–84

Hobbes, Thomas, 200, 272n.3, 290n.24
Hobsbawm, Eric, 252n.71
Hoens, Dominiek, 261n.54
Holmes, Rachel, 286n.54
home: correlated to the West's symbolic system, 106; loss of identity precipitated by tattoo and failure of, 106, 117; traversing fantasy of the other to reestablish desire for, 120
Home and Colonial Library series, 32, 103
homo economicus, 265n.8; Crusoe's brand of entrepreneurial individualism as literary birth of, 182
homo homini lupus, 200
homo sacer, 199, 200
honor, power of, located in an Other, 113, 114
Horkheimer, Max, 28, 303n.24
How to Read Lacan (Žižek), 286n.56, 288n.87, 288n.92
Hulme, Peter, 282n.8
Hurst, Andrea, 252n.69, 280n.64
hydrophasia, 28
Hyppolite, Jean, 278n.45

ideal citizen, Bob in Cooper's *The Crater* as, 183–84
ideal ego, dialectic between functions of ego-ideal and, 162–63
identity/identification: bifurcation between desire-to-be and, 92–93; built upon tenuous ground of nonbeing, 118; class identities, gap between, 34; dialectic between functions of ideal ego and ego-ideal and, 162–63; experience of the Other at heart of, 120; free choice and, 120, 281n.75; identity formation, 66–67, 68, 69; imaginary, 66–67, 68, 69; process of learning to desire original, Melville's *Typee* as, 116–17, 120; symbolic, 7, 66–67, 69; Tommo's fear of losing his, tattoos and, 101, 106, 110, 112–21; traversing the fantasy and, 119–20. *See also* national identification
ideology: ideological function of maritime narratives, 34; "inherent transgression" implicit in, 236; Marx's definition of, 9; modern cynical, 237, 245; relation between maritime craft and, 28–29, 256n.13; Žižek on, 9, 236
Imaginary, the: Lacan on, 6–7; Tommo's anxiety about tattoo on level of, 118
imaginary identification, 66–67, 68, 69
imaginary other, 118, 120
Imagined Communities (Anderson), 59
imperial gaze, 145
imperialism: American native heroines used in validation of, 137; the novel and, 15; sexuality as trope for power relations in, 128; shift from classical capital to imperial capital, 14–15
Imperial Leather: Race, Gender, and Sexuality in the Colonial Context (McClintock), 123, 132
impressment, English, 73, 265n.5, 268n.39
In Defense of Lost Causes (Žižek), 249n.38, 249n.42, 251n.59, 267n.22, 300n.94, 301n.12
individualism: American ideology of, 85; totalitarian superego as threat to, 216
industrialization, maritime labor market as outlet for artisans forced from jobs by, 44

infinite (feminine) jouissance, 170. *See also* feminine enjoyment/jouissance
Inhuman Race: The Racial Grotesque in American Literature and Culture, The (Cassuto), 100
Inquiry into the Nature and Effects of Flogging, An (anonymous), 228–29
Interpretation of Dreams, The (Freud), 5
Irigaray, Luce, 284n.38
Iron Men, Wooden Women: Gender and Seafaring in the Atlantic World, 1700–1920 (Creighton and Norling), 125
Israel Potter: His Fifty Years of Exile (Melville), 48

Jackson, Andrew, 192
Jack Tars (sailors), 29
James, C. R. L., 293n.8
Jameson, Fredric, 46, 80, 189, 251nn.56–58, 252n.65, 253nn.78–79, 262n.72; on abandonment of political and Utopian theories of past, 270n.61; on Adorno's mode of negative dialectics, 301n.9; on cognitive mapping, 15, 253n.79; distinction between deconstruction and dialectic, 12, 252n.69; on phases of capital, 14–15; the Real in Lacan and, 10, 251n.57
Jay, John, 187, 269n.49
Jefferson, Thomas, 193, 298n.88
Johnston, Adrian, 4, 8, 248n.13, 249n.41, 250n.45, 301n.13
Jolly, Margaret, 124, 282nn.4–5, 285n.38
Jones, John Paul, 85–86, 279n.63
jouissance (surplus enjoyment), 39, 129, 261n.55; access to knowledge precipitating correlative loss of, 41, 262n.56; as element lost with acquisition of language, 129, 130; female (feminine), 20, 124–25, 134–35, 136, 138, 140, 146–47, 170, 288n.80; Lacan's theory of sexuation and, 129, 130–33; master's discourse and desire for, 41–42; obtained vs. expected, 167; Other, 133, 149; phallic, 130–33, 138, 170, 288n.80; prohibition of, on basis of father's death, 215; sailors reduced to pure means for the Other's enjoyment, 223–24; from sailor's supposed experiences, 26; symbolic, 262n.58. *See also* feminine enjoyment/jouissance; women, native
Journal of a Cruise to the Pacific Ocean (Porter), 145–46, 275n.25, 275n.28

Kabris, Joseph, 97, 272n.2
Kaeppler, Adrienne, 277n.42
Kafka, Franz, 207
Kant, Immanuel, 200
Kaplan, Amy, 18, 254n.91, 283n.12, 293n.16
Kapor, Vladimir, 285n.48
Kazanjian, David, 17, 89, 254n.90, 271n.92, 302n.14
Kennedy, Gerald J., 59, 265n.9
Klein, Bernhard, 255n.93
knowledge: access to, precipitating correlative loss of jouissance, 41, 262n.56; Cartesian models of, 28; experiences "beyond the line," 4, 39, 247n.9; experiential, of sailor, 26–29, 39–43, 52, 264n.85; in Lacanian discourses, 39, 40; mediated by language, loss of

forbidden jouissance and, 129, 130; shift in domain of, 40, 41, 51–52; university, 40; Žižek on split between subject's and the Other's, 261n.52

knowledge, system of: bureaucracy and, 52, 264n.85; lack of totalizing master signifier filled in with totalizing, 211, 214, 216; in maritime world and nautical operations, authority within, 212; *Neversink* world as closed and mysterious, in Melville's *White-Jacket*, 211, 214, 233–34, 296n.54; of the West, vulnerability of, 106–8, 114–16, 279n.55

Kojève, Alexandre, 286n.51

Kopley, Richard, 272n.95

labor, maritime, 27–29; anxiety-ridden relationship between working-class maritime labor experience and authorship, 33–34, 35; Cohen's view of, 73, 256n.13, 268n.41, 269n.59; competing rhetorical paradigms of, employed by antebellum authors, 29; Cooper on potential strength of, 180; in Cooper's *The Pilot*, 73, 76–81; discharge of dead sailors, 222–23, 297n.68, 297n.70; divisions of, aboard *Neversink* in Melville's *White-Jacket*, 210–11, 214, 221, 234; divisions of, in Cooper's *The Crater*, 185, 291n.26; flogging, practice of, 219, 225–35; impressment of sailors, 73, 265n.5, 268n.39; as "know-how," 73, 268n.41; laboring to sound of fife, 297n.64; maritime labor market as outlet for artisans forced from jobs by industrialization, 44; pleasure taken in carrying out orders, in Melville's *White-Jacket*, 220–21, 224; process of proletarianization to fulfill maritime-related needs for, 29; relation between ideology and maritime craft, 28–29, 256n.13; relation between language and laboring station, 46–47; skin color and, race and class issues surrounding, 34, 259n.34; as special placeholders of system's (big Other's) needs, 221, 222, 223–24, 233–34, 297n.66. *See also* class; common sailor, fantasies of; common sailors

Lacan, Jacques, 4, 25, 55, 248n.13, 249nn.26–35, 261n.49, 261n.55, 284nn.31–34, 295n.38, 295n.42; antagonism between Derrida and, 280n.64; on big Other, 65–66; "Borromean knot" untying dimensions of the other, 118; Butler's critique of, 285nn.43–44; designation for subject ($), 249n.30; discourses, 39–43, 50, 51–52, 53, 113, 260nn.47–48, 279n.59 (*see also* master's discourse; university discourse); discourses, developing within historical progression, 50, 51; on ethics, 289n.10; exchange between students and, 265n.10; fantasy, formula for, 250n.46; fantasy, notion of, 5, 6–10, 12, 15, 36, 117–18, 239, 252n.70; fantasy, Žižek's modifications of notion of, 5, 8–12; on feminine enjoyment engendered from being not-whole, 152; gaze, notion of, 144–45, 166, 169; jouissance as term for surplus enjoyment, 129; lamella, discussion of, 279n.63;

Lacan, Jacques (*continued*)
law, conception of, 178; on love, 162, 163, 167; on "man of pleasure," 282n.8; master signifier (or *point de capiton*), notion of, 176–79, 187, 289n.12; on master–slave dialectic, 40, 41; modification of concept of phallus, 131–32, 284n.34; notion of woman as not existing and "not-whole," 129, 132–33; on object *a*, 10, 250nn.51–52; observations about honor and apparent loss of shame in modern world, 113; other, notion of, 117–18; Other's desire, notion of, 137, 286n.51; on perversion, 21, 198, 206–7; phallic jouissance, concept of, 130–33, 138, 170; on phallic mode of desire, 152; process of identification in dialectic between functions of ideal ego and ego-ideal, 162–63; on prohibition of jouissance on basis of father's death, 215; the Real in, 7–8, 10, 239, 251n.57, 251n.60, 251n.64; on relationship between language and enjoyment, 130; return to Freud, 249n.26; "sexuation," theory of, 20, 124–25, 129, 130–33, 135, 283n.23, 284n.33; on superego, 208; symbolic castration, notion of, 7, 9, 129, 130, 131–32, 290n.15; on symbolic functions conditioning imaginary ones, 267n.35; tattoo trope used by, 280n.70; "traversing the fantasy," notion of, 119–20, 138, 281n.74; work on Freud's beating-fantasy essay, 230

Lacan and the Political (Stavrakakis), 250n.50

Laclau, Ernesto, 241

lacunae at core of testimony, Agamben on, 264n.92

Lafayette, Marquis de, 271n.85

Lamb, Jonathan, 272n.3, 273n.5

lamella, Lacan's discussion of, 279n.63

Lamplighter, The (Cummins), 18

Land, Isaac, 202, 227, 271n.93, 298n.76

Lane, Horace, 30, 257n.21

Langsdorff, G. H. Von, 100, 101, 274n.21

language: jouissance as element lost with acquisition of, 129, 130; Lacan on function of, 7; Lacan on relationship between enjoyment and, 130; "plain style," 34, 46–47, 262n.73; relation between laboring station and, 46–47

Laplanche, Jean, 248n.15

Largier, Niklaus, 299n.90

Late Marxism: Adorno, or the Persistence of the Dialectic (Jameson), 301n.9

laughter, female enjoyment and excess in, 152, 154, 156–57

law: ability of sovereign to suspend, 201; as agency of the Other in subject formation, 178; apparent loss of, within democratic structures, 20–21, 176–77; constitutional law's relation to power and governance, issue of, 178; as divided subject in zone of exception, 206, 295n.36; as established set of sociosymbolic mandates, 178; fantasmatic appeal to distant and ideal Other of the Law, in Melville's *White-Jacket*, 235–36, 237; gap between parliamentary Articles of War and Crown's Printed Instructions, 201–2; historically codified, vs. transhistorical natural, 110–11, 287n.62; indistinction between

violence and, flogging as moment embodying, 232, 299n.93; Lacanian conception of, as symbolic function and effect, 178; lack of, within a martial state, 204, 208; master's loss of agency and waning reign of, Cooper's anxiety over, 186–88, 189, 190, 195; originary moment of, Derrida on, 205–6; rent war as defiance of contracts established in, 186–87; "of right," in Cooper's *The Crater*, 185–86, 193; state of exception as modus operandi of all legal functioning, 175; U.S. version of Articles of War, 201, 202–3. See also *Crater; or, Vulcan's Peak: A Tale of the Pacific, The* (Cooper); *White-Jacket; or The World in a Man-of-War* (Melville)
Law Magazine (periodical), 103
Lawrence, D. H., 262n.61
Leader, Darian, 230, 298n.85
Ledyard, John, 107
Leech, Samuel, 228
Lefebvre, Henri, 248n.11
Leggett, William, 30
Letter to His Countrymen, A (Cooper), 177, 191, 192, 193
Levander, Caroline F., 254n.89
Leviathan (Hobbes), 290n.24
Levine, Robert S., 254n.89
Levinson, Marjorie, 266n.22
Lévi-Strauss, Claude, 7, 109
liberty: associated with historical examples of resistance to power, 235; totalitarian superego as threat to, 216
libidinal energy, poles of, 82
Life in Feejee (Wallis), depiction of native women in, 146–47

Linebaugh, Peter, 18, 29, 82, 235, 247n.9, 255n.94, 256n.2, 282n.10, 300n.95
Lipsitz, George, 254n.89
Literary and Scientific Repository, The, 75
Literary Gazette, review of Melville's *Mardi*, 159
Littlepage Manuscripts trilogy (Cooper), 177
Lockwood, John A., 235, 300n.98
London Times, review of Melville's *Typee*, 32–33
loss, melancholia over, 164
love, Lacanian, 162, 163, 167
Lucy Ann (whaler), 99
Lukács, Georg, 59, 62, 265n.7
Luskey, Brian P., 257n.14

Mackenzie, Alexander Slidell, 1, 2, 247n.1
magazines, antebellum, 257n.19; calling for material that promoted maritime nationalism, 74, 75, 269n.54; sea narratives in, 14, 30
Magna Carta, 235
male fantasy(ies): contact-zone model, 124, 241–42, 301n.10, 302n.17; incompleteness and desperation of, 133–36; Melville's excessive women, 149–72; Pacific native women, phallic fantasies in nonfictional narratives of, 20, 125, 137–49; phallus and antebellum narratives, 125–36. See also phallic enjoyment; phallic fantasy; phallic jouissance
Manderson, Lenore, 124, 282nn.4–5, 285n.38
manhood: Nelson's conception of national, 18, 254n.92; Old Ushant as romantic model of, in Melville's *White-Jacket*, 232–33, 300n.94

Manifest Destiny: Cooper's coupling of Divine Providence and, 177–78, 182–83; spirit of, in U.S. economic maritime development, 13

Mardi and a Voyage Thither (Melville), 19, 114–15, 116, 123; excessive women and feminine desire in, 149, 150, 158–72; Hautia's complication of fantasy scenario, 165–71; ideal lost object (Yillah) in, 161–65, 167, 168–69; link between agency and possession of tattoos, 115, 279n.63; Melville's conception of project as romance, 159; women operating in positions of power within phallic economy in, 160, 166, 167, 170–71

Mariner's Library or Voyager's Companion, The, 27

maritime development, U.S., 2, 4, 13–14; process of proletarianization to fulfill labor needs, 29. *See also* labor, maritime

maritime narratives: authenticity issue and, 19, 26, 30–39, 42, 43, 44, 48, 99, 180–81; cognitive mapping of new global economic and social experiences through, 15, 253n.79; conflicts, contradictions, and tensions inherent in constructions of maritime national narratives, 19; desire to go to sea based on, 3; fantasmatically locating excess in experiential knowledge of common sailor's labor, 52, 264n.85; fantasy and antebellum, 13–21; frustration of knowledge as origin and necessary structural prerequisite for desire and fantasy in, 42; historical work on maritime themes, 242; ideological function of, 34; in magazines, 14, 30, 74, 75, 269n.54; national issues in, 58–61; "plain style" of, 34, 46–47, 262n.73; political import in antebellum era, 4; role of gender in antebellum, 125–36; as vehicles for subversive imaginary ideas, 3

Marquesas Islands, 99–100, 103, 117, 272n.2; ability to fend off complete colonial influence, 157–58; Melville's adventure in, 99; Porter in, 99, 145–46, 275n.28; Robarts in, 142–45, 146; tattooing patterns in, 109; U.S. foray into, 99–100; Western fantasies about, 102. See also *Typee* (Melville); tattoos in *Typee*

martial law: American Articles of War, 201–4, 225–26, 234–35, 236; men's inner space altered by, through flogging, 231; unconstitutionality of, 203–4

Martin, Henry Byam, 276n.32

Marx, Harpo, 288n.83

Marx, Karl, 232, 244, 252n.71, 286n.58; definition of ideology as false consciousness, 9; on historical analysis, 303n.24; on human relations in bourgeois society, 139, 286n.58; surplus value, notion of, 41, 129, 263n.85

masculinity, antebellum America and, 18, 254n.92

masochism, 230

master figure: in Cooper's *The Crater*, 183, 186–88, 189, 190, 195; differentiating performance of power of, 187–88

master's discourse, 39–40, 41, 113, 279n.59; as absolute monarchy, 260n.47; Cooper's *Ned Myers* and, 50, 51–54; fantasmic relation

between master and slave, 41, 261n.52, 261n.54; Lacan's formula for, 260n.48, 261n.54; narratives involving translation and transcription and, 44, 50, 51–54; social link with university discourse, 51–52, 53–54, 264n.89; structured by object *a* (surplus enjoyment), 41–42
master signifier, 39; constitutional democracy as central ideological, in Cooper's *The Crater*, 194; democracy as, 180; democracy as, Žižek on, 194–95, 290n.17; desire for, in Cooper's *The Crater*, 180; fantasy as veil that screens role of, 179; functions of, 178–79; Lacan's notion of *(point de capiton)*, 176–79, 187, 289n.12; lack of totalizing, filled in with totalizing system of knowledge, 211, 214, 216; of law, 177, 178; socioeconomic master as ideological, in Cooper's *The Crater*, 186; Tommo's refusal to relinquish his honor, 113, 114; totalitarian leader contrasted with, 207, 208
master–slave dialectic, 40, 41
Masur, Louis, 299n.90
matelotage, 272n.93
McClintock, Anne, 123, 128, 132, 278n.53
McCloskey, John C., 84, 271n.76, 292n.35
McCormick, Gladys, 254n.89
McGowan, Todd, 144, 166, 249n.30, 287n.66
McLaughlin, Kevin, 21, 255n.95
McLennan, Rebecca M., 231, 298nn.87–88
McWilliams, John P., Jr., 84, 269n.48, 271n.77, 289n.9

media: Cooper's view of, 190, 191; magazines, 14, 30, 74, 75, 257n.19, 269n.54; response to USS *Somers* incident, 2–3, 11
melancholia, 164, 288n.92
Melville, Herman, 14, 44, 123, 247n.6, 253n.85, 256n.97, 259n.32, 273n.6, 275n.28, 279nn.62–63; adventure in South Seas, 99; analysis and condemnation of Articles of War, 225–26, 234–35, 236; authenticity issue and, 30–31; books written for money, 197, 293n.2; challenge to romantic conceptions of sea experience, 3; condemnation of martial law, 203–4; "cultural grotesque," rethinking, 97–121; defense of Lord Paulet's actions in Sandwich Islands, 103–4; excessive women in writings of, 149–72; experience on board *Southampton*, 296n.55; full experience of enjoyment referred to in negative terms by, 129–30; mix of patrician heritage and family maritime experience, 33–34; "Pisgah View from the Rock" in *Encantadas, or Enchanted Isles*, 16, 17; public perception of, as experienced sexual authority, 123–24; retelling of yarn in *Moby-Dick*, 45; sympathy for executed seamen on USS *Somers*, 2; tattoo defetishized by, 108; tattooing presented as encounter with racial difference, 101; use of nonfictional accounts of Pacific encounters in novels, 149–50; warning about loss of law within modern antebellum nation-state, 204. See also *Encantadas, or Enchanted Isles, The*

Melville, Herman (*continued*) (Melville); *Israel Potter: His Fifty Years of Exile* (Melville); *Mardi and a Voyage Thither* (Melville); *Moby-Dick* (Melville); *Omoo: A Narrative of Adventures in the South Seas* (Melville); tattoos in *Typee*; *Typee* (Melville); *White-Jacket; or The World in a Man-of-War* (Melville)
Melville Anatomies (Otter), 100, 226–27
merchant class, Cooper's anxiety about rise of, 82–84
merchant-maritime infrastructure, development of, 2, 4
"Messianic Otherness," 116, 205, 280n.66
Metastases of Enjoyment: On Women and Causality, The (Žižek), 251n.63, 283n.23, 301n.9
Mexican–American War, 177
Miller, Christopher, 255n.93
Miller, Jacques-Alain, 113, 133, 279n.56, 288n.87, 292n.44; "zone between-two-deaths," 114, 117, 120
Miller, Perry, 257n.16
Milner, Jean-Claude, 170
Miriam Coffin: or, The Whale-Fishermen (Hart), 43, 127
missionaries, Christian, 100, 105, 147–49
Moby-Dick (Melville), 21, 55, 245, 304n.25; notions of class and representation in, 35; racial difference portrayed in, 276n.29; sea as mysterious and incomplete space in, 240; tattoos in *Typee* distinguished from tattoos in, 276n.38; "Town-Ho's Story," yarn/fantasy in, 45

"Modern Chivalry" (Sedgwick), 30, 126
modernity: American democracy as master signifier of, 180; crisis of, 4, 176
Modernity at Sea: Melville, Marx, Conrad in Crisis (Casarino), 18, 35, 91, 198, 247n.10, 256n.2, 259nn.36–38, 262n.66, 272n.97, 293n.5
Monikins, The (Cooper), depiction of masses in, 191
Monroe Doctrine, 253n.77
moral necessity of truth telling, Enlightenment-era rhetorical assumptions predicated on, 258n.23
Morgan, Gwenda, 259n.34
Morison, Samuel Eliot, 247n.7
Morrell, Abby Jane, 126, 283n.14
Morrell, Benjamin, 3, 58, 247n.4
mourning, melancholia vs., 164
"MS. Found in Bottle" (Poe), 42–43
Muller, John P., 280n.64
Murray, John, 32, 159
Mutiny Act, British, 201
mutiny plot aboard USS *Somers*, 1–2
Myers, Ned, 48–54, 264n.86. See also *Ned Myers; or, a Life before the Mast* (Cooper)

Nancy, Jean-Luc, 54, 264n.91
narcissism, Freud on, 295n.41
Narrative of Arthur Gordon Pym of Nantucket (Poe), 32, 44–45
Narrative of Four Voyages to the South Seas, A (Morrell), 3
Narrative of the Most Extraordinary and Distressing Shipwreck of the Whale-ship Essex (Chase), 58
Narrative of the United States Exploring Expedition (Wilkes), 146
Nash, Gary, 35

nation: expansion of, 57–58; internal contradictions of, convergence of, 92; modern bourgeois nation-state, development of, 59; perpetuation of, exploring, 60; state of exception in context of, 179; as theme of maritime narratives, 58–61. See also *Pilot: A Tale of the Sea, The* (Cooper); *Pirate, The* (Scott); national identification
national identification: Bhabha on anxiety affixed to national identity, 61; in Cooper's *The Pilot*, 62, 72–93; in Cooper's *The Pilot*, dangers of competing merchant/private and naval/national motivations and, 87–90, 92; in Cooper's *The Pilot*, national mandate and, 84–91; creation of national subjects and heroes, 92–93; distinction between "desire-to-be" and identification, 92–93; impressment irrespective of national identity, 73, 265n.5, 268n.39; romantic correlation between ship and state, 90; in Scott's *The Pirate*, 62–72, 93; time as foundational for, 60; Žižek on, 60
nationalism, War of 1812 and, 13, 30
nationalist fantasies: naval victories of War of 1812 as fodder for, 58; women in, 127
Nation and Narration (Bhabha), 59
native enjoyment: acknowledgement of qualitative difference in, 148–49; Ellis's denial of, 149. *See also* women, native
natives as Janus-faced tricksters, notion of, 104
native women. *See* women, native
natural law, 110–11, 287n.62

nature-versus-culture debates, eighteenth- and nineteenth-century, 110
nautical realism in Cooper's *The Pilot*, 31, 76, 81–82
naval force, 265n.5; construction of, 57; War of 1812 victories of, as fodder for nationalistic fantasies, 58
naval-reform rhetoric, relation of Melville's *White-Jacket* to, 227–35, 298n.76
Ned Myers; or, a Life before the Mast (Cooper), 19, 26, 48–54, 63; ambiguities of Cooper and Myers's collaboration, 52, 264n.86; ambiguous genre status of, 48; editorial preface to, 48–49, 50–51, 53; intended audience of, 49; as response to Dana's *Two Years*, 49; structure of yarn mimicked in, 49; transitional play between symbolic positions and domains of knowledge foregrounded in, 51–52
"negation of a negation," methodological, 278n.45
negative dialectics, 54, 301n.9
Negri, Antonio, 252n.71
Negro Seaman Act (South Carolina, 1822), 89, 227
Neill, Anna, 255n.93
Nelson, Dana D., 18, 254n.92
Nelson, Paul David, 90, 269n.54
Neo-Classicism, 274n.23
Nerlich, Michael, 267n.32
Netto, Priscilla, 286n.54
New American Exceptionalism, The (Pease), 60
Newbury, Michael, 29, 44, 257n.15
New Criticism, 244
New-England Magazine, 30
New Historicism, 243, 244

Newman, Simon P., 265n.5, 277n.42
New York Courier, 2, 3
New York Herald, 2, 3
New York political landscape in 1820s, Cooper and, 74–75
Nicol, John, 30, 257n.21
Nile Weekly Register, 30
Noble, David, 59, 254n.89
nomos (conceptual and judicial order) linking state territories and sea space, end of, 14, 253n.77
Norling, Lisa, 125, 255n.92, 282n.9
North American Review, 38
Notions of the Americans (Cooper), 84, 177, 191; as correction to European distortions of America, 83; on foreigners as common sailors, 88–89; on ideal nationalistic common sailor, 85; on profit motivation, 88–89
Novel and the Sea, The (Cohen), 18, 28–29, 73, 254n.91, 269n.59
Nussbaum, Felicity, 255n.93

object *a*, 10, 36–37, 250nn.51–52; common sailor invested with type of, in Dana's *Two Years before the Mast*, 37, 38–39; common sailor invested with type of, in Poe's "MS. Found in a Bottle," 42–43; flogging as means to force subject to act as, in relation to sovereign Other, 232; knowledge in position of agency addressing the other of, 51; Lacanian notion of gaze and potentially disruptive role of, 144–45; master's discourse structured by, 41–42; native women's bodies as source of, 141, 142–45; "the Other's desire for me" as central aspect of, 119, 137, 281n.74; as positive stand-in for lack of the Other in Lacan's theory of sexuation, 131, 133, 135, 284n.33; as stand-in for void in the Other, 131, 133, 135, 167, 168, 284n.33; traversing the fantasy to place of, to shape new fundamental fantasy, 119–20; Typees invested with, by Tommo, 117; Yillah as, in Melville's *Mardi*, 161–62, 164, 168; Žižek on, 259n.41, 260n.47

O'Brien, Patty, 137, 139, 282n.4, 285n.48
oceanic studies, 18, 242–44
O'Connell, James, 100–101
Oedipus, Antigone and, 113, 114
Olney, James, 258n.22
Olsson, Gunnar, 15, 253n.80
Omai (Tahitian), 100
Omoo: A Narrative of Adventures in the South Seas (Melville), 104, 105; excessive women and feminine desire in, 149, 150, 155–58; imprisonment of mutinous crew members in, 155–57; missionaries' laws against tattooing described in, 105; national issues in, 58–59
"On Semblances in the Relation between the Sexes" (Miller), 288n.87
"On Shame" (Miller), 113
oral narrative traditions, 44–55
"organic principle," romantic conception of, 46
Orientalism (Said), 128
Oriental travel texts, nineteenth- and twentieth-century, 15
Origins of Totalitarianism, The (Arendt), 199
Orr, Bridget, 272n.3, 273n.5
O'Sullivan, John L., 13

Other, the: agency of cultural other, vulnerability of West's symbolic schemas and, 114–16, 279n.55; as core aspect of Lacanian conception of fantasy and subject constitution, 117–18; experience of, at heart of identity, 120; fantasy as construction attempting to cover over lack in, 250n.50; flogging as means to force subject to act as object *a* in relation to sovereign, 232; imaginary, 118, 120; of the Law, Melville's appeal to distant and ideal, 235–36, 237; law as agency of, in subject formation, 178; object *a* as locus for the Other's desire for oneself, 119, 137, 281n.74; object *a* as stand-in for void in, 131, 133, 135, 167, 168, 284n.33; perverse structure of acting as object for an Other's will or desire, 206–7, 235–36; power of honor located in, 113, 114; visor effect as metaphor for emotive reality of being subject to enigmatic, 116; Žižek's overview of, 117–18. *See also* big Other

Other jouissance, 133; analogy between native enjoyment and, 149

other limit: of capital, 91; of cultural logic, Polynesian encounters and confronting, 108; of national narrative, Coffin in Cooper's *The Pilot* as, 91–93

Other qua Real (impossible Thing), 118, 120

Otter, Samuel, 18, 100, 198, 242, 255n.94, 274n.15; on analogy between sailor and slave, 226–27, 232; on flogging, 228; on jacket in Melville's *White-Jacket*, 209; on tattoos in *Typee*, 101, 102, 106, 108, 109

outer limit: of capital, 91; of cultural logic, Polynesian encounters and confronting, 108; of national constructs, 91–92

Oxenham, Ellen Astor, 123–24

Pacific: antagonism between symbolic systems of the West and Pacific cultures, 103–5; exploration of, 57–58, 274n.23; views on Pacific natives and racial difference, 104–5, 275n.28, 276n.29

Pacific islands, European eroticization of native women of, 136–49; antebellum nonfictional representations, 20, 137–49; Cook's portrayal of encounters with native women, 140–42, 287n.62; Cuneo's narrative of rape, 139; Edenic paradigms, 137, 285n.48; Ellis's missionary experiences, 147–49; in Melville's *Mardi*, 149, 150, 158–72; in Melville's *Omoo*, 149, 150, 155–58; in Melville's *Typee*, 149, 150–55; myths shaping views of, 137; in Porter's discussion, 145–46; racialized female body, 137–38; in Robarts's accounts, 142–45, 146, 166, 287n.64; Robertson's journal on trade for native women, 139–40; Wallis's depiction of native men and women, 146–47, 148; "wild woman" trope, 137–38; in Wilkes's comments, 146, 148. *See also* "porno-tropics"; tattoos in *Typee*

Pacific whale fishery, developing, 58

Paine, Thomas, 193, 194, 291n.24

parallax gap, 240, 300n.5

parallax Real, 8–9, 10, 65, 118

parallax view, notion of, 8

Parallax View, The (Žižek), 249n.37, 300n.5
paranoiac pole of libidinal energy, 82
Parker, Hershel, 32, 123, 258n.27, 273n.7
Paton, Diana, 299n.90
patroon system, 186
Paulet, Lord George, 103–4
Peasant's Revolt of 1381, 235
Pease, Donald, 60, 93, 253n.89, 254n.89
Peck, George Washington, 281n.1
Peck, H. Daniel, 73, 74, 83, 91, 268n.40
penal code of naval Articles of War, 201–3. *See also* Articles of War
perversion: acting as object for an Other's will or desire, 206–7, 235–36; flogging viewed as perverse scenario, 229–31; Freud's work on, 206, 295n.41; Lacanian conception of, 21, 198, 206–7; linking totalitarianism with, 204–20; perverse relations created by state of exception, 235–36, 299n.93; in relationship between objectified laborers and ship's broader systems of control in Melville's *White-Jacket*, 220–21, 223–24; sources of, 206–7; superego's involvement in perverse and totalitarian logic, 208, 215–20
Pflugrad-Jackisch, Ami, 254n.92
phallic desire: Melville's excessive women and, 149–72; in Southworth's *The Deserted Wife*, 134–36
phallic economy: Cook's perceptions conditioned by fantasy of, 142; in Melville's *Mardi*, women operating in positions of power within, 160, 166, 167, 170–71
phallic enjoyment, 42, 132, 262n.58; gender reversal in prison scene in Melville's *Omoo*, 157; native women located within bounds of, 150; role of object *a* within, 144–45; tension-wrought play between feminine enjoyment and, in Melville's *Mardi*, 167, 169, 171
phallic fantasy: female desires and enjoyment experienced by male narrators as threat to, 150; Lacan on women in scenario of, 133; in Melville's *Omoo*, 157; in nonfictional narratives of Pacific native women, 20, 125, 137–49. *See also* women, native
phallic jouissance, 130–33, 138, 170; limit of, 288n.80
phallus: antebellum narratives and, 125–36; beard as embodiment of Ushant's symbolic, in Melville's *White-Jacket*, 233; Lacan's modification of concept of, 131–32, 284n.34; woman as, Lacan's concept of, 133, 135, 285n.43
Phantasie, German, 5. *See also* fantasy(ies)
Philbrick, Thomas, 13, 75, 77, 81, 91, 252n.72, 257n.19, 268n.45, 270n.62, 292n.35
Pilot: A Tale of the Sea, The (Cooper), 19, 57, 62, 72–93; ambiguous figuration of American loyalists in, 269n.52; class mandate in, 76–77, 81–84, 89; Coffin and the "Other limit" of national narrative, 91–93; Coffin as ideal sailor in, 77–81; Coffin's death in, 90–91; Coffin's death in, as prerequisite for national narrative in, 72–76, 81; Coffin's motivations in, 87–90, 92, 93; as Cooper's first maritime novel, 31; dialectical shift and exchange of heroes in, 79–80;

distinctions between Coffin and other Cooper characters, 85–87; maritime labor and, 73, 76–81; national mandate in, 84–91; patriotism in, 75; preface (1823) to, 75, 269n.53; preface (1849) to, 19; preface (1849) to, emphasizing goal of nautical realism, 31, 76, 81–82; renarration of American Revolution, 180; shipwreck scene, 90–91

Pirate, The (Scott), 19; ambiguity of end of, 70–71; class notions in, 84; Cooper's emphasis on nautical realism in *The Pilot* as corrective to, 31, 76; desire for symbolic capital in, 63, 68, 70; entrance into political realm in, 64–72; as fantasy of modern national interpellation of past, 71; island's economic dependence on wrecking system in, 64, 267n.31; national identification and exclusion in, 62–72, 93; opening "Advertisement" to narrative, 71–72; plot of, 64–70, 72; women's positions in, 127

pirates: Barbary piracy narratives, 27, 256n.3; popular tales of infamous female, 125, 282n.10

place-as-experience, notion of, 16

Plague of Fantasies, The (Žižek), 250n.50, 250n.52, 250n.54, 253n.87, 278nn.51–52, 288n.94, 300n.99

"plain style," maritime, 34, 262n.73; in *The Female Marine*, 46–47; link between poetic "organic principle" and, 46

Plato, 129

Pocock, J. G. A., 98, 272n.4, 285n.48

Poe, Edgar Allan, 17, 42–43, 253n.88, 262nn.59–61, 272n.95, 275n.28; consciousness of desires surrounding narrative authenticity, 43; *Narrative of Arthur Gordon Pym* "hoax," 32

point de capiton, 176–79, 187, 289n.12. *See also* master signifier

political economy, popular views about, in eighteenth and early nineteenth centuries, 185–86

Political Unconscious, The (Jameson), 10

politics: antebellum racial, 226–27; apparent loss of law within democratic structures, 20–21, 176–77; transformed into modes of biopolitics, 199, 200, 201, 207, 231; Žižek's concept of economy and, 11, 302n.13

Polk, James K., 177

Polynesian encounters. *See* Pacific islands, European eroticization of native women of; "porno-tropics"; tattoos in *Typee*

Polynesian Researches (Ellis), 106; missionary experiences in, 147–49

polytropic man, figure of, 124, 282n.8

Pontalis, J. B., 248n.15

"porno-tropics," 123–72: Melville's excessive women, 149–72; Pacific native women, phallic fantasies in nonfictional narratives of, 20, 125, 137–49; phallus and antebellum narratives, 125–36; public perception of Melville as sexual authority and, 123–24

Porter, David, 58, 99, 273n.9, 275n.25, 275n.28; portrayal of native women, 145–46

Port-Folio, 74

power: constitutional laws relation to, 178; violence and, 215, 216, 219–20

Pratt, Mary Louise, 241, 301n.10

primum vivere, honor and, 113
Principles of Political Economy (Carey), 185–86
private property, rent war and institution of, 186–87
proletarianization, process of, 29
"Prospects of Oceanic Studies, The" (Blum), 243–44
psychoanalysis, 252n.69; as exotic science, Copjec on, 240; fantasy defined within, 5–6; Lacanian view of fantasy, 5, 6–10, 12, 15, 36, 252n.70
punishment: flogging as different from traditional modes of, 231–32; public, antiquated medium of, 231, 232. *See also* corporal punishment
Putzi, Jennifer, 102, 274n.22

Quirós, Fernández de, 99, 273n.8

race: analogy between sailor and slave, 226–27, 232; antebellum racial politics, 226–27; European ideas about, and conventions for representing non-white people, 102, 274n.23; as fantasmatic screen over other symbolic anxieties, 109, 277n.45; Melville's critique of martial flogging seen through lens of, 227–28; racialized and eroticized female body, 137–38; shipboard racial segregation, 227; skin color and labor, 34, 259n.34
racial anxiety, 106, 108
racial difference: Melville's presentation of tattooing as encounter with, 101; views of, 104–5, 275n.28, 276n.29
Radway, Janice, 60, 254n.89
Railton, Stephen, 270n.68
rape of native women, 139

Read, Mary, 125, 282n.10
Real, the: big Other stabilizing symbolic order in place of, 65–66, 130–31, 135; fantasy and, Žižek's conception of relationship between, 10–11; fantasy as protection for, 9, 11; in Lacan, 7–8, 10, 239, 251n.57, 251n.60, 251n.64; in Lacan, Žižek's linkage of economic absent cause to, 251n.60; Other qua Real, 118, 120; parallax Real, Žižek's conception of, 8–9, 10, 65, 118; Tommo's imaginary experience approaching, 118; Žižek's description of, 135
realism, nautical, as goal of Cooper's *The Pilot,* 31–32, 76, 81–82
reality: ideological, 9; linguistic field undergirding, Lacan on, 7
redemptive historiography, 266n.22
Redgauntlet (Scott), 63
Rediker, Marcus, 18, 29, 35, 82, 247n.3, 247n.7, 247n.9, 255n.94, 256n.2, 265n.1, 282n.10
Red Rover, The (Cooper), 2, 3, 11, 81; as Cooper's maritime masterpiece, 91; outer limit of national constructs in, 91–92; preface (1834) to, 31; women's positions in, 127
Redskins: or, Indian and Injin, The (Cooper), 177, 186–87, 193
reform rhetoric, Melville's *White-Jacket* and naval, 227–35, 298n.76
"Relation of the Poet to Day-Dreaming, The" (Freud), 6
religion: appeal to heavenly Law in Melville's *White-Jacket,* 237; Christian missionaries, 100, 105, 147–49; in Cooper's *The Crater,* Christian eschatological scenario, 182, 193–94; in Cooper's *The Crater,*

as threat, 189–90, 192; tattoos in Cooper's *Typee* and, 105
rent practices, Anti-Rent War of 1839–46 and, 177, 186–87
"Repossession of America: The Revolution in Cooper's Trilogy of Nautical Romances, A" (Peck), 73
representations of space, Lefebvre on, 248n.11
Resolution (ship), 107
Restuccia, Frances L., 284n.23
Ricardo, David, 186
Richardson, William J., 280n.64
Rime of the Ancient Mariner, The (Coleridge), 25
Rise of Totalitarian Democracy, The (Talmon), 199
Robarts, Edward, 142–45, 146, 166, 287n.64
Roberts, Captain, 99–100
Robertson, George, 139–40
Robinson Crusoe (Defoe), 182
Rogin, Michael Paul, 247n.2, 293n.8
romance: gender positions within maritime, 127–28; Melville's conception of *Mardi* as, 159; "romance of the sea," 247n.7
Rose, Jacqueline, 57, 248n.25
Rothenberg, Molly Anne, 207, 209, 295n.43
Rothman, David J., 298n.88
Rottenberg, Catherine, 92, 272n.101
Rousseau, Jean-Jacques, 235, 272n.3, 286n.48, 291n.24, 294n.31
Rowe, John Carlos, 241, 254n.89, 301n.10
Ruge, Arnold, 303n.24
Rush, Benjamin, 298n.88
Ruston, Peter, 259n.34
Rutherford, John, 97, 272n.2

"Sade" (Blanchot), 197
sadism of flogging, 228, 229
Said, Edward W., 15, 75, 128, 253nn.81–82
sailors, common. *See* common sailors
Saldívar, José David, 254n.89
Salecl, Renata, 129, 283n.22, 284n.23; on phallic signifier, 131–32
same-sex male encounters, 124
Samson, John, 110, 259n.33, 278n.46, 293n.8
Sandwich Islands, Paulet's actions in, 103–4
Santiago-Valles, Kelvin, 287n.62
Sattelmeyer, Robert, 253n.76
Saussure, Ferdinand de, 7
"savage," Western conceptions of, 98, 110
schizophrenic pole of libidinal energy, 82
Schmitt, Carl, 14, 175, 253n.77, 289n.1
science: shift in domain of knowledge and development of, 51–52; surgeon's use of injured sailor in Melville's *White-Jacket* for, 223–24
Scott, Walter, 19, 59, 84, 267n.25, 267n.30; Cooper's *Pilot* as corrective to, 31, 76; political positioning of, 62; universal conflicts in novels of, 62; voyage touring Scotland's islands, 62–63. *See also Pirate, The* (Scott)
Scutt, R. W. B., 277n.42
sea: as coherent cultural and imaginative space, problem of representing, 4; romantic accounts of, 247n.7; sea space as structurally incomplete, 240; as threshold between known and unknown, trope of, 39; "usage of the sea," 202–3, 215, 216

Seaman's Protection Certificates, 89
second death, 113, 114, 115
Sedgwick, Catharine Maria, 30, 126, 283n.13
Sekora, John, 258n.22
self and other: exotic force operating within self, 240; Tommo's formative notions of, in *Typee*, 112–21. *See also* Other, the
Sellers, Charles, 252n.71
semblances, women and, 288n.87
Seminar I (Lacan), 249n.26, 249n.31, 294n.34, 251n.64, 267n.35, 288nn.88–89, 296n.48
Seminar VII (Lacan), 260n.47, 282n.8, 289n.10, 290n.15, 296n49, 260n.47, 282n.8, 289n.10, 290n.15, 296n.49
Seminar XI (Lacan), 7, 144, 249n.29, 250n.47, 259n.41, 263n.81, 279n.63, 295nn.39–40, 297n.65; tattoo trope used in, 280n.70
Seminar XVII (Lacan), 25, 249n.26, 250n.51, 260nn.47–48, 261nn.49–50, 261n.54, 262n.57, 263n.83, 265n.10, 265n93, 279n.59, 284n.28, 284n.30, 296n.60
Seminar XX (Lacan), 129, 249n.35, 262n.58, 279n.59, 283n.21, 284n.24, 284n.33, 285n.39, 285n.41, 288n.81, 289n.97, 289n.110
Sexual Encounters: Pacific Texts, Modern Sexualities (Wallace), 124, 128
sexuality: colonial Pacific and, 281n.4; disruptive force of Polynesian, 124, 287n.80; same-sex male encounters, 124; as trope for power relations in imperialism, 128. *See also* "porno-tropics"
sexual violence against native women, 139

sexuation, Lacanian theory of, 20, 124–25, 129, 283n.23; object *a* as positive stand-in for lack of the Other in, 131, 133, 135, 284n.33; phallic jouissance and, 130–33
Shakespeare, William, 115
shame, 113; shame-induced death, 113; Tommo's feelings of, in *Typee*, 114
Shaw, Lemuel, 197, 293n.2
silence, feminine jouissance and, 170, 289n.101
Simpson, Mark, 44–45, 262n.68
Sites of Desire/Economies of Pleasure: Sexualities in Asia and the Pacific (Manderson and Jolly), 124
Skallerup, Harry R., 256n.3
skin art. *See* tattoo(s); tattoos in *Typee*
slavery, 59; analogy between sailor and slave, Otter on, 226–27, 232; ex-slave narratives, 257n.22; fantasmic relation between master and slave, 261n.52, 261n.54; in relation to naval flogging, 227–28, 232; *Zong* massacre (1781), 240
"Slavoj Žižek's Hegelian Reformation" (Johnston), 301n.13
Small, Elisha, 1
Smith, Adam, 185, 291n.29
Smith, Bernard, 274n.23
Smollett, Tobias, 26
Snell, Hannah, 125–26
social contract, 291n.24
Somers, USS, 1–2, 11, 226
Southampton (Atlantic liner), Melville's voyage on, 296n.55
Southworth, E. D. E. N., 134–36, 285n.45
Spanos, William V., 293n.16
Specters of the Atlantic: Finance Capital, Slavery, and the Philosophy of History (Baucom), 18

Spencer, John Canfield, 1–2
Spencer, Philip, 1–2
Spiller, Robert E., 186, 291n.32
Spivak, Gayatri Chakravorty, 34–35, 54, 259n.35, 261n.53, 278n.51
Springer, Haskell, 126, 283n.14
Spy, The (Cooper), 86
Stansell, Christine, 260n.42
state institutions, Cooper's warning about power of, 191–92
state of exception: Agamben on, 175–76, 199, 200–201; Articles of War and institutionalization of exception, 201–4, 212, 213, 232; Baucom's alternate model for conceiving of modern, 200; Cooper's vision regarding, 193, 194; as dominant paradigm of twentieth-century totalitarian and democratic governments, 175–76; flogging as manifestation of raw sovereign power behind and within, 232; legal rationales for exceptions to and in written law, 201; Melville's rendering of flogging as centerpiece of portrayal of life in martial, 226; Melville's *White-Jacket* prefiguring modern America's move toward, 198; perverse relations created by, 235–36, 299n.93; tension between two ambiguous zones of command on *Neversink* as, 213–15; "usage of the sea," 202–3, 215, 216; Žižek on sovereign power's right to proclaim, 179. See also *White-Jacket; or The World in a Man-of-War* (Melville)
State of Exception (Agamben), 175
state of nature, distinction between civilizing contract and savage, 272n.3

States of Emergency: The Object of American Studies (Castronovo and Gillman), 243, 302n.14
States of Fantasy (Rose), 57
Stavrakakis, Yannis, 7, 249n.33, 250n.50
Stedman, Raymond W., 137, 286n.49
Stern, Milton, 110, 278n.46
Steward, Samuel M., 277n.42
Stewart, Charles, 100
Stirling (merchant ship), 48, 268n.39
St. Lawrence (merchant ship), 33
Stoler, Ann Laura, 282n.4, 286n.53
Studies in Classic American Literature (Lawrence), 262n.61
subaltern subjectivities, gap between discourses used to represent them and, 34–35, 259n.35, 261n.53
subject and the big Other, relation between, 261n.52. See also master's discourse
subject formation: Lacanian conception of, 50; law as agency of the Other in, 178
subjective violence, 228
Sublime Object of Ideology, The (Žižek), 10, 250n.43, 250n.49, 262nn.55–56, 267n.33, 286n.58, 289n.12
Summer on the Lakes, in 1843 (Fuller), 46
superego: difference between normal supplemental and totalitarian, 216; involvement in perverse and totalitarian logic, 208, 215–20; Lacan on, 208
surplus enjoyment. See jouissance (surplus enjoyment)
surplus value, Marx's notion of, 41, 129
symbolic capital, 63, 68, 70
symbolic castration, Lacanian notion of, 7, 9, 129, 130, 290n.15; Lacanian phallus correlated with subject's relation to, 131–32

symbolic identity/identification, 7, 66–67, 69
symbolic jouissance, 262n.58
symbolic order: big Other and, 65–66, 130–31, 135; "failure of the limit" of, 152
symbolic register, Lacan on, 7
symbolic systems of the West: antagonism between Pacific cultures and, 103–5; cross-cultural maritime encounters mediated by, 98; incorporation of Polynesians through ethnographic work, 109; vulnerability of, 106–8, 114–16, 279n.55
symbolic violence, 228
Symposium (Plato), 129
systemic violence, 228

Tahiti, 59, 99, 103; accounts of native women of, 137, 141, 146, 155–58; behavior of Wallis's crew on (1767), 139–40; Christian missionaries in, 100, 105; Cook's 1769 visit to, 97, 107, 141; French and British vying with each other over, 156; Melville's *Omoo* recounting adventures on colonial, 104, 105, 155–58; political condition of, role in phallic fantasies, 157
Tahitian tattoos, 97, 100, 275n.25
Talbot, Anne, 125–26
"Tale of the Ragged Mountains, A" (Poe), 17
Talmon, J. L., 199, 293n.11
tattoo(s), 20; "aggressive" cultural practice of tattooing, 110; association of blackness and, 101; banned by missionaries in Tahiti, 105; European sailors with, 107, 277n.42; as form of lure, traditional view of, 106, 276n.34; haunting agency and possession of, link between, 115, 279n.63; invasive agency of, 108, 110, 112; Marquesan, patterns of, 109; Polynesian myth about origin of, 106; Tahitian, 97, 100, 275n.25; "te patu tiki," meaning to "wrap in images," 273n8; used as means of corporal punishment, 105, 276n.32; Western fascination with, 97, 100; West's anxiety about being disfigured by, 98, 99, 100, 101–3, 106–8, 110–11, 274n.25
tattooing, Polynesian, 20
Tattooing in Marquesas (Handy), 109
tattoos in *Typee*, 20, 97–121; distinguished from tattoos in *Moby-Dick*, 276n.38; historical break induced by, 111, 112–13; tattoo transference and refracted freaks, 99–109; Tommo's anxiety over loss of identity and, 101, 106, 110, 112–21; Tommo's "face divine," 104, 109–21, 277n.45
"Theses on the Philosophy of History" (Benjamin), 290n.14
Thing: national subjectivity and desire for fantasized relation to national, 93; Other qua Real (impossible Thing), 118, 120
Third Space of Sovereignty, The (Bruyneel), 302
Thirty Years from Home (Leech), 228
Thomas, Nicholas, 107, 277n.39
Thompson, Rosemarie Garland, 100, 273n.13
Thoreau, Henry David, 14
Tiffany, Sharon, 286n.53
time as social and historical object of study, 60, 265n.11
Tiresias, 137

Tocqueville, Alexis de, 13–14, 190, 252n.73, 292n.37, 293n.16
Toll, Ian W., 265n.1
totalitarianism/totalitarian state: democracy and, totalitarian modes of power manifest in, 199–200, 203; the *Neversink* and the modern, 198, 199–220; perversion and, 204–20; scholars interrogating concept of, 199; state of exception as dominant paradigm of twentieth-century, 175–76; superego's involvement in perverse and totalitarian logic, 208, 215–20; totalitarian bureaucracy, 207, 214; Žižek on, 205, 207, 296n.47
Totem and Taboo (Freud), 137–38
trade/commerce: Atlantic-maritime empire of, 2; "heads-for-weapons," 97; as most corrupt and corrupting influence of life, Cooper on, 189; for sex with native women, 139–42, 146
translation and transcription, narratives involving, 44–55; agency and, 44, 54; Cooper's *Ned Myers*, 19, 26, 48–54, 63; as fantasy, 54; struggle with cultural and literal translation, 105, 276n.30
"Traveling Genres" (Cohen), 73
travel narratives, 15, 18, 258n.23
"traversing the fantasy," Lacan's notion of, 119–20, 138, 281n.74
Tristes Tropiques (Lévi-Strauss), 109
Two Years before the Mast (Dana), 1, 3, 19, 26; common sailor invested with type of object *a* in, 37, 38–39; defense of corporal punishment at sea, 89, 298n.76; foregrounding of issue of class in, 36–39; as paradigmatic context of Cooper's *Ned Myers*, 49; positioned as first realist sea narrative, 31; "vital contact" notion in, 260n.42; yarn telling in, 47
Tyler, John, 2
Tyler, Royall, 58, 253n.86
Typee (Melville), 14, 19–20, 103; appendix to, 98, 101, 103–4, 105, 106, 107, 130; authenticity issue, 32–34, 99; establishing fantasy structures within social reality of native life, 157–58; excessive women and feminine desire in, 149, 150–55; fantasy structure reconstituted by Tommo at end of, 117–21; historical analyses of, 109–13; meaning of "Tommo" in Marquesan, 121; national issues in, 58–59; negated alternative in *White-Jacket* similar to, 237–38; process of learning to desire original Western identity in, 116–17, 120; public perception of Melville as sex symbol after release of, 123–24; public relations difficulties with, 32–34; queen of Nukuheva's display of tattooed buttocks to French colonials in, 150–51; reframing aggressive-grotesque in, 99–109; subversive element of, 120–21; tattoos in, 20, 97–121; Tommo's experience of feminine excess in, 153–55; Tommo's "face divine" in, 104, 109–21, 277n.45; Tommo's fantasies of natives in, 116–17; "whihenies" swimming to greet crew in, 151–53

United States, USS, 99, 197, 229
United States Exploring Expedition (1838), 15, 58, 146
United States Magazine and Democratic Review, article on flogging, 235

university discourse, 39, 263n.82, 263n.85; antebellum era seen as completing transition into, 40; social link of master's discourse with, 51–52, 53–54, 264n.89
unjust enemy, Kant's conception of, 200
"usage of the sea," 202–3, 215, 216

Van Rensselaer, Stephen, 186
Vatel, 113
Vattimo, Gianni, 303n.24
View from the Masthead: Maritime Imagination and Antebellum American Sea Narratives, The (Blum), 18, 27–28
Vincennes (ship), 100, 146
violence: divine, Žižek on, 295n.36; flogging, 202–3, 219, 225–35, 299n.90, 299nn.92–93; indistinction between law and, flogging as moment embodying, 232, 299n.93; "lawmaking" and "law-preserving" functions of, Benjamin on, 299n.93; power and, 215, 216, 219–20; ritualized, 215, 219, 220; sexual, against native women, 139; Žižek's distinctions among "subjective," "symbolic," and "systemic" forms of, 228. *See also* corporal punishment; flogging; Foucault, Michel; slavery
visor effect, Derrida's notion of, 115–16, 280n.64, 280n.67
"vital contact," notion of, 260n.42
Voltaire, 137
Voyages and Travels (Langsdorff), 101

Walcott, Derek, 240
Walden (Thoreau), 14
Wallace, James D., 75, 269n.48
Wallace, Lee, 124, 128, 136, 255n.92, 282n.4, 287n.80

Wallerstein, Immanuel, 252n.71
Wallis, Mary Davis, 126, 274n.25, 275n.28, 283n.14; account of Manicola men, 133; portrayal of native women, 146–47, 148
Wallis, Samuel, 139–40
War of 1812, 2, 25, 27; maritime nationalism spawned by, 13, 30; naval victories as fodder for nationalistic fantasies, 58
Water-Witch: or, The Skimmer of the Seas, The (Cooper), 77, 82–83; women's positions in, 127
Watson, Nicola, 63, 267n.27
Watt, Ian, 265n.8
Waverley (Scott), 63, 64, 72
Way, J. T., 254n.89
West, the: anxiety about being disfigured and racially marked by natives' ink, 98, 99, 100, 101–3, 106–8, 110–11, 274n.25; penetrating natives' physical and symbolic space in attempt to control it, 161
West, the, symbolic systems of: antagonism between Pacific cultures and, 103–5; cross-cultural maritime encounters mediated by, 98; incorporation of Polynesians through ethnographic work, 109; vulnerability of, 106–8, 114–16, 279n.55
White, Joanna, 277n.40
white-collar workers, burgeoning middle class of, 29
White-Jacket: or The World in a Man-of-War (Melville), 2, 19, 20–21, 44, 176, 177, 197–238, 244–45; Captain Claret, description of, 211–13; challenge to romantic conceptions of sea experience in, 3; complex universe of *Neversink* in,

210–15, 233–34, 296n.54; condemnation of martial law and Articles of War in, 203–4, 225–26, 234–35, 236; Cooper's *The Crater* compared to, 208; customary Fourth of July celebration in, 218–19; dialectic between extrastructural and authoritarian desire in, 217–20; discharge of dead sailors in, 222–23, 297n.68, 297n.70; division of labor aboard *Neversink*, 210–11, 214, 221, 234; flogging, as discipline acting on two levels simultaneously, 232; flogging, individuals refusing to submit to, 232–35; flogging, practice of, 219, 225–35; floggings, first detailed account of, 229–31; grog system in, 216–19; Jack Chase, description of, 210; jacket's role of differentiation in, 208–10, 221–22; from labor to the lash, 220–38; Melville's allusion to sailors' specialized discourse, 263n.73; negated alternative (White-Jacket's imaginary attack on Claret) in, 235–36, 237–38, 300n.101; *Neversink* and modern totalitarian state, 198, 199–220; numeric–symbolic schema required aboard *Neversink*, 211; objectified laborers and ship's broader systems of control, perversion in relationship between, 220–21, 223–24; Old Ushant as romantic model for manhood, 232–33, 300n.94; perversion linked with totalitarianism in, 204–20; prefiguring modern America's move toward state of exception, 198; relation to antebellum reform rhetoric, 227–35, 298n.76; ritualized violence in, 215, 219, 220; "subterranean parts" of *Neversink*, depiction of, 218; superego in perverse-totalitarian schema of, 208, 215–20; surgeon's (Dr. Cuticle) use of injured sailor for scientific knowledge, 223–24; system of authority aboard *Neversink* in, 211–15; White-Jacket's fantasmatic appeal to distant and ideal Other of the Law in, 235–36, 237

Wiegman, Robyn, 254n.89

"wild woman" trope, 137–38

Wilkes, Charles, 15, 16, 51, 58, 253n.83, 275n.28, 276n.30; portrayal of native women, 146, 148

Williams, Eliza Azelia, 126, 283n.14

Wittig, Monique, 284n.38

women: antebellum narratives written by captains' wives at sea, 126, 283n.14; cross-dressing sailors, 125–26; excessive feminine desire, notion of, 127–28; Lacan's notion of woman as not existing and "not-whole," 129, 132–33; Melville's excessive, 149–72; norms of female domesticity, 125, 126; popular tales of infamous female pirates, 125, 282n.10; positions within maritime romances, 127; semblances and, Miller on, 288n.87; woman as phallus, Lacan's concept of, 133, 135, 285n.43

women, native, 149–72; bodies as source of object *a*, 141, 142–45; desire of, in Melville's *Mardi*, 149, 150, 158–72; desire of, in Melville's *Omoo*, 149, 150, 155–58; desire of, in Melville's *Typee*, 149, 150–55; existence of desire of the other (and Other) within, 143; phallic fantasies in nonfictional narratives of Pacific, 20, 125, 137–49; Tahitian women,

women, native (*continued*)
accounts of, 137, 141, 146, 155–58; used as commodities, 139–42, 146; "wild woman" trope, 137–38
Women Adventurers (Dowie), 126
Wyandotté (Cooper), 177

Yaeger, Patricia, 302nn.16–17; on oceanic studies, 242–43
yarns, telling, 44–55; content and form as dialectical whole, 45–47
Yellin, Jean Fagan, 258n.22
Young Americans' association, 30–31

Zabala, Santiago, 303n.24
Ziser, Michael, 300n.101
Žižek, Slavoj, 51, 93, 217, 244, 247n.8, 248n.13, 249nn.37–39, 250nn.43–45, 250n.50, 251nn.62–64, 266nn.16–17, 280n.69, 281n.75, 283n.23, 285n.47, 290n.13, 292n.44, 298n.79, 301nn.12–13; on access to knowledge and loss of enjoyment, 262n.56; on artifice of true art, 16–17; on Butler's reading of Lacan, 285n.44; criticism of liberal-democratic multicultural perspectives on cultural analysis, 241, 301n.12; on democracy as master signifier, 194–95, 290n.17; description of the Real, 135; distinctions among "subjective," "symbolic," and "systemic" forms of violence, 228; on "divine violence," 295n.36; on entering sociosymbolic order via fantasy, 66; on external difference overlapping internal difference, 241, 301n.13; on fantasy as semblance for Lacan, 288n.87; on flogging, 299n.92; on fully identifying with fantasy, 120; on the gaze, 289n.96; on Harpo Marx, 288n.83; on hidden, nonrealized potentials of the past, 267n.22, 303n.24; on ideology, 9, 236; Lacanian critique of "Messianic Otherness," 205, 280n.66; on Lacan's *point de capiton* or master signifier, 178–79; on lamella, 280n.63; on limitation of Adorno's mode of negative dialectics, 301n.9; linking economic absent cause to Lacanian Real, 251n.60; on loss of desire, 164; on Marx's view of social relations in bourgeois society, 286n.58; on melancholy, 164, 288n.92; modifications of Lacanian notion of fantasy, 5, 8–12; on national identification, 60; on notion of history and historical breaks, 111–12; on object *a*, 259n.41, 260n.47; on ontological difference, 249n.42; on the Other, 117–18; on "pacifying intervention of external social law," 224; on parallax gap, 300n.5; parallax Real, conception of, 8–9, 10, 65, 118; perverse totalitarian rule, notion of, 211, 214; on power and violence, 215, 216; presymbolic X, 250n.45; on relationship between economy and politics, 11, 302n.13; on shift in Lacan's conception of object, 250n.52; on sovereignty and right to proclaim state of exception, 179; on split between subject's knowledge and the Other's knowledge, 261n.52; on subjects as "gaps in positive order of being," 118, 281n.71; on totalitarianism, 205, 207, 296n.47; on university discourse, 263n.85; use of examples, 251n.64
Zong massacre (1781), 240
Zupančič, Alenka, 170, 289n.100

JASON BERGER is assistant professor of English at the University of South Dakota.